Human Development Across the Life Span

Educational and Psychological Applications

Edited by
Ralph L. Mosher, Deborah J. Youngman,
and James M. Day

Westport, Connecticut
London

Library of Congress Cataloging-in-Publication Data

Human development across the life span : educational and psychological
   applications / edited by Ralph L. Mosher, Deborah J. Youngman, and
   James M. Day.
         p.   cm.
      Includes bibliographical references and index.
      ISBN 0–275–96457–4 (alk. paper)
      1. Developmental psychology.   I. Mosher, Ralph L.   II. Youngman,
   Deborah J., 1950–   .   III. Day, James M., 1955–   .
   BF713.H835   1999
   155—dc21   98–44538

British Library Cataloguing in Publication Data is available.

Library of Congress Catalog Card Number: 98–44538
ISBN: 0–275–96457–4

First published in 1999

Praeger Publishers, 88 Post Road West, Westport, CT 06881
An imprint of Greenwood Publishing Group, Inc.
www.praeger.com

Printed in the United States of America

The paper used in this book complies with the
Permanent Paper Standard issued by the National
Information Standards Organization (Z39.48–1984).

10 9 8 7 6 5 4 3 2 1

Copyright Acknowledgments

The editors and publisher gratefully acknowledge permission to reprint from the following:

Excerpts reprinted by permission of the publisher from *Raising Their Voices* by Lyn Mikel
Brown, Cambridge, Mass.: Harvard University Press, Copyright © 1998 by Lyn Mikel Brown.

Adapted material from *Journal of Family Psychology,* 1992, *5,* 379–402. Copyright © 1992
by the American Psychological Association. Adapted with permission.

James M. Day and Myriam H. L. Naedts, "Convergence and Conflict in the Development of
Moral Judgement and Religious Judgement." *Journal of Education,* 177, no. 2 (1995): 1–29.

Jeanne S. Chall and Roselmina Indrisano, "Literacy Development." *Journal of Education,*
177, no. 1 (1995): 63–83.

Carole Greenes, "Mathematics Learning and Knowing: A Cognitive Process." *Journal of
Education.* 177, no. 1 (1995): 85–106.

Eileen Nickerson, Ph. D., was one of three of my colleagues who contributed to the conception of this book. Her influence lay in at least three areas: her examination of the theoretical and practical links between developmental, counseling, and educational psychology; her interest in the effect of gender on formal and self-reflective thinking; and, perhaps most importantly, her passionate devotion to the idea of equal opportunity—race, class, and gender notwithstanding. Through these, her spirit is reflected within these pages.

Eileen was my closest senior colleague for more than twenty years at Boston University. I had known her previously at Harvard in the early 1960s and remember her for both her vision and her drive.

Eileen was a consummate professional. Her rare talent was a gift to her students and to her field. She mentored a whole generation of young professionals in New England, a great many young women among them. They are her greatest legacy.

Her care and concern for her family, her students, her colleagues, and her clients were always evident. Her sense of stewardship towards her profession emerged not only in her teaching but also in her administration of a women's specialization program, and in her national and international leadership in the field of counseling psychology in centers as disparate as the South side of Chicago, Europe, and South America.

In all these endeavors, Eileen displayed an unfailing sense of humor. She enjoyed the everyday ironies of leadership: her enthusiasm, resilience, and optimism buoyed us all.

We were, thus, shaken and deeply saddened by Eileen's untimely death. This book was brought to a halt for some time as we struggled to capture her ideological and pragmatic positions. Her concern for its completion was one of the last topics she shared with us, her colleague editors. We cared deeply for Eileen and are the richer and wiser for having known her.

Ralph Mosher

Contents

Acknowledgments

We are profoundly grateful to Kathleen Dunlap, Professor of Physiology at Tufts Medical School in Boston for her generous and unfailing support of this project. Her invaluable contributions of time, technical expertise, patience, encouragement, and wisdom have carried this book forward.

We would also like to express our deep thanks to the indefatigable Jessica Mosher for her warm support and her able and discerning help with communications.

Further acknowledged is the always graceful and judicious manner in which our Department Chair, Professor Lee Indrisano, continues to provide her colleagues with those conditions of workplace and relationship which potentiate both personal and professional development. We are indebted.

Finally, unending thanks to Monty Carlos Grob for keeping the hearth warm and the table laid, throughout.

Introduction: An Historical Perspective of Life Span Development

Deborah J. Youngman

Philosophical and literary references dating to antiquity document pre-scientific recognition of human development across the life span. Proto-Grecian and Platonic formulae for successful living were subsumed within Aristotle's logical conceptualization of propriety, which, though temporarily obscured by the metaphysics of the Middle Ages, has evinced authority since Classical times, informing even contemporary notions of evolution as hierarchical and teleological. Throughout Western history, prominent developmental indices have furthermore been, more or less, characterized by biological determinism and a prescriptive intent; age-differentiated tasks have been presumed to define the human condition while refining the social order.

Intellectual heir to emerging scientific methodology as well as to the eighteenth-century philosophical construction of human agency and spontaneity, the French scientist Quetelet (1796-1874) can justly be considered the founder of life span psychology. Employing systematic cross-sectional technique, Quetelet demonstrated that human variance and quantitative change over time is influenced not only by age but by constitutive features of the physical and social environment as well. Likewise of significance for our purposes here was the work of his predecessor, Pestalozzi (1746-1827), who had promulgated, as later did William James and John Dewey at the end of nineteenth century, the role of education in the purposive development of the whole human being toward prosocial ends. Interestingly, such considerations adumbrate more recent theoretical pursuits after an intervening period during which relatively less significance was attached to these themes.

Diverse, proceeding contributions by Goethe, Galton, Preyer, Darwin, and others across the disciplines laid the ground for the pioneering work of theorists such as Baldwin, Binet, Mead, Hall, and Buhler (1893-1974) a century later. In a notable departure from prevailing cross-sectional studies, Charlotte Buhler collected longitudinal data on

250 individuals, analyzing the quantitative data of their life histories by qualitative means. Emergent among her interpretative findings was the conclusion that humans are essentially motivated by the will to mark their existence by achievement of one or another variety and that this imprimatur rises from life-long processes of expansion and restriction of possibility and competence.

The prodigious study of human development during the first three quarters of the twentieth century did not, alas, continue to build, at least in any cohesive manner, on the sensible pluralism of Buhler's theory and research methodology. Specialists focusing on a particular phase of life, a functional domain, or on the nosological features of development gone awry have pursued their interests in relative isolation from one another and without benefit of any unifying theoretical consensus. Such continues to be the case despite periodic integrative efforts such as those of Neugarten, Baltes, and Schaie.

Before World War II, developmental psychologists were primarily devoted to descriptive observations of infants and children, longitudinal designs in time providing adolescent data as well. While G. S. Hall's publication in 1922 of wide-ranging, miscellaneous remarks on senescence initiated further enquiry into the associated matters of aging, and psychoanalytic theorizing drew further attention to the problems of adult adjustment as a function of mother-child socialization processes, scholarly vision was still primarily directed toward the explanation of early developmental characteristics, in large measure for the purposes of refining child guidance procedures. Practical objectives implied by the study of mental measurement, clinical genetics, educational psychology, and behaviorism led collectively to an atmosphere in which, given the technological advances made during and after World War II, increasing scientific rigor could be, needed to be, and was applied to the research that would inform derivative public instruction, primarily with regard to raising and educating children and adolescents.

As Americans next (and rather belatedly, at mid-century) came to appreciate Piaget's discoveries relative to language and cognitive development, quantitative investigations in these domains soon became the pre-eminent objective of developmental psychology, again strengthening the preoccupation with early life processes. Constructive theories in other domains (e.g., moral, social, and ego) were also generated as the heuristic appeal of stage models increased their popularity in the advanced classroom.

Pedagogical advantages notwithstanding, stage theories have presented certain methodological and theoretical problems, particularly from the perspective of developmentalists interested in the entire life course. Similar to the maturational and biomedical models they resemble, stage models imply that development in adulthood conforms to an evaluative trajectory, the distal end of which is either characterized by decline and constriction or is thought inapplicable to late adulthood on the assumption that optimal growth is achieved at some earlier phase in life. Precise replication and definitive empirical confirmation of stage models, however, have not been easy or possible, which has rendered them vulnerable to criticism as being value-laden and biased in particular and singular directions.

Stage model conceptualizations presume a fixed, universal sequence in the development of successive competencies. They differentiate qualitatively distinct stages and ways of functioning. They postulate that achievement at one stage is largely dependent on the successful negotiation of the previous stage. Development is assumed to be unidirectional in its orientation. While such models appear to provide salient, even robust explanatory power for development in certain domains (for example, in the area of literacy or numerical development) or temporal periods (much of infant development is relatively universal), they have been found wanting, particularly of late, both by those who seek comprehensive and coherent theories of contextualized development across the life span and by those who pursue more discerning and naturalistic research methods among participants who can articulate as well as conceal, rationalize, and transform their own self-perceptions.

Much effort has been made in this anthology of current writings in human development to be all of these: coherent, discerning, and comprehensive in the discovery and interpretation of what it is that develops, how, why, and under what conditions. In a spirit of intellectual flexibility, each of the contributing authors, while assuming the theoretical position most appropriate to the investigation and analysis of their particular interest, also recognizes the larger field, its traditions as well as its evolving sensibilities. The contribution of each reflects certain shared assumptions about what constitutes development.

Each would acknowledge, for instance, that not all change is developmental in nature; various criteria apply. There must, to begin, be qualitative and/or quantitative change and relative irreversibility. On these conditions alone, the onset of intransigent pathology of an endogenous origin might (inaccurately) be said to be developmental. Freud noted the correlation between personality and pathogenesis as well as the manner in which certain exogenous circumstances could provoke or subdue manifestations of illness. It is now, however, widely considered reductionist to assume that specific environmental conditions alone differentially potentiate pre-existing pathology or normative development. Even were there evidence of some correlation, neglect, abuse, and trauma can't adequately account for variation in development. Recent research into the protective factors that comprise resilience, and growing knowledge of other intervening and interactive variables suggest the actual complexity involved.

A more comprehensive, ecological understanding, then, is that the physical/social environment and heritability potentiate each other in an ongoing, dynamic interaction. From a life span perspective that generally assumes that change must move in the direction identified as mature, adaptive, increasingly complex, differentiated, and well-integrated, some changes associated with psychological regression cannot be judged developmental, although their therapeutic address may and perhaps should be. In their historical overview of clinical-developmental psychology, Speicher and Noam undertake a discussion of such non-normative change and the paradoxical emergence of complexity that is neither mature nor adpative. Cayten provides retrospective accounts of unorthodox self-labeling and deviant behavior as actually being formative in the adolescent ego development of tenured women faculty. Relying on a similar qualitative methodology, the systematic advantages of which are located by Tappan within the context of postmodern hermeneutic studies in a separate chapter, Brown explores variance in expressions of agency among socioeconomically differentiated adolescent school girls. As the impact of so complex an environment cannot be objectively measured nor the process and content of meaning-making conferred from without, such articulate participants are requisite to interpretative research.

The facilitating conditions for healthy progress and adjustment in the interactive domains of cognitive, socio-emotional, and motor development are delineated in Parson's description of efforts to develop aesthetic sensibility, Dupont's account of the systematic movement of children toward the reconstruction and more appropriate expression of affect, and Zaichkowsky and Haberl's opening chapter emphasizing the several ways in which physical development is fundamental to optimal growth in other domains.

Even as they focus on the emerging cognitive competencies requisite to literacy and numeracy, authors Chall, Indrisano, and Greenes impart their understandings of the multidirectional, multidimensional influence of ontogenesis and environment. Increasing attention has been paid in the last few decades as to which behavioral changes actually represent development in a particular domain, and which causes of change may represent a developmental influence. Current life span theories, having integrated both biodeterminism and socio-cultural emphases, conceive of the individual as an organizer of its own experience who is nonetheless subject to the restraints of contextual transactions. We now must consider not only age, genetics, and immediate instructive efforts, but the entire biopsychosocial life course experienced to date within interactive multiple contexts of history, geography, access to opportunity, timing, and the impact of preceding generations as they collectively and potentially influence the development of competencies such as literacy.

In adulthood, the variables that are considered to influence development become increasingly diverse secondary to the passage of time and the idea that all experiences until the moment of death can be formative ones. While operationalizing such ambiguities is certainly problematic, rather than to abandon the certainty of integrated complexity because research design is yet inadequate, we must instead pursue this complexity through the invention of more sensitive methods of enquiry that are comprehensive enough to account for multiple dimensions and directions of development but enough exacting so as to discover real evidence. Preliminary efforts at theoretical integration (dialectical, transactional, contextual) have been promising and are reflected here in chapters that present various aspects of adult development.

Day and Naedts detail the potentially transformative course by which religious maturity may be pursued; Sprinthall, Reiman, and Sprinthall report educational strategies designed to effect moral understanding in teachers; and Schrader describes the promotion of reflective thinking in adults. Levant and Demick, respectively, reconceptualize the processes by which males might construct or perhaps reconstruct their masculinity and parents learn, in part through being taught by children, to effectively parent. Through such chapters, the reader is reminded that, while in some domains continuity and evidence of accumulation over time are characteristic, the processes of conscientious selection, compensation, optimization, and/or discontinuous transformation are central to others.

The primary objective in the study of life span development and its implications for education and psychology is to increasingly understand interindividual similarities and differences as well as the range and degree of plasticity, level of organizational capacity, rate, direction, and properties of change, conditions which constrain or facilitate, importance of timing, and the impact of contextual transactions, meaning-making potential, and intent in ontogenesis over time. The emergent schematic Ralph Mosher originally visualized is a colorful, multistrand, multi-dimensional helix symbolizing an ontogenesis. To this image of the evolving individual (a significant departure from the two-dimensional matrices and staircases illustrating traditional theory), I add that of endless concentric spheres representing the interactive contexts in which the embedded developmental helix realizes its meaningful existence.

With such an image in mind and incorporating the concepts and research methods of various disciplines—anthropology, history, sociology, psychology, literary studies, and biological science—together we further enable the complex enquiry wanting. In closing, it is noted that there is common theoretical ground among these diverse approaches to the study of life: all scholarship, in recognition of the ultimate subjectivity of perception, concedes that we participate in our own definition. Development likewise intends itself and, as biography witnesses in the following pages, we are, furthermore, told from without.

Part I

Theory and Practice in Educating for Development

1

Cross-Domain Implications of Motor Development

Leonard D. Zaichkowsky and Peter Haberl

Since Bloom and colleagues constructed their taxonomy of educational goals in the mid-1950s (Bloom, Englehart, Hill, Furst, & Krathwohl, 1956), it has been generally acknowledged that there are three unique, yet interactive antecedents to behavior—those generated in the cognitive, the affective, and the psychomotor domains. A perusal of the literature, however, reveals that, in terms of human development, very little has been written about the motor domain. This omission was true when we wrote the textbook *Growth & development: The child and physical activity* (Zaichkowsky, Zaichkowsky, & Martinek, 1980), and it remains true nearly two decades later. In her recent text, Bee (1995) shares this view on what we called the "missing domain" (Zaichkowsky & Larson, 1995): "developmental psychologists have often placed too little emphasis on physical growth. We describe it briefly and then take it for granted" (Bee, 1995, p. 104). This chapter attempts to heighten reader awareness about the importance of physical and motor development in children and youth for life-long functional adaptation. We begin by describing the influences of Montessori and Piaget on our thinking regarding early sensorimotor experience in children, particularly as it relates to the development of the cognitive domain. We then discuss the potential psycho-social benefits of participation in sport and exercise with particular emphasis on the work of Csikszentmihalyi. We conclude with a brief discussion of the importance of early motor skill development in promoting the development of physical fitness in children as well as the formation of exercise habits that persist into adulthood and old-age.

Sports for children and youth reflect deeply entrenched values in many countries of the world. In the United States alone, approximately 48 million children between the ages of five and seventeen years participate in either agency sports, club sports, recreational sports, or interscholastic sports (Ewing, Seefeldt, & Brown, 1996). A prerequisite for participation in such physical activities is the development of adequate motor skills.

The development of motor skills precedes the development of sport-specific skills. Continuous development of competence in both motor and sport-specific skills enable participation in life-long physical activity that serves to promote a healthy lifestyle.

The primary questions we seek to address are: What does research say about the importance of motor development in children and youth? Is motor skill development related to the development of cognitive and psycho-social skills? If so, when are children ready to engage in certain physical activities, or in competition, and how should the environment be structured to provide for the optimization of potential benefits?

On an anecdotal basis, the example of the golf phenomenon, Tiger Woods, who started playing golf before he was two years old, not only seems to highlight the importance of early development of motor skills to ensure future success in a motor task, but also points to possible cross-domain implications (psychological and socio-cultural) resulting from this very early involvement in physical activity, namely the development of self-worth, confidence, concentration, coping skills, a perception of self as a role model, an achievement orientation, and so forth. The study of Tiger Woods' development provides a guiding case for our discussion of questions as to when (how early) to engage children in physical activities (talent development), why to engage them in these activities in the first place (cultural goals), and how some children develop their motor skills to such an extent that they become exceptional performers, whereas others never fully develop their potential.

BENEFITS OF MOTOR DEVELOPMENT AND SPORTS PARTICIPATION

The importance of play, exercise, and sport has been acknowledged since the early Classical period. While documentation of the precise relationship between physical and motor development and the development of the cognitive domain has remained elusive, few question the importance of sensorimotor activities in the development of cognitive abilities early in life. Montessori (1912) recommended the use of perceptual-motor and gross motor activities in the early education of children, and this practice is still recommended today. The work of Piaget (1952) has perhaps had the largest impact on our thinking about the value of early motor experiences for child development. Based on his observations of infants, Piaget (1952) concluded that the child's interaction with environmental forces and objects, the movements that such interactions require, and the resulting mental images that are formed constitute the basis for conceptual and symbolic thinking. The meanings the child attaches to object configurations, weights, textures, time, and space come primarily through sensory modalities dependent in large measure on motor interactions with the environment. Other theoretical writers and researchers have also argued for the importance of early motor experience for the development of cognitive abilities. For a more complete discussion, the reader is referred to Rarick, 1980, and Zaichkowsky and colleagues, 1980.

The data show that large numbers of American children and adolescents now participate in sport. Smith and Smoll (1996) point out that, since this participation is likely to be a permanent feature of life in this culture, it is crucial to know its impact on children (and on adults, for that matter). The discussion concerning the costs and benefits of participation in sport and physical activity continues. On the one hand, Kohn (1992) argues that a strong case can be made against sport participation due to the potentially negative effects of early competition. On the other hand, Smith and Smoll (1996) argue that physical play is a natural training ground where children can learn important life skills, the potential benefits including both physiological and psycho-social components.

What does the research say about the psycho-social implications of sport participation? Although it is relatively easy to obtain personal testimony and anecdotal reports from the professional and the popular press regarding the psycho-social benefits of sport, little definitive empirical research exists. But there are, in fact, a few well-conducted studies demonstrating the psycho-social value of sport participation for youth. The most complete summary of this research is to be found in a publication commissioned and published by the Carnegie Corporation of New York (Poinsett, 1996). Several conclusions can be reached from this collection of research papers:

(1) There are barriers to participation in sport that include intellectual snobbery, racism, sexism, threats to safety, and lack of access due to socio-economic factors, inadequate education, and insufficient personal and/or parental motivation to acquire competence.

(2) Participation in sport alone does not result in the development of positive social and emotional characteristics. As Weiss (1995) similarly pointed out, positive development can only be derived through sport involvement that fosters positive experiences and minimizes negative ones. As such, coaches and leaders are entrusted with a huge responsibility. Unfortunately, because these involved adults are often inadequately trained regarding child development and motor skill acquisition, children in their care receive less than optimal instruction and psychological support.

(3) The concepts of fair play, sportsmanship, and moral maturity are learned through the consistent and appropriate responses of coaches, parents, and other models and teachers. Moral behavior appears to be enhanced through imitating the just and prosocial behavior of others and through exposure to the moral reasoning articulated by parents, coaches, and other responsible adults and older children (Ewing et al., 1996; Youngman & Mosher, 1997).

(4) Participation in sport can provide a safe alternative to activities involving violence and intimidation. Sport can provide a direct alternative to gang membership by providing immediate opportunities for affiliation, enhanced self-worth, companionship, and the learning of effective ways to cope with frustration. In these ways cognitive strategies for psycho-social development are facilitated.

Csikszentmihalyi (1990) and Csikszentmihalyi, Rathunde, and Whalen (1993) contend that sport, due to its inherent structure, can provide the type of optimal experiences that they consider crucial for personal growth. Csikszentmihalyi (1990) calls such optimal experiences "flow," noting that they are characterized by an intense, complete involvement in the activity at hand: "Flow is a subjective state that people report when they are completely involved in something to the point of losing track of time and of being unaware of fatigue and of everything else but the activity itself. . . .The depth of involvement is something we find enjoyable and intrinsically rewarding" (Csikszentmihalyi et al., 1993, p. 14).

One's abilities are stretched to the limit through such experiences of intrinsic reward. To have this experience again, however, it is necessary to identify new challenges; the development of new skills adequate to these challenges, likewise, enables one to manage the anxiety increasing challenges may generate. For Csikszentmihalyi and his colleagues, flow experiences lead to a more complex self as a result of the dialectical process of "differentiation" (finding new challenges) and "integration" (integrating new skills into one's repertoire to meet these challenges) (Csikszentmihalyi, 1990, 1993; Csikszentmihalyi et al., 1993). Resultant psychological complexity serves as an endpoint model for optimal human development (Csikszentmihalyi, 1997; Csikszent-mihalyi et al., 1993).

The potential benefit of motor development and related athletic participation lies in their inherent ability to provide flow-like experiences at all levels of skill development. Whether one is a novice or an expert performer, physical activity and sport, especially when there are clear rules, goals, and immediate feedback, can provide new challenges that necessitate the growth of skills. This balance between challenge (differentiation—finding new challenges) and skills (integration into one's repertoire) stretches personal limits leading to the possibility of optimal experiences and a more complex self (Csikszentmihalyi et al., 1993). Sport can be an early training ground for developing a complex self that can then be transferred to other life domains.

Csikszentmihalyi and colleagues (1993) assume that to develop any talent it is necessary to direct attention (a cognitive skill) to something for extended periods of time. This is a habit that is probably best developed early in one's life, and it requires a supportive environment. Motor development, exploring one's physical surroundings, and later on developing specific sport skills allow for focused attention and provide goals and feedback—the ingredients of an optimal experience characterized by enjoyment. Developmental psychologist Jerome Bruner (1970) pointed out that the development of a motor skill is a cognitive problem solving venture for the child, one in which basic units or subroutines are organized in the proper sequence to achieve a performance goal. The required sequence of movements ultimately becomes automated and reflects "skilled" behavior—like Tiger Woods' golf swing.

REASONS FOR PARTICIPATION

Current research in sport psychology shows that children participate in sport for a variety of reasons, namely the pursuit of competence, affiliation, health and fitness, competition, and enjoyment (Ewing & Seefeldt, 1989; Weiss 1995; Gould & Horn, 1984). Participation ceases if children no longer enjoy themselves, are dissatisfied with their social environment, or perceive themselves to be lacking in competence (Gould & Petchlikoff, 1988). Lacking competence is synonymous with lacking skills and it is difficult to find enjoyment in an activity when one lacks the skills to be proficient in it. Children are, however, motivated to be competent in their social environment. This is accomplished by engaging in mastery attempts (Harter, 1978, 1981). Eventual, successful mastery leads to perceptions of competence and an increased internal locus of control which, in turn, lead to positive affect and related behavior. Competent children engage in achievement behavior that is, furthermore, characterized by appropriate attributions for success and failure, intrinsic motivation, and positive affective states (Weiss, Bredemeier, & Shewchuk, 1986; Weiss, McAuley, Ebbeck & Weise, 1990; Weiss & Horn, 1990).

These research findings align with the major tenets of Csikszentmihalyi's model of optimal experience. Mastering the challenges of one's environment by developing necessary skills leads to optimal experiences and a sense of competence. This striving for competence highlights the emphasis on developing skills rather than focusing on competition and winning/losing. If competence is not developed (and kids drop out for that reason), this means that skills were not taught, were taught at the wrong time, or were taught in the wrong way. Those that drop out of sport do not reap the potential positive benefits of participation; they are also exposed to the potential negative effects of non participation such as boredom, anxiety, low self-esteem, learned helplessness, and/or later avoidance of sports and physical activities, perhaps throughout the rest of their lives. These negative effects preclude enjoyment of skilled motor activities and can lead to health problems. This raises the question as to when children are ready to learn general motor and sport-specific skills.

WHEN TO START PARTICIPATION?

There is much information available on when children are ready to learn movement skills (Seefeldt, 1996). It is impossible, however, as Thomas, Thomas, and Gallagher (1993) point out, to cover so broad a topic in so short a chapter as whole books have been written on the matter. Nevertheless, some general implications do need to be addressed here. The ability to learn new motor skills is determined by the physical and cognitive maturational level of the child, observable in behavioral responses that indicate how well previous proficiencies manage current stimuli presented by the environment (Seefeldt, 1996). Although maturation is a biological process, the importance of cognition and the interplay of cognitive and motor development cannot be ignored.

Seefeldt (1996) points out that Piaget's developmental sequence highlights this interplay. With the onset of locomotion, the potential for sensory stimulation increases. A cyclical relationship evolves as the response to sensory stimulation leads to increased motor responses and further exploration of sensory stimuli (Seefeldt, 1996).

Optimal periods of learning exist when the child has acquired the necessary maturational level of the neuromuscular system, when the child has been exposed to the requisite previous skills (e.g., throwing before pitching), and when the child is motivated enough to engage in the activity (Magill & Anderson, 1996). Learning occurs with the greatest effectiveness and efficiency during such periods. Learning cannot occur in the absence of neuromuscular maturation; it would be futile to teach skills before the neuromuscular system is ready. Once maturation (which occurs at different rates) necessary for a given motor skill is achieved, learning can occur if the prerequisite cognitive and physical skills have been previously developed. Learning may occur in the absence of structured teaching, however, learning will not occur in the absence of motivation (Magill & Anderson, 1996). Since neuromuscular maturation is a naturally occurring biological process over which people have no direct influence, the focus in the following section will be on motivation as the crucial aspect that guides the learning of motor skills. Csikszentmihalyi and colleagues (1993) consider teaching someone who is not interested, and hence not motivated, generally wasteful.

IMPORTANCE OF MOTIVATION IN SKILL DEVELOPMENT

Tiger Woods was exposed to golf, a series of specific motor skills, at a very early age. His example seems to indicate that early exposure is necessary to the eventual achievement of expertise, although it does not provide much data regarding the development of less expert levels of performance. A great deal of information as to when children are ready to learn fine and gross motor skills is available (Seefeldt, 1996), but the evidence for when it is ideal to introduce sport-specific skills is not so clear.

Magill and Anderson (1996) refute the notion that early exposure is a key element in skill development. Ericcson, Krampe, and Tesch-Römer (1993), on the other hand, consider an early start crucial in developing expertise. The question of early exposure goes hand in hand with the question of developing superior motor skills. How is it that some children become exceptional in sports or other performance fields? How is it that some develop superior skills whereas others simply do not? Is talent, motor or otherwise, largely genetic or is superior performance largely a product of training and support variables? A number of researchers have recently shed new light on the nature versus nurture controversy with regard to talent development (Bloom, 1985; Csikszentmihalyi, Rathunde, & Whalen, 1993; Gardner, 1993; Ericcson, Krampe, & Tesch-Römer, 1993; and Ericcson & Charness, 1994). In Gardner's (1983, 1993) theory of multiple intelligences, the exceptional performance of an individual in a specific domain is attributable to a biological proclivity or "talent" that greatly facilitates learning.

It appears that Gardner considers the role of nature to be very salient in the explanation of talent. In his view, exceptional performance is determined by the close match between the particular intelligence profile and its domain. This is not a viewpoint shared by Ericcson, Krampe, and Tesch-Römer (1993) or by Ericcson and Charness (1994). They argue that, counter to societal beliefs, expert performance is "predominantly mediated by acquired complex skills and physiological adaptations" (Ericcson & Charness, 1994, p. 725). Expertise in various domains, they claim, is the result of "deliberate practice" starting at a very early age, over extended periods of time (at least ten years and 10,000 hours). Deliberate practice is defined as an activity that is "effortful" and motivated by the goal of increasing performance. It is not inherently motivating like play, nor does it lead to immediate extrinsic rewards, like work (Ericcson, Krampe, & Tesch-Römer, 1993). With the exception of height, the difference between expert and amateur performers is due to differences in acquired knowledge and skills or due to physiological adaptations that are the result of extensive training, rather than of genetics. What might be genetically influenced are those factors that might predispose an individual toward deliberate practice (Ericcson & Charness, 1994). Should their position be the more accurate one, the implications for education, support, and training are both numerous and optimistic.

As discussed previously, optimal periods for learning motor skills are best viewed from a multidimensional perspective (Magill & Anderson, 1996). This is a notion that also applies to other types of learning and to the larger question of talent development. Neither Csikszentmihalyi and colleagues (1993) or Bloom (1985) deny the presence of innate, inherited abilities as playing a role in talent development, but to them, as to Ericcson and coauthors, it is not the size of the individual gift that matters but rather what one makes of it. Many talented people never fully develop their talent. It is not a question of nature versus nurture, but rather one of how to nurture that which nature gives us.

This returns us to the importance of motivation. Neither Gardner (1993) nor Ericcson and Charness (1994) emphasize the matter of motivation, either in developing inherited abilities to their fullest or in deliberately practicing a skill until expertise is achieved. Csikszentmihalyi and coauthors (1993), however, view talent from a multidimensional perspective highlighting the role of motivation. They consider talent to be a social construction rather than a natural category since different cultures value different talents and, unless talent is valued by a culture, it is nonexistent. For these authors, talent is made up of three elements: individual traits, cultural domains, and social fields. Individual traits are partly inherited and partly developed as one interacts with the environment. Cultural domains refer to the rules that define a performance as meaningful, and social fields comprise the institutions and individuals that decide the value of a performance.

Csikszentmihalyi and colleagues (1993) acknowledge that personality traits, whether inherited or developed, play a role in talent but emphasize that these individual traits need to be nurtured in order for the inherent gift to blossom. They consider motivational and socio-emotional aspects just as important as underlying cognitive and biological ones to the development of talent. In order to nurture talent, the environment needs to provide information (knowledge tools) and the individual needs to be motivated and disciplined. This notion of discipline is closely linked to Ericcson and coauthors' (1993) concept of deliberate practice across a long time span. Where Ericcson and his collaborators (1993, 1994) differ from Csikszentmihalyi and his (1993), however, is that the former consider deliberate practice to be devoid of intrinsic rewards, neither work nor play, and not an activity to be enjoyed. However, deliberate practice need not be viewed as being contradictory to the flow model of optimal experience.

According to the flow model, deliberate practice refers to the discipline that is necessary such that a person who studies long enough can develop superior skills. However, in order to understand motivation, it is not enough to look at personality habits such as discipline, or at the properties of the environment alone. The quality of experience one derives from an activity also needs to be considered. The ability to focus attention over long periods of time is influenced by the quality of experience we have as we engage in activities that we find enjoyable, rather than boring or anxiety-producing (Csikszentmihalyi, 1990; Csikszentmihalyi et al., 1993). The quality of experience plays an important role in talent development as we continue to seek activities that provide a sense of enjoyment. In order to continue to enjoy an activity, it is necessary to find new challenges that help us to avoid boredom and to develop new skills that assist us in avoiding anxiety. Thus does flow lead to complexity of self. It is the desire to keep enjoyment alive that helps to makes us more complex. This requires differentiating new challenges and integrating anew the skills that prepare us to meet these challenges (Csikszentmihalyi et al., 1993). Durand-Bush and Salmela (1996) further suggest that the process of differentiation—of continuously finding new challenges—may be identical to the notion of deliberate practice. The phase of differentiating new challenges is then followed by the integration of those new skills required to meet these challenges. This closes the circle and provides an optimal experience, leading to a more complex self.

Csikszentmihalyi and colleagues (1993) oppose the ideology that insists there is a clear difference between hard work and fun:

The profile of committed students indicates that it is erroneous to believe that serious goal-directedness cannot be united with a sense of enjoyment and excitement over the task at hand...The committed students in our study defy easy description. They enjoyed their talent work, but they were not hedonists who avoided hardships and discipline. Indeed, they worked very hard, but they were not anxious and pressured while doing so. (Csikszentmihalyi et al., 1993, p. 240)

For them, developing talent meant enjoying work in their talent area. Research into the lives of people who have been highly creative in their respective fields (such as science, mathematics, and art) also shows that people derive a great deal of enjoyment from their work (Csikszentmihalyi, 1996). The intrinsic rewards of enjoyment and personal satisfaction must take precedence over extrinsic rewards if talented children are to acquire the single-minded dedication that is necessitated by the rigors of talent development. This requires that teachers and coaches know how to make learning intrinsically rewarding (Csikszentmihalyi et al., 1993).

ENVIRONMENTAL EFFECTS ON MOTOR DEVELOPMENT

Another important topic to consider here is that of the crucial role the environment plays in inter-domain development; we now understand that motivation itself, for example, is influenced by encouragement and support. Although Csikszentmihalyi and coauthors (1993) consider intrinsic motivation virtually paramount, they do not discount the salience of external sources of motivation for the development of skills. Their research shows that immediate as well as long-term extrinsic rewards that include recognition and praise from significant others are very important for developing talent. Again, it is not a question of intrinsic *versus* extrinsic motivation, but rather a question of how extrinsic motivation can enhance intrinsic motivation. Deci and Ryan's (1985) research on cognitive evaluation theory has shown that extrinsic rewards are useful in developing a sense of self-competence and self-determination if they are perceived as informational rather than as controlling. That is to say, if the external rewards provide information regarding one's competence and skill in a given task, rather than being perceived as controlling behavior on the part of an involved other, they may promote internal motivation toward the goal of improved performance.

Extrinsic motivation points to the importance that the environment plays in developing skills. Praise, support, and encouragement come from significant others such as parents, teachers, and coaches. The amount and quality of support from such role models are central to the development of talent (Bloom, 1985). For talent to develop, years of nurturance, education, training, and commitment are necessary and this requires a great investment of resources, especially on the parents' side. Bloom (1985) considers parental involvement with a focus on process rather than on achievement crucial in the early years of talent development. In the middle and later stages, the role of coaches and expert teachers becomes more important. However, unless there is consistent parental support encouraging self-determination and intensity, talented teenagers have a hard time overcoming the many obstacles that can prevent them from engaging in enjoyable experiences that also require effort (Csikszentmihalyi et al., 1993). Complex families that are integrated and differentiated enhance the "attentional capacities for finding challenges and for mastering them" (Csikszentmihalyi et al., 1993, p. 174).

Although there has been some emphasis in this chapter on the development of expert levels of motor performance, the objective of youth sport is not to cultivate Olympic champions alone, but rather to support the range that stretches from the Olympian on the one side to simply providing positive leisure experiences for participating children on the other (Smith & Smoll, 1996). However, even when we shift the focus to motor development for the sake of providing a pleasant leisure experience, the above findings point to the importance of matching skills with challenges and feedback. Smith, Smoll and their associates, in studying the interactions between youth coaches and their athletes, have shown that these interactions leave significant impressions and determine the children's sense of self-worth, enjoyment, level of performance anxiety, drop-out behavior, and cohesion. Positive coaching, with a focus on teaching skills, rewarding effort and persistence, and giving mistake-contingent feedback (rather than punishment) results in increased self-belief, satisfaction, continued sport participation, enhanced enjoyment, and positive regard for teammates and coaches (Smith, Smoll & Curtis, 1979; Smith & Smoll, 1990; Smith, Smoll, & Barnett, 1995).

CONCLUSIONS

Discussed research findings support the notion that not only are the potential negative stressors of sport participation greatly reduced if the focus is on teaching skills within a supportive environment, but that sport participation can become a source of enjoyment and personal growth for less as well as highly talented individuals. For life-long learning and continued engagement to occur, sport and exercise need to be enjoyable. Since motor development is closely linked to cognitive development and since it precedes sport-specific skill development, it is important to make sure that the learning of motor skills is enjoyable if future engagement in physical activity and learning are to be fostered. The emphasis ought to be on teaching for the development of a variety of skills. To balance challenge and skills, it is necessary to structure the environment to meet the physical characteristics of its participants (Magill & Anderson, 1996). A supportive environment and an activity that provides clear goals, while requiring a balance of challenge and skills, allow the young athlete to become completely absorbed, providing for a sense of enjoyment and a desire for future participation.

The need for future, life-long participation in sport and exercise is, furthermore, crucial for ensuring long-term health as emphasized by the Surgeon General's Report on Physical Activity and Health (Superintendent of Documents, 1996). There is undisputed evidence that physical activity is positively related to the short-term control of childhood obesity, elevated blood pressure, high density lipoproteins, blood lipid levels, and skeletal health (Zaichkowsky & Larson, 1995). Inactivity, it is now understood, leads to immediate and long-term negative health consequences across the life-span. The development of motor skills, it is reiterated, leads to participation in exercise and sports, which leads in turn to the acquisition of knowledge, attitudes, and habits that will serve our youth throughout their adult futures. Like Rudyard

Kipling (1935), we can scarcely overemphasize the importance of fitness for both individual and society:

Nations have passed away and left no traces,
And history gives the naked cause of it
One single, simple reason in all cases
They fell because their people were not fit.

Nothing on earth—No Arts, No Gifts, nor
Graces—No Fame, No Wealth
Outweighs the want of it.
This is the law which every law embraces—Be fit—Be fit!
In mind and body
This is the lesson of all Times and Places
One changeless truth on all things changing writ,
For boys and girls, men, women, nations, races:
Be fit! Be fit! and once again—Be fit!

REFERENCES

Bee, H. (1995). *The developing child.* (4th ed.), New York: HarperCollins.

Bloom, B. S. (1985). *Developing talent in young people.* New York: Ballantine.

Bloom, B. S. , Englehart, M., Hill, W., Furst, E., & Krathwohl, D. (1956). *Taxonomy of educational objectives. The classification of educational goals.* New York: Longwood.

Bruner, J. (1970). The growth and structure of skill. In K. Connolly (Ed.), *Mechanisms of motor skill development.* New York: Academic Press.

Csikszentmihalyi, M. (1990). *Flow—the psychology of optimal experience.* New York: Harper and Row.

Csikszentmihalyi, M. (1993). *The evolving self: A psychology for the third millennium.* New York: HarperCollins.

Csikszentmihalyi, M. (1996). *Creativity: Flow and the psychology of discovery and invention.* New York: HarperCollins.

Csikszentmihalyi, M. (1997). *Finding flow. The psychology of engagement with everyday life.* New York: HarperCollins.

Csikszentmihalyi, M., Rathunde, K., & Whalen, S. (1993). *Talented teenagers. The roots of success and failure.* New York: Cambridge University Press.

Deci, E. L., & Ryan, R. M. (1985). *Intrinsic motivation and self-determination in human behavior.* New York: Plenum.

Durand-Bush, N., & Salmela, J. H. (1996) Nurture over nature: A new twist to the development of expertise. *Avante, 2,* 87-109.

Ericcson, K. A., & Charness, N. (1994). Expert performance. Its structure and acquisition. *American Psychologist, 49,* 725-47.

Ericcson, K. A.; Krampe, R. T., & Tesch-Römer, C. (1993). The role of deliberate practice in the acquisition of expert performance. *Psychological Review, 100,* 363-406.

Ewing, M. E., & Seefeldt, V. (1989). *Participation and attrition patterns in American agency-sponsored and interscholastic sports*: An executive summary. Final Report. Sporting Goods Manufacturer's Association, North Palm Beach, FL.

Ewing, M. E., Seefeldt, V. D., & Brown, T. P. (1996). Role of organized sport in the education and health of American children and youth. In A. Poinsett (Ed.), *The role of sports in youth development.* New York: Carnegie Corporation of New York.

Gardner, H. (1983). *Frames of mind: The theory of multiple intelligence.* New York: Basic Books.

Gardner, H. (1993). *Multiple intelligences: The theory in practice.* New York: Basic Books.

Gould, D., & Horn, T. (1984). Participation motivation in young athletes. In J. M. Silva & R. S. Weinberg (Eds.). *Psychological foundations of sport* (pp. 359-70). Champaign, IL: Human Kinetics.

Gould, D., & Petchlikoff, L. (1988). Participation motivation and attrition in young athletes. In F. Smoll, R. Magill, & M. Ash (Eds.), *Children in sport* (3rd ed. pp. 161-78). Champaign, IL: Human Kinetics.

Harter, S. (1978). Effectance motivation reconsidered. *Human Develop-ment, 21,* 34-64.

Harter, S. (1981). A model of intrinsic mastery motivation in children: Individual differences and developmental change. In W. A. Collins (Ed.), *Minnesota Symposium on Child Psychology: Vol. 14* (pp. 215-55). Hillsdale, NJ: Erlbaum.

Kipling, R. (1935). *Land and sea tales: For scouts and guides.* London: MacMillan & Co.

Kohn, A. (1992). *No contest: A case against competition.* Boston: Houghton Mifflin.

Magill, R. A., & Anderson, D. I. (1996). Critical periods as optimal readiness for learning sport skills. In F. L. Smoll & R. E. Smith (Eds.), *Children and youth in sport. A biopsychosocial perspective* (pp. 57-72). Dubuque, IA: Brown & Benchmark.

Montessori, M. (1912). The Montessori method. New York: Frederick A. Stokes Co.

Piaget, J. (1952). *The origins of intelligence in children* (2nd ed.). New York: International Universities Press.

Poinsett, A. (1996). *The role of sports in youth development.* New York: Carnegie Corporation of New York.

Rarick, G. L. (1980). Cognitive-motor relationships in the growing years. *Research Quarterly for Exercise and Sport, 51,* 174-92.

Thomas, J. R., Thomas, K. T., & Gallagher, J. D. (1993). Developmental consideration in skill acquisition. In R. N. Singer, M. Murphy, & L. K. Tennant, Eds.), *Handbook of research on sport psychology* (pp. 73-105). New York, NY: Macmillan.

Seefeldt, V. (1996). The concept of readiness applied to the acquisition of motor skills. In F. L. Smoll & R. E. Smith (Eds.), *Children and youth in sport. A biopsychosocial perspective* (pp. 49-56). Dubuque, IA: Brown & Benchmark.

Smith, R. E., Smoll, F. L., & Curtis, B. (1979). Coach Effectiveness Training: A cognitive-behavioral approach to enhancing relationship skills in youth sport coaches. *Journal of Sport Psychology, 1,* 59-75.

Smith, R. E., & Smoll, F. L. (1990). Self-esteem and children's reactions to youth sport coaching behaviors: A field study of self-enhancement processes. *Developmental Psychology, 26,* 987-93.

Smith, R. E., Smoll, F. L., & Barnett, N. P. (1995). Reduction of children's sport performance anxiety through social support and stress reduction training for coaches. *Journal of Applied Developmental Psychology, 16,* 125-42.

Smith, R. E., & Smoll, F. L. (1996). *Way to go coach! A scientifically-proven approach to coaching effectiveness.* Portola Valley, CA: Warde Publishers.

Superintendent of Documents. (1996). Surgeon General's report on physical activity and health. Washington, DC: Department of Health and Human Services.

Weiss, M. R. (1995). Children in sport. An educational model. In S. M. Murphy (Ed.), *Sport Psychology Interventions* (pp. 39-70). Champaign, IL: Human Kinetics.

Weiss, M. R., Bredemeier, B. J., & Shewchuk, R. M. (1986). The dynamics of perceived competence, perceived control, and motivational orientation in youth sports. In M. R. Weiss & D. Gould (Eds.), *Sport for children and youths* (pp. 89-101). Champaign, IL: Human Kinetics.

Weiss, R. M., & Horn, T. S. (1990). The relation between children's accuracy estimates of their physical competence and achievement-related characteristics. *Research Quarterly for Exercise and Sport, 61,* 250-58.

Weiss, M. R., McAuley, E., Ebbeck, V., & Wiese, D. M. (1990). Self-esteem and causal attributions for children's physical and social competence in sport. *Journal of Sport and Exercise Psychology, 12,* 21-36.

Youngman, Deborah & Ralph Mosher (1997). Personal communication.

Zaichkowsky, L. D., & Larson, G. A. (1995). Physical, motor, and fitness development in children and adolescents. *Journal of Education, 177,* 55-79.

Zaichkowsky, L. D., Zaichkowsky, L. B., & Martinek, T. J. (1980). *Growth and development: The child and physical activity.* St. Louis: C. V. Mosby.

2

Emotional Development: A Constructivist Approach

Henry Dupont

"In truth, there is as much construction in the affective domain as there is in the cognitive."

—Piaget,1981, p.12

INTRODUCTION

Many advances in psychology follow the discovery of a new way of observing or measuring human behavior. The IQ test and the interest inventory, for example, produced remarkable advances in the study of intelligence and vocational interest, respectively.

In his study of thinking, Piaget's use of the interview led to great advances in our understanding of cognitive development. My effort to study emotions and their development has led me to the creation of the Structured Emotional Development/Well-Being Interview (SEDWI) as a research tool (Dupont, 1994).

The SEDWI assumes that, in the course of development, as a part of our personal and interpersonal intelligence, we acquire a meaning for each of our emotions that is shared by the other persons in our family, community, and culture. This meaning is acquired by each of us through the process of our socialization. Perceptions, values, beliefs, and reason come to shape affect. The meaning of children's emotions becomes evident as they answer the SEDWI's short sequence of questions.

According to Stearns and Stearns (1986), a school official notes that perhaps the emotion that causes the most problems is anger, especially in the schools, so it is to anger that I will give special attention in this chapter.

Using the emotion of anger as an example, then, the SEDWI questions proceed as follows:

(1) Do you ever feel angry?

(2) When?
(3) Why?
(4) What do you do when you feel angry for that reason?
(5) Why that?
(6) How does that work for you, or how does it turn out when you do that?
(7) Is that what you want?
(8) How often do you feel angry?

In my experience, most children and adults answer these questions with considerable interest and candor.

This sequence of questions is repeated for fear, shame, guilt, and sadness. Questions 1 through 5 are also asked for pride and happiness. After subjects have described what they do when they feel proud (or happy), they are asked:

(6) Do you ever deliberately do something to feel proud (or happy)?
(7) Why, or why not?

This change in content is necessary because, whereas the negative feelings of fear, anger, shame, guilt, and sadness are problems in living to be solved, feeling proud and happy are positive affective states to be sought after and enjoyed.

Subjects' answers to the "why" questions reveal their system of values. Many subjects are totally unaware of how their feelings and actions are related to their values and other cognitions, so these questions challenge them to become conscious of this relationship. Simply asking "why" can be confrontational, so for Question 3, I often actually ask, "Please help me understand why you felt angry about that" and for Question 5, "Why does that seem like a thing to do?".

Many subjects will have the event and their feeling about it so strongly linked together that they will give you information about both in answer to Question 2. As they answer Question 5, many will believe the actions they describe are so strongly linked to a reason that they will provide data about both action and reason in answering Question 4. Younger children will often say, "Well, I hit him back to get even," as if the action and the reason for the action were self-evident. The action may be repeatedly described as an answer to the "why" question, as if the reason for the action is evident in the action.

THE SEVEN STAGES OF ANGER

The logic is different for the experience of each emotion. For anger, the logic centers around a threat to one's identify and well-being and how this threat is to be managed. In our culture, the psycho-logic of anger appears to undergo seven transformations in the course of a person's development. These transformations can be thought of as Stages in the individual's developing capacity to manage anger.

1. Distress and Impulsive Acting Out

The subject acts as if saying, "This can't be happening" or "Why can't I do this?". Subjects may cry and holler at the same time, and their actions may be random and disorganized. There is no reasoning as such; there are only sensory-action schemes that are essentially inborn survival reactions.

2. Frustration and Appeal to Authority

"We aren't allowed to do that." "I'll tell on you." "I can't do it; I need help." Here there is upset and an appeal to authority. Reasoning is simple, concrete, and dependent.

3. Protest and Opposition

"You can't!" "You shouldn't!" "If you hit me, I'll hit you!" At this stage, there is often retaliation in kind. Reasoning is concrete and inflexible, but increasingly autonomous in its authority.

4. Objection and Appeal to Fairness and Reciprocity

"That's not fair!" "That bothers me." "That's not something I would do." "You wouldn't like it if I did that to you." "You shouldn't say that—take it back." Objections and a fuss are made, including a demand for change retraction. Reasoning is in transition from the concrete to the abstract; there is an appeal to reciprocity and a suggestion of beginning capacity for reversibility in thinking.

5. Conflict over Autonomy

"I have a right to do what I want to do, go where I want to go, and be what I want to be. I can't let you control me, so stop it or I'll have to leave." There is a need to be self-defining, self-directing, and autonomous. Reasoning is abstract, but it can be rigid and inflexible.

6. Discomfort and the Differentiation of Feelings and Related Response

"That is irritating/annoying/disgusting/contemptible!" "Something has to change." There is increasing differentiation of value-informed reasons for feelings and reasons for actions. Reasoning is more consistently abstract. Reversibility is now consistently evident and increasingly flexible.

7. Confrontation, Discussion, and Exploration

"I'm not comfortable with that. We've got to talk about it." Verbal address with a desire to discuss and explore the situation. Abstract self-reflective reasoning and reversible, flexible thinking with a discussion of options and alternatives characterize this stage.

At maturity, the logic of anger includes a consciousness of our higher level needs for relationships and for mutuality in these relationships, and it will often reflect spiritual and ethical considerations as well. My research suggests that something of this nature occurs in the construction and development of each of our emotions (Dupont, 1994).

SEDWI PROTOCOLS

The SEDWI takes us into the center of an individual's emotional life, as the following interview protocols will illustrate. Two individuals' responses centering on anger will be reviewed (I = interviewer; R = respondent).

David (Age 11)

I: David, do you ever feel angry?
R: Sometimes.
I: When?
R: Every day.
I: Why do you feel angry?
R: Because my mama whips me.
I: Why does that make you feel angry?
R: Because I'd like to run away.
I: Why would you do that?
R: So I can get away from her.
I: Would that help?
R: No.
I: Why not?
R: Because.
I: Why because?
R: Because if I run out the door she'd give me a whipping.
I: Do you ever feel angry for any other reason?
R: No.
I: How often do you feel angry?
R: Every day.

Note that David, who is likely to be operating at Stage 2, is quite frustrated and helpless.

Mary (Age 15)

I: Mary, do you feel angry?
R: Not really. I don't get mad very easily.
I: Do you ever feel angry though?
R: Yes, when something happens that I don't want to happen. When somebody goes and says things about me or wants to start something with me or does something I don't like, I get angry.
I: Why do you suppose you get angry about those things?
R: Because it bothers me.

I: Bothers you. What do you mean by that?

R: Because I want to do something about it, and I don't know what to do about it, so it makes me mad.

I: What do you do when you feel angry for those reasons?

R: I don't know. Sometimes I don't do anything about it, just walk away from it.

I: Apparently other times, you do something. When you do something, what do you do?

R: I cry or get mad. I tell somebody sometimes.

I: Why do you suppose you do that?

R: Because I want something done about it. I don't know why. Because it bothers me.

I: How does it turn out when you do that?

R: Sometimes good, sometimes the same, sometimes bad.

I: Doesn't always work then?

R: Yes.

I: Are you saying that when you're angry, it often doesn't turn out too well?

R: Yes. Usually I say things I don't mean, and I do things I don't mean to do.

I: How often do you feel angry?

R: Not very often.

I: Once a week? A couple of times a week? Once a day? All the time? Almost never? Once in a great while?

R: Once in a great while. I don't get angry very easily.

Mary, probably using Stage 4 abilities, tries to manage matters by herself, but sometimes she tells somebody about it. Notice that both sets of responses could easily be converted into stories that could be used to further the respondents' understanding of themselves and others.

There is always a psycho-logic that links the feeling and its biochemistry to its object and the action to the feeling and its object. I regard this entire sequence (as do Rosenzweig, Leiman, and Breedlove, 1996) as constituting the emotions.

THEORY

Over the past twenty years, work with various editions of the SEDWI has led me to the theory of emotional development presented below:

• **Our needs and values are the motivating force in the construction of our feelings and emotions.**

Needs and values are organized into a cognitive grid through which we filter all of our experience (Dupont, 1994).

• **Feelings provide the link between our system of values and our emotions.**

Feelings are an integral part of each of our emotions as transitional adaptations. Positive feelings produce positive emotional states such as joy, happiness, and contentment. Negative feelings produce negative emotions such as fear, anger, shame, guilt, and sadness. Over the course of our emotional development, feelings play an increasingly important role.

- **Feelings are energy-regulating evaluations.**

Our perception and evaluation of events become built into the logic and vocabulary of our feelings, and we have feelings about everything! As we develop and interact with the objects that make up our world, we are constantly assigning value to these objects, and this value becomes built into our representations for these objects. Then, our response to these objects—how we feel about them and how we act upon them—is automatic; we give it little attention but our thought provides the structure for our behavior. We consciously re-evaluate only when we become aware that our constructions are not working for us.

The more significant an event is for our survival or well-being, the more energy we mobilize for use in confronting that event. This very primitive ability to evaluate objects as well as events and situations is elaborated, differentiated, and integrated into every functional repertoire of feelings that becomes a part of our personal-social competencies. Our energy mobilization and utilization varies with the operation of this social capacity. This is the "energetics" referred to by Piaget (Piaget & Inhelder, 1969, p. 114).

- **Energy mobilization and utilization are different from our respective emotions.**

As Piaget (1951, 1981) suggests, both our intelligence (cognition) and our affect are adaptive. In the course of development then, we learn to modulate our energy use according to our needs.

Pert has advanced a theory that each living person is a "psycho-somatic communication network" that is coordinated by the mind (1993, p. 178). This coordination is achieved through a system of neuropeptides and their receptors, and neuropeptides are essentially information molecules that direct energy.

In Pert's theory, these neuropeptides and their receptors are the biochemicals of emotion so that with each change in our feelings, there is a change in our (internal) biochemistry. Emotions, then, previously thought to be purely psychological are now thought to be linked to chemical processes taking place throughout the entire body; that is, they affect the functioning of all systems of the body including the immune system.

These findings have contributed to the development of that field of study known as psychoneuroimmunology, and they have enormous implications for our emotional well-being and health. There seems to be, for example, growing evidence that fear, anger, and depression, typically evident as responses to prolonged stress, negatively affect our immunity and make us vulnerable to a number of diseases.

With development, feelings and emotions become two functionally integrated constructions: Feelings become energy-regulating evaluations and emotions become actions, informed by feelings, that restore our equilibrium. Our utilization of energy varies with our feelings and the acts we initiate to realize our intentions.

• **With development, each emotion becomes a cognitive biosocial construction with a distinctive structure or psycho-logic.**

Both Averill (1980) and Harré (1986) regard emotions as social constructions; I do as well (Dupont, 1994). The implications that follow from this social construction hypothesis are simply enormous! For example, the construction of each of our feelings and emotions is dependent upon the acquisition of a particular self-in-relationship-with-others conception or logic that is acquired as a product of development and our social experience in the family, at school, in the community, and in a culture.

My studies of the reasons children have for their feelings and the reasons they have for their actions upon the objects of these feelings strongly suggest that emotional development is a social phenomenon; between ages five and fifteen, there is a convergence toward a limited number of reasons for each feeling-action linkage. With development and socialization in a particular social system, children increasingly share the system of meanings sanctioned by that social system. This should not surprise us, because without shared meaning, they (and we) could not communicate at all (Dupont, 1994).

• **There is both conservation and transformation in the construction of our feelings and emotions.**

In data collected over the past two decades, I have found clear evidence that we conserve the meaning of fear, anger, shame, guilt, sadness, pride, and happiness in the constructions we develop for these respective emotions. The meanings that are conserved across objects, feelings, and actions are essentially as follows:

(1) *Fear.* There are threats to one's physical safety that must be avoided, dealt with, or recovered from.
(2) *Anger:* There are threats to one's identity or well-being that must be confronted and managed.
(3) *Shame:* There is the threat of exposure of and embarrassment about one's flaws or wrong-doings that must be avoided or addressed in some way.
(4) *Guilt:* One has done wrong or harmed others for which restitution must be made.
(5) *Sadness:* There has been a loss or failure that must be mourned and then replaced or corrected.
(6) *Pride:* Something has been accomplished that must be celebrated.
(7) *Happiness:* Being well and doing well is to be enjoyed.

These are the meanings or psycho-logics that I have found for these emotions. As we say with anger, there are transformations in these psycho-logics that have stage-specific characteristics; thus, each emotion is the same and different at different times during development and in response to different objects.

- **Both our emotions and our consciousness are constructed in discourse with others.**

In discourse with their caretakers (parents), siblings, peers, and teachers, children construct the cognitive biosocial adaptations we call feelings and emotions. Social experience, discourse, and dialogue are absolutely essential for emotional development. There is construction and reconstruction in the course of emotional development. This discourse and dialogue also contribute to the construction of our consciousness, which is another essential element in the emotional development process.

Self-regulation is further important to the course of development. Piaget's (1976) work suggests four levels of consciousness significant for the kinds of self-regulation they make possible: (a) biochemical communications that permit what we experience as internal auto-regulations; (b) an action level "know how" that can be regulated through rewards and reinforcements; (c) a self-other consciousness that is cognitively concrete, but permits the regulation of feelings and actions in thought; and (d) a self-reflective psychosocial consciousness that is cognitively abstract and that permits our highest level of self-regulation. We know ourselves, other selves, and how we affect each other.

TEACHING, COUNSELING, AND PSYCHOTHERAPY

Teachers can stimulate and guide cognitive, biosocial, emotional development through classroom discussion that focuses on the real-life problems that are the object of children's feelings and the discovery of more effective, better-reasoned ways of responding to these problems. Then, too, the children's responses to the questions in the SEDWI are easily converted into stories that can be used for discussion, perspective-taking through role playing, and dramatization to facilitate this inter-domain development. *Toward Affective Development* (Dupont, Gardner, & Brody, 1974) and *Transition* (Dupont & Dupont, 1979) were efforts to develop programs of this kind. School counselors have been conducting affective and psychological education activities for years and more of these, responsibly directed, may yet be needed.

The focus in these activities is *not* on helping children cope with their emotions. Rather, it is on helping them discover more effective reasoning and ways of acting upon the objects of their feelings, thus changing their emotions. I have found this same focus to be helpful in counseling and psychotherapy.

Counseling as active listening could easily focus more on the construction of consciousness and the cognitive reconstruction of maladaptive feelings and emotions. The client's consciousness is easily influenced by such directives and questions as:

(1) What happened?
(2) How did you feel about it?
(3) What did you do?
(4) How did others react?
(5) How do you feel about it now?

(6) Is that what you want?
(7) What action might have produced a better result?

I am no longer comfortable just letting clients ramble on and on. Those of us practicing psychotherapy these days are under pressure to make the process less time-consuming and more effective. I have found the SEDWI to be an excellent assessment procedure, and because it is, in fact, a mini-therapy session, it is an excellent entrée into the treatment process. It takes therapist and client right into the place where the client lives. I have also found it a very good way to start the treatment of many Axis I and personality disorders. I believe its use is also compatible with many of the narrative (Aftel, 1996) and constructive (Hoyt, 1994) therapies. Its greatest value, however, may be as a research tool.

In constructing the theory of emotional development presented here, then, my goal has been to create a normative model of cognitive, biosocial, emotional development that anticipates the achievement of a mature, self-reflective consciousness and a repertoire of those socially relevant and effective feelings and emotions necessary for fully adaptive human interaction.

REFERENCES

Aftel, M. (1996). *The story of your life: Becoming the author of your experience*. New York: Simon & Schuster.

Averill, J. R. (1980). A constructivist view of emotion. In R. Plutchik & H. Kellerman (Eds.), *Emotion: Vol. 1. Theory, research, and experience* (pp. 305-39). New York: Academic Press.

Dupont, H. (1994). *Emotional development, theory, and applications: A neo-Piagetian perspective*. Westport, CT: Praeger Publications.

Dupont, H., & Dupont, C. (1979). *Transition*. Circle Pines, MN: American Guidance Service.

Dupont, H., Gardner, O. S., & Brody, D. (1974). *Toward affective development*. Circle Pines, MN: American Guidance Service.

Harré, R. (Ed.). (1986). *The social construction of emotions*. Oxford, England: Basil Blackwell.

Hoyt, M. G. (Ed.). (1994). *Constructive therapies*. New York: Guilford Press.

Pert, C. (1993). "The chemical communicators." In B. Moyers (Ed.), *Healing and the mind* (pp. 177-93). New York: Doubleday.

Piaget, J. (1951). *Play, dreams and imitation in childhood*. New York: W. W. Norton.

Piaget, J. (1976) *The grasp of consciousness: Action and concept in the young child*. Cambridge, MA: Harvard University Press.

Piaget, J. (1981) *Intelligence and affectivity: Their relationship during child development*. Palo Alto: Annual Reviews.

Piaget, J., & Inhelder, B. (1969). *The psychology of the child*. New York: Basic Books.

Rosenzweig, M. R., Leiman, A. L., and Breedlove, S. M. (1996). *Biological psychology*. Sunderland, MA: Sinauer Associates.

Stearns, C. Z., & Stearns, P. N. (1986). *Anger*. Chicago: The University of Chicago Press.

3

Literacy Development

Roselmina Indrisano and Jeanne S. Chall

How literacy develops has been of interest to scholars and practitioners of literacy for at least the past century. The first theoretical constructs of reading development appeared in the 1930s during the beginnings of the scientific study of education. Analyses of literacy development advanced somewhat from the 1960s through the 1980s, and reached an unprecedented level of refinement in the 1980s and 1990s.

In Part I of this article, we present selected definitions of literacy followed by an overview of some of the early and more recent views of literacy development. We suggest how they contribute to the learning and teaching of reading and to the interventions designed for those whose progress lags behind the expected.

This is followed by a recent model of reading development and suggestions for using the model to gain insights into the developmental nature of both the texts that can be read with comprehension and the cognitive, linguistic, and reading abilities of the readers. The implications of the stage theory for teaching learners at-risk are described. In Part II, we focus on literacy instruction, from research and theory to practice.

LITERACY DEFINED

In 1981, the International Reading Association published *A dictionary of reading and related terms*, a reference intended by its coeditors, Theodore L. Harris and Richard E. Hodges, "to define in one volume salient terms in reading and in the related disciplines and supporting fields of study from which the vocabulary of reading is drawn" (Harris & Hodges, 1981, p. viii). In 1995, the same scholars *published The literacy dictionary: The vocabulary of reading and writing*. The changes in the new dictionary, with the inclusion of writing as well as reading, reflect more than a decade of developments in literacy research, theory, and practice.

It is in the earlier work that the reason for beginning this article with a consideration of definition is found. Within the discussion of definitions of reading, Harris and Hodges (1981, p. 264) cite Strang's conclusion that a theoretical point of view affects instruction. Strang suggests, "If we think of reading primarily as word recognition, we will drill on the basic sight vocabulary and word recognition skills" and "If we think of reading as a thinking process, we shall be concerned with the reader's skill in making interpretations and generalizations, in drawing inferences and conclusions."

How is literacy thought of in 1995? In the later volume, as in the earlier work, the first definition of literacy is "the ability to read" (Harris & Hodges, 1995, p. 140). In the essay that follows the definition, a feature in the new dictionary, Venezky (1995, p. 142) provides a more elaborate explanation, again emphasizing writing, as well as reading:

Literacy is a minimal ability to read and write in a designated language, as well as a mindset or way of thinking about the use of reading and writing in everyday life. It differs from simple reading and writing in its assumption of an understanding of the appropriate uses of these abilities within a print-based society. Literacy, therefore, requires active, autonomous engagement with print and stresses the role of the individual in generating as well as receiving and assigning independent interpretations to messages.

Venezky's thoughtful essay on literacy, and Harris and Hodges' wisdom in including this feature in a dictionary, address the concerns of philosophers who are wary of the isolated symbol. Langer (1971, p. 135) writes,

language is much more than a set of symbols. It is essentially an organic, functioning system, of which the primary elements as well as the constructed products are symbols. Its forms do not stand alone, like so many monoliths each marking its one isolated grave; but instead, they tend to integrate, to make complex patterns, and thus to point out equally complex relationships in the world, the realm of their meanings.

Consistent with the definition of literacy offered by Venezky (1995, p. 142), this chapter will focus on "the individual's active, autonomous engagement with print" and on the instruction that is a reflection of this view of the reading process. In adopting this definition, the authors acknowledge other definitions of literacy, including those that include the processes of listening, speaking, writing, thinking, and numeracy; and the work of those who suggest that the complexities of the phenomena associated with literacy and advances in technology require the use of the term "literacies." For a more detailed discussion of these ideas, the reader is directed to the work of Venezky and colleagues (1990) and Gee (1990).

I. THEORIES OF READING DEVELOPMENT

This section is concerned with how reading develops, from its beginning to the most advanced forms, and is based on several of Chall's writings (with some modifications): *Stages of reading development*, 1983, 1996; *The reading crisis: Why poor children fall behind*, 1990 (with Jacobs and Baldwin).

The first developmental or stage theory of reading in the United States was presented by William S. Gray in 1925. The initial scheme, which was refined in 1937, included five stages, each accompanied by descriptions of goals and expected achievements; (1) readiness; (2) learning to read; (3) rapid progress in fundamental attitudes, habits, and skills; (4) extension of experience and increases in efficiency; and (5) refinement of attitudes, habits, and tastes.

In 1947, Arthur I. Gates presented a stage theory in his textbook on the teaching of reading. Similar to Gray's, his stage scheme included the characteristics of learners, their capabilities, limitations, and anticipated achievements. Gates' scheme proposed eight stages, as follows: (1) prereading, (2) reading readiness, (3) beginning reading, (4) initial independence, (5) advanced primary, (6) transition from primary to intermediate, (7) intermediate, and (8) mature reading.

David Russell's (1961) stages were based on research on child development. For each of his stages, Russell described the cognitive characteristics of the learner and the possible implications for the teaching of reading. The following stages were described: (1) prereading, (2) beginning reading, (3) initial stage of independent reading, (4) transition, (5) intermediate or low maturity, and (6) advanced (Chall, 1983).

Chall's (1983) model of reading development also views reading as a complex of abilities and skills that change with development. Thus, reading is viewed as essentially different for the preschooler, first grader, fourth grader, high school student, and adult. The tasks set by the school differ at various stages of reading, and the abilities and skills needed by readers to meet these tasks also differ.

Chall's stages were first presented in 1979 and elaborated in the book *Stages of reading development* (1983 and 1996). These stages may be seen in the different texts that students are able to read at different levels of their development, and in the developing language and cognitive abilities needed to comprehend these increasingly more difficult texts.

Selection from typical materials at each succeeding stage contains more unfamiliar or low-frequency words, longer and more complex sentences, more difficult syntax, and more difficult ideas. The topics and language become more abstract and more removed from common events and experiences at successive levels. The differences in language, in concepts, and in syntax between Stage 1 and 2 as opposed to those in Stage 3 and beyond (around fourth grade and above) are that Stages 1 and 2 contain familiar, high-frequency words, and short, simple sentences, whereas in Stages 3, 4, and 5, the ideas and language become more abstract and more subtle and the vocabulary and syntax are less familiar.

The language and cognitive abilities of readers need to advance to meet the increasing demands of these stages. Generally, reading ability advances more slowly than language comprehension. Thus the first graders, who can understand about 6,000 words when heard, can read only about 300 to 500 words at the end of the grade—less than 10 percent of the words they can understand when heard. By the end of Stage 2 (grade 3), reading moves up toward the level of listening; but still only about one-third of the words known from listening can be read. Only sometime toward the end of Stage 3 (grade 8) does reading catch up to listening comprehension.

An overview of the major qualitative characteristics and masteries at each stage suggests that a useful way to conceptualize these elements is in terms of the relative emphasis of the two major aspects of reading: the medium, or word recognition (alphabetic writing that corresponds to the sounds of words), and the message, the meaning (the story, the textbook, the recipe, the legal document) that is read. Generally there is a shift that takes place at the successive stages—from learning the medium, that is, recognizing the printed words and learning the alphabetic principle in the early stages to acquiring a more extensive, abstract, less familiar meaning vocabulary and more advanced syntax in the later stages. A considerable change takes place at Stage 3, when the major task shifts from learning the medium to learning the message.

These developmental characteristics fall into six stages—from Stage 0 (prereading) to Stage 5 (the most mature, skilled level of reading, in which readers construct and reconstruct knowledge from their own reading). Generally, in Stage 0 (from birth to about age 6) the child learns some simple concepts of reading and writing—reading of signs, giving the names of the letters, writing one's name, and pretending to read books. Stages 1 and 2 (typically acquired in grades 1, 2, and 3) can be characterized as the time of "learning to read." In Stage 1 (grade 1 and beginning grade 2), children learn the alphabetic principle—how to recognize and sound out (decode) words in print—and they read simple texts. In Stage 2 (grades 2 and 3), children acquire fluency and become automatic in reading familiar texts—those that use language and thought processes already within their experience and abilities. Stages 3 to 5 can be characterized roughly as the "reading to learn" stages—when the texts read in school go beyond what the readers already know, linguistically and cognitively. At Stage 3 (grades 4 to 8), the students use reading as a tool for learning, and texts begin to contain new words and new ideas beyond the scope of the readers' language and knowledge of the world.

Stage 3 is distinguished from Stages 1 and 2 in that the reading tasks incorporate increasingly unfamiliar material. From then on (stages 4 and 5—high school and college), the texts and other materials typically read become ever more varied and complex in content, language, and cognitive demands. In order to read, understand, and learn from these more demanding texts, the readers' knowledge, language, and vocabulary need to expand, as does their ability to think critically and broadly.

Teaching Those Who Have Difficulty

The causes and treatments of reading difficulty have been a concern of psychologists, teachers, neurologists, and psychiatrists for nearly a century. A huge literature exists on the topic. We can touch only on some of it here, and we focus on interventions that can be implemented by teachers. These are presented in two sections—difficulty with decoding and difficulties of children from families with low incomes.

Difficulties with Decoding

The accumulated research confirms that difficulty with decoding and word recognition is probably the most common problem among students who have reading difficulty during early stages of reading (Share and Stanovich, 1995). Such students' language and cognitive development is usually ahead of their ability to recognize and decode words. Generally their listening comprehension is above their reading ability. Their difficulty is usually not with the understanding of ideas—with the message—but with the medium—the print.

Clinical and classroom experience suggests that these children have greatest difficulty with Stage 1, particularly with decoding. They have great difficulty in associating letters with sounds and even greater difficulty with blending sounds to form words. Many also have trouble learning to recognize whole words at sight.

Those who have these problems with print at Stage 1 usually have trouble with Stage 2, not because the stories they are expected to read are too hard to understand but because their word recognition and decoding are insufficient for the task. Their decoding is not sufficiently fluent and automatic to make concentration on the content possible.

Compared with others of similar chronological age and cognitive development, the transition of these children from Stage 1 and 2 is more difficult and takes longer. It may take some children several years before they are comfortable reading the simplest book. At an age when most move into the fluency of Stage 2, they are either glued to the print or they ignore the print and guess wildly. The difficult transition from decoding (Stage 1) to fluency (Stage 2) was noted by many of the early investigators of reading difficulty, among them, Gray, Gates, Orton, and Fernald (Reviewed in Chall, 1983).

An overlong stay in Stage 1 is serious. Aside from the impression these children and others may get that they cannot learn to read, they also fall behind in acquiring the substantive knowledge that others more advanced gain from their reading. Therefore, provision needs to be made for the pupil's continued conceptual and informational development, which, in most schools, comes from reading printed materials. If this is not provided while the reader is still learning to read and cannot yet use his reading for learning, the student may also lose out on the knowledge, vocabulary, and concepts needed for further education and also as background for reading at Stage 3 and beyond. Students may fall behind in their cognitive development, although their original problem may have been with decoding alone (Stanovich, 1986).

Difficulties of Children from Families with Low Income

That poor children lag behind in reading has been known and reported in the pedagogical literature for many decades (Eppenstein, 1966). In a recent study by Chall, Jacobs and Baldwin (1990), low SES second graders had reading and word meaning scores similar to those of middle-class children. But their scores started to decelerate around grade 4. This "fourth-grade slump," reported by teachers of poor children (and reported recently by Garibaldi, 1993), started first with word meaning. The low-income children in our study—in grades 4 through 7—had greatest difficulty defining less common, abstract, academic, and literary words as compared with a normative population. In grade 4, the children were about a year behind grade norms on word meaning. By grade 7, they were more than two years below norms. Next to decelerate were their scores on word recognition and spelling. Oral reading and silent reading comprehension began to decelerate later, in grades 6 and 7.

Thus, if we view reading as composed of the three basic components proposed by Carroll (1977)—cognition, language, and reading skills—cognition seemed to be a lesser problem for them than language and reading skills. In grades 4 to 7, they did best on the reading tests that relied on context and required understanding—reading comprehension and connected oral reading.

Our population seemed to do well on measures of basic language abilities through the third grade. After the third grade, they began to decelerate first in knowledge of the meanings of words, especially the less common, more academic words found in books used in the intermediate and upper elementary grades and higher. Further, their basic linguistic competencies, as shown in their grammar and language awareness scores, were stronger than their word knowledge, especially after the third grade.

Language and Literacy Connection

A useful way to view the instructional needs for literacy development among children and adults—those who are making normal progress as well as those who are having difficulty—is to assess their abilities in the various language areas. That is, are they more proficient in language, particularly in vocabulary, in knowledge, or in print skills—word recognition, decoding, and spelling? Or the reverse? Knowing a student's strengths and weaknesses in the various language areas helps in planning an effective instructional program (Roswell & Chall, 1992, 1994).

The following section discusses the connection between the various language areas with special emphasis on the reading development of the low income children we discussed earlier. More specifically, we will be concerned with the kinds of instructional emphases that lead to literacy development.

Generally, we found that those who received practice that was developmentally challenging made better progress. Thus teachers' awareness of how literacy and language develop, important concepts for all teachers, is critical for those who work with learners at-risk. As the earlier students start to slip in their literacy and language development, the further behind they fall in each successive grade (Chall, Jacobs & Baldwin, 1990; Stanovich, 1986).

Indeed, a follow-up study of our low-income children, five years later when they were in grades 7, 9, and 11, found patterns of decelerating scores similar to those they exhibited when they were in the elementary grades (see Snow et al., 1991). On most tests, their scores were below the norms; and the discrepancies between their scores and norms were larger in each succeeding grade. By grade 11, their reading scores were in the twenty-fifth percentile—considerably below their relative achievement in grades 4 through 7.

Preventing the Fourth-Grade Slump

In order to prevent the deceleration in vocabulary found in the fourth grade and higher, we recommend a systematic program for vocabulary development that would start early, in first grade or even kindergarten. Our proposal is based on the premise that, unless children are exposed to language that is beyond their everyday experience, they may have little opportunity to learn it.

Thus, we propose that the language of low-income children in grades 1-3 (and perhaps earlier) be stimulated by reading to them text that is considerably more advanced than they can read on their own. Such texts should be generally within their listening comprehension but contain words that are not yet in their listening and speaking vocabularies.

The research literature offers reasons why it is important to read texts *to* children that are difficult enough to challenge their existing language knowledge. Chomsky (1972) found that children, whose parents read books to them that their parents had read to them as children, were the best readers. Such books exposed the children to language that was beyond their everyday oral—language and that was beyond their reading ability.

Feitelson and her colleagues (1993) examined the mismatch for Arabic children between their home language and literate language. They found that, for kindergarten-aged children, reading them challenging stories that contained more literate vocabulary and language structures than they used in their oral language helped the children make the transition between the two forms of language. Their listening comprehension, in particular, increased as did the richness of their vocabularies and proportion of clauses they used.

John Carroll's recent studies of factor analyses of language (Carroll, 1993, p. 193) supports Feitelson's work. He wrote, "There are many influences that govern individual's rate and extent of language development—exposure to increasing levels of language complexity through exposure to model speakers, reading of increasingly difficulty material, etc."

Research on the relation between language, listening, and reading comprehension also supports the value of reading challenging texts to children. There has been a consensus in the research that children's understanding of spoken language (i.e., their listening comprehension) is more advanced than their reading comprehension. Chall's model of reading development (1983) discussed earlier reports that, by the end of the first grade, children know about 6,000 words (when heard), yet they read only about 600. Curtis (1980) found that, at grade 2, children's listening comprehension was nearly twice as high as their reading comprehension. By grade 5, while their listening and reading comprehension abilities become more similar, their listening comprehension still exceeds their reading comprehension. Even at the eighth grade, most students can understand better the same material when it is read to them than when they read it. It is not until about the high-school level when reading comprehension is at about the same level as listening comprehension (Sticht, 1979).

Borrowing from Feitelson, Carroll, and others, we thus propose that schools develop vocabulary in the earliest grades (as early as kindergarten and preschool), as well as in later grades by reading to children books that challenge their listening vocabulary and syntax. Teachers can play a vital role in such instruction by reading to children stories containing words and concepts beyond the students' everyday experiences. Follow-up activities would include having children discuss what was read, act it out, and respond to it in other forms (see Feitelson, Goldstein, Iraqi, & Share, 1993). Teachers can encourage children to use more difficult words in their speech as well as in their writing—especially in content-area instruction.

The Importance of Challenge

Challenge is a critical factor in language development—whether heard or read, for adults as well as for children. For reading, the low-income children in our study who received instruction using books on a challenging level made better gains in all aspects of reading—word recognition, comprehension, and word meanings—than those whose text-based instruction was not as challenging (Chall, Jacobs, & Baldwin, 1990). This finding is consistent with the conclusions of previous studies (Chall & Feldmann, 1966; Chall, Conard, & Harris, 1977; Chall, Conard, & Harris-Sharples, 1983; Chall & Conard, 1991; Hayes, Wolfer, & Wolfe, 1993). The findings on the importance of challenge confirm Vygotsky's (1962) theory of the zone of proximal development—that, when instruction is provided by the teacher (or by knowledgeable peers), it should precede rather than follow the child's level of development (c.f., Chall & Conard, 1991).

Thus, the reading to children of books that use more complex and difficult language than students can read helps build the vocabulary they will need for reading and writing in the fourth grade and beyond.

Educators have long recommended the reading of books to children. Unfortunately, once children begin to read on their own, it becomes unclear which books are appropriate for listening and which for their own reading. Further, the teaching of reading methodology has made little distinction between books that challenge children's language development and those that challenge their reading development.

Using the same reading materials for both language and reading development may not be equally effective. If the material is challenging for language development, it will usually be too difficult for reading. If it is challenging for reading, it will usually be too easy for developing language.

Thus, for developing language we propose a set of materials of greater difficulty to challenge, especially, their meaning vocabularies—texts from which they can learn the language forms, concepts, and words that they do not already possess. The texts that challenge language will usually be too difficult to read on their own. It is questionable, particularly in the early grades, whether the same texts can be used to meet the requirements for learning to read and for developing language.

In the following section we focus on literacy instruction, from the viewpoint of both theory and practice. We present recent thinking on optimal instruction to bring readers from the very beginning of reading ability to the highest levels of strategic reading.

II. LITERACY INSTRUCTION

At the dawning of the twentieth century, *The psychology and pedagogy of reading* (Huey, 1908) was published. This work marked a shift in the focus of psychologists who were the first researchers to study reading. To the early investigations of reading as behavior, Huey added studies of reading as behavior that is affected by instruction. Now, in the twilight of the twentieth century, the accumulated studies of the reading and writing processes and the instruction that contributes to their acquisition and refinement defy reasonable inventory. As in other human endeavors, the quality of the research and theory is as varied as the abilities and opportunities of those who have studied these complex phenomena.

In recent decades, several resources have made the daunting task of studying the accumulated knowledge and research more amenable to the beneficiaries of the work of leading scholars. Since 1970, the International Reading Association has published four editions *of Theoretical models and processes of reading* (Singer & Ruddell, 1970, 1976 and 1985; and Ruddell, R. B., Ruddell, M. R. and Singer, 1994). These volumes, which have grown in wisdom and in weight over the years of their development, are themselves a rich history of reading theory, research, and practice. While the first volume focused on theoretical models of the reading process, with minimal attention to practice, the most recent volume focuses on the processes of reading and literacy and is rich in information about instruction. In 1984, the *Handbook of reading research* edited by Pearson, Barr, Kamil, and Mosenthal was published, followed in 1991 by the second volume, edited by Barr, Kamil, Mosenthal, and Pearson. Again, the progress of the field is evident in the contents of these works, with the emphasis on reading in the first volume expanded to include literacy in the second volume. A joint effort of the International Reading Association and the National Council of Teachers of English resulted in the *Handbook of research on teaching the English language arts* (1991), edited by Flood, Jensen, Lapp, and Squire. In this volume, a comprehensive definition of literacy forms the basis for explorations of language, listening, speaking, reading, and writing.

We have turned to the most recent of these works for the summaries that are presented here in a form we hope will be useful to teachers and administrators. In doing so, we acknowledge that even the most conscientious reporter will not do justice to the original texts, and urge the reader to refer to the chapters from which the information was drawn.

In planning a synthesis of research on teaching, one option is to focus on instructional models. However, Farrell (1991, p. 63) suggests that, "Because of the complexity of the curriculum (or curricula) of the English language arts, any single instructional model, particularly a monolithic one, will perforce distort what takes place in the classroom." An alternative approach was offered by Mandel, cited by Farrell (1991, p. 63), who calls "for a true and strict eclecticism: selection from what appears to be the best in various doctrines, methods, or styles." Here, then, are summaries of the writers' analyses of the best thinking from which readers may make their selections. While the authors acknowledge the significance of the writing process in the acquisition and development of literacy, the limitations of space require the selection of most fundamental aspects of the reading process for emphasis: word knowledge, comprehension and learning, and response.

Word Knowledge

In their chapter in the *Handbook on teaching the English language arts* (1991), Mason, Herman, and Au focus on word identification and vocabulary knowledge, emphases that reflect the classic and current research on how children develop the ability to read text.

Word Identification

The recommendations for word identification instruction are based on two major themes within the context of children's overall literacy development: (1) "children learn to identify words more effectively if they are presented within a larger, more meaningful context" and (2) "the complexity of written English requires children to develop a number of different strategies for learning to identify words" (Mason et al., 1991, p. 726). Consistent with developmental theories of reading acquisition, the authors focus their recommendations for word identification instruction on the kindergarten and primary grades and advise teachers of younger learners to:

1. Shift from the view that literacy learning begins in the first grade to the idea that because literacy develops earlier, kindergarten children can benefit from "context-supported reading and writing activities" (Mason et al., 1991, p. 726).

2. Shift from isolated approaches to teaching words and skills "in the context of a wide range of meaningful reading and writing activities" (Mason et al., 1991, p. 726).
3. Understand that because word identification skills are acquired over several years, "new literacy concepts should be built upon those already learned and understood" (Mason et al., 1991, p. 726).
4. Understand that children acquire strategies for rapid, accurate identification of common words and analysis of letters and word patterns in unfamiliar words through a wide range of reading experiences.

Vocabulary Knowledge

Mason, Herman, and Au (1991) suggest that when reading and writing, mature language users draw upon their extensive vocabularies and their understanding of the systems of the English language. They cite Miller, who described vocabulary as "a coherent, integrated system of concepts" (Mason et al., 1991, p. 727), and they suggest that an understanding of and appreciation for the "systematicness" (Mason et al., 1991, p. 729) and regularity of the English language contribute to word identification and vocabulary knowledge.

Consistent with these principles, Mason, Herman, and Au (1991) offer these suggestions to guide instruction in vocabulary knowledge:

1. Because children cannot be taught all the words they will require for reading and writing, they need to expand their vocabularies through wide reading in and out of school. This approach affords students meaningful opportunities to learn new words and the concepts they represent, and perhaps, to develop the reading habit.
2. When vocabulary instruction is appropriate, effective approaches include assessing prior knowledge, relating the known to the new, and placing the new words in the overall schema or "network of concepts."
3. Older students who have been taught to understand English morphology, root words and affixes, are better able to comprehend groups of related words.
4. At all levels, an age-appropriate understanding of English grammar will assist students to infer both the identity and the meanings of unfamiliar words.
5. Frequent reading and discussion of a variety of books at school and at home are recommended for improving comprehension and expanding word knowledge.
6. Students benefit from opportunities to apply the strategies they have learned when reading unfamiliar text.
7. An interest in and a curiosity about language and words are critical ingredients in vocabulary development and are "within the inspirational power of teachers" (Mason et al., 1991, p. 729).

Comprehension and Learning

Based on their review of the research in reading comprehension instruction, Flood and Lapp (1991) present three types of information for teachers: a process for explicit comprehension instruction; a description of the behaviors that characterize effective, strategic readers; and a summary of the instructional practices that foster comprehension.

Explicit Comprehension Instruction
There is increasing evidence that explicit instruction is effective when the teacher uses a four-stage process that gradually shifts responsibility to the student. The stages include: (1) introducing the task and its purpose, (2) modeling or demonstrating how the task is accomplished, (3) providing guided practice and feedback as students attempt the task that has been demonstrated, and (4) providing opportunities for independent practice of the task in new situations. The shift in responsibility occurs when, following the teacher's assuming the major responsibility during the first two stages, the responsibility is shared by the teacher and the student(s) in stage three, and assumed by the student(s) in stage four.

In comprehension instruction, as in other aspects of the literacy curriculum, teachers can be guided by Vygotsky's (1978) concept of the "zone of proximal development," that place between the learner's current understanding and/or competence, and the place where progress can be made with expert guidance. (See earlier section on reading challenging texts.) In this view, teaching, learning, and assessment are considered dynamic, rather than static processes, and the teacher's decisions are based upon an understanding of the learner, the process to be learned, and the domain of knowledge. Assessment is conducted by observing the learners as they engage in authentic literacy tasks and by providing appropriate intervention at the point where students will benefit from teacher guidance. The effectiveness of the interventions suggests the type of instruction that should be provided to the learner.

The Strategic Reader
The approach described here derives its authenticity from the observed behaviors of competent or strategic readers before, during, and after reading (Flood & Lapp, 1991).

Before reading, strategic readers: (1) preview the text, noting text features and relating their predictions of text content to their existing knowledge and experience; (2) activate and/or build appropriate background knowledge, and note the vocabulary and the structure of the text; and (3) set purpose(s) and pose questions to guide their reading.

During reading, strategic comprehenders: (1) paraphrase the text to check their understanding, (2) monitor their comprehension by engaging in creative and critical thinking about the text, and (3) integrate what they have learned with what they already know, and revise their purposes for reading, as appropriate.

The activities strategic readers engage in after reading include: (1) summarizing the information presented in expository text or retelling the story after reading narrative text, (2) evaluating the writer's ideas, and (3) applying and/or extending the ideas presented by the writer.

Instructional Practices
Consistent with the view of the reader as actively engaged in generative thinking in order to construct the meaning of the text, Flood and Lapp (1991) recommend several instructional practices.

1. Preparing for reading. Students can be taught to prepare for reading activities by learning to become actively engaged with the text, by calling to mind the

relevant knowledge and experience that the author presumes they will bring to the text, and by determining a purpose and a plan for reading.

2. Developing vocabulary. Since the vocabulary of the text is the author's symbolic system for conveying meaning to the reader, students must be prepared to understand the language of the text, its relevance to the central concepts, and its subtleties and nuances.

3. Text structure. Since the structure of a well-written text reflects the author's thought patterns while telling the story or conceptualizing the informational content, a reader's awareness of the organizational pattern of the text can contribute to comprehension and recall.

4. Questioning. Teaching students to work cooperatively to construct and answer questions about the text, and to determine whether there is an explicit or implied relationship between the question and the answer can lead to increased independence in reading and learning from text.

5. Meta processing. Teaching students to understand their own learning processes through determining what they know, what they want to know, and what they need to know forms the basis for metacognitive processing whereby readers become responsible for selecting, monitoring, checking and correcting their own strategies for learning from text.

6. Summarizing and

7. Notetaking. These two processes exert similar cognitive demands on the reader, but impose different demands on the writers. While the summary requires a cohesive presentation of the significant ideas in a text, notetaking permits a simple or interrelated listing of these ideas. However, both procedures are useful in teaching students to select and reflect on the significant ideas in the text.

8. Voluntary/recreational reading. The opportunity to select books and materials consistent with the reader's interests and curiosities is known to enhance both comprehension and attitude toward reading.

In their chapter, Flood and Lapp (1991) present for each recommendation complete descriptions of instructional activities. The reader is invited to consult the original work for these detailed descriptions.

Response

Decades of investigations in reader response conducted by literary theorists, philosophers, psychologists, and educators have been analyzed by Squire (1994). Based on the findings of this body of research, Squire offers a series of principles to guide instructional practice of teaching literature.

1. "The teaching of literature must focus on the transaction between the reader and the work" (Squire,1994, p. 640). The task of the teacher is to guide students in thoughtful and aesthetic response to the central ideas in the text. Ultimately, the teaching of literature should assist students to deepen and strengthen the literary experience and to develop "sound literary insight" and "aesthetic judgment" (Squire,1994, p. 640).

2. "Response is affected by prior knowledge and prior experience" (Squire,1994, p. 640). Since the literary experience is dependent upon the cognitive and affective backgrounds of the reader, the teacher will need to understand and consider the characteristics of the reader when selecting

books and other reading materials. Timeless classics as well as contemporary high quality literature are the teacher's reservoir for introducing students to particular works at the optimal time in their young lives.

3. "Response differs with time and place" (Squire,1994, p. 641). Students' capacity for comprehension and response is limited by their knowledge and experience. Introducing literature that will extend students' knowledge and understanding beyond their immediate circumstances is a responsibility of the teacher.

4. "Response to literature varies with the rhetorical model—narrative or non-narrative, efferent or aesthetic" (Squire,1994, p. 642). This finding suggests that teachers "introduce young readers to the many modes, genres and conventions" of literature (Squire,1994, p. 642). Further, because the ability to read literary text that evokes a primarily aesthetic response does not assure the ability to read informational text, which generally evokes an efferent response, students need to learn to read and respond to a variety of genre.

5. "Readers generally have a common response to a literary text, yet no two responses are identical" (Squire,1994, p. 642). When guiding students to respond thoughtfully to a text, consideration must be given to the central tendency imposed by the text and the varied responses that will be unique to the individual reader.

6. "Works of genuine literary quality can evoke richer, more meaningful experience than can "pseudoliterature'" (Squire,1994, p. 643). Since the quality of the literary experience is dependent upon the quality of the text, Squire advises teachers to select works that offer readers rich opportunities for response. He cites Dixon, who suggested that a real literary text is "a poem, a novel, a play", "is an event in the life of a reader. It is an experience s/he lives through, part of the ongoing stream of life" (Squire,1994, p. 643).

7. "It takes two to read a book" (Squire,1994, p. 644). Squire suggests that the literary experience is enhanced when readers talk and write about their responses from their earliest school days. When individual readers discuss their responses orally or in writing, they are actively engaged in extending and refining their ideas in response to those of their listeners or readers.

8. "Important developmental differences can be seen in the ways children respond to literature" (Squire,1994, p. 645). At various age levels students differ in their responses "to such text elements as character, theme and point of view" (Squire,1994, p. 645). Differences are evident in both the form and the content of the responses. Once again, knowledge of the reader, the process, and the text are critical to instructional planning.

9. "The sounds of words are often as important as their sense" (Squire,1994, p. 645). A neglected aspect of the literary experience for students is reading and hearing text read aloud. Poems, plays, and stories written for the human voice are particularly amenable to enhanced response when experienced orally.

10. "The ways in which we teach literature will permanently affect our students' responses" (Squire,1994, p. 645). It follows, then, that we must emphasize, in school, the kinds of responses we think most important to develop for a lifetime. If we use literature only to teach reading skills or strategies, we will prevent children from growing in their understanding and appreciation of literature (Squire,1994, p. 645).

THE STATE OF THE ART

Scholarly reviews of the literature provide an opportunity to consider the progress that scholars have made in understanding and teaching the complex phenomenon that Huey (1908, p.6) described as "the most remarkable specific performance that civilization has learned in all its history." While individual interpretations will vary, we suggest that the century of investigations that was initiated with Huey's work has culminated in approaches to instructional practice that have several characteristics in common.

1. Reading is considered a transaction between a reader and a writer through the medium of the text. The reader uses a lifetime of knowledge and experience in order to construct meaning.

2. Literacy begins to develop at the beginning of a child's life, not when the child enters school. Thus experiences with living and language, as well as reading and writing, contribute to the child's ability to acquire and develop formal literacy abilities in the school years.

3. Since the literacy processes are thought to be recursive and interactive rather than linear and molecular, instruction that is informed by an understanding of the learner, the process to be taught, and the domain of knowledge is preferable to approaches that depend upon a presumed sequence of isolated skills.

4. The ultimate goal of reading instruction is to assist the learner to be a purposeful, competent, and thoughtful reader who uses the strategies they have been taught in the service of comprehension, learning, and response.

5. Literacy abilities are cumulative and develop over time, thus effective instruction builds from the known to the new.

6. Comprehension and learning from text depend on the reader's activities before, during, and after reading. Comprehension is not synonymous with response, but response is dependent upon comprehension.

7. The task of the teacher in strategic learning is to provide instruction that gradually shifts the responsibility from the teacher to the student(s) through direct instruction, scaffolded practice, and finally, independent application. In this model, students learn to be in control of their own learning by understanding what to do, how to do it, and when to do it again, and to use this knowledge to monitor and refine their efforts.

8. The task of the teacher in encouraging reader response is to provide students with high quality texts in a variety of genre, and to guide students to respond orally and in writing in both aesthetic and efferent modes.

9. In planning instruction, teachers are guided by Vygotsky's (1978) concept of the "zone of proximal development," that place between the learner's current understanding and/or competence, and the place where they can function with expert guidance. In this view, teaching, learning, and assessment are considered dynamic rather than static processes.

10. The development of competent, thoughtful, and committed readers is "within the inspirational power of teachers" (Mason, Herman, & Au, 1991, p. 729).

CONCLUSIONS

We have presented an overview of ways of looking at the development of reading and literacy over the past approximately seventy years. Starting with changes in the definitions of reading and literacy, we turned to various developmental schemes of reading and literacy development. A recent developmental view of reading was described together with ways in which it can help explain how reading develops and the instructional needs of those who make normal or below normal progress. This was followed by an overview of new theories, research, and practices that relate to bringing readers to ever higher levels of proficiency—from beginning reading to advanced strategic reading.

REFERENCES

Barr, R., Kamil, M. L., Mosenthal, P., & Pearson, P. D. (Eds.). (1991). *Handbook of reading research. Vol. II.* New York: Longman.

Carroll, J. B. (1977). Developmental parameters of reading comprehension. In J. T. Guthrie (Ed.*), Cognition, curriculum, and comprehension.* Newark, DE: International Reading Association.

Carroll, J. B. (1993). *Human cognitive abilities: A survey of factor-analytic studies.* New York: Cambridge University Press.

Chall, J. S. (1983). *Stages of reading development.* New York: McGraw Hill.

Chall, J. S. (1996). *Stages of reading development.* 2nd ed. Fort Worth, TX: Harcourt Brace.

Chall, J. S., & Conard, S. S. (1991). *Should textbooks challenge students: The case for easier or harder textbooks.* New York: Teachers College Press.

Chall, J. S., Conard, S. S., & Harris, S. (1977). *An analysis of textbooks in relation to declining S.A.T. scores.* New York: College Entrance Examination Board.

Chall, J. S., Conard, S. S., & Harris-Sharples, S. (1983). *Textbooks and challenge: An inquiry into textbook difficulty, reading achievement, and knowledge acquisition.* A final report to the Spencer Foundation. Cambridge, MA: Harvard University Graduate School of Education.

Chall, J. S., & Feldmann, S. (1966). First grade reading: An analysis of the interactions of professed methods, teacher implementations and child background. *The reading teacher, 19,* 569-75.

Chall, J. S., Jacobs, V. A., & Baldwin, L. E. (1990). *The reading crisis: Why poor children fall behind.* Cambridge, MA: Harvard University Press.

Chomsky, C. (1972). Stages in language development and reading exposure. *Harvard Educational Review, 42,* 1-33.

Curtis, M. E. (1980). Development of components of reading skill. *Journal of Educational Psychology, 72,* 656-69.

Eppenstein, J. M. (1966). Efforts to teach reading to the culturally deprived child throughout history: Seminar paper for selected problems in the teaching of the language arts. Unpublished manuscript, Harvard Graduate School of Education, Cambridge, MA.

Farrell, E. J. (1991). Instructional models for English language arts. In J. Flood, J. M. Jensen, D. Lapp, & J. R. Squire (Eds.), *Handbook of research in teaching the English language arts* (pp. 63-84). New York: Macmillan.

Feitelson, D., Goldstein, Z., Iraqi, J., & Share, D. L. (1993). Effects of listening to story reading on aspects of literacy acquisition in a diglossic situation. *Reading Research Quarterly, 28,* 71-79.

Flood, J., Jensen, J. M., Lapp, D., & Squire, J. R. (Eds.). (1991). *Handbook of research in teaching the English language arts.* New York: Macmillan.

Flood, J., & Lapp, D. (1991). 34 B. Reading comprehension instruction. In J. Flood, J. M. Jensen, D. Lapp, & J. R. Squire (Eds.), *Handbook of research in teaching the English language arts* (pp. 732-42). New York: Macmillan.

Garibaldi, A. M. (1993). Creating prescriptions for success in urban schools: Turning the corner on explanations for academic failure. In M. Tomlinson (Ed.), *Motivating students to learn: Overcoming barriers to high achievement.* Berkeley, CA: McCutchan.

Gee, J. P. (1990). *Social linguistics and literacies: Ideology in discourses.* New York: Falmer.

Harris, T. L., & Hodges, R. E. (Eds.) (1981). *A dictionary of reading and related terms.* Newark, DE: International Reading Association.

Harris, T. L., & Hodges, R. E. (Eds.) (1995). *The literacy dictionary: The vocabulary of reading and writing.* Newark, DE: International Reading Association.

Hayes, D., Wolfer, L., & Wolfe, M. (1993). Was the decline in SAT-verbal scores caused by simplified school texts? Paper presented at the annual meeting of the American Sociological Association, Miami Beach, FL.

Huey, E. B. (1908). *The psychology and pedagogy of reading.* New York: Macmillan.

Langer, S. K. (1971). *Philosophy in a new key: A study in the symbolism of reason, rite and art.* (3rd ed.). Cambridge, MA: Harvard University Press.

Mason, J. M., Herman, P. A., & Au, K. H. (1991). Reading 34 A. Children's developing knowledge of words. In J. Flood, J. M. Jensen, D. Lapp, & J. R. Squire (Eds.), *Handbook of research in teaching the English language arts.* (pp. 721-31). New York: Macmillan.

Pearson, P. D., Barr, R., Kamil, M. L., & Mosenthal, P. (Eds.) (1984). *Handbook of reading research.* New York: Longman.

Roswell, F. G., & Chall, J. S. (1992, Updated Edition, 1994). *Diagnostic assessments of reading and teaching strategies.* Chicago: Riverside.

Roswell, F. G., & Chall, J. S. (1994). *Creating successful readers.* Chicago: Riverside.

Ruddell, R. B., Ruddell, M. R., & Singer, H. (Eds.) (1994). *Theoretical models and processes of reading.* (4th ed.). Newark, DE: International Reading Association.

Russell, D. H. (1961). *Children learn to read.* (2nd ed.). Boston, MA: Ginn.

Share, D. L., & Stanovich, K. E. (1995). Cognitive processes in early reading development: A model of acquisition and individual differences. *Issues in Education, 1..*

Singer, H., & Ruddell, R. B. (Eds.). (1970). *Theoretical models and processes of reading.* Newark, DE: International Reading Association.

Singer, H., & Ruddell, R. B. (Eds.). (1976). *Theoretical models and processes of reading.* (2nd ed.). Newark, DE: International Reading Association.

Singer, H., & Ruddell, R. B. (Eds.). (1985). *Theoretical models and processes of reading.* (3rd ed.). Newark, DE: International Reading Association.

Snow, C. E., Barnes, W. S., Chandler, J., Goodman, I. F., & Hemphill, L. (1991). *Unfulfilled expectations: Home and school influences on literacy.* Cambridge, MA: Harvard University Press.

Squire, J. R. (1994). Research in reader response, naturally interdisciplinary. In R. B. Ruddell, M. R. Ruddell, & H. Singer (Eds.), *Theoretical models and processes of literacy.* (4th ed.). Newark, DE: International Reading Association.

Stanovich, K. E. (1986). Matthew effects in reading: Some consequences of individual differences in the acquisition of literacy. *Reading Research Quarterly, 21,* 360-407.

Sticht, T. (1979). Applications of the Audread model to reading evaluation and instruction. In L. B. Resnick & P. A. Weaver (Eds.), *Theory and practice of early reading.* (pp. 209-26). Hillsdale, NJ: Erlbaum.

Venezky, R. (1995). Literacy. In T. L. Harris & R. E. Hodges (Eds.), *The literacy dictionary: The vocabulary of reading and writing.* (pp. 721-31). Newark, DE: International Reading Association.

Venezky, R., Wagner, D., & Ciliberti, B. (Eds.) (1990). *Toward defining literacy.* Newark, DE: International Reading Association.

Vygotsky, L. S. (1962). *Thought and language.* (E. Hanfmann & G. Vaker, Eds. & Trans.). Cambridge, MA: MIT Press.

Vygotsky, L. S. (1978). *Mind in society: The development of higher psychological processes.* (M. Cole, V. John-Steiner, S. Scribner, & E. Souberman, Eds. and Trans.). Cambridge, MA: Harvard University Press.

4

Mathematics: Learning and Knowing

Carole Greenes

Everyone knew that Bryan was smart—his teacher, his fellow classmates, in fact, most of the fifth grade students at Oak Elementary School. That's why it came as such a surprise when Bryan did not raise his hand when the following problem was posed: *Mr. Clark drove 300 miles in 6 hours. How many miles did he drive each hour?* Bryan's teacher was perplexed. Her students had reviewed division with whole numbers the previous week, and this was just a simple division example. She decided to question Bryan about his lack of response—did he understand the question? Bryan indicated that, yes, he understood the question, but that there was a problem with the answer. "There isn't just one answer," stated Bryan.

Prompted by the teacher, Bryan went to the chalkboard to explain his thinking. He established two columns of numbers. The first, he said, were the hours, 1 through 6, and the second were the miles traveled each hour. Bryan explained that any six numbers that "made sense" could be used for the miles as long as the total was 300. "So," said Bryan, "maybe Mr. Clark stopped for gasoline here (pointing to Hour 1) so he only went 30 miles. Then in this hour (pointing to Hour 2) he didn't make any stops so he drove 55 miles. That's the fastest you can go . . . you know, the speed limit. Or maybe he went 53.62 miles. You can use decimals and have lots of different numbers, so there are lots of different answers. There are an infinite number of answers!"

Why did Bryan respond that way? What other mathematics does Bryan know? How did he come to know it? While not domain-specific, questions like these have been of interest to learning theorists and cognitive psychologists for hundreds of years. More recently, researchers in education, curriculum developers, classroom teachers, and test designers have turned their attention to these types of questions in order to orchestrate a reform in the teaching and learning of mathematics and other subjects, as well. The goal of this reform is to teach for understanding.

One way to teach for understanding is to avoid instruction of isolated facts, and, instead, focus on the "big ideas" in mathematics that have application in many disciplines and relate them to experiences relevant to the learner at his or her particular stage of cognitive development. A theory of cognitive development that can be usefully applied to pedagogical and assessment methodologies for teaching the big ideas is constructivism. This paper will introduce the constructivist theory and illustrate its application in a curriculum focusing on big ideas.

In the first section of this paper, how knowledge is constructed, how concepts mature and become more robust, and what it means to learn and to know mathematics are presented. A portion of the discussion is devoted to a summary of the constructivist-based theories of Piaget and Vygotsky. In the second section, the reform in mathematics curriculum with its dual focus on the big ideas in mathematics and the investigative processes (i.e., strategies for approaching and learning mathematics) are described. Ways in which the big ideas can be explored using the investigative processes are exemplified.

In the third section, pedagogical implications of adopting a constructivist perspective on knowledge and learning are considered. Two instructional models are presented and the role of the teacher in this type of learning environment is described. Key to good teaching is knowing what students know and their degree of understanding, and using that information to plan appropriate learning experiences. For this reason, in the final section of the paper, the various methods of assessment that enhance the construction of knowledge are examined.

CONSTRUCTIVISM: THEORY OF KNOWING AND LEARNING

In the last ten years, the theory of constructivism has dominated research efforts in mathematics education (von Glaserfeld, 1991; Steffe & Gale, 1995), and has fueled the reform in mathematics curriculum, pedagogy, and assessment (NCTM, 1989; 1991; 1995). Based, in part, on the constructivist epistemology of Jean Piaget (1970; 1980; von Glaserfeld, 1991), constructivism is defined as a dynamic and interactive conception of learning in which all knowledge is constructed; it is a product of the cognitive acts of the individual. Knowledge may be constructed by innate cognitive structures (Chomsky, 1971) or by structures that are, themselves, the results of developmental construction (Piaget, 1953; 1970; 1971).

Learning is "triggered by disequilibrium," or what the French psychologists call "obstacles epistemologiques" (Simon, 1995). Learning occurs when children's conceptions are challenged by more complex situations, different contexts, or by conflicting data or information. Overcoming obstacles, therefore, is a central part of conceptual development. Understanding evolves as children try to make sense of new information, of complexity, of conflict. Concepts are enriched as children abstract the salient features of new experiences, and incorporate them into existing mental structures, thereby changing those structures.

To "know" mathematics, children make constructions using "mathematical objects in a mathematical community" (Davis, Maker, & Noddings, 1990). "Mathematical objects" are the repertoire of concepts, skills, and strategies that the child is able to bring to bear at the appropriate time to think about and answer questions or to solve problems. The "mathematical community" are the students, the teacher, and any other adults in the classroom. In order to operate in the community, the children and teacher need to know the community's language, customs, typical problems, and tools. Because opportunities for constructing knowledge in a classroom arise from interactions with the teacher and with classmates, constructions in this, or for that matter, any mathematical community are not arbitrary. Constructions are constrained. Children have to develop interpretations that fit those of their peers. Communication about personal experiences, and the negotiation of a fit among them results in a taken-as-shared understanding of concepts (Cobb, Wood, & Yackel, 1990).

Cognitive structures are always in the process of development as children interact with their environment and with others. The experiences children have and the constructs formed are greatly influenced by their "cognitive lenses," that is, their current developmental levels, previous experiences, and existing constructions (Confrey, 1990).

Piaget and Levels of Intellectual Development

Piaget was instrumental in establishing levels of intellectual development, from the random responses of infants to the complex mental operations inherent in the abstract reasoning of adults (Piaget, 1970). From a Piagetian perspective, intelligence is the effective adaptation to one's environment. The evolution of intelligence involves the complementary processes of *assimilation*, the fitting of new information into existing cognitive frameworks, and *accommodation*, the modifying or developing of new structures. The development of intelligence, then, is a dynamic evolution of more complex mental structures. Concepts cannot be simply planted in a child's mind. Rather, the child must filter the information, construct a mapping between the new information and past experiences and constructs, and reorganize existing mental structures to assimilate and accommodate the new ideas: "I think that human knowledge is essentially active. To know is to assimilate reality into systems of transformations. I find myself opposed to the view of knowledge as a copy, a passive copy, of reality" (Piaget, 1970, p. 15).

Although Piaget is identified as a constructivist epistemologist and has provided us with a scheme for interpreting children's current developmental levels from their actions, he has not given us any insight into the types and degrees of development between stages. Nor has he considered the influence of instruction and other types of human interactions on children's thinking.

Vygotsky and The Zone of Proximal Development

Vygotsky, a Russian psychologist and constructivist, proposed a different theoretical framework for analyzing intellectual development, one that relates cognitive and social phenomena, and that attends to the development between stages. Vygotsky distinguished between two levels of development: (1) what the child knows now (i.e., the functions that have matured) and (2) what functions are in the process of maturing. The first level is determined through unassisted problem solving; the second, through assistance with the problem solving activity. Assistance may be in the form of, for example, demonstrations, leading questions, or strategies for getting started on a problem. The "distance between the actual developmental level as determined by independent problem solving and the level of potential development as determined through problem solving under adult guidance or in collaboration with more capable peers" was referred to by Vygotsky as Zone of Proximal Development (ZPD) (Vygotsky, 1935/1978, pp. 85-86). Thus, the ZPD is defined by both the child's psychological developmental level and the social environment. Group interaction, with its social and linguistic components, is critical to the development of mental operations. Vygotsky describes the maturation of intellectual constructs in terms of his two levels: "What lies in the Zone of Proximal Development at one stage is realized and moves to the level of actual development at a second. In other words, what the child is able to do in collaboration today he will be able to do independently tomorrow" (Vygotsky, 1934/1986, p. 206).

Thus, the ZPD provides a way of gaining insight into children's capabilities and the type of instruction required for them to realize their potential. It also implies that teaching should not wait until all mental functions required for independent performance are fully developed. Although Vygotsky wrote a great deal about children achieving higher levels of mental functioning with assistance and collaboration, he did recognize that a child's current level of functioning limits the types of behaviors that are possible, and influences how the child interprets the content of the assistance provided by a teacher or peer.

MATHEMATICS CURRICULUM

Since the 1970s, mathematics education, its curriculum and teaching, have been severely criticized for fostering rote learning without understanding. Criticisms have come from various sectors of society including colleges, which are providing remedial courses in mathematics for at least 25 percent of their freshman (Greenes & Fitzgerald, 1991), and from the workplace, in which the number of low-level mathematics training programs is growing exponentially, while, concomitantly, the need for technologically, scientifically, and mathematically literate workers is on the increase (SCANS, 1991). The criticisms are best summarized in the report of the American Association for the Advancement of Science (AAAS, 1989, p. xvii):

The present curricula in science and mathematics are overstuffed and undernourished. They emphasize the learning of answers more than the exploration of questions, memory at the expense of critical thought, bits and pieces of information instead of understanding in context, recitation over argument, reading in lieu of doing. They fail to encourage students to work together, to share ideas and information freely with each other, or to use modern instruments to extend their intellectual capabilities.

The Big Ideas

Because of the bloated nature of curricula, mathematics educators are increasingly in agreement on the view that mathematics curricula should treat a limited number of topics in depth, rather than survey a vast range of content in a cursory fashion. Curriculum should focus on the learning of large conceptual structures rather than on large collections of isolated (and unrelated) bits of information. Further, they are recommending that arithmetic, algebra, geometry, probability, statistics, trigonometry, discrete mathematics, and calculus should not be treated as separate courses. Rather, the fundamental concepts or constructs that undergird these areas should be identified, and be the organizers of the curriculum. This would result in the integration of disciplines, and would demonstrate, to students, the power of key mathematical ideas.

Among the key or big ideas that have been identified by the National Council of Teachers of Mathematics in their *Curriculum and Evaluation Standards in School Mathematics* (NCTM, 1989) are proportionality, function, representation, and computation. These ideas are big because they have applications in all of the disciplines of mathematics and in other content areas, as well.

Proportionality, for example, is the basis for fractions and unit-price analysis in arithmetic, percentages in algebra, slopes of lines and similar figures in geometry, estimates of likelihood in probability, Chi Square in statistics, and right-triangle relationships in trigonometry. We also see applications of proportion in other fields. There are map scales in geography, dosages in medicine, timelines in history, blueprints in architecture, transposition in music, and break-even analysis in economics. Even on the highway, there are examples of proportions. The road sign, "Hill: 4% grade," means that the drop in elevation is proportional to the horizontal distance traveled, or for every 100 feet traveled on the road, the descent will be 4 feet.

The Investigative Processes

Not only must the curriculum focus on the big ideas of mathematics, but it also must provide an environment and opportunities for students to learn and to employ the various cognitive processes that facilitate investigation and exploration. Learning mathematics, thinking mathematically, and solving mathematical problems are complex, nonlinear procedures involving at least five cognitive processes: (1) observation and formulation of questions, (2) gathering of information, (3) analysis of information, (4) evaluation of conclusions, and (5) communication of procedures and results. Each of these processes involves all of the others, and may be revisited several times during investigation, exploration, and learning. The diagram in Figure 4.1 illustrates these relationships.

Figure 4.1
The Investigative Process

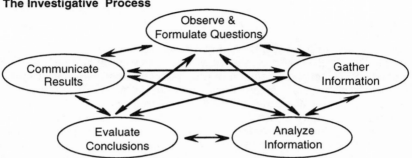

Observation and Formulation of Questions
The formulation of questions often occurs as a result of observing ambiguities or inconsistencies, or patterns and relationships among data or information that are puzzling (i.e., cognitive conflict) and thus provoke the questions, "Why?" or "How?". Other questions arise from visualizing or imagining "What if?"—what would happen to results or outcomes as a consequence of changes or variations in conditions or parameters? Thus, observation, questioning, and problem formulation involve the gathering and analysis of information and data, the hypothetical testing (i.e., thought experiments) of relationships, and the communication or posing of questions.

Although the ultimate goal is for students to make conjectures, question the official record or formulate other questions, this formulation takes time and instructional coaching to develop, and requires a model (the expert) to emulate. Without instruction and models, students tend to note only surface features and ask trivial questions or no questions at all. The nature of students' questions helps teachers assess, on-the-spot, what students know. I shall discuss this further in the section devoted to pedagogy and assessment.

Gathering of Information
A careful observation and analysis of a problem or question often results in the identification of information that is relevant or could be relevant to the solution. Students must think about what they already know; what previous knowledge they can bring to bear to the solution of the problem or to the answer to the question. Information may be culled from various resources; generated through simulation, interview, experimentation or survey; or obtained as a consequence of the decomposition or simplification of a problem or situation. Central to the process of gathering information is the ability to represent the information in such form(s) as to facilitate analysis.

Analysis of Information

Analysis is the process of evaluating data and other information in terms of whether or not they make sense in the context of the problem/question and are relevant to the solution, recognizing patterns, making inferences, generalizing relationships, and synthesizing results. Analysis involves observation, questioning, evaluating, and communicating (perhaps, having a conversation with oneself!), and the ability to move back and forth, or translate, between a situation and its abstract representation (e.g., model, theory).

Evaluation of Conclusions

The evaluation of conclusions and solutions is a sense-making process that requires observation, analysis, communication, and most importantly, questioning. Is the answer or solution reasonable within the context of the problem? Does the solution make sense to me (the student) personally? Are the data, results, and solution consistent with the findings, solution, and opinions of others? Is the answer robust (i.e., will it "stand up" if the question or problem is approached in another way)? Does the analysis and/or solution prompt other questions or problems for investigation?

Communication of Procedures and Results

Finally, findings and conclusions must be communicated. The purpose of communication may be to explain the choice of solution strategy; describe the model or theory; document thinking steps and activities followed to resolve the problem; provide justification for the solution, and/or solution method; or suggest implications of results and identify other questions or problems to be considered. Some presentations may be oral, others may be written, and still others may be dramatizations.

Investigating the Big Ideas

Exploration of the big ideas by means of an investigative approach enables students to actively construct knowledge about the concepts, skills, and strategies related to the big idea and to the investigative process. An example can best illustrate this exploring process.

One of the topics in geometry and measurement at the sixth-grade level is the circle. In traditional, noninvestigative classes, students identify diameters and radii, and memorize the formulas for circumference ($C=\pi d$) and area ($A=\pi r^2$). Typically, understanding is determined by student success in using the formulas in straightforward problems of the type, "What is the area of the circle with a radius of 2?" Using this "tell-practice-test" approach, students do not often realize that the circumference of a circle is proportional to its diameter. They often do not understand why the area formula has an r^2 factor, nor do they learn much about that mysterious factor, π, which appears in both the circumference and area formulas.

Consider, instead, an exploration of circle relationships with students actively involved in constructing their understanding of circumference and area. In such an exploration, students are prompted into activity with a "find-out" type of question: *How is the circumference of a circle related to its diameter?*

Students are supplied with cans of different diameters, string, paper, scissors, and rulers. They trace around one end of a can, cut out the circle, fold it in half, measure the length of its diameter (the fold line), and record the diameter length in a table. They then wrap a string around the can, measure the length of the string, and record this circumference in the same table. After repeating this measurement activity with cans of different sizes, students analyze the pairs of data in their tables, and speculate as to the relationship between the diameter and the circumference of a circle. Students may combine data with others in the class, and continue to conjecture about the relationship. What they will discover is that the circumference is always a little more than three times the diameter. The number that is a little more than three is π. (π is about 3.1416.)

Similarly, to discover the relationship between the radius and the area of a circle, students are provided with paper, compasses, rulers, and scissors. Their job is to construct a circle and several squares whose sides are equal in length to the radius of the circle ("radius squares"). They then cut out the radius squares and use them to "cover" the circle. Some radius squares may need to be cut so that the pieces can be used to cover the circle completely, without overlap and without extending beyond the border. The number of radius squares needed to cover the circle is recorded in a table along with the area of the circle computed using the formula, $A=\pi r^2$. Students follow the same procedure using circles with different length radii, and look for relationships between area and number of radius squares. Once again, the number of radius squares needed to cover a circle is always a little more than three (π).

The big ideas in mathematics can be investigated by students at various levels of cognitive development. At early stages, exploration of the big ideas takes on a more concrete form, in which students manipulate objects, experiment with models, and make conjectures based on their observations. At later stages, students reason symbolically, using, for example, algebraic expressions and structures. Ultimately, students reason logically to construct proofs of mathematical relationships. The reform movement in mathematics education is strongly endorsing exploration of the big ideas by all students at all levels of logical development.

Problem-Based Curricula: Big Problems

A major goal of mathematics education is for students to realize and appreciate that mathematics is not only a powerful tool for understanding the world, but that it is also a powerful tool for discovering the world (Silver et al., 1990). Understanding and discovery are facilitated by a curriculum that has a strong component of exploration and investigation and is problem-based. With such a curriculum, students learn important mathematical concepts, skills, and strategies as they deal with problems that may come from mathematics or physics, chemistry, biology, earth or space science, economics, political science, engineering, business, art, architecture, sports, or music.

The problems are not solved by simply applying one computational procedure. Rather, they may require the application of a variety of mathematical concepts, skills, and strategies for their solutions. Because of the complexity of the problems, the solution processes may not be immediately nor easily determined. As a consequence, students need to work collaboratively to formulate hypotheses; plan investigations; make observations and conjectures about their observations; collect, organize, and analyze data; construct models; determine the best means of displaying their data; test cases; identify variables; draw conclusions; generalize results; and formulate new problems—in other words, use the investigative process. From now on, I will refer to these problems as "big problems." (Big problems and big ideas are omnipresent in mathematics education!)

To differentiate these big problems from traditional types of problems (e.g., the Mr. Clark problem at the beginning of this article), consider the following three: the Flying Problem for intermediate-grade students, the Manute Bol problem for middle-grade students, and the Seizure Problem for high school students. After each problem is a summary of how students grappled with and solved the problem.

Flying Problem: A plane is flying over Chicago at an average speed of 500 miles per hour. After 45 minutes, the plane is flying over another large city. What is the city? Initially the fourth grade students found a map of the United States, located Chicago, and proceeded to look for other big cities they estimated to be about 500 miles away. One student pointed out that the plane couldn't be 500 miles away since the plane was flying for 45 minutes, not for one hour. Thus the next job was to figure out the number of miles the plane did travel. After several false starts, someone suggested dividing 500 by 60 to find the number of miles per minute (a little proportional reasoning), and then multiply that number by 45. While some of the students thought there had to be an easier way, they agreed that this procedure would work, and with a calculator, the computation would not be difficult. After computing the distance traveled, students returned to the map, and realized that they would have to convert the actual distance to the map-scale distance (some more proportional reasoning). They then used a compass set on the map scale equivalent of 375 miles, and using Chicago as the center, drew a circle around Chicago. They knew that the big city had to lie on the circle. To their surprise, they discovered that there were several cities on the circle. They returned to the problem statement, and noticed the words "large city." Using an almanac and other resources, they found the populations of all of the larger cities, and identified the largest.

Manute Bol Problem: At 7 feet 7 inches, Manute Bol is the tallest player in the National Basketball Association. If Manute Bol is standing under a regulation height net, can he reach up without jumping and put the ball into the basket? After presenting this problem, the grade 8 students realized that, to answer the question, they needed to know the length of Bol's arm. One student suggested that we call Bol to get that piece of data. I suggested that it would be more cost effective if we used mathematics to estimate the length of Bol's arm. One student thought that we could use a proportion (that big idea, again) to estimate the length of Bol's arm. To do that, we would need the height of a person in the class, the length of that person's arm, and the height of Bol, which we already knew. There was a great deal of conversation about whose height and arm length to use. Some students recommended that we measure the tallest person in the class; others suggested using the average height and arm length of the male students. After a lengthy discussion about averages (i.e., which average to use, the arithmetic mean, the median, or the mode) and the relationship between heights and arm lengths (students were amazed to discover that the relationship between height and arm length varied little; taller people generally have longer arms), students finally decided to use the measurements of the tallest male, and with a proportion were able to estimate Manute Bol's arm length. Subsequently, a student pointed out that one just cannot add the length of the arm to the height of the body, because there is a part of the arm that overlaps a part of the head-to-toe height. Once again, the students used a proportion to find this top-of-head to top-of-shoulder length, and subtracted that length from the sum of the body height and arm length. But the question was still not answered for the students. They were concerned about the size of Bol's hand; was it big enough to hold the ball? And so, the exploration continued. While proportion is a big idea, it is a difficult concept to understand, but not as difficult when it is related to a memorable application.

Seizure Problem: Often, outside of theaters, we see signs that indicate that a stroboscope will be used during the productions. People disposed to having seizures are warned that the stroboscopic flickering of the light might trigger a seizure. There are other flickerings that can trigger seizures, as well. Some years ago there was a multi-car pileup on the German autobahn. While trying to determine the cause of the accident, investigators noticed that along the side of the highway, trees had been planted equidistant from one another for a stretch of several miles. The investigators concluded that the flickering of the sun's light between the trees in the late afternoon triggered a seizure in the driver of the first car, who lost control of the car, and caused the accident. On federal highways in the United States., there are broken white stripes that separate the lanes of the highway. The lengths of the stripes are 10 feet and the lengths of spaces between stripes are 30 feet. Tiny glass beads are added to the paint to make the stripes reflective during night driving. Driving at fast speeds, the stripes and spaces cause a flickering phenomenon. At what minimum speed could this flickering trigger a seizure in someone disposed to having seizures? To solve this problem, high school students first obtained information about seizures and how they are triggered. They discovered that when the flickering caused by some external activity coincides with a person's alpha rhythm of 10 cycles per second, and that person is disposed to seizures, a seizure could be triggered. Subsequently, students decided to go to a federal highway to verify the stripe and space lengths. They were quite certain, from their driving experiences, that the stripe and space lengths had to be shorter. (That, of course, is how they appear at faster speeds!) Once they had all of the data, students brainstormed ways in which the problem could be approached and solved. Although they realized that they only had to do lots of multi-digit computations and that they could use calculators, determining the speed in miles per hour from data presented in feet and seconds was puzzling. They decided to make a drawing to help visualize the situation. Students saw that for every stripe there is one space, so they could think of stripe-space as one unit, 40 feet in length. To trigger a seizure, a driver would have to see 10 of these units per second, or travel 400 feet per second. This would mean that the driver would travel 288,000 feet or 272.72 miles in one hour; an obvious impossibility. But, this raised another question. What length stripe and space could trigger a seizure if a driver was traveling at the legal speed limit of 55 mph? To solve this new problem, students decided to use a proportion. They estimated that 55 was about one-fifth of 272.72. Therefore, the stripe and space lengths would be about one-fifth their actual lengths. To trigger a seizure at 55mph, the stripe and space lengths would be 2 feet and 6 feet, respectively. Interestingly, no one at the Department of Transportation knew how the stripe and space lengths were determined!

PEDAGOGICAL IMPLICATIONS

Constructivism does not specify a particular model of instruction. The construction of knowledge proceeds whether or not a teacher is present. However, leaving students to their own devices or placing them in groups is no guarantee that they will be learning mathematics or the cognitive processes that facilitate mathematical explorations, investigations, and learning. Several educators have explored the implications of constructivism on various models of instruction.

Instructional Models

Steffe (1990), interpreting and extending the developmental theories of Piaget and Vygotsky to mathematics, identified three "global" periods in the teaching-learning process: (1) Constructive Period, (2) Period of Retroactive Thematization, and (3) Period of Assimilating Generalization.

Constructive Period

In this first period, faced with a challenging question or problem, children come to grips with the nature of the problem, rephrase the problem or represent it in different ways (e.g., pictorially, symbolically, through modeling), identify the givens and other information that is needed, determine sub tasks to be completed, devise a plan for solving the problem, carry out the plan, and verify the solution in the context of the problem. These activities bear a great resemblance to those described by George Polya (1945) in his four-step plan for solving problems: understand the problem, design a solution plan, carry out the plan, and look back to verify the solution.

The responsibilities of teachers during this period are many. They must have a rich collection of problems of varying levels of complexity. And, they must be excellent problem posers. Prior to posing a problem, teachers must identify the concepts, skills, and strategies needed to solve the problem, and the sub tasks the students need to complete in advance of tackling the problem. Teachers must decide if the students have the relevant backgrounds to have a good chances of solving the problem, either alone, or as described by Vygotsky, with more capable peers. The teacher also must coordinate the discussion of the problem and facilitate students' reflection on solution paths in order to enhance their abilities to connect the problem and its solution with other problems of similar structure during the next period.

Period of Retroactive Thematization

With teacher mentoring, students review the solutions to several (related) problems, examining their representations and solution strategies in order to identify common elements. From this examination of different problems, and the ensuing discussion and reflection, students develop deeper understanding of the concepts.

One of the most powerful problem-solving strategies involves reasoning by analogy, that is, by a process of Piagetian abstraction, recognizing that two problems have similar structures or representations, and applying the solution strategy from one to the other. During the period of retroactive thematization, students learn to classify problems with similar structures.

Period of Assimilating Generalization

During this period, the concept is reconstructed as students apply it to new, more complex problems. The salient features of these new problems, contexts, and solution strategies are identified, and contribute to the maturation or robustness of the concept. The matured concept now includes the new problems that can be solved. Through discussion and analysis of new problems, teachers can help students generalize the concept and recognize its power to solve large classes of problems.

The instructional model proposed by the Biological Science Curriculum Study (1993) gives a more detailed breakdown of Steffe's first period, the Constructive Period, and provides a scheme for the development of lessons to enhance student understanding of mathematical concepts, skills, and strategies, and to help them advance to more abstract cognitive levels. The model has five stages: Engagement, Exploration, Explanation, Elaboration, and Evaluation.

Engagement stage. Students' curiosity is provoked by a problem, conflicting information, or a challenge. Students make connections between the problem information and what they already know that may be relevant to the solution.

Exploration stage. During this stage, the concepts, skills, and strategies necessary to solve the problem are developed. Students often work collaboratively to conduct the explorations and activities.

Explanation stage. Once students have had numerous opportunities to explore the concepts, the teacher brings the students together, and through discussion and reflection, helps them focus on particular critical aspects of their experiences. It is during this period that students negotiate and renegotiate meaning to develop taken-as-shared knowledge, as described by Cobb, Wood, and Yackel (1990), which becomes the basis for their future explorations, communications, and constructions.

Elaboration stage. To extend students' understanding of the concepts, skills and strategies, students are challenged to use these ideas in more complex situations.

Evaluation stage. By means of self-assessment through reflection and analysis of their documented thinking steps and solution methods, and feedback provided by teachers and others (peers, experts), students get a sense of their degree of understanding. Results of the evaluation may direct students back to any one of the previous stages, or to the exploration of new ideas.

Role of The Teacher

It is necessary (for the mathematics teacher) to provide a structure and a set of plans that support the development of *informed* exploration and *reflective* inquiry without taking initiative or control away from the student. The teacher must design the tasks and projects that stimulate students to ask questions, pose problems, and set goals. Students will not become active learners by accident, but by design, through the use of the plans that we structure to guide exploration and inquiry. (Richards, 1991 p.38)

The teacher has many roles to play. She is a mentor, guiding students in their explorations and investigations, continually assessing their progress, providing feedback and advice, and adapting activities and instruction to their needs in order to help them with the transition between stages of development (Vygotsky, 1935/1978). Some adaptations will require the use of different materials for exploration (e.g., blocks, computer simulations) or instruction (e.g., audio or video tapes, computer presentations). Others may require modifying the instructional sequence. Still others may involve changing the classroom structure by assigning students to work on their own, in small groups, or with the entire class.

The teacher is a model of a mathematical investigator, practicing the mathematical behavior, the investigative processes she expects from her students. She is a resource, assisting students with the location of relevant tools, information, and other materials. She is the architect of the classroom environment that will provoke students' curiosity about phenomena such that they formulate questions, wrestle with ideas, gather information, analyze data, draw conclusions, and communicate results.

To engineer this environment, they should select problems that will engage students and cause them to conduct explorations. The problems need to be challenging in order to move students beyond their comfort zones to new concepts, skills, and strategies. The problems should be moderately novel, having some connection to students' past experiences. The problems should offer conflicts or complexity, and ideally, have multiple solution paths. Finally, the problems should be in contexts that are interesting to students. Research has shown that assimilation and interest are intimately related; students are more likely to tackle and persevere with problems that tweak their interest (Baroody & Ginsburg, 1990).

To nurture the development of students' conceptual knowledge, and help them form more powerful constructions, the teacher can:

- connect new ideas to other ideas or concepts. For example, while studying rates (e.g., miles per hour), the teacher could relate this proportional relationship to other applications of proportion, such as unit prices and similar triangles, that had been explored earlier;
- provide multiple contexts for the development of a concept. For example, the concept of slope can be developed geometrically by examining lines of varying steepness, or algebraically, by analyzing equations of the form y=mx+b that model real-life situations in which m represents variable cost and b represents fixed cost;
- offer counter-examples to challenge students' generalizations or conclusions;
- challenge students to use different representations to illustrate relationships. For example, students might describe the same relationship using tables, graphs, diagrams, three-dimensional models, simulations, symbols, or text;
- change one or more of the parameters in a problem, or representation, and probe students' understanding of the consequences of those changes (i.e., What will happen if?);
- require students to reflect on their solution strategies and solutions, justify the choice of strategies, retrace and document their thinking steps, and provide rationales for their solutions;
- prompt students to generate new questions/problems (Cobb, Wood, & Yackel, 1993).

IMPLICATIONS FOR ASSESSMENT

Embracing a new theory of learning that has as its core the active involvement of students in the construction of concepts requires a new method of assessment, one that is dynamic rather than static, one that presents a profile of the student's current level of functioning and insight into the types of instruction that might facilitate development rather than a snapshot of a single performance (e.g., score on a test). Traditional quantitative measures do not tell the whole story.

As noted by Vygotsky, students differ in their current states of development in ways that cannot be determined by assessing performance as they work alone. Rather, techniques must be employed for determining what students are capable of doing in collaborative activities, either with peers or with teachers.

Not only are students at different levels of development, they often do not do mathematics the way they were taught (Davis, 1984; Ginsburg, 1989). They frequently use their own invented methods for solving problems, methods teachers need to know about in order to identify difficulties, gaps, or ingenious approaches, and to provide appropriate follow-up experiences. This is yet another reason to look at assessment strategies that provide detailed information on children's thinking. Among such strategies are: interviews, "think-alouds," performance tasks, and journal conversations.

The *interview technique*, used extensively by Piaget and Vygotsky, involves a dialogue between student and teacher about some mathematical concept, strategy, or exploration. Through questioning, the teacher attempts to assess the students' depth of understanding of important mathematical ideas, and gain information about what students can do with varying degrees of assistance (i.e., Level 2 of Vygotsky's framework for intellectual development). When interviews are conducted after the completion of an exploration or project, teachers can gain information about students' abilities to plan investigations; collect, organize, and analyze data; reason mathematically; and communicate ideas. Teachers also can probe students' understanding of the factors/conditions that might affect an outcome or limit a generalization.

The *think-aloud strategy* also involves a one-to-one teacher-student format, and is particularly useful for getting a handle on methods students use to solve problems. The teacher poses a problem or question, and the student talks aloud as she is solving the problem, describing her thinking. The teacher may intervene with prompts or probes. "Prompts" are comments that encourage the student to continue to speak (e.g., "Keep talking"). "Probes", by contrast, are interventions that cause the student to provide additional information (e.g., "Where did that 4 come from?") or reflect on what they were doing (e.g., "Why did you decide to do that?").

Performance tasks may be completed by students working on their own or in groups. In either case, students are presented with an activity or problem, and are given, generally, from twenty minutes to an hour to respond in writing to the various questions. Responses could be documentation of thinking steps, persuasive arguments for particular solution strategies, justifications for solutions, or rationales for representational formats (e.g., why a bar graph is preferable to a circle graph). In most performance assessments, student responses are evaluated using a scoring rubric that assigns points based on levels of proficiency. For example, the state of Wisconsin recently instituted a performance assessment with five scoring levels: advanced, proficient, nearly proficient, minimal, and attempted. Teachers, trained in using the rubric, score the responses (MSEB & NRC, 1995).

Some performance tasks are designed to evaluate students as they work in groups to solve long-term project types of problems that require formulation of plans, development and testing of alternatives, and evaluation of results. Through observations, teachers gain insight into students' abilities to: identify factors, conditions, or variables that may affect the solution or problem solving process; use appropriate mathematical concepts, skills, and strategies; recall similar (analogous) problems; make conjectures based on observations; recognize and generalize patterns among data in tables, graphs, and schematics; recognize how changes in one representation affect other representations of the same relationship; draw false conclusions from data; and identify constraints on conclusions. In addition, communication and collaborations skills can be evaluated. Do students use the language of mathematics correctly? Do they clarify or explain ideas and procedures to others? Do they listen to and show respect for other students' ideas? Do they participate in brainstorming activities (Greenes & Schulman, 1996)?

Mathematics journals or logs are another way of capturing students' thinking. In journals, students communicate their thoughts, ideas, feelings, and questions through writing and the production of various visual displays. The writing may be in response to a question posed by the teacher or another student (e.g., "Why did you choose to use that solution strategy?"); or the writing may be open-ended in that students write about anything of interest or concern to them related to their mathematics learning (e.g., "I don't see how you can have more than 100 percent of something"). Sometimes students do a combination of prompted and open-ended writing as they describe experiments and observations of phenomena; record information obtained from references and resources; document their thinking steps; or construct persuasive arguments, proofs, or justifications for solutions and solution strategies.

For both prompted and open-ended communications, the teacher responds in writing in the journal, so that, in effect, the journal serves as a "conversation" or "talk" on paper between student and teacher. From journals, teachers can identify misconceptions and gaps in students' knowledge, and can obtain information about the students' abilities to link new knowledge to that which is already known. In journals, students often identify their own strengths and weaknesses with respect to learning. By doing this, they develop greater awareness of themselves as learners. Students also gain confidence as the result of the specific feedback to their questions and comments. They know that their difficulties and concerns will be given attention. They know that someone will be sharing in, responding to, and celebrating their discoveries and insights.

Student Self Assessment

"Involving students in the assessment process is essential to the development of their abilities to reflect on their own work, to understand the standards to which they are held accountable, and to take ownership of their own learning" (Greenes et al., 1995, page xiv).

The self-assessment process is particularly relevant when students are working with other students on long-term projects or explorations. After the completion of the project, students can evaluate the procedures used and comment on what they would do differently if they repeated the exploration, identify the mathematical ideas they learned as well as those they still find confusing, and describe their greatest accomplishment. Students also can assess the contributions of various team members as well as of themselves to the solution process. These reflection pieces can be maintained in students' portfolios along with other productions.

While the above strategies are often referred to as "alternative" techniques to standardized tests, one cannot substitute for the other. The assessment strategies cited above are designed to explore students' understanding, to enter students' minds in order to obtain rich views of their cognitive process. Standardized tests, by contrast, are intended to be restricted and focused, and evaluate products as either "right" or "wrong" with no concern for process. For some goals, the standardized test may be the evaluation tool of choice, as for example, having students identify sets of equivalent fractions. On the other hand, if students experience difficulty with equivalent fractions, teachers may want to delve into their procedural difficulties in determining equivalency by using think-aloud methods. Whichever techniques are used, the ultimate goal of assessment is to obtain a comprehensive understanding of what students know, how they know it, and what appropriate instruction will enhance their understanding.

CONCLUSIONS

Concern with students' poor performance on mathematical and problem-solving tests in schools and colleges, and the need for remediation at workplace sites, have stimulated a reform in all aspects of mathematics education, curriculum, pedagogy, and assessment. Influencing this reform is a constructivist theory of learning that holds that students come to understand big ideas and concepts in mathematics as they experience them in different contexts and with varying complexity. With each new experience, the concepts change; they are redefined, reorganized, elaborated, and become more robust. To facilitate this construction of knowledge, curriculum must change from a large collection of isolated facts to a cohesive development of a few big ideas, ideas that undergird all areas of mathematics and have application in other disciplines. Problem-based curricula that engage students in problems for which there is no easily identifiable solution strategy provide opportunities for students to develop expertise with the investigative process while concurrently becoming more competent with mathematical concepts, skills, and strategies.

To ascertain what students know, to gauge their depths of understanding, and to identify appropriate curricula and instructional approaches, different types of assessment strategies are required. Some of the strategies will prompt and probe students' thinking as they are solving problems, in order to gain information about what they can do with support. Other strategies will evaluate their products or performances, carried out with no assistance. Still other strategies will identify their contributions to group problem solving efforts. The role of the teacher in such a constructivist-based program is multifaceted. She must know mathematics well and know what her students know about mathematics. She must design learning environments that provoke students' curiosity and challenge them to explore new ideas. She must mentor students during their explorations. She must be the convener and architect of the mathematical learning community.

REFERENCES

American Association For The Advancement of Science (1989). *Project 2061: Science for all Americans.* Washington, DC: Author.

Baroody, A. J., & Ginsburg, H. P. (1990). Children's learning: A cognitive view. *Journal For Research in Mathematics Education, Monograph 4* (pp. 51-64). Reston, VA: National Council of Teachers of Mathematics.

Biological Science Curriculum Study (1993). *Developing Biological Literacy* (pp. 38-41). Dubuque, IA: Kendall Hunt.

Chomsky, N. (1971). *Language and mind.* New York: Harcourt Brace Jovanovich.

Cobb, P., Wood, T., and Yackel, E. (1990). Classrooms as learning environments for teachers and researchers. *Journal For Research in Mathematics Education, Monograph 4* (pp. 125-46). Reston, VA: National Council of Teachers of Mathematics.

Confrey, J. (1990). What constructivism implies for teaching. *Journal For Research in Mathematics Education , Monograph 4* (pp. 107-22). Reston, VA: National Council of Teachers of Mathematics.

Davis, R. B. (1984). Learning mathematics: The cognitive approach to mathematics education. Norwood, NJ: Ablex Publishing Co.

Davis, R., Maher, C., & Noddings, N. (1990). Constructivist views on the teaching and learning of mathematics. *Journal For Research in Mathematics Education, Monograph 4* (pp. 1-3). Reston, VA: National Council of Teachers of Mathematics.

Ginsburg, H. P. (1989). Children's arithmetic (2nd ed.). Austin, TX: Pro-Ed.

Greenes, C., & Fitzgerald, W. (1991). Mathematical performance of non-math majors at the college level. In R. Underhill (Ed.), *Proceedings: Thirteenth Annual Meeting, Psychology of Mathematics Education* (pp. 98-104). Blacksburg, VA: Virginia Tech.

Greenes, C., & Schulman, L. (1996). Communication processes in mathematical explorations and investigations. In P. Elliot (Ed.), *1996 NCTM Yearbook: Communication in mathematics, K-12.* Reston, VA: National Council of Teachers of Mathematics.

Greenes, C., Schulman, L., Spungin, R., Chapin, S., Findell, C., & Johnson, A. (1995). *Math explorations and group activity projects (MEGA): Teacher resource guide (5).* Palo Alto, CA: Dale Seymour Publications.

Mathematical Sciences Education Board & National Research Council (1995). *Assessment in practice newsletter, Vol. 2,* Spring. Washington, DC: Author.

National Council of Teachers of Mathematics (1989). *Curriculum and evaluation standards for school mathematics.* Reston, VA: Author.

National Council of Teachers of Mathematics (1991). *Professional standards for teaching mathematics.* Reston, VA: Author.

National Council of Teachers of Mathematics (1995). *Assessment standards for school mathematics.* Reston, VA: Author.

Piaget, J. (1953). *Logic and psychology.* Manchester, England: Manchester University Press.

Piaget, J. (1970). *Genetic epistemology.* New York: Columbia University Press.

Piaget, J. (1971). *Biology and knowledge.* Chicago: University of Chicago Press.

Piaget, J. (1980). *Adaptation and intelligence: Organic selection and phenocopy.* Chicago: University of Chicago Press.

Polya, G. (1945). *How to solve it: A new aspect of mathematical method.* Princeton, NJ: Princeton University Press.

Richards, J. (1991). Mathematical discussions. In E. von Glasersfeld (Ed.), *Radical constructivism in mathematics education* (pp. 13-51). Dordrecht, The Netherlands: Kluwer.

Secretary's Commission on Achieving Necessary Skills (1991). *What work requires of schools: SCANS Report for America 2000.* Washington, DC: U.S. Department of Labor.

Silver, E., Kilpatrick, J., & Schlesinger, B. (1990). *Thinking through mathematics.* New York: The College Board.

Simon, M. A. (1995). Reconstructing mathematics pedagogy from a constructivist perspective. *Journal for Research in Mathematics Education, 26,* 114-45. Reston, VA: National Council of Teachers of Mathematics.

Steffe, L. (1990). On the knowledge of mathematics teachers. *Journal For Research in Mathematics Education, Monograph 4,* 167-84. Reston, VA: National Council of Teachers of Mathematics.

Steffe, L., & Gale, J. (Eds.) (1995). *Constructivism in education.* Hillsdale, NJ: Lawrence Erlbaum.

von Glasersfeld, E. (1991). *Radical constructivism in mathematics education.* Dordrecht, The Netherlands: Kluwer.

Vygotsky, L. S. (1978). Interaction between learning and develop-ment. In L. S. Vygotsky, *Mind in society: The development of higher psychological processes* (M. Cole, V. John Steiner, S. Scribner, & E. Souberman, Eds. and Trans.) (pp. 79-91). Cambridge, MA: Harvard University Press. (Original work published 1935).

Vygotsky, L. S. (1986). Thinking and speech. In L. S. Vygotsky, *Collected works: Problems of general psychology, Vol. 1.* (N. Minick, Trans.). New York: Plenum. (Original work published 1934).

5

On the Development of Understanding Art

Michael J. Parsons

The arts, we can say, are cognitive now. Since the 1960s, the arts in education have been increasingly thought of as a matter of intelligence and understanding. Not only do we now see artworks as complex, symbolic, and often multivocal reflections of our common life, we also—persuaded by Rudolf Arnheim[1]—regard perception itself as a matter of thinking—of selection, analysis, synthesis, abstraction, and so forth. Today this view has found a secure place in our schools. More and more, educators think of the arts as a matter of intelligence, involving the development of ideas, solving of problems, transfer of learning, critical thinking, self-reflection, and so on.

This paper takes a cognitive view of the arts for granted and it would hardly be worth mentioning, except that it stands in such contrast to the view that prevailed before the "cognitive revolution" of the 1960s[2]. The previous view, which can still be found in some of our schools, divided mental life into two kinds: the cognitive and the affective. The arts (along with morality) fell on the "affective" side. They were considered a matter of feeling and intuition, highly subjective, suitable for the development of creativity and self-expression, perhaps also of sensitivity and perception, related to "values," which were also considered noncognitive. But they were not thought of as requiring intelligence or as leading to the kinds of understanding fostered by other school subjects. This noncognitive view of the arts was no doubt a major reason for their traditionally marginal place in the school curriculum in the United States (as opposed to Europe). Similarly, the present change toward a cognitive view of the arts suggests that they deserve an important place in the curriculum and in any serious consideration of human development.

There have been a number of efforts in the last thirty years to develop art curricula based on the cognitive view, curricula that have substance and are intellectually demanding. Some of these efforts have continued to focus on making art, regarding it now more as a matter of intelligence, communication, and reflection than of self-expression and creativity. Other curricula have signaled an interest in a general understanding of art, often adding other art "disciplines" to the curriculum, especially art history, art criticism, and the philosophy of art. It is fair to say that a major unsettled issue today is how to relate these two kinds of study—art-making and the study of artworks—to serve the overall purpose of understanding art and artworks in general. It is an assumption of what follows that both art-making and talking about artworks are necessary in any art curriculum.

There has also been renewed interest in studies of children's development in the arts. These studies can also be divided into those that address the abilities required in making art—especially drawing and painting, but also working with ceramics and other media—and those that are involved in understanding artworks. There is a long history to the investigation of children's abilities to make art and this area has continued to receive most attention.[3] The systematic study of children's understanding of artworks, on the other hand, is relatively new and still at a beginning stage.[4] In both areas there is much still to be learned. In what follows, I will focus on the latter—the development of children's abilities to understand art—and I will confine the discussion to understanding of the visual arts only.

When children in nursery school are given crayons and paper, they experiment with them eagerly. But they are usually more interested in the process of making marks on the paper than in what the marks look like when they have finished. They will try different crayons, different movements, and different colors. They enjoy the activity but will also end it abruptly in favor of other activities. Characteristically, they do not pay much attention to the result of their activity. In this situation, as must have happened innumerable times, an adult may point to some marks on the paper and ask: "What is this?" And the child will go along with the question, inventing answers as they come to mind: "This is a house. And this is Mom."

Before the "cognitive revolution" of the 1960s, it was common to disapprove of this question, on the grounds that it might impose adult conceptions on the child's natural creative activity and so distort it. Now, we would more likely praise it, on the grounds that it helps the child construct some basic ideas that are fundamental to understanding art.[5] One such idea is that the child has produced something that is "finished," a product that is to be looked at. This is one root of the idea of an artwork. Another idea is that the marks on the paper picture or represent something. This is the beginning of the idea that an artwork is meaningful.

This latter idea may need explanation. Artworks, after all, are more than pieces of paper with marks on them. They have meanings. They are always *about* something. This means that they must be understood and require interpretation, implicit or explicit, on the viewer's part. Of course, they do not have to picture something to have meaning. And surely they do not, as sentences do, carry propositions about the world that can be judged true or false. They have meaning in their own way, as artworks, using their own medium and requiring to be understood in their own terms. And this is quite compatible with having a strong or a sophisticated emotional content; indeed, on the cognitive view they can express emotion only because they are meaningful. The emotional content is often (part of) the meaning.

In our culture, we have several ways of speaking and thinking about the meanings of art, ways that can be distinguished from each other but that nevertheless overlap in various ways. Children must learn to use these ways of speaking and thinking to make sense of artworks. Development in understanding art has to do with how children learn these ways of speaking and thinking.

I have chosen to focus here on the early acquisition of three basic ways of speaking about art in our culture: what we might call the ways of beauty, of representation, and of expression. The ideas involved are central in understanding art and virtually everyone in our culture learns them at some level. Moreover, they have to do with more than art. They also play a part in our understanding of self and society, and in this way, they illustrate the role that art plays in life in general. Understanding art is always about understanding more than art, because art is about fundamental themes, about beauty, reality, and identity.

This latter point—that understanding art is always understanding more than art—is especially important today because of the greater prominence in our society of visual materials. Visual images, usually presented in the context of words, surround us in quantities and forms that never existed before: in books, photographs, advertisements, movies, television, and now on the computer screen and through the internet. Reality comes to us increasingly in a mediated form. We learn who we are and how we relate to each other increasingly through a combination of visual images and texts. If we put this fact together with the other thought with which I began—that art is cognitive and requires understanding—it seems inevitable that art will gradually become more and more important in the school curriculum.

One common way of speaking about art connects it with beauty. In this way of speaking, an artwork is supposed to be beautiful, or at least beauty earns it the highest praise. Beauty, in turn, is understood to be what is appealing, glamorous, pleasant, uplifting, and it applies ambiguously to both art and people. Thought of this way, then, beauty has an undeniable tendency to embody a conventional set of values. This idea of beauty has a long history, coming down to us from at least as far back as the Renaissance. It persists today in our culture, in spite of the fact that art has long had an eye for tragic and difficult themes and, often, a distaste for the conventional. Children usually learn to speak about art in terms of beauty during the elementary school years.

Consider, for example, what twelve-year-old Katie said.[6] She was looking at a work by Ivan Albright titled *Into the World Came a Soul Called Ida*, which she thought very ugly:

Interviewer: Is this a subject you'd expect a painter to choose?
Katie: No

I: Why?

Katie: Well, if a painter was going to paint something—most painters paint beautiful women, or they really look nice in beautiful surroundings, and this just—it so contrasts with that—

I: It's not a beautiful painting?

Katie: I don't think so.

I: What should a painting do?

Katie: Entertain people. Like, I won't look at a painting like that—well, I will look at it because it's so disgusting—but I'll pass it up and go and look at beautiful scenery or a woman sailing a boat or something. Something beautiful.

For the same reason, Gloria, who was ten years old, did not approve of Goya's *Lo Mismo* (from the *Disasters of War*).

Interviewer: What feelings are in the picture?

Gloria: Sadness, help. . . . I don't like having some of these things, when you look at it.

I: Is it good to paint paintings about war?

Gloria: No. Not unless . . . it doesn't show any dead people or anything like that. If the war has just barely started, then that's OK.

Of course, Gloria is not alone in this preference and there are many war paintings that she would like, paintings that focus on heroic soldiers seated on horses, dressed in impressive uniforms, at some distance from the fight. There are more of these, by far, than those which dwell on the horrors of war.

In this way of speaking, ugliness is the opposite of beauty and is considered inappropriate in art. Where it is undeniably there, as in the Goya and the Albright, young children find it hard to make sense of. Katie, for example, having said that Ida "sort of looks like a witch," was asked:

I: Why do you suppose the painter painted it?

Katie: He was angry with his mother-in-law. (She laughs) I don't know, I don't know. He just felt like it. He saw some lady going down the street and he said: "That looks sickening," and so he decided to paint her. He was angry at her for some reason.

Derek, who was fourteen years old, had a similar strongly negative response to Ida. He said:

I: What was the artist's feeling when he painted this?

Derek: Well, I'm sure . . . he felt angry at her, seeing her wondering: "Oh, why am I like this . . . ?"

I: What are your feelings about the painting?

Derek: I don't like it. No one wants to look at some fat cellulited lady sitting there and keep powdering, all slobbed out. You don't like to think of things like that.

Godfrey, also fourteen years old, spoke in the same way and thought he knew why the artist was angry:

I: Then why did the artist paint this?

Godfrey: To show what people are like. People do this all the time, and they just
sit around and vegetate and dwindle away. And they look in the mirror and
wonder why. "Oh, I'm so depressed! Look at me now!" You know. She should
fight it. It wouldn't be a bad time to start. She not dead yet. Let me tell you, my
mom goes to a health spa . . .

Clearly, this rejection of ugliness in art, so common in elementary
school children, is both emotional and cognitive at the same time. It is
cognitive in that these children understand the work as ugly and can give
good reasons why. Basically, it is that they have learned some
conventional expectations about beauty and ugliness, about age and
being overweight, in people, especially with respect to women. These
stereotypes may be unsympathetic but they are clearly cognitive and are
undeniably part of our society.

This way of thinking about beauty in art is obviously linked with
thinking about the painting as a picture, or a "representation." To these
children a painting is obviously about the people and other items it
pictures. Most elementary school children, when asked: "What is this
painting about?" will respond with a description of what is depicted. For
them, to talk about the meaning of a painting is to talk about what it
represents. This is the basis of what I call the representational way of
speaking about art. It constructs the painting as if it were a window
through which one can look at the objects pictured. It positions the
viewer to look not at the windowpane (the painting itself and the way it is
painted) but at what lies beyond it (what is represented), as if the viewer
were looking at actual people rather than at paintings that represent
people. In the extracts above, the persons depicted (the two men
fighting in the Goya; Ida in the Albright) are described and responded to
as if they were actual people: ugly, dying, too lazy to take exercise.

Of course the children are aware of the difference between a person
and a painting. They are not confused. But their way of speaking does
not facilitate this awareness: they speak as if they are *not* aware of the
difference, as if there is no difference. This manner of referencing
structures the emotional character of the children's' responses in a
particular way. Derek is offended and Godfrey is indignant, and their
emotions are directed more at Ida the person than at the painting.
Godfrey's indignation notably seems to contain an element of moral
judgment when he says: "She should fight it. It wouldn't be a bad time to
start; she's not dead yet. Let me tell you, my mom goes to a health spa." It
makes little sense, when you come to think of it, to direct moral
indignation at a painting. Indignation is more properly directed at persons
than at paintings. Of course—this is the point—Godfrey does not come
to think of it. To do so would be to speak in a different way, a way that
builds on—rather than obscures—an awareness of the artificial and
symbolic character of artworks, or, what is much the same thing, of the
origins and character of one's own emotions. A related observation is that
the stereotypes about beauty and ugliness in people that are reflected in
these responses are also an undigested mixture of aesthetic and moral
attitudes. It is their undigested character—their lack of distinctions—that
gives them their strength. One of the educational opportunities that art of

this kind offers is—by working through these kinds of responses—to encourage the kind of self-awareness that is so notably lacking here.

There is an interesting exception to this analysis. It occurs in Katie's response to the Albright (quoted above). Katie was quite clear in her condemnation of the Albright and she talked consistently about art, beauty, representation, and Ida, in an extended interview. But she was also, apparently, an unusually self-aware and honest child; or perhaps she was at a very teachable developmental moment. For she said: "Like, I won't look at a painting like that—well, I will look at it because it's so disgusting—but I'll pass it up and go and look at beautiful scenery. . . . "

This appears to be an acknowledgment, however brief, of the fact that the Albright actually has a fascination for her. It is a powerful painting and this power is felt and interpreted in different ways by different people. Katie, it seems, has no adequate way to interpret its power because it runs counter to her way of thinking about it, a way that positions the viewer to attend primarily to the beauty of the work's subject matter. Consequently, she can only say that she would willingly "pass it up." But she is self-aware enough to acknowledge a fascination that can only appear paradoxical: "Well, I will look at it because it's so disgusting. . . . ". At this point, Katie's experience of the Albright appears to transcend her ability to speak about it.

In the above, I have described children as learning "ways of speaking" about art. We have several different ways of speaking about art. We can, roughly, distinguish these ways of speaking, though at times they interpenetrate each other. Ways of speaking are not like Piagetian stages, which are comprehensive in character and have a tight logical structure. They are looser and more rhetorical, collections of insights that hang together and make sense without obvious contradiction. These different ways of speaking about art make different cognitive demands of the speaker. Some are harder to learn than others, demand more self-awareness or other achievements than others. In this case, development consists in the progressive mastery of these ways of speaking, beginning, necessarily, with the less demanding.

Ways of *speaking* and ways of *thinking* are obviously closely related. Vygotsky, the Russian developmental psychologist, conceived this relation as one that runs from speaking to thinking and not the other way round.[7] Children, he argued, learn to speak by engaging in conversation with others. Adults and others who have mastered ways of speaking model and assist the child in speaking that way. Later, as children come to master a way of speaking, they "internalize" it, that is, they say it silently and only to themselves. The way of speaking has then become a way of thinking. At that point the only difference between a way of speaking and a way of thinking is that sometimes the thinker does not articulate the thought aloud. For this reason, when I say "ways of speaking," in this paper, I also mean ways of thinking.

Consider the example of the nursery school child whose teacher, looking at her scribbles, asks: "What is this?" The child answers: "This is a house. And this is Mom." The child is learning to speak of marks on paper as representations. In such conversations, the child learns what is a suitable kind of answer in this way of speaking. For example, one can hardly point at an empty space and say: "This is Mom." And if one were to point at a horizontal kind of scribble and say: "This is Mom," the question might come back: "Oh, why is she lying down?" or: "Where is her head?" In this way, the child learns that a picture—unlike, say, the alphabet or a map—requires a kind of visual similarity. It is odd to say: "This is Mom" if it looks more like a caterpillar. Similarly, adults are likely to say, of certain works and not of others: "Isn't it pretty!" and the young child begins to learn the language of beauty.

The elementary school age children quoted earlier have learned these ways of speaking—the one that positions the viewer before the work as if before a window and the one that focuses attention on the beauty of what is pictured—and they think in those ways when presented with works like the Goya and the Albright. Most children of their age would do the same. There are other ways of speaking about these same works that they have not yet learned. One of these, the expressive way, connects art closely with emotions. Other kinds of works may well evoke other ways of speaking about them. For example, one cannot easily use the language of either representation or expression about some wholly abstract paintings (Mondrian, for instance) or about earth-works. Mondrian might call for a language that focuses on the form and style of the work and on how its parts relate internally. In fact, the language of form and style is probably our major current alternative to those I discuss in this paper.

The advantage of conceiving development as the mastery of ways of speaking about art is that it reflects the role that culture plays in our understanding of art. Art is understood differently in different cultures and even in the same culture at different times. We, in what is often called "Western" culture, understand art differently than it was understood in pre-Colombian Mexico or in Europe in mediaeval times. Many would even say we understand art differently today than we did at the beginning of this century. And, of course, children everywhere take on the understandings of their own time and culture. The same is true of science and morality, no doubt, but it seems particularly clear with art that the culture determines the developmental direction of understanding.

The expressive way of speaking about works like the Albright and the Goya connects them with emotions. It speaks of art as basically the expression of emotions. This idea also has a long history in our culture, going back, more or less, to the romantic age. Learning to speak in this way can be an extended process because the expressive view of art can be quite complex.

The simplest way to locate emotions in artworks is to attribute them to the persons represented. For example, Ernest, seventeen years old, said this about the Goya:

Ernest: How brutal is the expression on the man's face, even though he's about to get him! It's like, does he really want to? Or is he just doing this to stay alive? Cause he has to, now that he's out there.
I: So it's about what war feels like?

E: Yes, because you can get pictures in a movie or magazines, but I imagine it's quite different when you're out there yourself.

Wendy, sixteen years old, talked about the Albright:

I: Would you describe what you see here?

Wendy: I see a woman who is way past her prime of life. . . . She looks like she's mourning for her lost beauty. You can tell when she was younger she was probably fairly pretty.

I: How can you tell?

W: Because I don't think that people that aren't pretty worry much about their looks. Just by her features and stuff you can tell, given that all her wrinkles were gone. I admire people who grow old with grace. I don't mean sit home and grow old but they aren't worried about not being young. They accept it.

I: Is she accepting it?

W: It looks like very reluctantly. It looks like something she doesn't want to deal with.

I: How can you tell she doesn't want to deal with it?

W: Because she seems to be looking in the mirror as though it's a glance. She's not admiring herself at all. It's kind of like: harsh reality dawns. It's pathetic, because she's wearing this pink silk thing and the high heel shoes, and she's just disgusting.

I: So there's a contrast between the clothes she's wearing and her physical aspect?

W: Yeah. But the lingerie and the shoes she's wearing are dumpy too. They're old like she is.

I: Anything else that points to her oldness?

W: Yeah, things seem run down. The top of the table is nice but things seem run down. . . . Is that a piece of paper burned on the floor? The flowers are dead. . . .

I: What is the subject of the painting?

W: It tries to put across the thing with beauty and it's all so superficial. You get old and it's putting across the pointlessness of the whole looks thing, the obsession with beauty.

I: Is that a good subject for a painting?

W: I like it because I think that this painting definitely does have a lesson to it. I mean, I can picture her thirty years earlier sitting in the same chair, doing the same thing and being absolutely beautiful, because she has such a woeful expression. I admire the painter, if that's what he was trying to put across, for seeing through that, because it's hard for people to do. I mean they know it but everyone is as guilty as the next person as being vain or concerned about how people look.

Ernest and Wendy both talk about the painting as if its meaning lies in the feelings it expresses. To talk this way positions one to look at the work somewhat differently, to look not so much for what is literally represented but for clues about feeling. Both Ernest and Wendy focus on the face and gesture: "She seems to be looking in the mirror as though it's kind of a glance. She's not admiring herself at all." The Goya and the Albright both invite this focus because of the way they represent persons. Other kinds of works, landscapes for instance, would not allow scrutiny of a face and might not so readily elicit this way of speaking.

Wendy also looks closely at other details of the painting, trying to relate them to feelings. She examines the clothes and the items on the top of the table and finds metaphors for her theme of aging: "things seem run down. . . . Is that a piece of paper burned on the floor? The flowers are dead." Finding these metaphors is a result of the search for clues to feelings, and one might even say that, for Wendy, Ida herself becomes a metaphor, or a symbol, for something more general: "the pointlessness of . . . the obsession with beauty." The younger children do not spontaneously find metaphors in these paintings, presumably because they are oriented toward them as literal descriptions. This may be why the expressive way of speaking appears later in development than the representational way. It is cognitively more demanding to regard items metaphorically because it requires seeing them in a double aspect, as both literal representations and as signs of something further.

Ernest and Wendy also demonstrate here what is perhaps the key feature of the expressive way of speaking: a kind of personal empathy, in this case an attempt to imagine the emotion of the person represented. This empathy is not a direct intuition of feeling so much as the result of an active search for it, brought about by the orientation toward the painting as expressive of feeling. It is a result of the coordination of two movements: the active imagining of how one would oneself feel in the situation represented and the scrutiny of the details of that situation. Ernest does this quite quickly by connecting the expression on the face in the Goya with his imagination that "it's quite different when you're out there yourself." Wendy takes longer. She searches the work for clues to Ida's situation and is also guided by her sense of the feelings she would have in that situation. She speaks, for example, of her admiration for those who "grow old gracefully" and it is clear throughout her interview that she is aware of her own concern for appearance, which she attributes to Ida. The interview ends with an explicit reference to her own feelings:

I: Is this a good painting?
W: Yeah, I like it. It puts a point across and I think there's a lot to it. It's like the first one [a painting that was previously discussed]. I guess they all have a point to them, but this one more than any other. It's closer, more intimate.
I: Closer to your own experience?
W: Yeah, because I can imagine myself looking like that. I just wouldn't want to feel like I'd lost everything when my looks went.
I: So this makes you anticipate the future?
W: Yes. And she also seems like she has nothing anymore, she's looking in the mirror like there's no more point to living.

We have here another clue as to why children usually learn to think about art as expression after learning to think of it as representation. The former calls for an attention to, and an awareness of, one's own feelings that younger children normally do not have. The younger children quoted here certainly *have* feelings in the face of the Goya and the Albright and they express them forcefully. But simply to have feelings is cognitively less demanding than to be aware of them. This latter ability is fostered and required by the language of expression, which encourages

Ernest and Wendy to search both the paintings and their own experience for clues about feelings in the paintings. It is a well-known theme in the expressionist school of aesthetics that art is ultimately a means of clarifying and communicating emotions, both one's own and those of others.[8] If there is truth in this, then understanding art in this way both requires and fosters the development of a wider emotional range and a more sophisticated emotional awareness than we would otherwise have. And, to repeat, this range and awareness is a cognitive achievement, requiring intelligence and displaying clear developmental trends in its acquisition.

It is easier to talk about the expressiveness of portraits than that of works that do not represent people, such as landscapes, still-lifes, abstract works, because one can attribute feelings to the persons represented. It is therefore interesting to ask how, developmentally, we move to understanding landscapes (etc.) as expressive. How do we learn to make sense of the expressiveness of a landscape?

There is a philosophical question here, which is: What sense does it make to say that a landscape expresses feeling? This is different from the developmental question, which is: How do we learn to speak of a landscape as expressive? The philosophical question has been much discussed in the philosophical literature, but, fortunately, we do not need to go deeply into this literature to answer the developmental question. After all, philosophy is (at least) an attempt to make sense of the way we speak and we do not need to do philosophy before learning to speak in that way. This means that learning to speak of art as expression is compatible with almost any philosophical account of how that way of speaking makes sense. It is worth noting, though, that adolescents are often aware of the conceptual puzzles involved and they struggle with them. For example, Flora, thirteen years old, said regarding her idea of expression: "Perhaps he [i.e., the artist] is thinking the same way it looks when you look at it."

And Frank, eighteen years old, said: "When you have strong feelings on a subject, to express it would be to paint a painting to portray your feelings, just the way you want them to be portrayed, straightforward, yet disguised in a way, so you have to look at it to see what he wants. He puts it down so other people can look at it and see part of him."

These statements suggest the difficulty that appears only after one has learned to speak of nonportraits as the expression of feelings. The difficulty is both practical—how to make sense of artworks—and philosophical—how to explain how artworks can express feelings. Understanding artworks and understanding philosophical problems are not the same thing, but they are related. One leads to the other and both are worth attention in school. For example, a teacher might well use statements like those above, and the artworks that provoked them, to provoke a philosophical discussion with students.[9]

But the main thread here is the developmental question: How do we learn to talk about the feelings expressed by landscapes? It seems that we learn first to speak of the feelings, not so much of the trees or mountains represented, as of the artist. We imagine what the artist felt or intended when she painted the landscape. We search the painting for clues to the feelings of the artist, just as earlier Ernest and Wendy searched for clues to the feelings of persons represented, and then we imagine how we would have felt, if we had been the artist, making that painting.

This appeal to the artist's intentions (or feelings) has a developmental history of its own, going back to the very beginning of our understanding of art. It is part of the basic structure of coming to see art as significant in the first place. Consider once more the situation in which young children are asked by an adult what their scribbles are about. One implication of these early conversations is, as we have seen, that marks on paper are expected to be about something. Another is that their maker is expected to determine their meaning. It seems that the marks are about what their maker intends them to be about. This intention determines, or at least affects, their significance very much as the intention of speakers determine what their speech means. This lesson is reinforced in other conversations that we, as young children, have with adults about other pictures, in picture books, for example. The discussion of such pictures often proceeds in terms that imply not only that the pictures are meaningful but also that behind them lies an artist who intended the meaning.

The result is that the idea that the artist's intentions influence the work's meaning is an early one. Its use in itself is not developmentally significant. What changes developmentally is the *kind* of intention imputed to the artist. As we have seen, young children begin by assuming that the meaningfulness of artworks takes the form of picturing things, so that a work is about what—in some sense— it looks like; and they also assume that the artist intended it to look like whatever it does look like. Thinking this way, we will make poor sense of the idea of the expressiveness of landscapes. The best we could do would be to approach it in terms of the items represented. For example, Denise, twelve years old, responded as follows:

I: Why do you think artists paint paintings?
Denise: Well, sometimes they do it to express, to let out their feelings and such.
I: Can you give me an example?
D: If they're angry, they do two people fighting, or something.

And Dunstan, also twelve years old, understands it the same way:

Dunstan: It gets out their feelings.
I: Gets out their feelings?
D: Yeah, in a way. If they're feeling sad and unhappy, they could make a picture of a sad and unhappy person. The reason they are unhappy, they will just sort of express it and that will help to get it out. . . . . Sometimes if I'm mad and angry, I draw a dragon. If I'm happy, I'll draw a meadow with some flowers and all sorts of things.

Both children use the word "express" but they understand it in terms of *what* is pictured, not *how* it is pictured. This, obviously, does not allow one to understand, say, a joyous (picture of a) fight or a moody (picture of) flowers; nor does it help much with landscapes.

If we go back to what Katie and Derek said about the Albright, we remember that they also spoke in terms of the artist's intention. But neither could imagine what that intention was. Katie persisted longest. She said: "He was angry with his mother-in-law. (She laughs) I don't know, I don't know. He just felt like it. He saw some lady going down the street and he said: 'That looks sickening,' and so he decided to paint her. He was angry at her for some reason."

The key difference between Katie and Wendy, as was claimed in the analysis above, is not in the appeal to the artist's intention. It is in the ability to imagine empathetically what someone else felt. Wendy focused mostly on the feelings of Ida, but she did also speak, a little hesitantly, of the artist's intention: "I admire the painter, if that's what he was trying to put across, for seeing through that, because it's hard for people to do. I mean they know it but everyone is as guilty as the next person [of] being vain or concerned about how people look."

Here, Wendy attributes to the artist the interpretation that she herself arrived at by imagining Ida's feelings. Later, she will be able to attribute intentions to the artist without first having to consider those of a person represented. Consider, for example, Henry, an undergraduate, as he searches for the meaning of Chagall's *La Cirque*:

Henry: Well, OK, you've got all the performers and everything else—but I think it has a deeper meaning than simply it being a circus. I get the sense that it isn't quite even close to being a circus. Such as this violin, or bass, with a bird's head and wings, the candelabra, the two-faced figure—that's different— the head on the bottom of the figure with the woman's head on top. This doesn't represent anything you can say.

I: Why are all those things there, do you think?

H: That's—I think he's trying to say something about the circus itself, but I can't pick out exactly what he is saying from it.

I: It is complicated.

H: OK, there's something in here he's trying to say with the juggler, or whatever, with the head. In fact it looks as if he's juggling his own head there. And the colors, too. The audience in the background is more of a muted, darker blue-purple color, whereas the performers are in colors that kind of stand out from the rest of the audience and everything else.

What Henry does here is to examine particular passages of the work and ask what the artist intended by them. He takes this way of speaking for granted, so that it seems equivalent for him to speak of the artist's intention and to speak of the work itself. He passes from one to the other without noticing the difference. For example, the reference of "he" shifts without warning from the artist to the juggler represented: "OK, there's something in here he's trying to say with the juggler, or whatever, with the head. In fact it looks as if he's juggling his own head there."

Several features of this way of speaking are worth noticing. To begin with, it suggests that the artist is making a work in order to express a particular meaning or emotion; that is, that the act of expression is deliberate and that the artist is aware of what he is trying to express.

Henry even speaks as if the artist has particular intentions for particular passages in the work, although Henry cannot quite imagine what they are. On the other hand, this speech does not acknowledge the activity of the viewer, the fact that Henry is imagining what *he* would have meant if he had invented a particular passage of the painting. This imaginative activity is analogous to Wendy's, when she attributed to Albright her own interpretation of Ida, and neither Henry nor Wendy acknowledge it. Neither Henry nor Wendy have yet mastered a way of speaking that acknowledges *both* the artist's and the viewer's active participation in constructing the meaning of a work. That is something still to come.

Before discussing that development, however, I want to note a further suggestion in Henry's way of speaking. It suggests that the artist is an ahistorical individual who knows not only what she wants to say but also freely chooses the means of saying it. In other words, the artist is not significantly affected by history or culture. To imagine what the artist intended, Henry does not have to consult the historical or cultural differences between them. His way of speaking suggests that such differences do not affect what is expressed nor how it is expressed, or rather it avoids raising questions about such differences. Consequently, Henry can imagine the artist to be very like himself. But, of course, what an artist expresses may well be shaped by his historical or cultural background, as, for example, Chagall's desire to escape the horrors of ethnic progroms. An artist may even be unaware of such feelings and yet they may be what are most strongly expressed in his work. And similarly, the *way* in which feelings are expressed is affected by history and culture. The circus is a potent symbol in early twentieth-century Russia, for instance, and Chagall uses color in part in reaction to its previous use in art history.

The general point is that to think of an artist as an individual not significantly affected by culture is again cognitively simpler than the alternative and is therefore developmentally earlier. To think of the artist as reflecting particular cultural formations would require one to imagine the historical concreteness of others and this, in turn, would mean grasping something of the way in which we all are structured by our own culture and of at least some of the influences that shape our personality and attitudes, much of which usually operates "behind our back." This awareness is a major achievement of cognitive development, a task that occupies us all and is never completed. The experience of art is a major way to develop this awareness and to continue its growth.

Most adolescents become aware of their own activity in their response to art. They develop various ways of speaking of their own experience, which is usually construed as a direct and emotional response to the work. Sometimes they contrast the character of their response with the more formalistic and reasoned response they attribute to critics and experts. This may be thought less honest, because it is more inferential and appears less directly experienced. For example, Harriett, an undergraduate student, said about a work by Picasso:

Harriet: No, I think it's so—it's your human feelings. I think you can say: "This one has great brushstrokes." You can say these things but when it comes right down to it, I think, from my point of view,— I don't know critics that well—I think it finally boils down to just your gut reaction to the painting.

I: Is that more an emotional than a cognitive thing?

Harriet: For me, it is. I don't know, I'm not exposed to a great deal of art. So for me it is a total emotional reaction, which is my reaction to stories or plays or anything. If I can connect with it somehow emotionally, then I can go with it and become one with it. But if there's no connection emotionally, I would—you know, it can be the greatest Picasso and I generally, with his abstract ones, I don't connect at all. And yet he is considered one of the greats. He is all this but I don't connect with it emotionally.

Speaking of oneself this way implies an awareness of one's own experience; that is, an awareness that one is having an experience of a particular kind, emotional or not. It also requires one to be aware that the character of what one sees is partly a function of one's own particular characteristics. This awareness amounts to the realization of the act of interpretation and the loss of the belief that one can simply see what is objectively there for everyone to see. It is no longer enough just to tell what one sees; one has to take into account the way one's own interpretation affects one's response. It takes considerable time, developmentally, to work through a discovery of this magnitude.

The discovery also suggests that other people, including the artist, have an experience of the artwork and that these experiences will similarly depend on their personalities. Hence, their interpretations may differ. And, hence, one has the task of relating one's own experience of the work with, or disentangling it from, the experience of others, especially the experience of the artist. One version, perhaps the simplest, is to assume that the experiences coincide when both viewer and the artist are successful. For instance, the following is from a conversation with Kathy, an undergraduate student:

Interviewer: Why do artists paint paintings?

Kathy: I've heard, and it makes sense to me, that they paint to express something, express dreams, explore fantasies. That probably makes the most sense to me that I've heard. Certain composers compose for the money. That makes sense to me and is more real to me. I'd rather think that they paint to express something and cause some feeling. That would be my wish.

I: Is it possible to paint a painting that is expressive without having a deep need to do that?

Kathy: I would think it wouldn't be real, genuine.

I: Can you tell that from the painting?

Kathy: I don't think, I don't think it would be [genuine] if the artist was painting to just put something on the canvas. I tend to see through things like that. I don't have a trained eye, I wouldn't know for sure whether it was intentional [i.e., genuine] on a how-it-was-done point of view. [But] from an inner sense of myself I would know the artist wasn't trying to express. I couldn't relate to it anyway.

I: You are saying you can tell by looking at the painting whether it's honest?

Kathy: Kind of an inner feeling about it.

This kind of talk—inner feeling, gut reaction— implies a certainty about knowing what one feels, a belief that one's experience is transparent to one's self and has a unity that makes it easy to identify. A somewhat more complex version of the relation between the experience of the viewer and of the artist is that they may be different from each other and that one might not be aware of such a difference. One can see Lewis, another undergraduate student, working some of this out in the following dialog:

Interviewer: You say he wants other people to get what he is trying to say. Then in a way the success of a painting depends on whether people can get what he is trying to say?

Lewis: Well, not necessarily success. But like, the artist, the reason he painted it is he just wanted to. He likes to paint and he wanted to get his thoughts and feelings on paper and, you know, that's the most important thing. And, like, another thing, I would imagine that an artist would like people to look at his picture and see, like, what the artist is trying to say. But they might not. They might see something he didn't think of. But that doesn't necessarily mean it's wrong. Like, that person's view could be just as important as the artist's.

I: So even if the artist had something in mind, you couldn't say someone else's view of it was wrong?

Lewis: Yeah, the artist knows what he's trying to say and he's painted it out. That's what's important to him. But, like, a person that sees it, he sees something completely different, you know, really meaningful to him. His point of view is going to be just as important as the artist's.

At this point, Lewis has realized that the viewer and the artist have particular and potentially different experiences regarding the artwork, and that this is true of all viewers. These insights raise questions about where the meaning of a work lies and how we can establish it, whether it is intersubjectively the same for all viewers, how determinant is the artist's experience versus the viewer's, all questions that have been much discussed in the philosophy of art. It may well be that, at this point, Lewis needs help in working these questions out. But we can say, minimally, that he understands the intrinsic ambiguity of art, that different people may have different interpretations of a work, and that it is not obvious that there is only one correct view of it. Such an understanding is cognitively quite complex and represents a considerable degree of cognitive development.

I will not pursue these developments in understanding art further. Instead, I will close by making explicit what the foregoing has implied: that development in the arts is closely connected with the development of a more general cognitive and emotional maturity and that we have good reasons for valuing this kind of maturity. Indeed I want to suggest that the cognitive abilities of this sort, which are developed by the study of art, are of central educational interest.

Development in the arts is valuable in itself, of course, just as the arts are valuable in themselves, and needs no other justification. But all knowledge is both an end in itself and also a means to something further. Art in particular cannot easily be confined within its own boundaries. It has always been linked with human values, with insight into self and others, and with questions of personal and collective identity. The developmental story indicated above suggests these same connections, couched in the idiom of the cognitive view of the arts. The story began with the discovery that some kinds of objects carry meanings and have been made by individuals for that purpose. Then these works were seen as embodying representations of reality and human values (such as beauty, ugliness, and violence), as being, in effect, symbols of good and bad. Next it was discovered that artworks somehow embody subjectivity—the feeling, thought, insight of an individual person, with whom one can empathize and share the same feeling, thought, insight. Finally, in the story told above, Lewis came to realize that artworks must be interpreted by the viewer and that there may be several reasonable and different interpretations of them. He wondered whether the artist or the viewer can determine once and for all which is the correct interpretation and he understood that interpretations are affected by the experience and background of the interpreter.

There is more, of course, for Lewis to discover. For example, he has not yet grasped the historical and cultural character of artworks and of his own interpretations. He has yet to grapple with the question to what extent artworks can be understood across cultural or historical differences, or to what extent we can learn about other cultures through artworks.

Many of us used to think that science—the rigorous, methodological, and objective search for truth—provides educators with our best paradigm of thinking. But I now believe that our times call for something more complex, contextual, and tolerant of multiple interpretations and ambiguity. This is especially so in a multicultural society like ours, which is characterized by multiple groups seeking and contesting the recognition of their values and where much of the communication occurs through charged visual images. It seems to me that such a society needs citizens who respond to symbolic objects in a way that is more like Lewis's than Godfrey's. Godfrey, after all, roundly condemned Ida for not conforming to some social stereotypes that he took for granted. Lewis learned to wonder whether his interpretation is the only reasonable one. The difference between them suggests that art may provide a better paradigm than science of the kind of thinking we need today: a kind of thinking that combines a sympathetic response to symbolic objects with the ability to entertain several interpretations of them and to understand that one's own interpretation may not be the best. The arts may not be the only vehicle for the development of such understandings but they are a principal one.

NOTES

1. Rudolph Arnheim's classic and most influential work is *Visual Thinking* (Berkeley: University of California Press, 1969).

2. For an account of the "cognitive revolution" of the 1960s, which has made so much difference to the arts, see Bernard J. Baars, *The cognitive revolution in psychology* (New York: Guilford Press, 1986) or Howard Gardner, *The mind's new science* (New York: Basic Books, 1985).

3. For a recent overview of related subject matter, see Claire Golomb, *The child's creation of a pictorial world* (Berkeley: University of California Press, 1992) and Ellen Winner, *Invented worlds: The psychology of the arts* (Cambridge, MA: Harvard University Press, 1982).

4. There are two systematic efforts to describe the development of understanding the visual arts. One is the work of Abigail Housen, *The eye of the beholder: Measuring aesthetic development* (unpublished doctoral dissertation, Harvard Graduate School of Education, Cambridge, MA). The other is my own: Michael Parsons, *How we understand art: A cognitive-developmental account of aesthetic experience* (Cambridge: Cambridge University Press, 1987).

5. This situation is discussed by Michael Cole as an example of the social construction of understanding in general in "Culture and cognitive development," *Culture and Psychology, 1*, 1995.

6. The extracts from discussions of artworks are taken from my book, *How we understand art*, cited above.

7. A good introduction to Vygotsky's thought is found in J. V. Wertsch, *Vygotsky and the social formation of mind* (Cambridge, MA: Harvard University Press, 1985).

8. The best statement of this view in English is still R. G. Collingwood's *The principles of art, third edition* (London: Oxford University Press, 1958).

9. Discussion of ways of teaching aesthetics is found in Lewis Lankford, *Aesthetics: Issues and inquiry* (Reston, VA: National Art Education Association, 1992) and in M. J. Parsons & H. G Blocker, *Aesthetics and education* (Urbana, IL: University of Illinois Press, 1993).

6

Metacognitive Reflection in University Students

Dawn E. Schrader

Colleges and universities have created a world that dominates the lives and thoughts of countless young people during the years in which their character and values are being formed. Under these conditions, students must get help from their universities in developing moral standards or they are unlikely to get much assistance at all (Derek Bok, April 15, 1988).

The mission of many colleges and universities includes two primary forms of education: academic excellence and character or moral education. Too often, moral and ethical development has been left to chance—to discussions in residence halls, or to the occasional moral philosophy course taken as a part of a liberal education curriculum. College is a time when students face, perhaps for the first time, values and perspectives other than the ones that their families espoused and have a chance to self-consciously reflect on their way of thinking about both those values and their moral meaning-making-system. Those conflicting values may arise during a philosophy course where students may begin to explore the question of whether God exists; whether democracy is a moral form of government; whether right to life is the highest moral value, or whether issues such as quality of life or self-determination may supersede such a value, and so on. Similar issues may arise in informal gatherings of students in residence and dining halls or student lounges.

How students in pluralistic colleges and universities make choices about right and wrong, good and bad is of concern to all of us. We are concerned about how students develop the ethical systems that they will use when they become the leaders of tomorrow. How do we explain incidents that clearly demonstrate that college students are nonreflective in their moral thoughts and actions?

The following two occurrences in Ithaca, New York, highlight our need to begin examining students' metacognitive or reflective awareness of their own moral thinking processes and developing educational opportunities to foster moral education in college settings. One fall, two college students engaged in a fist-fight—not an unusual occurrence after a Friday evening of drinking. One student died as a result of the injuries sustained in this argument about school affiliation. The student walking away from the incident said that the other student "deserved" to be beaten for the comments that he had made about his college, but did not know at the time that his last blow caused the student's death (Cornell Daily Sun, October 1989). In a separate incident, a recently graduated college student intentionally drove his car into the path of a woman walking along the side of a road. These incidents, though occurring within a locality usually considered to be a safe, quiet semi-rural town, are not isolated to one college or geographic area. These acts are morally reprehensible. They involve very low levels of moral reasoning, yet, also importantly, demonstrate low levels of moral metacognitive reflection. Unless we can encourage students to be aware of their moral thoughts and actions, reflect upon and evaluate them, a focus on moral and character development in the college years will not be achieved.

It is generally agreed that the academy plays an essential role in the moral development of its students, but what is the structure of the moral development programs that we have, how well do they work with college populations, and what can be done to improve our knowledge and practice in higher educational settings?

In high schools, moral educators have developed ethics curricula, instituted Just Community schools, centers of care and character education programs (e.g., Power, Higgins & Kohlberg, 1989). High school teachers and administrators encourage students to think about and discuss moral issues—both real and hypothetical—in homerooms and in academic classes.

But what about in college? We no longer have "homeroom" or easy ways to institute moral education programs college-wide other than in living-learning environments. Promoting care and respect for others is difficult when the social and academic lives of our students are so diverse that few students at large institutions even know people who live in different residence halls or off-campus, are non—traditional aged students (perhaps with families of their own), or are pursuing a different course of study. How, then, can students reflect on those differences and use such reflection to transform their moral perspectives?

What can be done? Have the institutions of higher education—whose goal and mission it is to promote ethical character and to develop good citizens capable of critical thinking—organized themselves in such a way that moral education, as we know it, is infeasible? Can anything be done? In this paper, I put forward the idea that we need to reconceptualize the moral judgment-moral action question in terms of moral development and conscious reflection on the metacognitive components of students' thinking so that there is (1) greater consistency between moral judgment and ethical moral action, and (2) there are increased opportunities for students' taking responsibility for reflective thought and, thus, moral development.

The literature on moral judgment and moral action, replete with examples demonstrating the relationship between moral stage and behavior, collectively finds that the higher the moral stage, the more likely a person is to engage in moral action. The preponderance of the studies indicate that the focus is in the direction of judgment to action. Kohlberg and Candee posit that the development of both moral judgment and moral action is a "single-track process" but that moral judgment arises out of moral action, and moral action can give rise to moral judgment: "A new stage of moral judgment may guide new behavior, whereas a new action involving a conflict and choice may lead one to construct a new stage of moral judgment" (Kohlberg & Candee, 1984, p. 53). The authors, however, also state that action itself must be seen in the context of reasoning in order to determine its relative morality. Thus, although the judgment-action question may begin with an observation of an action, in order for such action to be considered moral, the moral judgments and reasoning that underlie such action must also be considered.

Such has been the nature of the inquiry into the judgment-action question. With the exception of Blasi's insights, which highlight the importance of characteristics of the self and moral understanding (e.g., Blasi, 1990), and Turiel's (1990) discussion of moral judgment, action, and development as having ignored nonmoral and other social factors, the focus has been on moral judgment as the explanatory factor for people engaging in given action situations. While moral stage has been shown to be monotonically related to deontic action choice in many situations, Turiel (1990) correctly points out that this explanation is deficient and encourages the exploration of additional variables that better explain the moral judgment-action gap such as ego strength, autonomy (moral types), and judgments of responsibility.

THE QUESTION OF CONSISTENCY

In order to get at the notion of consistency between thought and action, there needs to be an awareness that the two are potentially at a disjuncture. The question of consistency would be best explored in the changing contexts in which decisions are made such as in practical matters and in hypothetical ones. These contexts can then be compared as to the differences in thought strategies individuals use when involved in action contexts. In practical matters, there is a lack of consistency between decision processes and the actions taken, and thought processes are changed depending upon the nature of the situation itself. For example, in the book, *Mind over Machine*, Hubert and Stuart Dreyfus (1986) provide an example that describes their approach to understanding expert systems of thought in an attempt to develop a computer program that replicates optimal decision making. The example given involves the decision of when to replace one's car. They describe the decision process as follows. First, there must be an examination of the factors involved (such as reliable performance, depreciation, pleasure in driving). Next, there is a weighing of the factors based upon the factors themselves and trade-offs between factors. Third, a sequence of decisions is generated that determines whether or not to replace the car. The Dreyfuses explained that this process was simply one of putting in all the facts, listing the pros and cons of the various factors, and allowing the computer program to make the sequence of decisions that would lead to a final decision.

However, a perplexing problem arose for the Dreyfuses when, instead of the usual response they received when they provided this example, such as "Oh, I understand," someone asked the question, "Oh, and is this the way you decide when you replace YOUR car?" Stuart Dreyfus replied quickly, "Of course not. That was only an example of how to use the formal procedure. Buying a new car is for me much too important to be left to a mathematical model. I mull it over for awhile, and buy a new car when it feels right" (Dreyfus & Dreyfus, 1986, pp. 9-10).

Moral decisions are reached in some very similar ways. A person may have an underlying structure of moral reasoning, or a parallel to what the Dreyfuses called the "formal procedure" for coming to moral or ethical decisions, but when a person is asked the question, "Is that the way you decide when you replace *your* car?"—make *your* moral decisions—the answer may be quite different.

In the moral domain, Kohlberg supposed that hypothetical situations elicited the structure of one's best reasoning capabilities, similar to those used in Dreyfus' formal procedure. When "real life" moral situations arise that call for moral actions, a person does not always translate his or her best reasoning to that personal moral situation. Something else exists that tells us that the formal procedure does not fit, that another procedure is called for, and that factors other than reasoning (as Blasi and Turiel discuss) are called upon to explain the lack of consistency. But while those factors may help explain the inconsistency, they are insufficient in explaining the relationship between judgment and action. The explanation, I believe, lies in the ability or inability for the moral decision maker to engage in metacognitive awareness of their thinking process. It is this awareness that leads to the possibility of engaging in a different moral action choice than was immediately made, and possibly, with experience and practice, this reflective awareness could lead to moral stage change.

THE MODEL

I propose that the bridge between moral judgment and moral action involves an understanding of the interconnectedness of judgment and action beyond the "unidimensional" approach Kohlberg & Candee (1984) outlined. I see a dynamic interaction that involves the following process:

(1) Judgment: One's epistemological framework (including one's ego, social, moral, and interpersonal development) influences one's interpretations of the action situation itself. This framework is likewise influenced by the social context in which the action situation occurs.
(2) Action: A situation is experienced and activates a decision-making process that leads to a particular action choice (similar to Rest's [1984] 4 component

model, or perhaps an emotional intuitive process). Utilized in the action component are the elements in Step1 and one's experience in prior action contexts.

(3) Metacognitive Reflection: The result of the action situation provides an opportunity for an individual to engage in reflection regarding his or her own thinking about their actions and moral judgments. Further provided is an opportunity for a person to reflect on the thought processes invoked by the action situation (metacognition). Such reflection provides fertile ground for the Piagetian equilibrative process to recommence (including the ego, social, moral and interpersonal epistemic domains), and may change one's epistemological framework, beginning the cycle of development and the quest for consistency between thought and action.

This interconnectedness of thought sets up the dynamic that illuminates the processes involved in the judgment-action gap. This dynamic interaction differs from that of Kohlberg and Candee's model, which states that "moral stage influences moral action in two ways: (1) through differences in deontic choice, and (2) through judgments of responsibility" (Kohlberg & Candee, 1984, p. 62). This proposed model incorporates a greater dialectic between stage and action, and utilizes the Piagetian equilibration processes in an explicitly conscious metacognitive activity rather than in the reflexive activity responsible for much of cognitive stage transition.

The judgment-action question is not only a one-way relationship nor is it simply a "unidirectional" model in which "moral judgment arises out of moral action itself" and where "a new stage of moral judgment may guide new behavior" (Kohlberg & Candee, 1984, p. 53). I propose that the relationship involves a dialectical interaction—judgment and action being at the core, but metacognition in the form of reflections on judgment and reflections on action being essential for the further development in each of the three components (namely, increased moral judgment stage, morally adequate action choices, and higher levels of metacognition).

In sum, a complete model of understanding the components involved in the translating of judgments to action and the influence of actions on the development of moral judgments (specifically, this is Kohlberg's unidimensional model) requires an understanding of the additional component of metacognitive awareness; of the individual as a social, moral, reflective action-agent. To illustrate the interactions between moral judgment, moral action, and metacognition, I will give an example of a college student involved in this process.

CASE EXAMPLE

Krista, a junior social science major at a large land grant institution, illustrates the complexity of the moral judgment and moral action question in her responses to hypothetical and real life moral dilemmas. She provides us with some evidence that, as Dreyfus and Dreyfus point out, the optimal way to buy a new car is not the way one actually buys one for herself. More precisely, Krista demonstrates that formal decision procedures differ from personal decision procedures in her moral decision processes. Krista demonstrates that moral judgment, moral actions, and metacognitive knowledge and experience are important in making moral decisions. The role of each of these factors differs in the context of the dilemma—whether formal, hypothetical, or real life. Her case further demonstrates that moral judgments play a central role in the decision-making process in all contexts, and that other factors are influential in her action strategies in a real life context.

Krista was interviewed using Form B of Colby and Kohlberg's (1987) Moral Judgment Interview (MJI), a Real Life Moral Dilemma Interview (patterned after Gilligan, 1982) and a Metacognitive Interview (Schrader, 1988). The metacognitive components of the interview involved three tasks: Krista was asked to engage in a standard metacognitive task—teaching someone else to do something—in this case, how to resolve a hypothetical dilemma. Next she was interviewed using the MJI. Krista was asked to talk aloud about her thinking (called the "think aloud" technique in metacognitive research) while she resolved the MJI dilemmas. Lastly, Krista discussed a moral dilemma that she faced in her own life. Excerpts from her interview follow. The metacognitive, formal procedure part of the interview asked her to think about how she would tell someone to solve a hypothetical dilemma (this parallels Dreyfus' "How would you go about buying a new car?" strategy) (I: Interviewer; K: Krista).

I: Could you just briefly summarize the steps that I would use in [resolving this dilemma]?
K: Okay . . . first you'd reflect on the problem from the characters' standpoints, bringing into account their roles in society and the expectations of the society that they're in their context. You should look over the outcomes of other such situations, either by looking through—reading books or seeing a movie on the topic. In that second step, the viewing, you could also discuss with other people and get their input and their ideas and draw from their value base. In the next step, you would bring your own values into play: what would you do if you were in that situation, as either—as any of the characters involved? When you find a solution that agrees with you, that you can live with and that you can use, you've done it.
I: Okay. Thinking over what you just told me, would you change any of your instructions about how I should solve the dilemma?
K: Well, I forgot to mention like writing down and . . . Somewhere in the steps where you're discussing it with other people or dealing [with] films or such, you should probably put down on paper or at least some sort of concrete form—maybe like record it or something—something that you can have to look at or to hear and revise again, until you come to something that sounds right or is right for you. Kind of like paper-revising, revising your ideas, or at least holding onto other people's ideas. That's where like books come into play, 'cause it's already there, or the movies or something. You should probably write it down so that you don't lose it in your head somewhere. Like if you're thinking about it when you're about to go to sleep, and then when you wake up in the morning it's gone. That sort of thing. I guess I'd stick that in!

In the quotes above, Krista demonstrates a formal decision-making method. This method involves thinking about the situation from a variety of perspectives, examining the context, referring to alternative experiences (such as actions used books, movies, etc.), discussing it with people in terms of their values and experiences, and then utilizing her values and experiences by invoking a rule of placing oneself in that situation. She also recommends a metacognitive strategy that allows her to recall her thinking at a later date (writing it down so you don't forget about it when you go to sleep). Thus, her formal strategy, revealed through her instructions to another person, involved the components of moral judgments (in the structure of role taking and a societal perspective), others' actions (in books, movies; from friends), and the use of a metacognitive strategy for retrieving her thought processes after the decision was made. This metacognitive strategy was used so that she could reflect back on her thought processes and strategies, presumably for later evaluation in another action context. Krista was next interviewed using Form B of the MJI and then asked to metacognitively reflect on her moral decision-making processes while she was actually resolving these dilemmas.

I: Thinking back over the [hypothetical] dilemmas that we just discussed, how did you know how to go about resolving the dilemmas?
K: Okay . . . mostly based on experience, both what I've experienced in my own life—like I brought some of my own thoughts into the sister conflict, and from what I've experienced in or through books, through talking with other people, through an eleventh-grade morality course!
I: That really helped?
K: Yeah, instruction in decision making, that's what . . . So that kind of experience gave me a base to use my values to make the decision.

In this excerpt, Krista immediately mentions two main factors that influenced her decision making in the hypothetical dilemmas: experiences in her own life and instruction in morality in eleventh grade. Thus we see that experience in instruction of moral decision making helped shape her judgments; it gave her "a base to use my values." Oser & Reich (1990) has called instruction in morality a metacognitive tool that he later demonstrated fostered higher stage scores on the MJI in his sample (although he taught his subjects Kohlberg's theory itself). In Krista's case, we also see an interplay between such a metacognitive experience in the making of moral judgments in hypothetical dilemmas:

I: As you think back over the [hypothetical] dilemmas and the way that you thought about them, would you change the approach to any of the ways that you went about thinking?
K: I'd want to have more input from either concrete sources like, well, books, materials, that sort of thing, and/or have more people sitting around discussing this topic, because I know there are things that I am not considering, only because they're not part of my experience. I'd also want to have—I guess I'm a concrete person. I like having paper or something in front of me, where I can write down their suggestions or their opinions and my own thoughts. Because when I'm just thinking things through or talking things out, I'll lose my train of thought. Or I'll say something and then forget I said it, and inconsistencies like that bother me. I like to work things out.

In this excerpt, Krista reflects on her decision-making processes and is aware that her experiences are incomplete ("I know there are things that I am not considering, only because they're not part of my experience"). She then utilizes a tool (such as having something concrete in front of her) to help her in her thought processes, to help her to "think things through" or "talk things out." These ideas were added to her moral decision strategy in use for the hypothetical dilemma, which then made the decision strategy in use more consistent with the formal moral decision strategy described above. She did not, however, spontaneously engage in that thinking while she was resolving the hypothetical dilemmas of the MJI. Thus, context of the dilemma (whether hypothetical or ideal) is seemingly important in understanding moral decision making and action choices.

The third part of the interview consisted of Krista discussing a moral situation in her own life. Krista told of a dilemma where she was trying to make a decision whether or not to have premarital sex with her boyfriend.

I: What were the moral issues for you?

K: Okay . . . first, do I adhere blindly to the [Roman Catholic] church's teaching that you're not supposed to have sex before marriage, and just base it solely on that? Do I go against everything I've been taught and decide to have sex with my boyfriend? Also taking into consideration my parents' and my family's reaction to that kind of relationship with my boyfriend: What would they say? What would they think? How would it change the way we react with each other? Because it would change; I know it would change. Do I—should I—okay, how would a sexually intimate relationship change what I have now with my boyfriend?

Okay, so I had to consider how that would affect our relationship. Had to consider how either following church teaching or going against them would affect my role in the church, because I'm very active in my church. Would I feel like I shouldn't be doing—would I feel like I'm not worthy to be standing up here serving as a lector or as a minister, because I've gone against the church? Would I be able to look other people in the eye—I mean if I go back to high school and see all my old teachers—my morality class teacher! Would I be able to say—to look them in the eye, just a dignity sort of issue.

In beginning to resolve this dilemma, Krista mentioned several considerations: church and family teachings, parents' reactions, and the impact of her decision on her relationship with her boyfriend. Then she began to make moral judgments about these considerations and exploring the effect her decisions would have on her own sense of dignity ("would I feel like I'm not worthy to be standing up here"; "its just a dignity sort of issue"). Krista began to frame the dilemma from a perspective of the self in relation to a variety of social systems, relations, and expectations as well as her own self-system, thereby utilizing the underlying structure of her moral judgment stage.

When further probed about her decision making—I: "Was there a method or an approach that you used while you were solving the dilemma?"— Krista replied:

K: Yes, I relied heavily on discussing with other people what my options would be, not only—obviously—with Sam, but I discussed sexuality and I discussed my relationship with Sam with a Catholic chaplain, who was able to provide not only what church teachings are, but helped me decide if I'm ready for this or if I want to do this—that sort of thing.

I: Did you consider the method to be the best for you?

K: Yes. I don't think I could have relied solely on my own—I certainly couldn't rely on my own feelings. If I did that . . . I don't know. I probably would have jumped in bed with lots of people! So I tamed my own feelings. I had to tame my own desires in this particular situation.

Krista's decision making involved a discussion with other people as well as a metacognitive awareness of the limitations of her own thoughts ("[the] chaplain provided not only what the church teachings were but helped me decide if I'm ready for this") and her own feelings ("I don't think I could have relied solely on my own feelings"). Thus, a reflective awareness of the limits of her thoughts (simple self-reflective level of metacognition) was involved, as was a strategy that she used in her ideal decision strategy and her reflections on her hypothetical decision strategies—specifically, discussion with others. Krista was then asked:

I: How did you know when you reached the solution?

K: "Well . . . okay . . . after we both sat down and discussed things, after we'd both talked to other people and gotten other people's input to the situation, we knew that the fact that we were hesitant about it in the first place meant that it might not be a good idea to include sexual intimacy into our relationship at this time. So after we started discussing it, it was obvious from the start: okay, we're having doubts about it; we shouldn't be doing it. And then we fleshed out reasons why, so it wasn't just based solely on feelings. So it was based on—so we knew that thinking had gone into it and discussing and caring about each other enough to listen to each other's insecurities or thoughts that we each had about it. I think that was very important.

In discussing her action strategy, Krista was very clear about the components involved in making this moral decision: obtaining information about the situation (talking with other people), reflecting on her metacognitive experiences of her action choice ("we knew that the fact that we were hesitant about it in the first place meant it might not be a good idea"), and reflecting on her reasoning strategies in making the decision ("we fleshed out reasons . . . so we knew that thinking had gone into it"). Krista further evidenced the relationship between moral judgments, experience and metacognition intersecting in response to this question:

I: Okay, thinking back on the situation that you described, not any of these dilemmas that we talked about, were you aware of your thinking about your decision process when you were making the decision?

K: Okay . . . I was . . . I realized that I was in a situation where my values and my experience were not sufficient to make the decision, so I realized that I needed to get more information and more people's input. And I knew that was part of the way I make decisions.

In her explanation of her cognitive decision-making processes, Krista indicated a reflective awareness of her thinking strategies and realized that her moral decisions involved both her own values (or moral judgments) and her own experience. She was metacognitively aware that her own experiences were insufficient for her to make a good moral decision and relied on a formal decision-making strategy to help her find a solution to her dilemma.

From a constructive developmental perspective, moral stage development is important in relation to social and cognitive development and behavior. That is, the monotonic stage and action relationship is strong, and the underlying structural cognitive properties across domains is evident. In the same spirit, the content of our experience and the socio-cultural environment provides fertile constructivist ground for growth to occur. Promoting moral stage development should not only provide role-taking opportunities but aid students in considering moral content such as care and responsibility—as mapped by Gilligan (1982) and others, and philosophically based moral content such as Kohlberg and his colleagues' conceptions of moral types (Tappan, Kohlberg, Schrader & Higgins, 1987).

IMPLICATIONS FOR MORAL EDUCATION

Since Blatt and Kohlberg's (1975) ingenious invention of moral education programs that use Socratic dialogue as an educational tool, students have been participating in dilemma discussions as an essential part of their moral education programs. While this method has proven to be effective in study after study (see Schlafli, Rest, & Thoma, 1985), we should examine this educational program for its failures (the "insignificant" number of students) as well as its successes to improve our conceptions of moral education. We should ask what is failing, for whom, and why? Perhaps we (or they) are not failing, but our methods of evaluating success may be in need of re-assessment.

But what is Socratic Dialogue? Is it what we're doing in our programs? To many, Socratic Dialogue means conducting an open-ended discussion of a problem while the teacher asks questions. Yet Socrates asked questions in a particular way. As with Socrates in the Meno, students are asked to reflect on and to think through their beliefs, assumptions—reaching into the inner workings of their mind to discover the natural truth that lies within the person. The questions are guided carefully, thoughtfully. Unfortunately, none of us are Socrates; and more unfortunately, most of us are not trained in the method. The moral education dilemma discussion programs conducted today are dilemma discussions pure and simple, and not Socratic. This is an important distinction since moral systems are actively constructed, not discovered; internal moral "truths" are not already present to be revealed.

Dilemma discussion works for stage development for several reasons. First is that most college students reason within one stage of each other. Given the stage norms from data that James Rest has collected over the years, this is a justifiable assumption. Next, we assume that moral reasoning development takes place through listening to and thinking about higher-stage arguments, which through the Piagetian process of accommodation stimulates thinking to the adjacent higher moral stage. This assumes that students listen to others' arguments in the discussion—peers' or authorities'—rather than focusing on the development of their own argumentation. Accommodation requires attention and relevance. We must examine whether students can identify something as a moral problem, care about (i.e., be motivated by) that moral problem, and cognitively act upon it. It is in this area where the field of moral reasoning has not joined with many other areas of social psychology (Turiel, 1990) or moral motivation (Blasi, 1990).

Third, we assume that professors reason at a higher stage than the students, and that they are thus able to promote moral stage growth through plus-one discussions and moral advocacy. With age, education and experience as correlates of higher stage development, this is a probable but insufficient reason for placing our best bets on professorial talents for creating a morally disequilibrating discussion and advocating the next higher stage. Often in classrooms, professors reject taking a moral stance or even presenting their own views for fear of influencing students because of their authoritative position.

Lastly, dilemma discussion is based on the Piagetian process of development: reflexive abstraction (assimilation, accommodation, equilibration)—an unconscious process. Since Kohlberg's stage model was based upon a Piagetian paradigm, we accept this notion. At the same time, a Socratic process involves encouraging students to engage in self-reflection and analysis. These two ideas—reflexive abstraction and Socratic reflection—have some components in common. Both claim that patterns of development exist within the person before one develops knowledge of them. Both require some activity to "discover" the way of making meaning. Yet the difference is that one (Piaget's) is an unconscious process that "just happens" when we operate on the world (including the world of morals), while the other must be self-conscious, active, reflective. I propose that the link is metacognition—applied to the moral domain. Metacognition is the conscious process of coming to take "as object"—to think about—the way that one thinks about—one's own thoughts and actions, operate upon them, develop toward the next (moral) stage, and use that more developed stage to make more adequate moral choices and act upon them.

CONCLUSIONS

I have argued in this paper that metacognition is an essential missing component in a model that helps narrow the gap between moral judgment and moral action, and helps explain the interactive effects of judgment on action and vice versa. Metacognitive components in moral decision making have been scarcely addressed in action and education contexts, and have only recently been the object of study. I believe that we must further develop the underlying cognitive and affective processes that stimulate moral stage transition and change, that we must examine the role experience plays in such transition, and look toward variables and interactions that shed light on the question of how judgments encourage moral actions, and how such actions provide the impetus for metacognitive reflection and change.

Ultimately, I agree with Blasi (1990) that reasoning and understanding is central to morality and that these are insufficient to motivate action. The solution, Blasi states, "must consist of making reason itself, knowledge, and understanding the object of one's motives and desires" (p. 55). I am saying that making such a "commitment to reason and to the result of one's cognition" and the process of "making reason itself knowledge" (Blasi, 1990) lies in the domain of metacognition; of being reflectively aware of one's thought processes (metacognitive knowledge) and being reflectively aware of one's affective experiences (metacognitive experience), and then integrating these metacognitions into one's cognitive structure of the moral world (moral judgments). But further, such awareness is necessary to incorporate in a model that includes a person's moral, social, and interpersonal epistemologies and their own action situations in context.

PROPOSAL FOR THE FUTURE

I propose two reforms of moral education in higher educational settings. I propose that (1) a more specific approach to moral dilemma discussion will assist students in developing the critical thinking skills needed to think about moral problems, and (2) individuals' metacognitive awareness of the ways in which they make moral decisions and experience moral dilemmas in action can be instrumental in drawing the connection between students' current moral reasoning and moral actions, as well as providing the impetus for promoting moral reasoning development.

We must refine the definition and use of dilemma discussion techniques to be less reminiscent of values-clarification exercises or persuasive debates in which one group of students (and the faculty member) try to "win" the other over to their point of view. I suggest that we utilize Rest's (1984) four-component model that encourages the examination of each component of a morality. By so doing, individuals can gather cognitive skills within the moral components and develop complex strategies that will assist in taking these "content" concerns as the "object" of their thinking. Thereby, moral education becomes more specific and directed toward the cognitive-moral processes that we are teaching.

In addition, I recommend that we utilize the concept of moral types (Tappan, Kohlberg, Schrader, & Higgins, 1987) and integrate the processes underlying the philosophical criteria in a directed method of questioning and analysis. Moral Type B (a) shows a relationship to the content of postconventional thinking and (b) has a high correlation with moral action (Kohlberg & Candee, 1984). Thus, the aim of educational programs becomes the development of critical and complex thinking, principled morality, and moral action—not principled reasoning alone.

Further, moral metacognition may be an essential element in the development of ethical reasoning and judgment in individuals. Many programs in higher education that Schlafli, Rest, and Thoma (1985) reviewed worked partly because an element of "personal reflection" was involved along with the dilemma discussion component. For example, the Alverno study (Earley, Mentkowski & Schafer, 1980) and the Sierra Project (Loxley & Whiteley, 1986; Whiteley, 1982) both had components in which students were asked to keep journals—a key mechanism for reflective thinking. Perhaps the involvement of personal reflection provided the impetus for students to then go back and think about their personal reflections—the latter of which is metacognition. If this is done in the moral domain, a person engaged in cognitively stimulating moral activity is engaging in conscious "reflective abstraction'—which results in cognitive restructuring.

If metacognitive strategies can be extrapolated from the critical reasoning processes people use in resolving ethical issues and dilemmas, we might design moral education programs that foster critical thinking and ethical development, as well as teach ethical components of subject matter. Since it is extraordinarily difficult for universities, particularly state-assisted universities, to teach particular ethical values. However, the mission of universities includes the development of the moral character of its students. An important way to develop such moral character is to teach students the processes and procedures of making ethically sound moral decisions, and encourage them to consciously reflect on their thinking processes.

Lastly, I propose that instead of relying on dilemma discussion and a combination of a host of other educational procedures (e.g., small groups, journal writing, living-learning environments) to transform the structure of their thinking from one stage of moral reasoning to another, we should examine the development of critical thinking through critical pedagogy and through the understanding of the development of metacognitive thinking processes and awareness. With this understanding, more specific programs can be developed to augment the reflective critical thinking processes that are used when engaging in moral decision making and participating in moral discussions. Then, ethical reasoning processes may be integrated into the curricula instead of being ancillary to the subject matter, and academically centered forms of moral education may be more successful.

In conclusion, to gain some sense of how to develop moral reasoning in college students, we must first understand the nature of development of our awareness of our ethical thinking processes so that those processes may be used as a basis for reflection and learning. Further, investigating the process of decision-making potentiates a clearer understanding of the components and the mental operations involved in making ethical choices. This knowledge will provide important information for developing programs of ethics education for students in various professions at the time when students are most open to learning—that is, during the college years when they are in the midst of defining themselves as moral citizens and adopting a self-chosen, but well considered, ethical value system.

REFERENCES

Blasi, A. (1990). Kohlberg's theory and moral motivation. In D. E. Schrader (Ed.) *The legacy of Lawrence Kohlberg.* San Francisco, CA: Jossey-Bass.

Blatt, M., & Kohlberg, L. (1975). The effects of classroom moral discussion upon children's level of moral judgment. *Journal of Moral Education, 4,* 129-61.

Bok, D. (April 1988). "Bok issues report on ethics in higher education" in *Harvard University Gazette, LXXXIII,* No. 3.

Colby, A., & Kohlberg, L. (1987). *The Measurement of moral judgment.* New York: Cambridge University Press.

Cornell Daily Sun, October (1989).

Dreyfus, H., & Dreyfus, S. (1986). *Mind over machine: The power of human intuition and expertise in the era of the computer.* New York: Free Press.

Earley, M., Mentkowski, M., & Schafer, J. (1980). *Valuing at Alverno: The valuing process in liberal education.* Milwaukee: Alverno Productions.

Gilligan, C. (1982). *In a different voice: Women's conceptions of the self and of morality.* Cambridge, MA: Harvard University Press.

Kohlberg, L., & Candee, D. (1984). The relationship of moral judgment to moral action. In Kohlberg, L. *The psychology of moral development.* San Francisco: Harper & Row.

Loxley, J. C., & Whiteley, J. M. (1986). *Character development in college students. Volume II: The curriculum and longitudinal results.* Schenectady, NY: Character Research Press.

Oser, F., & Reich, H. (1990). Moral judgment, religious judgment, world view, and logical thought: A review of their relationship; Part One. *British Journal of Religious Education, 12,* 94-101.

Power, C., Higgins, A., & Kohlberg, L. (1989). *Lawrence Kohl-berg's approach to moral education.* New York: Columbia University Press.

Rest, J. R. (1984). The major components of morality. In W. Kurtines and J. Gewirtz (Eds.) *Morality, moral behavior and moral development.* New York: John Wiley.

Schlafli, A., Rest, J. R., & Thoma, S. J. (1985). Does moral education improve moral judgment? A meta-analysis of intervention studies using the Defining Issues Test. *Review of Educational Research, 55,* 319-52.

Schrader, D. E. (1988). Exploring Metacognition: A description of levels of metacognition and their relation to moral judgment. Unpublished doctoral dissertation, Harvard University.

Tappan, M., Kohlberg, L., Schrader, D. & Higgins, A. (1987). Heteronomy and autonomy in moral development: Two types of moral judgments. In A. Colby,. & L. Kohlberg (1987), *The Measurement of moral judgment.* New York: Cambridge University Press.

Turiel, E. (1990). Moral judgment, action and development. In D. E. Schrader (Ed.), *The legacy of Lawrence Kohlberg.* San Francisco, CA: Jossey-Bass.

Whiteley, J. M. (1982). *Character development in college students. Volume I: The freshman year.* Schenectady, NY: Character Research Press.

Part II

Theory and Practice in Counseling for Development

7

Clinical-Developmental Psychology

Betsy Speicher and Gil G. Noam

INTRODUCTION

When Kohlberg (1963, 1968, 1969) integrated moral philosophy, symbolic interactionism, and cognitive-developmental psychology into a general constructivist theory of moral development, he was a lone innovator. Twenty years later, constructivism, built primarily on the theories of Baldwin (1902), Mead (1934), Werner (1957), Piaget (1929, 1954), and Kohlberg (1969), had become part of mainstream American psychology, and numerous social-cognitive theories and stage models had been introduced for a variety of domains, including ego development (Loevinger, 1976), faith development (Fowler, 1981), social-cognitive development (Selman, 1974, 1976, 1980), intellectual and ethical development (Perry, 1970), epistemological development (Broughton, 1975), personality and ego development (Kegan, 1982), and self development (Noam, 1988a).

Partly inspired by Kohlberg's moral development framework and by Loevinger's theory of ego development, a variety of *social-cognitive self theories* have also been put forward (e.g., Damon and Hart, 1982; Kegan, 1982; Noam, 1985). These structural theories examine the self in terms of an underlying logic of self-understanding, self-representation, or self-other differentiation. They differ in their definitions of the self and in their approach to the question of whether the self is a unitary process or is comprised of a number of sub-domains (e.g., cognitive, emotional, social self, etc.). The descriptions of the developmental sequences, however, are similar, even when the methodologies differ greatly.

Before we explore the educational and clinical applications of some of these theories, it is first necessary to understand the differences in underlying theory. The distinction between "minimalist" and "maximalist" structural theories (Noam, 1993) can provide a helpful starting point.

"MINIMALIST" AND "MAXIMALIST" STRUCTURAL THEORY

Following Piaget (1960), Kohlberg (1969, 1984) defined several underlying assumptions of cognitive-developmental theory in what he called a "hard-stage" model of development. He elaborated that a developmental stage theory is hard only when a precise distinction can be drawn between content and structure, and between competence and performance. Structural stages, according to Kohlberg, have to form an invariant and universal sequence, independent of cultural influences; stages must represent unified structural wholes and hierarchical integrations that involve increasing differentiation and integration in the structures of thought. Kohlberg included only Piaget's cognitive stages and his own moral judgment sequence as hard-stage theories. He repeatedly stated that structural theories of the self were "soft-stage" theories because self theories do not provide hard criteria for structural change and refer to the content and function of personality rather than to structures of cognitive operations.

However, it remained unclear why a conceptual focus on the self would yield fewer hard-stage distinctions than the study of moral judgment. The *cognitive-conceptual focus* on the self includes the distinction between physical and psychological categories, between the relationship of self and other, and between an egocentric and decentered perspective on internal and interpersonal psychological processes, all distinctions that can be explored following Kohlberg's hard-stage criteria. In order to insure such an analysis, broad personality dimensions, individual life history, and subjective experiences had to be "parceled out" to insure principles of self-development that can be generalized. As there seems no reason why the development of the self cannot be studied as a hard or soft phenomenon, we prefer the distinction between minimalist and maximalist. A minimalist position remains close to conceptual distinctions, focuses on cognitive dimensions of the self, and follows a careful cognitive analysis. A maximalist perspective freely integrates dimensions of personality, emotions, and life experience to achieve global distinctions in self-development.

Minimalist Structural Theory: Social Perspective-Taking

Strongly influenced by G. H. Mead's emphasis on the role of social experience and social perspective taking in intellectual development, Piaget's theory of cognitive development, and Kohlberg's theory of moral reasoning, Selman (1980) described and empirically validated developmental changes in children's ability to take the perspective of another (role-taking) from early childhood to adolescence. In addition to investigating interrelationships among social perspective-taking ability, cognitive development and moral reasoning in normal children, Selman also examined differences in developmental patterns in children whose interpersonal relationships were age-appropriate and in clinic children whose social-interaction patterns were diagnosed as immature.

Selman has described five developmental levels of social perspective taking based upon research with a normative sample of forty six female and 179 male subjects age four to thirty two, a longitudinal sample of forty eight boys ranging in age from six to fourteen, and a clinical-comparative sample of twenty one "emotionally disturbed" boys who were matched by age, sex, race, socio-economic status (SES), and IQ with twenty one of the boys from the normative sample. Subjects were presented with several social dilemmas; responses were assessed for conceptions of individuals, friendship, peer group, and parent-child relationships.

At Level 0, the "Egocentric Undifferentiated Stage of Social Perspective Taking" (ages 3-6), children view others egocentrically and are unable to differentiate their own perspective from that of others. A classic example is the four-year-old who thinks that her father would like a doll for his birthday because that is what she would want. Children at this stage are unable to separate physical and psychological characteristics of others, tend to confuse external behavior and internal feelings, and have difficulty differentiating intentional from nonintentional actions.

Level 1, the "Differential or Subjective Perspective-Taking Stage or the Social-Informational Role-Taking Stage," typically emerges between ages five to nine. Children now are able to recognize that their own perspectives may be different from that of others, are able to differentiate between actions and feelings, and can make inferences about the subjective states of others. However, they still have difficulty understanding the perspective of others, and assume that only one perspective is 'right' or 'true.' Children cannot maintain their own perspectives and simultaneously consider the viewpoints of others. They cannot judge their own actions from the viewpoint of another.

Between ages seven and twelve, children typically reason at Level 2, "Self-Reflective/Second Person and Reciprocal Perspective Taking." At this level, the preadolescent is able to take a self-reflective perspective on his/her own thoughts and feelings and is also able to realize that others can take his/her perspective. The child is now able to put him/herself in "another's shoes"—take the perspective of another, make inferences about the perspectives of others, anticipate how others may view the self's thoughts and behaviors, differentiate thoughts and feelings, and distinguish between external behavior and internal psychological states. Social relationships are viewed in terms of two-way reciprocity of actions, thoughts, and feelings. For example, friends are seen as individuals who act kindly toward each other or who do favors for each other.

Level 3, "Third-Person and Mutual Perspective Taking" normally develops during early adolescence. The main conceptual advance at this level is the ability to take a "third-person perspective" on relationships and interpersonal interactions. This means that adolescents can view friendships as ongoing mutual relationships, and can simultaneously coordinate the perspectives of all participants from a generalized other perspective. The concept of friendship goes beyond simple reciprocity toward interpersonal mutuality based on trust, respect, and shared expectations. From a clinical perspective, the adolescent is capable of having an "observing ego."

Finally, Level 4, "In-Depth and Societal-Symbolic Perspective Taking," typically develops between adolescence and adulthood. Perspective taking rises to the level of the shared point of view of the generalized other or social system. The mutuality that first developed at Level 3 is expanded from the dyadic relation to the group perspective. At this level of abstract perspective taking, consideration of a general social system perspective on interpersonal relationships facilitates communication and understanding.

Like Kohlberg's longitudinal sample, Selman's samples were primarily male; his clinical sample was exclusively male. Also like Kohlberg's stages of moral judgment development, there is strong empirical support for the reliability and construct validity of Selman's levels of social perspective taking (Selman, 1980). Furthermore, the levels of interpersonal understanding described by Selman meet many of the formal criteria of cognitive-developmental theory (invariant sequence, clear structure/ content distinction, etc.), providing a strong example of a minimalist perspective.

Maximalist Structural Theories

A second group of theorists has taken the constructivist paradigm in a different direction. They have not tried to distinguish a carefully delineated domain of the cognitive self. Instead, they have used structural principles in order to address broad dimensions of personality and ego development (e.g., Kegan, 1982; Loevinger, 1976; Noam, 1985). In the process, the more strictly defined social-cognitive focus has become a more loosely defined frame of thinking and feeling, judging and acting, and closeness with other people.

In Loevinger's and, more recently, Kegan's work on ego and personality development, there are numerous noncognitive, affective, and behavioral processes and dimensions incorporated into the stage definitions but with an assumption of an underlying structural paradigm. In an earlier publication (Noam, Kohlberg, & Snarey, 1983), it was shown that Loevinger's stage model includes both structural and content dimensions. Loevinger defines stages of ego development partly in terms of structures; equally important, however, are psychological functions and motives pertaining to self-enhancement, coping, and defense. For example, the self-protective stage (Delta) is characterized primarily by an interpersonal style that functions to defend the self and, less so, by the stage-specific structures used to understand the world. This has led to the repeated criticism that Loevinger's ego stages are not guided by an underlying logic (Habermas, 1979; Broughton & Zahaykevich, 1977). Without that logic, it is difficult to justify a sequence of hierarchical stages. What makes one stage higher, more mature, more adequate, more adaptive, or better than another? Thus, it remains unclear why Loevinger chooses a Piagetian model over other possible developmental theories to account for the mixture of structural, functional, and motivational elements that make up her stages.

Robert Kegan (1979, 1980, 1982, 1983, 1986b) introduced a set of similar ego stages, each defined by a logical structure of self-other relationships, outlined in more general terms by Kohlberg (1969) and later by Selman (1980). Like Kohlberg's moral judgment stages and Selman's social cognitive stages, each of Kegan's stages contains an underlying perspective on the self and social relationships with each higher stage of ego development consisting of a more differentiated and complex social perspective. According to Kegan (1986b), Kohlberg's stages represent a structure that is more general than moral reasoning and that is present in all cognitive-developmental stage descriptions. This more general, holistic, and unitary structure, manifest in various personality domains, is, for Kegan, the ego.

One way of understanding Kegan's work is to note that he has translated Kohlberg's stages of moral development into stages of the self, creating descriptions similar to Loevinger's ego stages. And, like Selman, he focuses on social perspective taking and describes the perspectives on which the self is capable and on which the self relies at different developmental positions. Kegan generalizes from these perspectives to issues of personality and identity development, including impulse control, needs, and quality of interpersonal relationships. It is this integration of so many aspects of the self that typifies a maximalist position.

In Kegan's neo-Piagetian model, subject-object relationships are the unifying functional force of the ego. The "object" is created through a lifelong, evolutionary process, not, as in psychoanalytic object relations theory, from fundamentally important early childhood experiences. The logic and the process of self-other relations in Kegan's theory suggest that ego development might be best represented by a helix in which personality swings back and forth between two poles of development. This model interprets growth and adaptation as a process of polar differentiation and integration. Each stage is perceived as a new balance and organization between the wishes and needs for inclusion or affiliation and the wishes and needs for autonomy or differentiation.

Whereas psychoanalytic theory has emphasized how people internalize objects during childhood, Kegan describes a number of internalizations over the life span by focusing on the structure of balance in the relationship between the self and "person objects." Kegan's conception of ego development as a process of self-other differentiation refers not only to the relationship between an individual and other persons but also to ways the self understands itself and the meaning that real relationships have in the social world. Thus, the theory addresses: a perspective of a self on "itself"; a perspective of important others that have been internalized and are part of an "inner dialogue"; and a perspective of real others with whom the person is interacting and the understanding of those others in relationship to the self. Each differentiation of the self results in a qualitatively more extensive object and involves a succession of negotiated balances that organize experience in qualitatively different ways.

Unlike Kohlberg's and Selman's domain-specific structural stages, Kegan's broad, unitary stages of ego and personality development ("self organization") were not derived from empirical research. Rather, Kegan's stages of ego and personality development were theoretically constructed from an integration of constructive developmental theories, psychoanalytic ego and object relations theories, and phenomenological and existential theories. Kegan's more theoretical and conceptual approach, his unitary conception of ego and personality development, and his orientation toward a hierarchy of biological and social organizing principles such as reflexes, impulses, needs, and interpersonal relationships raise important questions. Are these constructs structural-developmental? Is Kegan inappropriately applying hard-stage principles to a soft-stage theory? Does Kegan's model linking constructive developmental processes and behavior have empirical support? Is ego development a unitary process in which stage transformations reorganize all aspects of the self as suggested by Kegan's clinical theory? Why should the development of impulses (Stage 1) or needs (Stage 2) or interpersonal relationships (Stage 3), or an ideological self-system (Stage 4) or an inter-subjective process (Stage 5) be united by one function? Are perhaps each of these processes a psychological function with its own developmental line (e.g., impulse control, pursuit and negotiation of needs, development of intimacy, of autonomy, etc.)? Any one of these processes may exist throughout the life span and undergo important developmental changes.

Like Loevinger (1976), Kegan has used hard-stage structural principles, applied by Kohlberg and Selman in the empirical validation of developmental changes in specific social-cognitive domains, in order to address broad dimensions of personality and ego development. Also, like Loevinger, but for different reasons, Kegan seems to give up the important cognitive-developmental distinctions between judgment and action, content and structure. In the process, the circumscribed social-cognitive focus has become a more loosely defined frame of thinking and feeling, judging and acting, and intimacy with people. Kegan's meaning-making structures are thus characterized both by how a person lives and acts in interpersonal relationships as well as by the framework of meaning a person gives to the self and life situations.

A full assessment of the implications of Kegan's model will require careful validation through the development of a clinical and research methodology. Kegan has begun to address the need for empirical validation by the development of a subject-object interview and assessment procedure. A longitudinal research program with a diverse sample of children and adults is currently underway. Although inter-rater and test-retest reliability for this measure are reported to be good, Kegan will need to provide evidence of construct validity (e.g., longitudinal stage sequentiality), as well as of criterion-related validity (e.g., research linking constructive, affective, and behavioral processes).

Schemata: Self Perspectives and Development of Self-Complexity

Gil Noam (1985, 1986a, 1986b, 1988a, 1988b, 1990) is critical of both the minimalists and maximalists for ignoring each person's unique life story, or biography, in constructing theories of the self. For investigators in the Piaget-Kohlberg tradition, the unique experiences, as well as the typical biographical paths, are considered mere content in comparison to structure that provides the "royal road to the conscious" (Noam, 1990). This position, according to Noam, has led to two problems. The minimalists shied away from exploring the issues of biography by restricting the structural model to overly conceptual dimensions of the cognitive self. The maximalists, on the other hand, embraced a form of "structural imperialism" where almost any new content was viewed as grist for the structural mill. Both approaches share the same problem. These cognitively based theorists have overlooked life history and, instead, defined the epistemic self as the sole representative of structure. Life history became content to the structure of the epistemic self. Said differently, the five or six generalized perspectives that define ego or self development were viewed as the organizing principles of that which makes meaning in a person's life. Epistemology replaced life history.

Out of the principles introduced by Mead and Baldwin, Noam has schematized a developmental line of self-other complexity. Through continuous assimilation and accommodation between organism and the environment, the self is challenged to establish increasingly more complex views about itself and important others. Each position brings out new strengths and opportunities to rework past vulnerabilities. But each new system of self complexity can also lead to new weaknesses or to more complex forms of dysfunction. For that reason, Noam does not assume that higher stages of self-complexity are necessarily better, truer, or more mature psychological adaptations. For example, self-complexity can be applied in the service of further self-deception and self-entrapment. Nonetheless, the hierarchical ordering of self-complexity points to the potential of a life-long transformation of the ways we view ourselves and important others (Noam, 1988b).

Themata: Biographical Dimensions of the Self

Despite situational variability and powerful developmental discontinuities, each person has core existential issues that help organize the many events, relationships, and contexts encountered in a life. Because of the basic organizing nature of these themes, Noam views them as biographical structures and calls them "*themata.*" Themata refer to life themes that create a frame of knowing, experiencing, and relating in the ongoing relationship between person and environment. They convey four additional points: (1) the multiple life experiences are organized into key interpersonal and intrapsychic patterns of adaptation; (2) these patterns can be described and defined in terms of some basic existential themes; (3) they have enduring qualities spanning across time and space; and (4) they contribute to the organization of behavior, cognition, and affect.

Themata provide structuring frames for our basic ways of knowing the world and are constructions of meanings about the self's evolution, not objective accounts of life history. It is the meanings people attribute to these events that make them formative, powerful, or traumatic. Furthermore, only those meanings that have an enduring quality should be labeled as biographical.

This leads Noam back to the issue of internalization. The reason why biography continues to shape experience long after original events have occurred and social environments have ceased to exist is because experiences and actions become internalized. Interestingly, this is the same process through which *schemata* get established. Schemata, however, are defined by a generalizable logic of knowing, understanding, role-taking. Themata structures are concerned with internalization of specific events, relationships, and relationship patterns.

For this reason, it is natural to assume that themata refer to one life rather than to many. Since internalization and social construction always occur from the self's perspective on important others in friendship, family, and community, themes emerge individually. They are the stamp of identity, making the one life different from all others. Nonetheless, there are patterns that can be generalized. For each life, one can generalize to the many lives that solidly embed the individual in his or her cohort, and in the "historical moment" (Erikson, 1968).

Uncovering the relationship between the specific and the general, the biographical self, and the epistemic self makes this work particularly challenging. The theory of biography and transformation posits that early life history does not just get replayed. Thus, we cannot find life history that is not also filtered through the most mature developmental self position. There is also no expression of self-complexity that is abstracted from its genesis. Each level of organization requires its own descriptions and explanations. The two structures, themata and schemata, have their own shape and properties, yet each structure affects the other. The experiences in one structure will reframe the experience of the other. Each frame is by definition incomplete and thus we are required to focus on both for an encompassing view of self development and the process of educational and clinical practice.

While these issues are important in the theoretical evolution of developmental thought, the observations were made among clinical populations. The implications are, therefore, also clinical. Of course, some problems emerge because an individual is unable to resolve new tasks or issues. But frequently, present-day problems are tied to a person's biography. To avoid having to view psychopathology as purely primitive, shaped by a psychology of early childhood, it is important to understand the continued development of the self throughout life. This means that we cannot fully understand the present-day function and shape of psychopathology without a full exploration of a person's biography. It is the goal of the theory of biography and transformation to overcome the unproductive split between a hermeneutic theory of cognition focused only on the 'here and now' and the equally hermeneutic approach of psychoanalysis which focuses primarily on the continued power of early experience in human development.

INTERVENTIONS: PSYCHOLOGICAL EDUCATION

The first applications of structural-developmental theory to psychological practice were undertaken in the early 1970s by several educational and clinical researchers who were strongly influenced by the theories of Baldwin (1902), Mead (1934), Piaget (1929, 1932, 1954), Kohlberg (1963, 1969), and Loevinger (1976). As an historical overview, the research and psychoeducational interventions of Mosher and Sprinthall (1971), Perry (1970), Selman (1974, 1976, 1980), and Whiteley (1982) are briefly presented here as representative (not exhaustive) early examples.

We turn first to Selman. His research demonstrates how an understanding of the social-cognition can guide educational and clinical interventions with children and adolescents. Selman's approach emphasizes how developmental differences in children's social conceptions give meaning and help to shape social behaviors. Since the same behavior can reflect different levels of social cognition, knowledge of how the child perceives psychological and social qualities of persons and relationships is critical for understanding and dealing with overt behavior. Furthermore, knowledge of age-appropriate levels of social understanding and perspective taking is also critical in differentiating developmental psychopathology from age-appropriate social reasoning and behavior (Selman, 1980).

Selman, who, like Kohlberg, assumes that the mechanisms of development are exposure to conceptual conflict and slightly more advanced reasoning, developed psychoeducational interventions for elementary and junior high school students using the dilemma approach to stimulate discussion among the children. For example, to facilitate discussion among preadolescents, Selman developed a set of filmstrips that present a series of social dilemmas, for example, whether to buy a friend a new puppy for his birthday in spite of the fact that the friend has just lost his beloved dog and says he never wants another one. By stimulating discussion among peers, these interventions highlight Selman's belief in the importance of peer group experiences in the development of social reasoning. Through the peer group discussion process, children should develop a greater understanding of social relationships, increased social sensitivity, awareness, and problem-solving skills.

Finally, Selman also stresses that it is important that teachers recognize the social-cognitive stage of each child so that they can better understand the child's behavior and how the child views social relationships. With both socially immature clinic children and normal children in the classroom, an understanding of the child's cognitive and affective capacities assists in the setting of developmental goals.

For older adolescents, Mosher and Sprinthall (1971) developed a high school curriculum in human development and counseling designed to directly affect personal development. Their objective was to make personal and human development, and in particular the development of morally and emotionally sensitive human beings, the primary focus of education, rather than a second-order curriculum concern. Influenced by the developmental theories of Piaget (1952b), Kohlberg (1968), Elkind (1967), and Erikson (1968), Mosher and Sprinthall (1971, p. 13) defined the central processes of personal development in adolescence as: "the development of more complex and more integrated understanding of oneself; the formation of personal identity; greater personal autonomy; a greater ability to relate to and communicate with other people; the growth of more complex ethical reasoning; and the development of more complex skills and competencies—in part by trying pre-vocational and 'adult' roles."

The Mosher and Sprinthall curriculum combined academic content in life-span human development, the psychology of interpersonal relations and marriage, the psychology of work, and a seminar in counseling, along with experiences in the application of psychology such as practicum in nursery schools and institutions for the elderly and mentally retarded, a practicum in counseling, and participant observation in several occupations. Students participating in the psychological development program showed significant gains in moral judgment and ego development, learned to counsel other students as well as practicing professionals, and learned more effectively from personal experience than from exposure to psychological knowledge (Mosher and Sprinthall, 1971).

An example of a similar curriculum intervention in higher education is the Sierra Project at the University of California, Irvine (Whiteley, 1982). Specifically designed to promote character development in college students, the Sierra Project is a residential learning program that emphasizes values, close relationships among faculty, staff, and students, intense small group discussions, curricular experiences modeled on developmental theory, and a general humanitarian environment. Character development, defined as the progression in the individual's capacity for understanding what is right and good in increasingly complex forms, and the willingness to act in accordance with conceptions of morality, was assessed by developmental changes in Kohlberg moral judgment stages and Loevinger ego development stages.

In another university setting, Perry (1970) and his colleagues at the Bureau of Study Council at Harvard University were struck by the variety of ways in which students who presented themselves as having academic concerns responded to the relativism and pluralism of values in the university's academic and social environment. For example, the thinking of some students was dualistic, concrete, and simplistic. These students tended to view knowledge and morality in absolutist terms of right and wrong and sought to memorize "right answers" handed down from Authority. Others viewed *all* knowledge and values contextually and relativistically. Still others were engaged in a continuing search for their own commitments and responsibilities in the world of pluralism and relativistic values.

Perry, recognizing that what appears to be personality differences may be reflected differences in developmental maturity, undertook a study of the development of intellectual and ethical thinking over the four years of college among undergraduates at Harvard and Radcliffe. From this research, he devised a developmental scheme with nine "positions" that describe structural aspects of how students perceive and interpret the world at different points in development.

Perry's scheme has been formatively influential in other epistemological models of adult development, including Parks' (1986) exploration of faith development in young adulthood and Basseches' (1984) descriptions of dialectical thinking and adult development. The scheme also has implications for curriculum design, educational group-ing, teaching methods, advising, and counseling. Fleck-Henderson (1991, p. 17) summarized the contribution of the scheme to counseling and therapy:

The Perry scheme is useful in both clinical formulation and clinical action. In the former it directs our attention to the formal characteristics of clients' assumptions about knowledge. In clinical action, the scheme constitutes constructs in the clinician's mind which are a source of response, especially of metaphor. The empathic clinician is "pulled" toward the client's epistemology. Especially where that differs from her own, clinical reflection using Perry's ideas about epistemology may help her to make sense of her responses.

These developmental schemes have important societal implications. How the student developmentally adapts to the pluralism of values and to the cultural diversity in the university environment is, as Perry asserts, critical to the future of a democratic society. For example, students from traditional secondary schools who may perceive the world dualistically will be more comfortable with a factual lecture format of instruction and will require "calculated incongruities" to stimulate their development. Perry found, however, that for the majority of students, the environment that most supported their development was one in which the student could derive a sense of community with other students who had concerns and questions like his/her own and with faculty who were open in their own thinking, doubts, and search for commitment. This was the type of higher-education environment that Parks (1986) views as critical for the development of mature adult faith and that Whiteley (1982) deliberately promoted in the Sierra Project.

Since the 1970s, applications of constructivist theory to psychoeducational practice have continued but with a more clinical focus upon counseling and therapeutic interventions. One example is Levant's (1989) model for training spouses and parents in psychological skills such as interpersonal communication, perspective taking, problem solving, and conflict resolution. As a client-centered family therapist, Levant focuses on each family member's constructive processes, that is, on how each member constructs his/her own reality and how they coconstruct their relationships. According to this model, once an individual feels understood, defenses loosen and the individual becomes more able to integrate experience and take the perspective of others.

Strongly influenced by Mosher and Sprinthall's (1971) model of "deliberate psychological education," Levant emphasizes individual development and the ability to take the perspective of others as a prerequisite for systemic change in the family. According to this view, family dysfunction represents problems in living, and psychological skills such as empathy, assertiveness, communication, problem solving, and negotiation can be actively taught. Levant teaches mutual perspective taking by assisting spouses to assertively express their own feelings, reflect the feelings of others, check the reality of their empathic understandings, and recognize the others' pain and vulnerability. Carl Rogers' influence is also evident in Levant's approach.

Parent education programs for foster parents, fathers, single parents, and step-parents have focused upon preventing problems and facilitating development in at-risk families. For example, in a typical course on fatherhood, fathers are actively taught child development, child management, and communication skills, how to listen to and respond to children's feelings, how to constructively express their own feelings, and how to appreciate the child's point of view.

In summary, developmental theories have provided models of psychoeducational interventions for children, adolescents, young adults, and parents. In addition to emphasizing psychoeducational applications, these models share with client-centered and behavioral models an emphasis upon scientific methods and empirical validation. Grounded in the empirical tradition of the University, many of these applied researchers including Mosher and Sprinthall (1971), Whiteley (1982), and Selman (1974, 1976, 1980) took the positive step of measuring and evaluating developmental change. However, control groups were notably lacking, a methodological limitation that one hopes would be addressed in the evaluation of future programs.

The psychoeducational models described here were all strongly influenced by the underlying assumptions of Piaget's theory of cognitive development and Kohlberg's theory of moral judgment development. However, each model has moved beyond a strictly cognitive approach to developmental change and toward an emphasis on the importance of social relationships in the developmental process. Repeatedly echoed are emphases on social perspective taking, interpersonal understanding, interpersonal communication, social sensitivity and awareness, social insight, close interpersonal relationships, sense of community, empathy, problem solving, negotiation, constructive expression of feelings, and empathic responses to the feelings of others. The change in focus from the cognitive to the social-cognitive first seen in the psychoeducational interventions of the 1970s, further expanded into a more integrative theoretical perspective, "clinical-developmental psychology," in the 1980s.

CLINICAL-DEVELOPMENTAL PSYCHOLOGY AND DEVELOPMENTAL PSYCHOPATHOLOGY: IMPLICATIONS FOR CLINICAL PRACTICE

The emergence of clinical-developmental psychology in the 1980s represented a change in theoretical and empirical focus. While structural-developmental psychology and psychoeducational interventions of the 1970s were concerned with understanding normal developmental processes and with interventions for nonclinical populations, clinical-developmental psychology has focused upon the application of theories of social-cognitive and ego development to the understanding of personality, psychopathology, and psychotherapy. Clinical-developmental theories and research paradigms explore relationships between the development of social cognition and meaning systems, psychopathology, symptomatology, personality, object relations, affective phenomena, and conceptions of self, other, and interpersonal relationships.

While all clinical-developmental theories share the assumptions that an understanding of developmental psychopathology requires (1) knowledge of developmental transformations in mental representations of self and relationships and (2) that the same events will be experienced and understood differently depending upon the developmental level of the individual (Noam, 1991), there are differences among the various clinical-developmental theories, for example, in the conceptualization of developmental stages, psychopathology and mental health, and measurement of developmental change. To illustrate the differences in conceptions of psychopathology and therapeutic applications, the approaches of Selman (1980), Lyman and Selman (1985), Selman and Arboleda (1985), Selman and Schultz (1987, 1990), and Noam (1985, 1986a,1986b, 1988a, 1988b, 1988c, 1988d) will be described briefly.

Selman's theory of social cognition and descriptions of developmental levels of social perspective taking were further elaborated on the basis of many years' clinical research with children at the Manville School of Judge Baker Children's Center in Boston, Massachusetts, an alternative school for children with severe interpersonal problems. Selman and Schultz (1987) found that there are typical profiles of children and adolescents who have social and emotional problems and that the differences among these children have implications for therapeutic treatment. One profile, consisting of immature levels of thought along with immature levels of behavior, requires several years of intensive milieu treatment in an atmosphere of trust, safety, self-reflection, firm controls, and consistent limits. Two other profiles—more mature thought with immature action, and more mature thought with variable action—require approaches that stress the integration of thought and action. In order to therapeutically address these discrepancies between thought and action, Selman and Schultz devised a "pair therapy" approach aimed at linking feelings and reasoning in real-life interactions.

The pair therapy approach, which provides emotionally disturbed children with the opportunity to work together with a trusted therapist to integrate understanding, action, and affect during situations naturally arising in interaction with a peer, is described in detail by Selman and Arboleda (1985) and Selman and Schultz (1990). Briefly, a pair of children with peer relationship difficulties are matched for age, intelligence, level of social perspective taking, communication skills, ethnicity, social class, sex, and interests. The pair meets once a week with a therapist to work on social skills. Selman and Schultz also attempt to pair children with "complimentary fixed role orientations" (e.g., children who try to transform themselves and children who try to transform others in social interactions). This pairing results in an initial power disequilibrium, but gradually, as the children become more comfortable with each other and the therapist, they are able to try out the role orientation of the other.

A primary focus of the therapy is to help the children mature in their level of social perspective taking by helping them to use conflict resolution strategies that transform both the self and the other. In a safe and supportive environment, the therapist gives the children repeated opportunities to resolve and negotiate conflicts, provides a third person perspective on the interactions of the pair, encourages children to reflect on their own behavior and on the behavior of their pairmate, helps them to take the perspective of their pairmate, and keeps the interactions free of psychological and physical harm.

Lyman and Selman (1985) differentiate three types of troubled children and the therapeutic goals of pair therapy for each group of children. One group, which is quite common, is characterized by inability to integrate interpersonal understanding and negotiation strategies; typically their behavior tends to regress under stress. In pair therapy, which provides children with a safe place to work on higher level strategies for recognizing and coping with stressors that lead to regression, this group makes dramatic gains. In a second group of children who are delayed in both social reasoning and behavior, the goals of pair therapy are to develop interpersonal reasoning and improve social competency by repeated practice at a more individualized pace. The third group of children, who are the most psychologically disturbed, show a pervasively unintegrated sense of self and a fluctuating ability to take the role of others and negotiate. The prognosis for these children is poor; the therapeutic goals are specific skills training and exposure to experimentation with higher level strategies. Extensive long-term individual and pair therapy is required.

While Selman's stages of social perspective taking and interpersonal understanding have been empirically validated, the effectiveness of the pair therapy intervention has been judged primarily through clinical observation. Lyman and Selman (1985) reported gains in level of both social understanding and behavior, but these results are confounded by the milieu environment at the Manville School. It is difficult to isolate the unique contribution of pair therapy to developmental gains in social reasoning and behavior because the school, itself, provides comprehensive therapeutic interventions (Selman and Schultz, 1990). In spite of such methodological difficulties, Selman's careful research agenda has contributed substantially to our understanding of the linkage between social reasoning and behavior in normal and emotionally disturbed children.

Like Selman, Noam's model defines development as the aim of clinical intervention. If development can be related to more complex forms of pathology in addition to expanded mental health, one would be inclined to leave it to the schools to elaborate on development as the aim of education. Noam argues that if we broaden our view on development, however, we do not have to abandon our commitment to development as the aim of both education and clinical intervention. Until recently, all cognitive-developmental models, even when applied to the ego and self, have been unable to address central clinical dimensions because maturity and complexity have been used interchangeably. From this emerging clinical-developmental perspective, maturity and complexity should be viewed as very different ideas. For Noam, maturity implies insight and perspective with an adaptive quality. Complexity refers to the shape and form of the self's organization, not its adaptive value.

From this broadened developmental perspective, clinical-developmental practice can use knowledge about social and cognitive development to support a new and stronger sense of integration. Noam argues that this approach requires a serious interest in a person's biography and a knowledge about the possibility of "weaving-in" aspects of the self that have remained unintegrated. Each reorganization of self-complexity provides the opportunity for this process of weaving-in. For each developmental level, different tools are available, and the types of interventions necessary depend on the development of self-complexity. These ideas are described in detail in Noam (1992). Two levels are contrasted in terms of interventions in Table 7.1

In this model, both self-complexity and biographical themes, such as attachment history and traumatic experiences, become *integrated* into the overall self through the course of development. The interrelationships between self-complexity and self-integration are viewed to determine—at least in part—how well the person is adapted. A well-integrated person has more freedom to pursue new experiences in work and love and to explore and experiment in ways that produce enhanced self-complexity. This exploration, in turn, produces new windows of opportunity for bringing into focus earlier vulnerabilities and to finally overcome them. Addressing these issues then produces new freedom for exploration and emboldens the self to create deeper forms of intimacy and greater autonomy. Noam argues that it is this continuous cycle we should call development, rather than the stepwise progression from stage to stage that continues to mark cognitive-developmental models. In Noam's view, mental health is not the ability to function smoothly and to produce appropriately. Rather, mental health is developmental courage, vitality, and flexibility.

Table 7.1
Clinical-Developmental Interventions

	The Reciprocal-Instrumental Patient	The Mutual-Inclusive Patient
Insight	Emerging recognition that the world can be influenced in productive ways and that rejections by others do not have to be addressed in terms of revenge hostility Close relationships provide a possibility for beginning to view the world through a sense of mutuality and community	Beginning reflection is occurring in the relationship *as a pattern* Explore the problem Explore overly strong need for approval from others
Typical Therapeutic Binds	Patient confuses the therapist "being on his or her side" with jointly breaking rules (e.g., underage smoking in office). Fear of consequences can lead to a style of nondisclosure Difficulty in talking about problems emerging in the relationship, and past hurts as a biographical and transference focus has not yet developed	Silences in the treatment and feelings of rejection by therapist require impossible proof of acceptance (e.g., weekend visits) Clinician holds all the power to define convention and health
Treatment Focus	Milieu treatment with focus on issues of fairness and support for behavior that takes other people into consideration Central role for peer learning as struggles with authority figures are typical (e.g., Alcoholics Anonymous)	"Interpersonal Therapy" with focus on depression, suicidality, anxiety, and low self-esteem emerges in close relationships
Settings	Containment in residential setting needed, especially when antisocial trends are strong Despite seeming disinterest in individual therapy, one-to-one relationships are important for creating trust Family treatment with focus on fair rules, teaching parents limit setting	Individual treatment important (sometimes in conjunction with family treatment), group therapy, necessary short hospitalization (avoiding regressive hospitalizations)

CLINICAL-DEVELOPMENTAL PSYCHOLOGY: THEORETICAL ISSUES, EMPIRICAL EVIDENCE, AND DIRECTIONS FOR FUTURE RESEARCH

We conclude our discussion of clinical-developmental psychology, an area of study and application that is still evolving, by returning to three central theoretical issues, presenting research findings that address these issues, and suggesting directions for future research. We will explore two questions: (1) Is there a relationship between structural development and psychopathology? (2) Are higher stages more adaptive?

Structural Development and Psychopathology

There is strong evidence for a relationship between structural development and psychopathology. As previously noted, Selman (1980) found developmental delays in social perspective taking in his sample of emotionally disturbed adolescents at the Judge Baker Guidance Center. He measured developmental change and differences in the clinical and nonclinical groups by longitudinally analyzing responses of the two groups on individual interviews that posed social dilemma situations. These interviews were structurally assessed in four concept domains: concepts of individuals, friendship, peer-group relations, and parent-child relations.

When the clinic and normal children were compared on levels of social perspective taking and understanding, Selman found that, although there was little empirical evidence of a critical period in the development of social perspective taking in normal children, clinic children at age thirteen tended to lag two years in the development of social understanding. While not all clinic children were developmentally delayed, the better adjusted clinic children were more mature in interpersonal understanding. Clinic children were, however, inconsistent in their use of interpersonal understanding. Although they sometimes used higher levels of interpersonal reasoning, they also tended to regress more and use less mature reasoning than normal children. Selman concluded that the deficiencies and distortions in the thinking of the clinic children often reflected a lag in social-cognitive development and the interference of affective mechanisms that prevented the use of higher-level thinking.

A second group of researchers at McLean Hospital in Belmont, Massachusetts, have also found lags in the structural development of adolescents hospitalized for psychiatric reasons. These investigators (Hauser, Jacobson, Noam & Powers, 1983; Powers, Hauser, Noam, Jacobson & Houlihan, 1985) found that mental health status was strongly related to absolute levels of both moral and ego development and to patterns of change during adolescence.

Behavior disorders such as sociopathy and delinquency have been consistently associated with developmental lags in Loevinger's stages of ego development and in Kohlberg's stages of moral judgment development (Frank & Quinlan, 1976; Kegan, 1986a; Vincent & Vincent, 1979; Noam & Dill, 1991). Indeed, Kegan (1986a) argues that sociopathy should be viewed as developmental delay since individuals with this diagnosis, like preadolescents, are unable to coordinate their own perspective with that of another. However, much work is also needed to understand why many developmentally delayed adolescents and adults are *not* delinquent.

With the exception of sociopathy, studies that have examined the relationship between structural development and psychopathology during adulthood generally have not found a direct isomorphism between developmental level and formal psychiatric diagnoses such as clinical depression (Kegan, Noam, & Rogers, 1983) or borderline personality disorder (Noam, 1984). In other words, patients with the same diagnosis may be at different levels of structural development. However, in a study at Yale/New Haven Hospital, Kegan, Rogers, and Quinlan (1981) did find an association between developmental moral judgment stage and the subjective experience of depression and depression type. A self-sacrificing depression in which the patient is disturbed about being unable to satisfy needs and wishes is associated with Stage 2 moral reasoning. Patients at Stage 3 experience a dependent depression in which emotional upset is associated with affect surrounding the loss of relationships. Stage 4 reasoning is associated with a self-evaluative depression focusing on one's failure to live up to one's own self-concept and standards.

For borderline psychopathology, three different developmental positions were described (Noam, 1986 a,b). At each position (subjective, reciprocal and mutual), the typical borderline vulnerabilities of identity diffusion and relationship confusion were expressed differently. Blakeney and Blakeney (1987) have reported a wide spread of different stage responses in moral development in borderline youth. Much more work is needed if we are to pursue the promising task of "developmentalizing" existing psychiatric nosology. Better treatment modalities may be designed when the developmental organization of the patient is taken into consideration.

Although psychopathology may be manifest in individuals at all stages of structural development, there is growing evidence that ego and moral development are related to the form of psychopathology and to patterns of symptom expression. An association between externalizing symptoms at lower stages and internalizing symptoms at higher stages is a consistent finding. Noam and his colleagues investigated this relationship systematically in large samples of children and adolescents. In one study at McLean Hospital, Noam (1984) found that low stages of ego development were significantly associated with externalizing symptoms such as arguing, demanding attention, and aggression, whereas higher stages of ego development were related to internalizing symptoms (guilt, anxiety, and depression). In another study, Noam, Paget, Borst and Bartok (1994) grouped diagnoses into categories of conduct, affective, and mixed conduct/affective disorders. Using this typology, conduct and mixed conduct/affective disorders were found to be more prevalent among pre-conformist stage adolescents. In their sample of 277 inpatient adolescents, affective disorders were more commonly associated with female gender and conformist ego level stages.

Rogers and Kegan (1991) also report a relationship between Kohlberg's and Selman's developmental stages and the form of psychiatric symptoms. In a sample of forty five adolescent and adult psychiatric inpatients with serious thought and affective disorders, they found a relationship between structural development and the form of disturbance (symptoms, representations of self, and conflicts). With development, there is a shift from more immediate and behaviorally expressed symptoms to more cognitively mediated ideational symptoms.

There is further evidence that level of development is related to psychopathology in adults. Dill and Noam (1990) and Noam and Dill (1991) found, in a group of adult outpatients, that severity of diagnoses decreased with increased ego development. The variety of requests for treatment also changed. These findings implied that knowing the developmental level in adult patients can have important implications for defining and organizing treatment.

In summary, there is evidence for a relationship between structural development and psychopathology. In samples of children and adolescents, severe psychopathology was associated with developmental delay in ego development, moral reasoning, and social perspective taking; inconsistencies (scatter) in the use of more mature reasoning; lack of integration between structural competence and behavioral performance; and a tendency to regress in response to painful affect. In adult samples, there was a relationship between structural development and sociopathy and between forms of psychopathology and patterns of symptom expression. These conclusions, however, are based on studies comparing hospitalized or institutionalized individuals with severe psychiatric disorders to individuals with no diagnosed psychopathology. Future research should address how structural development interacts with dynamic formulations in individuals with various psychiatric diagnoses and should focus on individuals with varying degrees of adaptive functioning.

Structural Development and Adaptation

If psychopathology may potentially occur at all developmental levels, are higher stages more adaptive? Are individuals at higher stages just more adept at rationalizing their behavior, as argued by Bandura (1991)? To date, the studies that have examined the questions posed here again have focused on individuals with diagnosed psychopathology.

Rogers and Kegan (1991) and Noam (1984) argue that mental health and mental growth are not synonymous. In a critique of many structural theories that view higher stages as necessarily more adaptive, Noam maintains that higher stages, in fact, can give rise to more complex forms of psychopathology; the most mature ego states can lead to the most internalized and complex psychopathology (Noam, 1988b). To pursue this reconceptualization, Noam and his associates conducted studies on depression and suicidality. For example, Borst, Noam, and Bartok (1991) investigated the relationship between ego development, age, gender, and psychiatric diagnosis to serious suicidal ideation and attempts among 219 inpatient adolescents. They found that while suicidal ideation and behaviors were seen in the majority of pre-conformist and conformist inpatients, adolescents became more prone to suicidal ideation and attempts with increasing ego development. Noam and colleagues concluded that the self-protective and externalizing qualities of the earlier developmental positions put an adolescent at greater risk for impulsivity, conduct disorders, or delinquency, but might shield the youth from directing aggression against the self. The authors proposed two profiles of suicidality: the angry-defiant suicidal adolescents who are explicitly angry, impulsive, concrete, and often see suicide as revenge; and the self-blaming attempter who is more often depressed and concerned with socio-centric perspectives, and who views suicide in terms of loss and abandonment.

While some people function at more mature developmental levels and suffer from more internalizing disorders, others seem to recover in the process of structural development. In a longitudinal study of thirty seven psychiatrically hospitalized adolescents, Noam, Recklitis, and Paget (1991) found that higher ego development is more adaptive. Adolescents who progressed in ego development showed significant decreases in psychiatric symptoms compared to nonprogressors. The progressors also evidenced significant increases in their use of adaptive defense mechanisms and five adaptive coping mechanisms, including investing in close friends, solving family problems, engaging in demanding activities, seeking diversions, and self-reliance.

Noam's other studies of adolescent and adult psychopathology have also found positive associations between ego development and adaptation (Dill & Noam, 1990; Noam & Dill, 1991; Noam et al., 1984; Noam, Kilburn, & Ammen-Elkins, 1989). For instance, decreases in the severity of psychiatric diagnosis and symptomatology was found in a study of 140 adolescent inpatients (Noam & Houlihan, 1990) and eighty four adult outpatients (Noam & Dill, 1991). Individuals who experienced the greatest distress from their psychiatric symptoms functioned at the least mature levels of ego development while those functioning at the most mature levels experienced the least distress. In general, three trends have been found in this research (Noam, Recklitis, & Paget, 1991). First, with increased ego there is a decrease in overall symptomatology and severity of symptoms. Second, delayed ego development is significantly related to externalizing and aggressive behaviors. Third, more mature ego development is associated with internalizing symptoms and defenses.

A serious effort to further address the difference between those adolescents and adults who become more complex and more adaptive in their development from those who become more complexly maladaptive requires longitudinal research. One ongoing study follows adolescents with psychopathology into adulthood to find out more about patterns of recovery and the development of psychopathology. Clinical case studies of individuals with mature structural development and poor adaptive functioning are also clearly needed.

CONCLUSION

This chapter introduces a very exciting new direction in developmental and clinical psychology. A number of therapeutic traditions have focused on the role of cognition in psychopathology (e.g., cognitive behavior therapy) and the connection between meanings about the self and relationships to symptoms. For that reason, clinical-developmental psychology stands in a long tradition of theory, research, and practice. As a perspective steeped also in academic developmental psychology, however, it breaks new ground. Cognition and meanings are viewed in life-span developmental terms, the intrapsychic world is always related to the interactions with the world, and biography is as much a return to the past as it is a contribution to the present.

As a hermeneutic procedure, clinical-developmental psychology honors the role of theory, the interdisciplinary approach that integrates methodology and conceptualizations from philosophy, psychology, education, and so forth. As a discipline in psychology, the clinical-developmental perspective is dedicated to research, especially longitudinal analyses of psychopathology and recovery. As a form of application, the evolving ideas find a central corrective in the day-to-day work with patients. These three agendas make for an ambitious program. New research projects will shed light on the relationship between development, dysfunction, and, most importantly, recovery. The variety of clinical activities will produce new treatment forms as traditional techniques are reinterpreted, leading to added forms of deeper listening and responding.

While much lies ahead, more than ten years of productive work have given clinical-developmental psychology shape and direction. In conjunction with the fast-growing field of developmental psycho-pathology, clinical-developmental psychology has begun to influence how we think about our patients, what questions we ask in our research, and which theories we need to enhance our understanding. Such impressive developments never occur without debates and theoretical conflicts. If they are a sign of a vital and developing discipline, clinical-developmental psychology is alive and well—and growing.

REFERENCES

Baldwin, J. M. (1902). *Social and ethical interpretations in mental development.* New York: Grune & Stratton.

Bandura, A. (1991). Social cognitive theory of moral thought and action. In W. M. Kurtines & J. L. Gewirtz (Eds.), *Handbook of Moral Behavior and Development.* Hillsdale, NJ: Lawrence Erlbaum.

Basseches, M. (1984). *Dialectical thinking and adult development.* Norwood, NJ: Ablex.

Blankeney, C., & Blakeney, R. (1987). *A Logic to the Madness: Understanding Adolescent Moral Disorder.* Berkeley, CA: Institute for Clinical-Developmental Psychology.

Borst, S. R., Noam, G. G., & Bartok, J. A. (1991). Adolescent suicidality: A clinical-developmental approach. *Journal of the American Academy of Child and Adolescent Psychiatry, 30,* 796-803.

Broughton, J. (1975). *The development of natural epistemology in adolescence and early adulthood.* Unpublished doctoral dissertation, Harvard University.

Broughton, J., & Zahaykevich, M. (1977). Review of J. Loevinger's *Ego development: Conceptions and theories. Telos, 32,* 249-53.

Damon, W., & Hart, D. (1982). The development of self-understanding from infancy through adolescence, *Child Development, 53,* 841-64.

Dill, D. L., & Noam, G. G. (1990). Ego development and treatment requests. *Psychiatry, 53,* 85-91.

Elkind, D. (1967). Egocentrism in adolescence. *Child Development, 38,* 1025-34.

Erikson, Erik. (1968). *Identity youth and crisis.* New York: W. W. Norton.

Fleck-Henderson, A. (1991, December). *The Perry Scheme, Counseling and Therapy.* Paper presented at the Perry Conference, Washington, D. C.

Fowler, J. (1981). *Stages of faith.* New York: Harper & Row.

Frank, S., & Quinlan, D. (1976). Ego development and adjustment patterns in adolescent psychopaths. *Journal of Genetic Psychology, 85,* 505-10.

Habermas, J. (1979). *Communication and the evolution of society.* Boston: Beacon Press.

Hauser, S. T., Jacobson, A. M., Noam, G. G. & Powers, S. I. (1983). Ego development and self-image complexity in early adolescence: Longitudinal studies of psychiatric and diabetic patients. *Archives of General Psychiatry, 40,* 325-32

Kegan, R. G. (1979). The evolving self: A process conception for ego psychology. *The Counseling Psychologist, 8,* 5-34.

Kegan, R. G. (1980). Making meaning: The constructive-developmental approach to persons and practice. *Journal of Personnel and Guidance. 58,* 374-80.

Kegan, R. G. (1982). *The evolving self.* Cambridge, MA: Harvard University Press.

Kegan, R. G. (1983). A neo-Piagetian approach to object relations. In B. Lee & G. Noam (Eds.). *Developmental approaches to the self.* New York: Plenum Press.

Kegan, R. G. (1986a). The child behind the mask: Sociopathy as developmental delay. In W. H. Reid, D. Dorr, J. I. Walker, & W. Bonner, III (Eds.), *Unmasking the psychopath.* New York: W. W. Norton.

Kegan, R. G. (1986b). Kohlberg and the psychology of ego development. In S. Modgil & C. Modgil (Eds.). *Lawrence Kohlberg: Consensus and Controversy.* Susses: Falmer Press, Ltd.

Kegan, R. G., Noam, G. G., & Rogers, L. (1983) The psychologic of emotion: A Neo-Piagetian view. In D. Cicchetti & P. Hesse (Eds.), *Functional development: New directions in child development.* San Francisco: Jossey-Bass.

Kegan, R. G., Rogers, L., & Quinlan, D. (1981, August). *Constructive-developmental organizations of depression.* Paper presented at the eighty-ninth annual convention of the American Psychological Association, Los Angeles, CA.

Kohlberg, L. (1963). The development of children's orientation toward a moral order: I. Sequence in the development of moral thought. *Vita Humana, 6,* 11-33.

Kohlberg, L. (1968). The child as a moral philosopher. *Psychology Today, 2*, 24-31.

Kohlberg, L. (1969). Stage and sequence: A cognitive-developmental approach of socialization. In D. A. Goslin (Ed.), *Handbook of socialization theory and research.* Chicago: Rand McNally.

Kohlberg, L. (1984). *The psychology of moral development.* San Francisco: Harper & Row.

Levant, R. F. (1989). From client-centered family therapy to psycho-educational programs to strengthen the contemporary family. In F. Kaslow (Ed.). *Voices in family psychology.* Newbury Park, CA: Sage Publications.

Loevinger, J. (1976). *Ego development.* San Francisco: Harper & Row.

Lyman, D. R. & Selman, R. L. (1985). Peer conflict in pair therapy: Clinical and developmental analyses. In M. W. Berkowitz (Ed.), *Peer conflict and psychological growth.* San Francisco: Jossey-Bass.

Mead, G. H. (1934). *Mind, self and society.* Chicago: University of Chicago Press.

Mosher, R. L., & Sprinthall, N. A. (1971). Psychological education: A means to promote personal development during adolescence. *The Counseling Psychologist, 2*, 3-84.

Noam, G. G. (1984). *Self, morality and biography: Studies in clinical-developmental psychology.* Unpublished doctoral dissertation, Harvard University.

Noam, G. G. (1985). Stage, phase and style: The developmental dynamics of the self. In Berkowitz, M. & Oser, F. (Eds.), *Moral education: Theory and application.* Hillsdale, NJ: Lawrence Erlbaum.

Noam, G. G. (1986a). Borderline personality disorders and the theory of biography and transformation (Part I). *McLean Hospital Journal, X*,1, 19-43.

Noam, G. G. (1986b). The theory of biography and transformation and the borderline personality disorders (Part II): A developmental typology. *McLean Hospital Journal, X*, 2, 79- 105.

Noam, G. G. (1988a). The self, adult development, and the theory of biography and transformation. In D. K. Lapsley & C. F. Power (Eds.), *Self, ego, and identity.* New York: Springer-Verlag.

Noam, G. G. (1988b). Self-complexity and self-integration: theory and therapy in clinical-developmental psychology. *Journal of Moral Education, 17*, 230-245.

Noam, G. G. (1988c). The theory of biography and transformation: Foundation for clinical developmental therapy. In S. R. Shirk (Ed.), *Cognitive development and child psychotherapy.* New York: Plenum.

Noam, G. G. (1988d). A constructivist approach to developmental psychopathology. In F. D. Nannis & P. D. Cowan (Eds.), *Developmental psychopathology and its treatment.* San Francisco: Jossey-Bass.

Noam, G. G. (1990). Beyond Freud and Piaget: Biographical worlds interpersonal self. In T. E. Wren (Ed.), *The moral domain.* Cambridge, MA: The MIT Press.

Noam, G. G. (1991). Clinical developmental psychology. *International Society for the Study of Behavioural Development Newsletter, 19*, 1-4.

Noam, G.G. (1992). Development as the aim of clinical intervention. *Development and Psychopathology, 4*, 670-96.

Noam, G.G. (1993). Ego development: True or false. *Psychological Inquiry, 1, 3*.

Noam, G. G., & Dill, D. L. (1991). Adult development and symptomatology. *Psychiatry, 54*, 208-217.

Noam, G. G., Hauser, S. T., Santostefano, S., Garrison, W., Jacobson, A. M., Powers, S. I., & Mead, M. (1984). Ego development and psychopathology: A study of hospitalized adolescents. *Child Development, 55,* 184-94.

Noam, G. G., & Houlihan, J. (1990). Developmental dimensions of DSM-III diagnoses in adolescent psychiatric patients. *American Journal of Orthopsychiatry, 60,* 371-78.

Noam, G. G., Kilburn, D., & Ammen-Elkins, G. (1989). *Adolescent Development and Psychiatric Symptomatology.* Unpublished McLean Hospital Report.

Noam, G. G., Kohlberg, L., & Snarey, J. (1983). Steps toward a model of the self. In B. Lee & G. Noam (Eds.), *Developmental approaches to the self.* New York: Plenum Press.

Noam, G. G., Paget, K.F., Borst, S., & Bartok, J. (1994). Conduct and affective disorders in developmental perspective: A systematic study of adolescent developmental psychopathology. *Development and Psychopathology, 6,* 519-32.

Noam, G. G., Recklitis, C. J., & Paget, K. F. (1991). Pathways of ego development: Contributions to maladaptation and adjustment. *Development and Psychopathology, 3,* 311-28.

Parks, S. (1986). *The critical years.* San Francisco: Harper.

Perry, W. G., Jr. (1970). *Intellectual and ethical development in the college years.* New York: Holt, Rinehart & Winston.

Piaget, J. (1929). *The child's conception of the world.* New York: Harcourt, Brace.

Piaget, J. (1932). *The moral judgment of the child.* New York: Harcourt, Brace.

Piaget, J. (1952). *The language and thought of the child.* London: Routledge & Kegan, Paul.

Piaget, J. (1954). *The construction of reality in the child.* New York: Basic Books.

Piaget, J. (1960). The general problems of the psychobiological development of the child. In J. M. Tanner & B. Inhelder (Eds.), *Discussions on Child Development: Proceedings of the World Health Organization Study Group on the Psychobiological Development of the Child, 4,* New York: International Universities Press.

Powers, S. I., Hauser, S. T., Noam, G. G., Jacobson, A. M., & Houlihan, J. (1985, April). *Ego development in adolescence: A longitudinal study.* Paper presented at the meeting of the Society for Research in Child Development, Toronto.

Rogers, L., & Kegan, R. (1991). Mental growth and mental health as distinct concepts in the study of developmental psychopathology: Theory, research and clinical implications. In H. Rosen & D. Keating (Eds.), *Constructivist perspectives on developmental psychopathology and atypical development.* Hillsdale, NJ: Lawrence Earlbaum.

Selman, R. (1974). *The development of conceptions of interper-sonal reasoning based on levels of social perspective taking.* Harvard: Judge Baker Social Reasoning Project. Unpublished manuscript.

Selman, R. (1976). Social-cognitive understanding: A guide to educational and clinical practice. In T. Lickona (Ed.), *Moral development and behavior: theory, research and social issues.* New York: Holt, Rinehart and Winston.

Selman, R. (1980). *The growth of interpersonal understanding: Developmental and clinical analyses.* New York: Academic Press.

Selman, R. & Arboleda, C. (1985). Pair therapy with two troubled early adolescents. *McLean Hospital Journal, X,* 2, 84-111.

Selman, R. & Schultz, L. H. (1987). Interpersonal thought and action in the case of a troubled early adolescent. In S. Shirk (Ed.), *Cognitive development and child psychology.* New York: Plenum.

Selman, R. & Schultz, L. H. (1990). *Making a friend in youth: Developmental theory and pair therapy.* Chicago: The University of Chicago Press.

Vincent, L., & Vincent, K. (1979). Ego development and psycho-pathology. *Psychological Report, 44,* 408-10.

Werner, H. (1957). The concept of development from a comparative and organismic point of view. In D. Harris (Ed.), *The concept of development.* Minneapolis: University of Minnesota Press.

Whiteley, J. M. (1982). *Character development in college students.* Schenectady, NY: Character Research Press.

8

Adolescent Girls' Development

Lyn Mikel Brown

Much attention of late has been given to the struggles and losses in self-esteem and self-confidence girls sustain in adolescence, as well as to the connections between these losses and other psychological struggles endemic to this developmental period such as eating disorders, negative body image, and depression (AAUW, 1991; Allgood-Merton, Lewinsohn, & Hops, 1990; Attie & Brooks-Gunn, 1992; Brown & Gilligan, 1992; Harter, 1990; Peterson et al.,1993; Pipher, 1995; Renouf & Harter, 1990; Steiner-Adair, 1986; 1991). In addition, the myriad forms of gender bias girls endure, as well as their experiences of sexual harassment in public spaces such as cafeterias, hallways, and on school playgrounds, have taken center stage in both the research literature and the public imagination (Stein, 1992; Stein, Marshall, & Tropp, 1993; AAUW, 1992, 1993).

We know and understand very little, however, about those girls who resist these losses and retain their psychological resilience and invulnerability. Indeed, psychologist Michelle Fine and her colleague Pat Macpherson (1992) argue that feminist academics' writings

have been persistently committed to public representations of women's victimization and structural assaults and have consequently ignored, indeed misrepresented, *how well young women talk as subjects*, passionate about and relishing their capacities to move between [the] nexus of power and power-lessness. That is to say, feminist academics have forgotten to take notice of how firmly young women resist—alone and sometimes together (p. 178).

Such attention to the losses girls experience, while certainly pointing to the psychological effects of societal gender inequities, may inadver-tently contribute to an over-emphasis on passive indoctrination and an under-emphasis on girls' resistance that might inform educational and therapeutic strategies for encouraging and sustaining their voices and which may, in turn, effect social and moral change in their immediate communities.

In this chapter, I address the complexity of girls' psychological development, highlighting not only the costs of coming of age in patriarchal culture, but underscoring the possibility and potential of girls' resistance, whether it is an indirect, underground resistance or an open, angry refusal to accommodate to narrow conventions of idealized (i.e., white, middle-class) femininity. To illustrate such possibility and potential, I turn to the issue of social class and the often subtle relationship between discourse and power. Listening to girls from very different material and social locations create unique spaces for self-expression and develop strategies for resistance to idealized femininity reminds us that, as Valerie Walkerdine (1990) suggests, "socialization," in any simplistic sense, "does not work" (p. 198); that attempts at social regulation are often disrupted, reappropriated for one's own purposes, circumvented. Finally, I consider briefly what this all means for those of us working with—teaching, counseling, conducting research on—adolescent girls.

GIRLS' DEVELOPMENT

In a five-year study of girls and young women, Carol Gilligan and I explored the strength and power of younger girls' voices and underscored the need to preserve their observational capacities and their tendency to stay in touch with strong feelings like anger and frustration, to hold on to their propensity to express disagreement with confidence and self-assurance as they grow up (Brown & Gilligan, 1992). Through childhood, the girls we studied at Laurel School, a private day school for girls, had a lucidity and strength not often noted or elaborated in studies of female development. At the edge of adolescence—at ten and eleven and twelve—however, something happened. As girls moved into and against the dominant culture, as the people around them reacted to their changing bodies, and as they confronted new expectations and gained new capacities for understanding, reality as they experienced it in childhood began to shift. What they once knew and expressed, felt and thought or did no longer held the same meaning for, or had the same effect on, others. As the names for things— relationships, feelings, actions—changed, girls at the edge of adolescence struggled with the interpretation and definition of reality.

The usual psychological terms for such a shift into adolescence seemed both inadequate and inaccurate. This was not a negotiation or resolution of the Piagetian distinction between appearance and reality— girls were not simply experiencing the "normal" difficulties of moving away from childhood fantasy and accepting adult reality. As we listened, we came to understand that girls were questioning the very notion of reality itself. Girls' fight for their angle of vision, their insistence on staying with their experiences and evidence of their senses, their desire to name what was happening to them and around them, called into question the stability of the normative. Through their resistance, they asked, both implicitly and explicitly, whose construction of reality was to be named, given legitimacy and authority? It seemed to us that girls at early adolescence saw the patriarchal framework for the first time and named its effects on their lives: they would have to narrow their feelings, modulate their voices, control their expressive bodies if they were to make a smooth transition into the dominant culture and its social construction of feminine reality. Strong feelings like anger were no longer acceptable, would no longer move people to respond, but instead would move them away; full use of their bodies and their brains would make people uncomfortable.

The girls in our study described this awareness as a struggle between what they had known and experienced in childhood, and what was newly imposed and understood to be reality. To the degree that this broader cultural reality did not relate in satisfying ways to their thoughts and feelings, and to the degree that they felt pressed to adopt ways of acting and being in the world with little or no opportunity for discussion or rejection or critique, they experienced it as externally imposed, false, and out of relationship, and their adaptation or accommodation to it as pretense. Girls at this point in their development talked about knowing when they were being themselves and when they were pretending, performing, or impersonating the right kind of girl in order to maintain relationships or satisfy others' views of appropriate behavior; they spoke of the importance of being "discreet" if they were to pass as a nice or perfect girl in their relationships; they told us they felt themselves "disappearing," felt their thoughts and feelings were in "jeopardy" of being lost to them in such relationships. They became astute observers and judges of hypocrisy in themselves and others.

We were struck by the girls' capacity to articulate this process of dissociation and disconnection, and by their awareness of their own fear, sadness, and anger in the face of pressure to accommodate to conventions of white middle-class femininity. We were also struck by their capacity to appear as if everything was all right, as though nothing was happening. Although some were noticeably thin, for the most part their good grades, high test scores, and smiling faces gave no public indication of the struggle we were hearing in the privacy of the interviews. In fact, their performances would lead most to assume they were comfortable, even eager, to embrace the reality into which they were being socialized.

Thus, *before* we heard a loss of voice or shift into idealized relationships, before we observed a gap between experience and reality, before strong feelings became privatized, covered with public performances of idealized femininity, we witnessed an active struggle and resistance—sometimes in the form of quiet protest; sometimes in the form of outspoken angry outbursts. Developmentally, things went something like this: The lively curiosity and disruptive behavior of the younger girls gave way to the pointed observations, the sometimes cynical and angry resistance of girls on the brink of adolescence. As these girls began to comprehend fully the social and cultural expectations, as they came up against pressures to bury their astute observations of the world around them, to disown or contain their anger, to accommodate or capitulate in the service of appropriate femininity, their voices faltered and the political potential of their observations and feelings moved into the active underground. Those who resisted such a move, girls who carried their open voices of protest into middle adolescence, tended to be on the margins of their privileged, predominantly white girls' school, either because of color or class.

A *Difference* That Makes a Difference

Partly because of a growing awareness of the significance of my own working-class background on my interpretations of girls' voices and experiences and partly through my relationship with a white working-class girl from Laurel whom we called Anna, I began to wonder at the struggles and challenges and the intensity of feelings these early adolescent resisters faced in their determination to remain whole, lucid, and in touch with themselves and their experiences. Specifically, I wished to know more about the relationship between class location and girls' active resistance to the often imperceptible forces that threatened to bury or pathologize their insights, to move them out of touch with their experiences, their thoughts, and feelings.

And so I began to construct a study that would, to borrow bell hooks' (1984) phrase, bring margin to center—a study that would bring the resistant voices of girls like Anna, specifically white girls from working-class and working poor families, into relationship with white girls from middle-class families; to bring the similarities and differences between their experiences and voices to the surface and into the on-going conversation about girls' and women's development, a conversation that still too often assumes that to be female is to be white and to be white is to be middle-class and privileged.

Over the course of a year, I videotaped two focus groups, one consisting of middle-class girls in a mid-size city in Maine that I refer to as Acadia, and one consisting primarily of girls from working-class and working-poor families who live in a small rural Maine town I call Mansfield. The eighteen girls who participated in these groups range in age from eleven to fourteen; all are white. Because I planned to explore the relationships among the girls' understandings of themselves, their expression of resistance and their views of conventional femininity, these girls were chosen for their outspokenness and strong opinions, and in some cases their critical perspective on and their behavioral resistance to dominant societal expectations of femininity. The groups met weekly in their public schools to discuss their feelings about themselves, their relationships with each other, their families, their teachers, and their reactions to pressures to meet societal expectations of appropriate femininity. Using a feminist qualitative method, a "Listener's Guide" (Brown et al., 1988, 1989, 1991), I began to outline a clearer picture of these girls as "resisters" and to explore how social class affects their resistance strategies.

Against the current climate of loss and capitulation in girls' development, my findings in this study suggest two things: First, girls' development in our current patriarchal culture is a complicated, gradual, layered process of "ideological becoming" (Bakhtin, 1981). Throughout this process, and particularly at early adolescence, girls struggle with and against the voices of conventional femininity—voices that endorse silence over outspokenness, passivity over active resistance, a pleasing ignorance over knowledge of the complexity and difficulty of lived experience and relationships, weakness over physical strength and aggressiveness. Moreover, girls from different material and social locations experience, understand, express, and enact this struggle in different ways.

Second, there is nothing simple or transparent about girls' behavior and expressions. Given the pressures and expectations of idealized femininity, given the prevalence of sexism, racism, classism, and homophobia that too often leads to emotional, psychological, or physical abuse, reading girls' lives and interpreting their voices is complicated business. Drawing useful, much less "truthful," conclusions on the basis of surface performances or simple responses is not possible, since in the face of pressures to not know and not speak, adolescent girls develop and employ subtle and creative forms and strategies of resistance. Even as they speak in soft voices, imagine female perfection, or fantasize about idealized relationships, the boundaries and limits and even the absurdity of the feminine ideal can often be observed in their facial expressions and their body movements. Indeed, the Mansfield and Acadia girls illustrate their capacities to resist idealized femininity by creatively inventing space for themselves and their constructions of reality in a variety of ways. One of the most compelling is their use of language.

RENEGADE VOICES

The Acadia and Mansfield girls' ideological struggles reveal the complex relationships between discourse and power, language and domination. They also reveal what bell hooks (1994, P. 167) calls the possibility of "outlawed tongues, renegade speech": "Like desire, language disrupts, refuses to be contained within boundaries. It speaks itself against our will, in words and thoughts that intrude, even violate the most private spaces of mind and body. Words impose themselves, take root in our memory against our will."

The Mansfield girls find strength in the renegade voices and outlawed tongues of those who refuse to be narrowly contained in or made invisible by the language and categories and expectations of conventional white middle-class femininity. These working-class girls convey their parents' mistrust of and irreverence for authority derived solely from material wealth or status, reiterate their parents' stubborn refusal to be dismissed, their predilection for expressing strong opinions openly. Her courage to speak out and criticize the way the school is run and the values it espouses, Susan says, for example, "comes from my parents. They always taught me if I had something to say, just say it."

Echoing their parents and other adults in their community, the Mansfield girls resist the middle-class notions of feminine behavior espoused at their school, particularly the pressures they feel to be passive and silent about their strong feelings. Speaking through their fathers and mothers, many of whom work more than one part-time job, the girls talk of the practical necessity of standing up for themselves, of committing to hard work and their willingness to do menial jobs and endure long hours of physical labor to achieve their dreams of having enough. Qualities fostered at home such as toughness, boldness, straight-forward expressions of thought and feeling that often label them as difficult and disruptive at school, connect them with each other, their families, and their community. Reprimands from teachers and administrators for such behavior, in turn, invite open critique and anger from their parents. Dana's mother is notorious at the Mansfield school for her support of her children's right to physically protect themselves or to fight for a just cause, for example, and has been to the school a number of times in Dana's defense. Dana and the other girls openly admire her for such physical and psychological toughness, qualities Dana, in particular, imitates. "You should see her arms," Dana exclaims with pride. "She's got muscles!"

In fact, Dana's admiration and love for her mother become apparent as she ventriloquates her mother's belief in self-protection and the defense of those weaker or less powerful, and enacts her devotion to her family, their sense of humor, and their beliefs about what it means to be a woman. Like her mother, Dana would protect those who "couldn't stop and defend" themselves; like her mother, she anticipates that one day she may have to go without or "take somebody's old stuff" for the sake of her children. Both fighting and nurturing fall comfortably within the realm of feminine behavior for Dana and her friends. For the Mansfield girls, other women too—aunts, cousins, friends—embody and give voice to constructions of femininity at odds with white middle-class ideals. Their outspoken, self-protective boldness holds the place for an economically successful, healthy, self-propelled life against the dire predictions they read in many of their teachers' faces and reactions.

So, too, over the course of the year, does a woman teacher, Diane Starr, provide a language and course of action through which the girls can effectively resist unfair school practices they encounter. The girls take in Diane's bold commitment to them, a commitment that interrupts the prevailing discourse in the school about these girls as difficult, "stupid," with "dim" futures, and complicates also the girls' too simplistic descriptions of all teachers and all administrators as uncaring, unpredictable, and unjust. The relationship between Diane and the Mansfield girls thus makes room for genuine dialogue and creates space for Diane to explicate the expectations, communicative patterns, rules, and norms of "the culture of power" (Delpit, 1995). Educating the girls in the way the school works and channeling their strong feelings and opinions into constructive avenues, Diane facilitates what becomes a formidable group of resisters over the course of the year.

Renegade voices from diverse sources thus enter and take root in the Mansfield girls' minds and bodies. Their over-sized T-shirts and baggy shorts, their slang—references to each other as "ho's" and bitches"—read negatively in one light, also loosely identify them with the sexuality, boldness, resistance, as well as the marginalization of Black rappers they listen to and watch on MTV[1], particularly their favorites, Salt 'n Pepa. These voices, mingled with the voices of their white working-class families and communities, seem in contradiction to and in constant tension with white middle-class feminine ideals and the relentless expressions of material abundance relayed through television— particularly the MTV shows the girls watch, such as "The Real World," "House of Style," and the popular but short-lived "My So Called Life."[2] Such tensions among voices and viewpoints open the Mansfield girls to an indeterminacy of meaning, to creative possibilities, alternative values, feelings, and thoughts, and also gives voice to longings and desires that contrast sharply with their material realities.

The Mansfield girls occupy that liminal space between childhood and adulthood where intentions are questioned and meanings are, indeed, indeterminate. In their struggles for personal truth and self-definition, in their desires to make the different voices they hear and take in coherent and understandable, to make them their own, they ferret out, expose, and wrestle with the contradictions, the limitations, the hypocrisies, the pretense around them. In their anger, expressed throughout their interviews and group sessions, they react stubbornly to the constraints white middle-class femininity, indeed, the traditional category "girl" or "woman," place on their personhoods, and to the frustrations they experience as they search for words to describe their difference, to speak what they know and who they might become.

There is, in this struggle, the possibility of an opening, of creative alternatives; the possibility that the languages they inherit and voice can be "possessed, taken, claimed as a space of resistance" (hooks, 1994, p. 169). Within the comfort and intimacy of their group sessions, for example, such alternatives to the dominant discourse emerge in the way the Mansfield girls interrupt conventional meanings and definitions of femininity, or playfully reappropriate such words as "slut" or "ho," and also in the way they collectively question their middle-class women teacher's interpretations of their experiences and behaviors.

But these girls struggle to know and trust these openings when they're in the public arena of school, a place where it seems, in Cheyenne's words, that "people don't listen because they don't like us," and where it feels always necessary to translate their teachers' commands and expectations to their own lived experiences; where their potentially creative moves, born of the interface of two disparate and sometimes contradictory realities, risk misunderstandings and confusion. And too, their distrust of their teachers and the lessons, the language, and behaviors promoted in school sit uncomfortably beside their desire for adult love and approval and for the future successes such lessons, well learned, promise. Against such contradiction, the Mansfield girls publicly voice their anger and frustration, distancing their teachers from the intimate group space that is creatively their own.

The Acadia girls, too, occupy this liminal reality; they, too, struggle with and against the gendered boundaries pressing upon their personhoods. But unlike the Mansfield girls, they embrace their education as the medium for refusal and resistance. The ease with which they play within and manipulate the conventions of language speaks to their comfort with, indeed their pleasure in, the privileged middle-class world of school they occupy. Experiencing the limits of "appropriate" speech and behavior, they create new unofficial ways of expressing themselves and their reactions. Robin, for example, introduces new words, as yet unpopulated with the intentions and meanings of the dominant culture, as a way to express her strong feelings and to carve out room for those pieces of her experience unfit for the public world of her classroom: "Teachers would be horrified by my opinions," she says, "they are very descriptive and colorful—even purple." "Purple," to Robin and her friends, means:

It's kind of really open. It's really flat out kind of sleazy. You know, not something too many people would like to hear . . . colorful in a way. I mean it definitely gets attention, but sometimes negative attention. A lot of times people don't want to hear it. It might offend somebody . . . I have a lot of fun with the guys that would say really nasty stuff, and I'll make some smart little retort . . . And it's like "ROBIN O'BRIAN!" If you can talk like that, so can I!

Robin's "purple" language allows her to play with, to have "fun" with, the passions she feels, to interrupt notions of her as a nice, sweet, white middle-class girl. Using this language to shock the boys, especially—to claim her right to out-"nasty" the "guys"—disturbs the boundaries of "normal" gendered expression. Thus, while the Mansfield girls appropriate socially unacceptable terms and endow them with their own meaning, the Acadia girls either create new words or boldly claim their right to define themselves in "masculine" terms, to occupy conventionally male spaces. Both groups of girls know the power of words to affect their teachers and their peers. But while the Mansfield girls speak a "double voiced discourse", simultaneously assuring a level of intimacy and trust with their friends and keeping their teachers at a distance, they often do so loudly and directly. The Acadia girls, however, tend to cultivate their creative language and shocking personas among themselves, underground.

And yet while Robin does not bring these feelings or this language into the public world of the school, her subterranean expressions hold a place for another identity, for another Robin. Anger, although not often seen above ground, is critical to such disruption of the ideal, to such possession and reclamation. Throughout her interview, thirteen-year-old Robin's anger is focused, her feelings intense. Anger is a justified emotion that permeates her life: "I express [anger] in my writing and in my art and stuff like that. And in my general personality," she says. "I mean I express a lot of anger at society and everything because a lot of this is—a lot of what makes me mad is a society that ideals (sic) the perfect woman. It really makes me mad."

For Robin and her classmates, white middle-class girls living in a post-modern world, the "picture . . . of what the good life for a woman consists in" (Scheman, 1980, p. 178) is no longer certain, no longer a given that over-determines their life-course. While such indeterminacy creates situations where these girls find themselves moving between categories and, as Robin says, "re-evaluating all my roles and what I was thinking," their anger serves as a kind of touchstone, a sign, "a clue that something is wrong in the relational surround" (Gilligan, 1991, p. 527). While Robin is sometimes shaken by the intensity of others' reactions to her "difference," for example, her anger moves her to question, to respond, and to judge others' attempts to define her in ever narrower terms.

As with the other Acadia girls, much of Robin's anger is directed at expectations that she will meet dominant middle-class fictions about femininity; much of her resistance is against being regulated and constrained by these fictions. In these moments of struggle, Robin calls on other voices, "outlawed tongues" that have "taken root in her memory" (hooks, 1994, p. 167): the voices of her mother, who some-times "thinks I'm too opinionated," but who nonetheless listens to and supports Robin, allows her daughter's "weirdness"—her dyed hair, unusual dress, her "multiple personalities" and "imaginary friends" ("It helps with acting and everything," Robin insists.); the voices from the different cultures she's traveled to when her mother was married to her military husband; the voice of her anti-establishment uncle, who's "really, really funny," who "paints," and who defends her actions to her parents when she wanders too far off the beaten path. Against the conformist voices of many of her classmates, the "wannabes" and the "posers," Robin hangs on the margins with her friends and listens to the "unusual music" of Prince, John Lennon, and Kurt Cobain; against boys' desires that she be appropriately submissive and attentive, she draws from "tough women" like Janice Joplin and Courtney Love: "She's a very strong person. She's very talented, you know. She hasn't free-loaded off her [late] husband's fame or anything; she's just a strong person." Against the constraints of "nice and feminine" voices, she draws from the bolder images on MTV and voices from magazines like *Skateboarder 90* where, she says, she picks up "good views of the world," views that are "insightful" and "candid." She listens to the voices of friends who, like her, claim their difference, and to the older actors in the city theater group to which she belongs. And she listens eagerly to the outlaw voice of a woman teacher who is funny and eccentric, sometimes embarrassingly original, but "cool," who "doesn't lie to us. She tells us the truth."

Like Robin, the other middle-class girls play with, appropriate, resist, and adapt to their own intentions, a language constructed to serve the interests of more powerful others. In their certainty of social place and simple ease of movement, they underscore their privilege, for such successful play and manipulation necessitates an insider's under-standing of the rules of the game. Their creative, often indirect, resistance, too, hints at their astute observations and understanding of the thin line between what is appropriate and acceptable and what is out of bounds.

In some cases, as Robin illustrates, being a girl who speaks like a boy itself creates new accents and possibilities, but more often these girls delight in disturbing expectations and meanings: they look words up in the dictionary, question their semantic and expressive intentions, break down or reconfigure their original meanings until, in their transformed context, they mean nothing at all. During a conversation about the derogatory names popular boys call them, for example, Jane jumps up and grabs the dictionary to look up the word "skid." The definition causes her to shriek with laughter:

Theresa: Is it funny?
Jane: Kind of, in the way that they use it. It's a log or plank for supporting something above ground (everyone is laughing) . . . Any device that slows up or retards movement . . . or the act of skidding, slide.
Lydia: We can tell them, "Oh, you mean a plank?"
Jane: You're calling me a sad plank?
Lydia: You're calling me a sad sliding movement?

Subverting language with language, outwitting the popular kids at their own game, the Acadia girls signify their cultural and class privilege through their expressed power to more "appropriately" or "correctly" interpret and also, then, to undermine social conventions. Subverting power from the "inside," they are backed by their families, friends, and at least some of their teachers. Their greater fluency in the meanings and terms of white middle-class experience allows them to play with, manipulate, laughingly reject the very language that would define and contain them.

In this way, the Acadia girls question and resist expectations and understandings of what it means to be a girl, engage in an active struggle to be "ourselves" against categorical entrapments and assumptions. "I don't want to be just like anyone," Kirstin insists. "I want to be myself." She knows this struggle to "mean it" brings her into conflict with "people who have a hard time dealing with changes," who "have a grudge against women having power . . . because when they were young women were lower and they've just remembered that way."

Thus, against different expectations and pressures and in quite different ways, the Mansfield and Acadia girls create space in language and culture for their expression of thoughts and feelings and for alternative versions of themselves. Experiences of struggle, ambiguity, and contradiction reveal the differing voices and identities these girls try on and sometimes embrace on the way to their own ideological becoming. Their ability to play and experiment allows for movement between categories of girl and woman and their perceptiveness, as well as their anger and resistance and desire for personal space and self-protection, motivates them to shift about, to experiment, to resist, and at times, to mirror what others desire and want from them. Whatever else these girls are, they are not deluded by, passive to, or easily indoctrinated with cultural prescriptions. On the contrary, their responses to the pressures they feel and the expectations they encounter from different people and in different contexts gives their lives the feel of creative, active performance.

CONCLUSIONS

Most recent psychological and educational portrayals of girls' development, cast broadly as capitulation to cultural ideals of white middle-class feminine behavior and appearance, are too simple and too pessimistic. They give the sense that most girls inevitably fall victim to media representations of ultra-thin bodies, that their voices are silenced by the sheer force of a monolithic sexist culture. They suggest that most girls give up and give in without a struggle and those who don't are somehow inherently different from other girls, specially gifted, embodying unique qualities of resilience. And they imply by their broad descriptive strokes that all girls have the same experience, encounter the same culture and the same pressures, and respond in the same ways.

Against such *simplicity*, I have been exploring the gradual, complicated, and very difficult process of ideological becoming; the different ways girls struggle with and against ventriloquating the voices of conventional femininity—voices that endorse silence over outspokenness, passivity over active resistance, a pleasing ignorance over knowledge of the complexity and difficulty of lived experience and relationships, weakness over physical strength and aggressiveness—and I have underscored the ways girls from different material and social locations understand and express this struggle.

Against such *pessimism*, I encourage researchers to focus on the subtle and creative forms and strategies of resistance girls employ in the face of pressures to not know and not speak; the ways they play with, in, and around the boundaries of appropriate expression to interrupt and disrupt the social construction of gendered reality and to invent spaces and possibilities for themselves. Such resistance and refusal does not deny the power of dominant cultural expectations and expressions of white middle-class femininity on girls' sense of themselves. On the contrary. But it does give back to girls the power of their *response*, the deep feeling, the frustration and anger, the cleverness, the potential for a different outcome that is rightfully theirs. Thus, while ventriloquation can be and has been a powerful tool for silencing, it can also be a process of creation, holding within it the possibilities of disruption, the potential to contest conventional categories and frameworks, offering up new discourse and language.

I have suggested here and elsewhere that the edge of adolescence constitutes a key developmental and political moment in girls' lives, a critical period, if you will, for such possibility and potential. Girls' struggles with the push and pull of often contradictory, fragmented voices telling them who, as young women, they are or should be, provides an opening, a juncture in the life cycle where the incongruity between the personal or experiential and the "externally authoritative" (Bakhtin, 1981) comes into focus and where the processes of ideological becoming are salient and pronounced. In their struggle with varying conceptions of what it means to be female, adolescent girls destabilize the categories of girl and woman, revealing them to be what Judith Butler calls "structures of impersonation," exposing the fact that gender is performative, a construct, "a kind of imitation for which there is no original," a phantasmatic idealization of what a woman is supposed to be in a given culture (Butler, 1991, p. 21). In their resistance to increased attempts to regulate or train their voices and actions, girls at this developmental juncture call attention in different ways to this idealization, and to the demands and costs of female impersonation. Their strong feelings and their questions are disruptive of the way things "naturally" go and anxiety-provoking for those who like things the way they are.

Listening to adolescent girls, I hear them struggle as they try on and reject, attempt to reframe and reinterpret the culturally inscribed and socially sanctioned notions of womanhood that specify the normal, the typical, the desirable, the good. In their conversations about who they are and who they are not, who they desire to be and who they wish never to become, they reveal their problematic relationship, deeply classed, raced, and cultured, with conventional definitions of femininity. When they ventriloquate the dominant expectations, stereotypes, and images of girls and women, even as they struggle to like themselves as girls, even as they resist the pressure to contain and constrain their own voices to fit such expectations, they reveal the contradictions that catalyze ideological conflicts. Their anger and frustration at the categorical limits imposed on their experiences and desires point to the heart of the matter: not only is there no possible way to account for or fit their varied experiences and understandings of themselves, the range of feelings they feel, their observations or the complexities of their relationships, into the dominant cultural construction of gender, there is also no adequate justification for the attempt.

Listening to these working- and middle-class adolescent girls suggests that we should more often encourage rather than discourage the expression of strong feelings as well as irreverence, play, humor, and absurdity. The experiences of the working-class girls, in particular, suggest that one woman willing to take seriously girls' feelings and thoughts can have a profound effect on girls' behavior, on their desire and motivation to be heard. Listening to these girls also underscores the influence material and social location has on what voices girls take in and what discourses they develop, and thus on the ways girls interact with each other and those around them, on what they see as possible and probable.

Adolescence for girls *is* a time of particular vulnerability; a time when girls risk losing touch with the specific—with their bodies, their feelings, their experiences; a point where a girl is encouraged to give over or to disregard or devalue what she feels and thinks, what she knows about the world of relationships, if she is to enter the dominant views of conventional womanhood. But we need also to keep in mind that girls' development is a conflictual, complicated, active struggle for voice and integrity. An emphasis on loss and capitulation, on the various structural assaults girls experience at the expense of acknowledging this complexity and this activity, at the expense of appreciating girls' "capacities to move between [the] nexus of power and powerlessness" (Fine & Macpherson, 1992, p. 178), is not only partial and inaccurate, but ultimately dangerous for girls.

NOTES

1. MTV is a music video television channel, popular with adolescents and young adults, that began in the early 1980s. Along with current music videos, it broadcasts the latest fashion trends, dating games, news and sports updates, occasional documentaries of rock music, as well as other shows of particular interest to its audience.

2. This show, about the coming of age struggles of a middle-class white adolescent girl, is a favorite of the Mansfield girls. Because MTV continuously re-runs the episodes, the girls know each episode nearly by heart.

REFERENCES

Allgood-Merton, B., Lewinsohn, P., & Hops, H. (1990). Sex differences and adolescent depression. *Journal of Abnormal Psychology, 99,* 55-63.

Attie, I., & Brooks-Gunn, J. (1992). Development issues in the study of eating problems and disorders. In J. H. Rowther, S. E. Hobfoll, M. A. P. Stephens, & D. L. Tennenbaum (Eds.), *The etiology of bulimia: The individual and familial context.* (pp. 35-50). Washington, DC: Hemisphere.

American Association of University Women. (1991). *Shortchanging girls, shortchanging America.* Washington, DC: AAUW Educational Foundation.

American Association of University Women. (1992). *How Schools Shortchange Girls*: Washington, DC: AAUW Educational Foundation.

American Association of University Women. (1993). *Hostile hallways: The AAUW survey on sexual harassment in America's Schools.* Washington, DC: AAUW Educational Foundation.

Bakhtin, Mikhail. (1981). *The dialogic imagination.* Austin: University of Texas Press.

Brown, L. M., Argyris, D., Attanucci, J., Bardige, B., Gilligan, C., Johnston, K., Miller, B., Osborne, R., Tappan, M., Ward, J., Wiggins, G., & Wilcox, D. (1988). *A guide to reading narratives of conflict and choice for self and relational voice* (Monograph no. 1). Cambridge, MA: Project on the Psychology of Women and the Development of Girls, Harvard Graduate School of Education.

Brown, L. M., Debold, E., Tappan, M., & Gilligan, C. (1991). Reading narratives of conflict and choice for self and moral voice: A relational method. In W. Kurtines & J. Gewirtz (Eds.), *Handbook of moral behavior and development: Theory, research, and application.* Hillsdale, NJ: Lawrence Erlbaum.

Brown, L. M., & Gilligan, C. (1992). *Meeting at the crossroads: Women's psychology and girls' development.* Cambridge, MA: Harvard University Press.

Brown, L. M., Tappan, M., Gilligan, C., Miller, B., & Argyris, D. (1989). Reading for self and moral voice: A method for interpreting narratives of real-life moral conflict and choice. In M. Packer & R. Addison (Eds.), *Entering the circle: Hermeneutic investigation in psychology.* Albany: State University of New York Press.

Butler, J. (1991). Imitation and gender insubordination. In D. Fuss, *Inside/out: Lesbian theories, gay theories.* New York: Routledge.

Delpit, L. 1995. Other people's children. New York: The New Press.

Fine, M., & Macpherson, P. (1992). Over dinner: Feminism and adolescent female bodies. In M. Fine, *Disruptive voices.* Albany, NY: SUNY Press.

Gilligan, C. (1991). Joining the resistance: Psychology, politics, girls, and women. *Michigan Quarterly Review, 29,* 501-36.

Harter, S. 1990. Self and identity development. In S. Feldman & G. Elliott (Eds.), *At the threshold: The developing adolescent.* Cambridge: Harvard University Press.

hooks, b. (1984). *Feminist theory from margin to center.* Boston, MA: South End Press.

hooks, b. (1994). *Teaching to transgress.* New York: Routledge.

Peterson, A., Compas, B., Brooks-Gunn, J., Stemmler, M., & Grant, K., (1993). Depression in adolescence. *American Psychologist, 48,* 155-68.

Pipher, M.. (1995). *Reviving Ophelia.* New York: Ballantine.

Renouf, A. G., & Harter, S. (1990). Low self-worth and anger as components of the depressive experience in young adolescents. *Development and Psychopathology, 2,* 293-310.

Scheman, N. 1980. Anger and the politics of naming. In S. McConnell-Ginet, R. Borker, & N. Furman (Eds.), 174-87. *Women and language in literature and society.* New York: Praeger.

Stein, N. (1992). *Secrets in public: Sexual harassment in public (and private) schools* (Working Paper No. 256). Wellesley, MA: Center for Research on Women, Wellesley College.

Stein, N., Marshall, N., & Tropp, L. (1993). *Secrets in public: Sexual harassment in our schools.* Wellesley, MA: Center for Research on Women, Wellesley College.

Steiner-Adair, C. (1986). The body politic: Normal female adolescent development and the development of eating disorders. *Journal of the American Academy of Psychoanalysis, 14,* 95-114.

Steiner-Adair, C. (1991). When the body speaks: Girls, eating disorders and psychotherapy. *Women and Therapy, 11,* 253-66.

Walkerdine, V. (1990). *Schoolgirl fictions.* London: Verso.

9

Meta-Development in Tenured Women Faculty

Marianna Lawrence Cayten

In this chapter, I consider data from a recent study that examined developmental assumptions concerning women, identity, and power. The resulting exploration of women's own definitions of power and how they came to accept its privileges and constraints is reported, in part, here. In so doing, I argue that the experiences reported by these research participants is of particular relevance for those who would revise traditional notions concerning development, especially notions of how it is that women claim intellectual talent and desire in the transition from adolescence to adulthood (Cayten, 1989).

The discourse on women and power has predominantly occurred within the confines of traditional paradigms of power and of women (Keller, 1983). The traditional study of power has assumed that power is structural, static, and individual. The study of women has been based on several assumptions that require analysis in order to avoid constricted interpretations of female development. Affiliation and relationship have been promulgated as aspects of women's lives that are undervalued and often denigrated by traditional developmental theories (Belenky, Clinchy, Goldberger, & Tarule, 1986; Gilligan, 1982). If such affiliative processes are relevant to the development of girls and women, an analysis could be offered that would integrate and celebrate the construct rather than merely present yet another constricting interpretation.

The women in this study spoke retrospectively about their childhood experiences of empowerment. The issues of femaleness, divergence from the norm, affiliation, and empowerment were woven together to challenge traditional paradigms, to create paradoxes for developmental theories and for the women themselves.

THEORETICAL FRAMEWORKS

The Issue of Paradigm

The assumption that true scholarship is objective and depersonalized has been the foundation of the Western pursuit of knowledge for centuries. That the investigator, researcher, scholar removes the self from the process has been the acceptable mode when conducting scientific investigation. Recent research, however, documents and challenges such a position (Belenky et al., 1986).

An even more fundamental assumption has been made regarding the essential substance of science; questions as to the content and worth of documented knowledge have rarely been posed. Thomas Kuhn (1970) contradicted this traditional assumption with his claim that all investigators and all investigative endeavors are influenced by ideologically based paradigms. Evelyn Fox Keller (1983) applied this issue of paradigm specifically to the influence of gender in the study of science. She stated that gender ideology has constructed the scientific paradigm to such an extent that the entire premise on which the scientific process is based must be transformed. She questioned the legitimacy of the debate of subjectivity versus objectivity, claiming objectivity as a false concept, and science as a "highly personal" endeavor. Adrienne Rich (1979) spoke more specifically about paradigms when she claimed that "the great weight of patriarchal scholarship is in need of reevaluation." Carolyn G. Heilbrun (1979) stated that the researcher must look to history and transform it, so that we might transcend the "male-gender boundaries" of the intellectual pursuit.

The Traditional Study of Power

The study of power has also operated within a constricting and little-challenged paradigm. McClelland (1975) defined four stages of power that were predicated on Freud's (1923) and Erikson's (1959) stages of development. The absence of the experience of females in the formulation of Freud's and Erikson's stages of development brought into question the relevance of their theories to the study of women. McClelland reified the individualistic developmental approach by discussing power and self only in terms of dependence/independence or domination/subordination. He assumed the hierarchical paradigm, excluding alternative expressions of power and empowerment. In addition, McClelland dichotomized the need for power and the need for affiliation, which, in fact, may not be conceptually accurate for the study of women (Harlan & Weiss, 1980).

Woman as Victim

A third paradigm detrimental to transforming the understanding of women's development has been that of woman as victim. Traditionally, within the hierarchical construct of power, woman has been perceived as powerless. And even those who are considered "feminists" have positioned women as such. Simone de Beauvoir (1953) documented woman as victim in *The Second Sex,* articulating the historical and contemporary status of women. Her intellectual contributions brought the experience and position of women into international consciousness. By naming man as "subject" (actor) and woman as "other" (acted upon), she brought into stark relief the hierarchical dimension of the power dynamics of Western culture shaping women's and men's experiences.

De Beauvoir's (1953) intention was to delineate the reality of women's experience. However, within the last twenty five years, the assumption of woman as powerless has formed the basis for much of the study of women as reflected in popularized phrases now applied to them: Seligman's (1975) work on "learned helplessness," Dowling's (1981) theorizing on the "the Cinderella complex," and Horner's (1972) much-debated "fear of success" typify. This emphasis on the surface of behavior and attitude must be critiqued and challenged.

Alternative Views Of Power

Scholarship is developing, however, toward a new vision and integration of women and power, including new definitions, reinter-pretations, and expanded options for women. Miller's (1982) definition of power was the first step in this exploration of the female experience of power. Basing her work on Gaventa (1980), she has described power as "the capacity to produce a change, that is to move anything from point A or state A to point B or state B, including one's own thoughts or emotions" (Miller, 1982, p.2). This conceptualization expanded the traditional idea of power beyond control over another person.

Miller (1982) also addressed another essential aspect of the description of power: that of community. Developmental theorists' traditional equation of autonomy with development, according to Miller, was an illusion that perpetuated the exclusion of women from the so-called highest stages of development (Kohlberg, 1981) and narrowed the boundaries in which women could be considered powerful. She stated that the concept of "community" must be inserted into the analysis of power and development. Women's involvement in furthering the development of others as an aspect of community has not been named as powerful. She maintained that these supportive behaviors must be included in an expanded definition of power. However, as power is redefined to include community, the self must not be ignored. Miller's research challenged the potential dichotomy of self and others, allowing for the possibility of a less polarized analysis: a dialectic between the individual and the collective processes of power and empowerment.

However, feminist scholars do not agree that affiliation and community are necessary components in women's experience of power. Nannerle Keohane (1985) questioned whether women do and will exercise power in this communal mode. She suggested that dominance and autonomy could be as prevalent among women as men, or that there might be a synthesis, as yet undescribed. Her query raised the essential issue of limitations imposed upon women if there were assumed restrictions on their mode of being powerful. To assume that women's experience of power is necessarily different from men's could be as constricting as an assumption of similarity or of their nonexistent power.

The concept of a women's college may also be important in the empowerment of women. Florence Howe (1984) stated that "women's colleges are beginning to reconsider their special mission as colleges recover their feminist histories, and plan for the future development of their students in a changing world" (p. 136). Her emphasis on the intent and content of the academic experience spanned their effect on students and on faculty. She assumed a reciprocity between the two that involved "knowledge, consciousness, and ultimately, power" (p. 136). Howe (1984) visualized women's colleges as essential in projecting her definition of power as "deriving from Gandhian conceptions, as instrumental, not controlling, as an essential strategy for change: a feminist instrument born out of consciousness and knowledge and used most effectively to empower other women to free themselves" (p. 140).

METHODOLOGY

The three major areas I addressed in this research were: (1) The woman's conceptualization of power and her placement of herself within its structure. How did she define power for herself? Were there varying concepts of power? If so, what were they? Did she consider herself powerful? How, or how not? Has this perception evolved? If so, how? (2) The development of the woman's power. How did others (her family, peers, etc.) influence her sense of power? What historical factors had an impact on her development? Was/is the feminist movement important to her? How and how not? (3) The woman's analysis and actions regarding empowerment of self and others. How have her professional commitments affected the empowerment of self? Did the woman value power for herself and other women and men? If so, how did she act on such a belief? Did she perceive herself as a mentor to others? If so, how? How did she think of herself professionally in relation to other women? Did she "network"? How? In terms of power, was there an individual focus? Was "community" an issue related to power? The segments of the research included for this publication are the woman's perceptions of the development of her power during childhood and adolescence.

Design

In order to expand the paradigms prevalent in psychological inquiry concerning women (Keller, 1983; Harding, 1986), in-depth multi-case studies within the mode of qualitative research were utilized (Levinson, Darrow, Klein, Levinson, & McKee, 1978; Bogdan and Biklen, 1982; Fetterman, 1982; Erickson, 1986; Baruch, Barnett, & Rivers, 1984; Gilligan, 1982; Yin, 1984; Belenky et al., 1986). The phenomenological approach was important in discovering the meanings of behaviors (Giorgi, 1985), rather than merely recording those behaviors (Fetterman, 1982; Erickson, 1986).

Participants and Procedure

The participants were twenty two randomly selected tenured women faculty, eleven from a women's college, and eleven from a university. Tenured women were chosen so as not to focus on structural power, which might become paramount in a comparison between those with and without tenure. Participants were chosen from two prestigious East Coast institutions of comparable academic standing. The two different types of institutions were chosen in order to examine possible contextual influences on the women faculty's empowerment: the College is comprised of women students, and the University has women and men as students. As of 1987, at the University, in Arts and Sciences, from which the participants were chosen, there were forty eight women among the tenured standing faculty (331 tenured male faculty), comprising 13 per cent of the total number of tenured standing faculty in the Arts and Sciences (*Almanac*, 1988).

At the College, there were sixty tenured women faculty, 47 per cent of the total number of tenured faculty (67 tenured male faculty) (*College Bulletin*, 1986-87). The difference between the percentages of tenured women faculty at the two institutions is marked.

The participants were randomly selected from the list of tenured faculty from each of the two institutions. The University list was developed from departments that would have comparable departments at the women's College (e.g., there were no participants chosen from the medical faculty of the University).

In addition to being stratified by their present institutional affiliation, the participants were stratified by the date of receiving their Doctoral degrees. The stratification into two groups permitted an examination of the possible salience of the contemporary feminist movement on the participants' experience of empowerment.

Half of the participants received their Doctoral degrees through 1969 (subsequently referred to as "senior women"); the remaining half received their degrees after 1969 (subsequently referred to as "junior women"). 1969 was a pivotal year in the evolution of the feminist movement (Deckard, 1979; Robbins & Kahn, 1985), and thus serves as a marker for distinguishing between those who achieved their Doctoral degrees before a broad, cultural impact was felt by society and those who attained the degrees as the movement was expanding.

I, as the researcher, conducted a semi-structured interview with each participant. I developed the system for the data analysis, coding the women's statements and deriving themes from their experiences.

RESULTS

Rebel/Misfit: Resistance and Marginality at a Young Age

Two thirds of the women of this study, when asked what had affected their sense of themselves, their sense of empowerment while they were growing up, responded by naming themselves as "rebel" and/or "misfit."

The label and conceptualization were independently generated by many of the participating women; research questions did not make any such inference. The prevalence of this particular response and its relatedness to subsequent, explicitly named marginality in adulthood have made its inclusion relevant, thus, to the broader inquiry.

Rebel/misfit pertained to the self-perceptions of the women as young girls. Those who referred to themselves as misfits felt that they did not fit into the prescribed expectations of their cultures, whereas, the self-named rebels refused to accept certain requirements of their environments. An additional aspect of these perceptions of self was the hiding of one's intellect. This was not universal, but, for some, was a particular example of the rebel/misfit construct as they developed into their adolescent years, and, in one case, into college.

In addition to the self-labeling as either rebel or misfit, there were other distinctions between the groups of participants regarding the dates their Doctorates were received and their institutional affiliations. All but one of the senior women from the University included themselves in the rebel/misfit category, whereas only two of the senior women from the College did so. Three of the senior women were subsequently involved, as adults, in transformative processes in their scholarship and collegial relations. That they perceived themselves as different from other females when they were younger might have allowed them to continue the process of being different by being exceptionally competent as they grew into their adult identities.

Between the senior and junior women from the College, there was a marked difference. All of the junior women described themselves as rebels or misfits; this contrasted with the fact that only two of the senior women described themselves as rebels or misfits. The distinction was between those who received their formal education before and after the major influences of the feminist movement. Perhaps the younger women were more able to name and pursue their nonconformity because of the sanctions lifted by the feminist movement. Theoretically, in the broader culture, women were raising their voices and speaking out. The proclaiming of female experience in the wider culture perhaps provided a more receptive environment in which the younger women could speak.

The slightly different connotations of misfit and rebel permitted the separate examination of each. And yet, as will be seen, the distinctions were not always clear. Within the category of misfit were the responses of those who saw themselves as socially outside the mainstream; others felt different from other girls intellectually. One woman even expressed her sense of herself at a more basic level by saying she was of "the wrong sex. [There] wasn't the means to do what I wanted to do." There was in this remark the voice of an incipient rebel who could not figure out how to change her life in the direction she desired.

A junior woman from the College, whose intellect was valued, "never got the social graces of school". "I wasn't hated in high school and people were plenty nice to me and friendly in classes and stuff, I just didn't get invited to the dances after school. But I didn't want to go anyway. My sister was just normal, and I was a little too weird for her. I just wanted to do what I wanted to do."

Another junior woman, also from the College, described how intellectual activities separated her from her peers: "I felt I just didn't belong, and I didn't belong. I was brighter than the kids I was in school with, most of them." Alternatively, she was "attractive to boys," despite her and her mother's ambivalence about the boys' intellect. There was "ambivalence that she and I felt about running around with these sort of moronic boys, most of them empty and vacuous."

A senior woman from the University described another manifestation of misfit, in which the intellectual and social merged:

I was not, I think, an extraordinarily happy kid, socially, and through adolescence. I felt like a misfit, that what I wanted to do and what I was interested in was not what the people around me were interested in. And I very quickly acquired the sense that I wanted to do something else. And about the only way I ever figured out to do something else was through education. I liked to read and I read an enormous amount, fairly difficult stuff fairly early on. None of my friends were reading in grade school, were reading the same things, or interested in the same things. I just felt that the life around me of a lot of people was just very constricted. There weren't any ideas, there weren't things going on. It was partly, that I was small and shy with glasses. And the last thing I ever wanted was to get married and join the country club and sit around in Ohio, doing not much of anything, except taking care of a house. I thought, "That's for the birds; clearly I've got to get out of this."

She felt as though she did not belong, and in fact, did not want to belong. But, through books and education, she could expand her world into a more appealing place.

The perspective of the rebel was a slightly more active one, in which the child chose to confront that which she opposed. A junior University woman stated her case bluntly: "I've always been rebellious, not wanting anybody having power over me and wanting to make my own decisions. I fought with my mother. She complains because I didn't let her pick out the dress that I was to wear to kindergarten, that I put it back and got a different dress."

A Senior woman from the College described her resistance to prescribed behavior. The imposition of a model irrelevant to her required her noncooperation:

I can remember in grade school thinking it was important to insist on certain things and not cooperate with certain things. I don't know what gets a child into that, but you sort of have a sense that somebody else has some idea of how things should be that isn't yours and that you don't necessarily think that it's a good one to cooperate with. I don't know where one gets into that. Maybe agency starts in stubbornness. I think that may come from a sort of sense that a model is going to be imposed. I would think that this would be true of many women who don't necessarily buy into the existing model totally. That they would at some point realize that there is something there that they would resist. That has to be some kind of exercise of one's own self-assertion.

A senior woman from the University described her intellectual difference from others. "I grew up convinced I was a great genius . . . and so, in the second grade, since I finished my work quickly and then was a smart-ass and it was disruptive, my teacher thought it would be very enriching for me and probably peaceful for her, if I were to go upstairs to the high school library and read through much of the day. So this was a special privilege I was given, which convinced me of my great genius." The juxtaposition of "genius," "smart-ass," "disruptive," and "privilege" underscored the contradictory messages she received. Her difference resulted in her disrupting the regular class, which then resulted in special treatment. She valued herself as "genius" and yet it was viewed as problematic.

Another senior woman from the University experienced a profound sense of exclusion from society, which contributed to her anger and rebelliousness. She spent her early years in a home for girls because her single mother could not challenge her religious convictions and keep her daughter:

I felt powerfully lonely in those institutions. The loneliness was really very great and the loneliness had a lot of power in it, it was very great. I just had very strong motivations to do certain things ever since I was a child, and I've always done them. I guess you would say that is power. When I was confronted with the inability to do something I really wanted to do, it enraged me and forced me to work very hard to overcome those obstacles. All that encouraged me, in a way; it might not have encouraged me in other circumstances; and also it created the conditions for a tremendous sense of rage at society for doing that to her and to me. If I had grown up in a family, a sweet and loving family, I probably wouldn't have the same motivations that I have, a sort of do it my way and fight the system despite what the system had done to me. I guess, in a way, my birth was my first obstacle I had to overcome.

A junior woman from the College traced her sense of rebelliousness through her childhood. She first was courageous, then in adolescence became fearful of voicing her thoughts:

I certainly had a sense of outrage as a little girl when I was told I couldn't be on a team in the neighborhood or something, and really fought my way onto those teams. And I have a sense of being pretty fiery about things like that in grade school, resenting when I felt I was not allowed to do the things the boys did. I'm sure I thought of myself as an individual, not as a girl. I also have a sense of having been a much more risk-taking, adventurous, decisive person as a pre-schooler and in grade school than I was later. It was Carol Gilligan who said that something terrible happens at puberty, and I really think that's true. I got much more cautious, much more cowardly, afraid to speak up, all of that. And I know I have felt in the last ten years a lot of resurgence of that old speaking up. I feel a lot like my pre- eleven-year-old self. Occasionally, just a little bit, she'll just float into my head. I can sort of feel myself being the best high jumper in sixth grade. But, more, it's this not being so afraid, which I think I was for a long time, afraid to stand up and speak up.

Her rebelliousness and courage shifted into the need to hide her intellectual competence: "I remember trying to shape my vocabulary so it would sound less erudite, and so I certainly hid things in order to belong. I couldn't even allow myself to see that; I couldn't allow myself to get angry about it." She rebelled as a young child, and retreated somewhat in her teenage years, as she experienced a sense of not belonging.

I felt I just didn't belong, and I didn't belong. I was brighter than the kids I was in school with, most of them. [Where] I went to junior high and high school we were sort of more prosperous than most of those families. And then, in the midst of my junior year in high school, I was sent to a private school for girls, a day school, taken out of the great big high school. It was a much better place for me. But, there, I was one of the poorest of the kids because these people were all bankers, and I was terribly shy. I was a very shy kid and got along much better with adults than with children. And so that private school was difficult for me because I was so shy, and because so many of them had known each other forever. On the other hand, it was just wonderful. It was the first time I'd ever been in a school where anybody cared about your brains or your work, or where that was regarded as being a positive thing. People didn't make fun of you if your words were too long, or if you read books. So that school was, in that way, a good experience. It made all the difference to me, because I don't know what would have become of me if I hadn't gone there.

Economically, she was first "more prosperous," then less affluent. In both cases, she felt excluded. The private school, however, finally provided her with a contradiction to earlier attempts to hide her intellect. She further described the confusing, contradictory assignation by her mother to be the socially adept daughter:

I felt that I was being assigned, and I don't know when this became clear to me, but probably as an adolescent. I was being assigned the role by my mother of the cute, the attractive, social one. Because the brain role had already been handed out (to my sister). Not that they didn't think I was smart, they did, and certainly didn't put me down. But, my sister was not very good socially. Certainly if you go to Smith at fourteen, it's a little tricky to be good socially. So I think my mother loved it that I had lots of boyfriends. I wasn't too good with girls, but I had boyfriends always and I did all those things, going to proms. . . . After I hit puberty and began to go out with boys, I probably belonged a good deal better than I had before in the sense that I was attracted to boys and that, then, gave me some popularity with girls.

The contradictions between her social and intellectual needs constructed a polarized view of reality. As her colleague at the College stated it, "the social marketplace and the intellectual marketplace weren't the same."

Of the remaining women, two senior women described themselves respectively as a "good girl" and "spoiled brat." They did not rebel and did not perceive themselves as misfits. The five other women did not discuss these issues as part of their childhood/adolescent experience.

IMPLICATIONS

This study demonstrates the necessity of examining the lives of girls when postulating developmental theories. Relying on the experience of boys alone creates an inadequate paradigm of limited applicability. Traditional developmental theories promulgate *independence* as the developmental task of childhood (Erikson, 1959). However, the women in this study perceived their "independence" as a form of resistance to normative development for girls; with such resistant behavior, furthermore, came feelings of marginality. Gilligan, Lyons, and Hanmer (1990) describe a similar process by stating that for girls to "develop a clear sense of self" means "to take on the problem of resistance."

Perceiving oneself as a misfit creates a paradox for developmental theory. Merely adopting an affiliative model (Gilligan, 1982; Miller, 1982) for girls is, however, as inappropriate as assuming the universality of the traditional model formulated on the lives of boys. The participants in this study were aware of the possibility of relationship; however, in viewing themselves as different from other girls, the affiliative mode seemed largely unavailable to them. What is required of our developmental theories is a de-emphasis on traditional gender behaviors and expectations so that individual transformation to a broad range of "normal" possibilities can occur. Furthermore, because transformation is a slow process, children, adolescents, and those around them need encouragement to affirm so-called "deviations" from the norm. This mirrors, of course, the "feminist standpoint," which focuses on the "liberating possibilities" of girls' and women's experience (Hartsock, 1985, p. 232).

Mentoring

Evolving from such a reality for girls is the need for women and men who can name the girls' difference and resistance as empowering rather than denigrating. The concept of mentor in professional life has received extensive attention as potentially providing this affirmation. Levinson and colleagues (1978), in their study of forty men, and Kanter (1977) concluded that having a mentor in a wide range of careers was essential to achievement. In academia, however, there is conflicting evidence for the worth of this arrangement whose cultural popularity is now widespread (Speizer, 1981). This study of tenured women faculty explored mentoring as a possible component of empowerment. Only three of the twenty two tenured women participants had female mentors, and being a "mentor" was not relevant for sixteen of the twenty two. That almost three-quarters of the women did not perceive themselves as mentors could have been related to the absence of female mentors in their own development. It also could be the repudiation of the hierarchical model implied in the mentoring process. In fact, many of the women in the study alternatively developed communities of scholars in which they supported each other. How such a "community" of mutual empowerment can be created in the lives of children and adolescents, where the power and status differential is evident, is the challenge for educators.

The resistance and rebellion of the girls/women in this study also could imply the possibility of more transformative and transforming lives as adults. Challenging norms of female behavior at an early age could well have contributed to these women's continued intellectual development and achievement despite the traditional limitations imposed by society.

However, a contradictory aspect of the empowering advantage of being a rebel was, for some women, the perceived importance of camouflaging their intellectual capacities. This corroborates previous research that described early adolescent girls becoming quiet and voiceless (Gilligan, 1982). Its importance lies in the carry-over into adult life where, rather than being rewarded for obscuring their intellect, their participation in the academy required that they display intellectual competence. Such a contradiction between early experience and adult expectations could be confusing and debilitating. Despite their accomplishments, there was evidence that some of the women had retained a need to obfuscate their competence.

Such a possibility for self-denigration introduces another aspect relevant to educational reform: the assessment of educational efficacy. What many have considered an adequate generic curriculum and pedagogy is now being shown to be inadequate and discriminatory for girls (AAUW, 1992). The women in this study, by naming themselves rebels and/or misfits, challenged with varying results the educational systems of their childhood and adolescence. However, these challenges have not been considered normative for girls. Worthy effort and achievement, however unorthodox, must be prized; methodologies must be created and content chosen so that girls and boys can be educated to their fullest potential.

REFERENCES

Almanac (1988). *34*, 2.

American Association of University Women Educational Foundation. (1992). *How schools shortchange girls*. Washington, DC.

Baruch, G., Barnett, R., & Rivers, C. (1984). *Lifeprints: New patterns of love and work for today's women*. New York: New American Library.

Belenky, M. F., Clinchy, B. M., Goldberger, N. R., & Tarule, J. M. (1986). *Women's ways of knowing: The development of self, voice and mind*. New York: Basic Books.

Bogdan, R. C., & Biklen, S. K. (1982). *Qualitative research for education: An introduction to theory and methods*. Boston: Allyn & Bacon.

Cayten, M. L. (1989). *Women and empowerment: Conceptualization and process among tenured women faculty*. Unpublished doctoral dissertation, University of Pennsylvania, Philadelphia.

de Beauvoir, S. (1953). *The second sex*. New York: Alfred A. Knopf.

Deckard, B. S. (1979). *The women's movement: Political, socioeconomic and psychological issues*. New York: Harper & Row.

Dowling, C. (1981). *The Cinderella complex: Women's hidden fear of independence*. New York: Summit Books.

Erickson, F. (1986). Qualitative methods in research on teaching. In M. C. Wittrock (Ed.), *Handbook of research on teaching* (3rd ed.) pp. 119-161. New York: Macmillan.

Erikson, E. H. (1959). *Identity and the life cycle*. New York: W.W. Norton & Company.

Fetterman, D. M. (1982). Ethnography in educational research: The dynamics of diffusion. *Educational Researcher, 11* , 17-22.

Freud, S. (1923). *The ego and the id.* (J. Riviere, Trans.). New York: W.W. Norton & Co.

Gaventa, J. (1980). *Power and powerlessness: Quiescence and rebellion in an Appalachian valley.* Urbana: University of Illinois.

Gilligan, C. (1982). *In a different voice.* Cambridge, MA: Harvard University.

Gilligan, C., Lyons, N. P., & Hanmer, T. J. (Eds.) (1990). *Making connections: The relational worlds of adolescent girls at Emma Willard School.* Cambridge, MA: Harvard University.

Giorgi, A. (Ed.) (1985). *Phenomenology and psychological research.* Pittsburgh, PA: Duquesne University.

Harding, S. (1986). *The science question in feminism.* Ithaca, NY: Cornell University.

Harlan, A., & Weiss, C. L. (1980). *Sex differences in factors affecting managerial career and advancement.* (Working Paper). Wellesley, MA: Wellesley College, Center for Research on Women.

Hartsock, N. C. M. (1985). *Money, sex and power: Toward a feminist historical materialism.* Boston: Northeastern University.

Heilbrun, C. G. (1979). *Reinventing womanhood.* New York: W.W. Norton & Co.

Horner, M. S. (1972). The motive to avoid success and changing aspirations of college women. In J. M. Bardwick (Ed.), *Readings on the psychology of women* (pp. 62-67). New York: Harper & Row.

Howe, F. (1984). *Myths of coeducation: Selected essays, 1964-1983.* Bloomington: Indiana University.

Kanter, R. M. (1977). *Men and women of the corporation.* New York: Basic Books.

Keller, E. F. (1983). *Reflections on gender and science.* New Haven: Yale University.

Keohane, N. (1985, June). *Women and power.* Paper presented at reunion, Wellesley College, Wellesley, MA.

Kohlberg, L. (1981). *Essays on moral development.* San Francisco: Harper & Row.

Kuhn, T. S. (1970). *The structure of scientific revolutions.* Chicago: University of Chicago.

Levinson, D. J., Darrow, C. N., Klein, E. B., Levinson, M. H., & McKee, B. (1978). *The seasons of a man's life.* New York: Alfred A. Knopf.

McClelland, D. C. (1975). *Power: The inner experience.* New York: Irvington Publishers.

Miller, J. B. (1982). *Women and power.* Wellesley, MA: Stone Center for Developmental Services and Studies, Wellesley College.

Rich, A. (1979). *On lies, secrets and silence.* New York: W.W. Norton & Co.

Robbins, L., & Kahn, E. D. (1985). Sex discrimination and sex equity for faculty women in the 1980's. *Journal of Social Issues, 41,* 17-28.

Seligman, M. E. P. (1975). *Helplessness: On depression, development, and death.* San Francisco: Freeman.

Speizer, J. J. (1981). Role models, mentors and sponsors: The elusive concepts. *Signs: Journal of Women in Culture and Society, 6,* 692-712.

Wellesley College Bulletin, (1986, September). *76,* pp. 249-63.

Yin, R. K. (1984). *Case study research: Design and methods.* Beverly Hills, CA: Sage Publications.

10

Toward the Reconstruction of Masculinity

Ronald F. Levant

BACKGROUND AND RATIONALE

A Brief Introduction to the Psychology of Men

The new psychology of men is an emerging area, part of the larger field of men's studies[1]; while space here does not permit me to provide a thorough summary, it is important to sketch a few basic points with which many readers may not be familiar. From a theoretical point of view, Pleck's work (1981, 1995) is central. Pleck demonstrated that the paradigm that has dominated the last fifty years of research in this area, the Gender Role Identity Paradigm, is inadequate in accounting for the observed data, and he has proposed a new paradigm, the Gender Role Strain Paradigm.

The Gender Role Identity Paradigm assumes that people have an inner psychological need to have a gender role identity, and that their personality development hinges on its formation.[2] The extent to which this "inherent" need is met is determined by how completely they embrace their traditional gender role. In this paradigm, the development of appropriate gender role identity is viewed as a failure-prone process; and failure for men to achieve a masculine gender role identity is thought to result in homosexuality, negative attitudes towards women, or hypermasculinity. This paradigm springs from the same philosophical roots as the "essentialist" or "nativist" view of sex roles—the notion that there is a masculine "essence" that is historically invariant (Connell, 1991; Kimmel, 1991).

In contrast, Pleck's Gender Role Strain Paradigm proposes that gender roles are contradictory and inconsistent; that the proportion of persons who violate gender roles is high; that violation of gender roles leads to condemnation and negative psychological consequences; that actual or imagined violation of gender roles leads people to overconform to them; that violating gender roles has more severe consequences for males than for females; and that certain prescribed gender role traits (such as male aggression) can be dysfunctional. In this paradigm, gender roles are defined by gender role stereotypes and norms, and are imposed on the developing child by parents, teachers, and peers who subscribe to the prevailing norms and stereotypes. This paradigm springs from the same roots as social constructionism—the perspective that notions of "masculinity" and "femininity" are relational, socially constructed, and subject to change (Kimmel, 1987).

What are the norms of the male role? Based on a review of the literature, Levant and colleagues (1992) proposed a set of seven traditional male role norms: avoiding femininity, restrictive emotionality, seeking achievement and status, self-reliance, aggression, homophobia, and nonrelational attitudes toward sexuality.

Pleck's Gender Role Strain Paradigm has stimulated research over the past decade. Space does not permit more than a brief mention of a few points. First, a number of instruments have been developed to assess aspects of the male role. For a review, see Thompson and Pleck, 1995. In addition, two investigators have developed instruments to measure male gender role strain, and have developed productive research programs using these instruments: Eisler's (1995) Masculine Gender Role Strain Scale and O'Neil's (O'Neil, Good, & Holmes, 1995) Gender Role Conflict Scale.

The Crisis of Masculinity

To many men, particularly mid-life men, the question of what it means to be a man today is one of the most persistent unresolved issues in their lives. Raised to be like their fathers, they were mandated to become the good provider for their families, and to be strong and silent. They were discouraged from expressing vulnerable and tender emotions, and required to put a sharp edge around their masculinity by avoiding anything that hinted of the feminine. Unlike their sisters, they received little, if any, training in nurturing others, or in being sensitive to their needs, or in being empathic with their voice. On the other hand, they received lots of training in problem-solving, logical thinking, risk-taking, staying calm in the face of danger, and assertion and aggression. Finally, they were required at an early age to renounce their dependence on their mothers and accept the pale substitute of their psychologically, if not physically, absent fathers.

For the past two decades, men of this generation have had the experience of attempting to fulfill the requirements of the masculine mandate in the midst of criticism that has risen to a crescendo. Men feel that they are being told that what they have been trying to accomplish is irrelevant to the world of today. Since women now work and can earn their own living, there is no longer as much need for Mr. Good Provider. Furthermore, society no longer seems to value, or even recognize, the traditional male way of demonstrating care, through taking care of his family and friends, by looking out for them, solving their problems, and being one who can be counted on to be there when needed. In its place, men are being asked to take on roles and show care in ways that violate the traditional male code and require skills that they do not have, such as nurturing children, revealing weakness, and expressing their most intimate feelings. The net result of this for many men is a loss of self-esteem and an unnerving sense of uncertainty about what it means to be a man.

A Reconstruction of Masculinity

What is needed? What will help? This chapter will propose a reconstruction of masculinity—which brings us to a problem. The social construction of masculinity has collapsed before it has been systematically "deconstructed" by men's studies scholars, as recommended by Kimmel (1987) and Doherty (1991). Aspects of masculinity have been deconstructed by feminists, such as Dinnerstein (1976) and Ehrenreich (1983), in their compelling analyses of the relationship between gender and power. Sexual aspects of masculinity were vividly deconstructed by television during 1991, in the broadcasts of Anita Hill's allegations of sexual harassment against Clarence Thomas and the subsequent Senate Hearings, in the William Kennedy Smith date rape trail, and in "Magic" Johnson's revelation that he has been infected by the HIV virus due to a sexually promiscuous heterosexual lifestyle. While it would be wonderful if men *en masse* were to examine masculinity and say "these stereotypes don't fit our reality; we are better than that" (Doherty, 1991, p. 30), I don't think that is going to happen in the current climate. The collapse of masculinity has resulted in defensiveness and demoralization. I therefore think that it is important to develop a positive image of masculinity that can restore men's self-respect, one that does not revert to an outmoded model of aggressive, dominant, and disconnected manhood nor to the Gender Role Identification Paradigm. The pitfalls of thinking of masculinity as inherent and of creating rigid norms and stereotypes must be avoided.

Thus, this is a reconstruction that must adhere to a fine line, intellectually. But above all, this reconstruction must be one that responds both nondefensively to the feminist critique of patriarchy and empathically to men. It thus must also walk a fine line in terms of crediting men for what is valuable about masculinity on the one hand, and helping men come to terms with what must be changed on the other hand. Finally, this reconstruction must attempt to inspire men to find the courage to undertake the "modern hero's journey" (Napier, 1991, p. 10), which is an inner pilgrimage, involving the confrontation with one's own emotional demons.

In keeping with these aims, this reconstruction will separate out the aspects of the traditional male code that are still quite valuable and celebrate these, and identify those aspects that are obsolete and dysfunctional and target those for change. Some of the positive attributes that will be celebrated are: a man's willingness to set aside his own needs for the sake of his family; his ability to withstand hardship and pain to protect others; his tendency to take care of people and solve their problems as if they were his own; his way of expressing love by doing things for others; his loyalty, dedication, and commitment; his stick-to-it-iveness and will to hang in until the situation is corrected; and his abilities to solve problems, think logically, rely on himself, take risks, stay calm in the face of danger, and assert himself. These traits are natural results of the male role socialization process, attributes of the male code that are still quite valuable, but which have been lying around in the dust ever since the edifice of masculinity collapsed. We need to express our appreciation for these traits, so that men can regain some of the lost esteem and pride associated with being a man.

Then there are the other traits, those parts of the male role that are obsolete and dysfunctional, which include: men's relative inability to experience emotional empathy; men's difficulty in being able to identify and express their own emotional states; the tendency for men's anger to flip into rage and result in violence; men's tendency to experience sexuality as separated from relationships; men's difficulties with emotional intimacy; and men's difficulties in becoming full partners with their wives in maintaining a home and raising children. These traits are results of the male role socialization process. Rectifying them requires learning new skills and doing emotional work.

A recent study suggests that the time may be ripe to undertake this reconstruction of masculinity. Using the Male Role Norms Inventory, Levant and colleagues (1992) found that their respondents (mostly undergraduates) tended to not endorse many of the traditional norms of the male role: the requirement to avoid all things feminine; the injunction to restrict one's emotional life; the emphasis on achieving status above all else; nonrelational, objectifying attitudes toward sexuality; and fear and hatred of homosexuals. However, the respondents did endorse the norms of self-reliance and aggression. These results are similar to those of Thompson, Grisanti, and Pleck (1985). Using the Brannon Masculinity Scale (Brannon & Juni, 1984) with a sample of undergraduate males, the investigators found that their respondents tended to not endorse the norms of "No Sissy Stuff" (avoidance of femininity and concealing emotions) and "The Big Wheel" (The breadwinner and admired and respected), but tended to endorse the norms of "The Sturdy Oak" (toughness, the male machine) and "Give 'em Hell" (violence and adventure). Although the results from both studies are encouraging, it is still somewhat disheartening to find that both samples endorsed the norm of male aggression.[3]

The New Man

What form will the new masculinity take? What will the new images look like? Who will be the new role models? For contemporary men, the John Wayne/Gary Cooper model of masculinity that suited our fathers clearly does not work, but neither does the pro-feminist "sensitive man" for which Alan Alda served as the caricature. The search for appropriate images of what it means to be a man is a central issue today. The journalist Ellen Goodman (1991, p.22) nominated General Norman Schwarzkopf for the model man of the 1990s: "This complicated character seems to synthesize conflicting and changing male images. Introspective but decisive, caring yet competent, one of the guys and a leader. Not stuff that always comes in the same male packages." There is a certain amount of irony in suggesting a military man as a role model to mid-life men—the "Viet Nam generation"; however, Goodman (1991, p. 22) points out, by contrasting Schwarzkopf with Colonel Oliver North, that military men come in various shapes and sizes.

However you might feel about Schwarzkopf as a role model, a new combination of values is increasingly in evidence among public figures and opinion-makers. When he was stricken with lymphoma in 1984, former Senator Paul Tsongas left the U. S. Senate because of his concern that his two-year-old daughter might never know her father. Senator Tom Harkin of Iowa spoke openly of his feelings of sadness and empathy for his brother Frank, who was ridiculed as a child for his deafness. And President Bill Clinton revealed with quite a bit of feeling that his mother was widowed three months before he was born, and that his grandfather stepped in to fill the void of the father he never knew. These are significant changes in the posture of public figures, especially when you recall the tears shed by Ed Muskie, the former Senator from Maine, during an emotional campaign speech in 1968 as he realized his presidential chances were melting away.

So what will the new man, the man of the 1990s and beyond, be like? He will possess a combination of old and new traits. He will still be strong, self-reliant and reliable. He will show care by doing for others, looking out for them, and solving their problems. He will be good at solving problems and in being assertive. He will be logical and live by a moral code. But he will no longer be a stranger to emotions. He will have a greater appreciation of his own emotional life and an ability to express his emotions in words. His emotional life will be also be richer and more complex. Anger will retreat to an appropriate level, and he will be more comfortable with sadness and fear. He will feel less afraid of shame. He will be aware of the emotions of others, and adept at reading their subtle nuances. He will have a better balance in his life between work and love. He will be a better husband and lover because he will be able to experience the true joys of intimacy, and come to prefer that over disconnected lust. He will be the father that he wanted for himself.

RESTRUCTURING MASCULINITY

This section of the article will outline a proposal for the reconstruction of masculinity. Space limitations do not allow the intensive treatment of each topic, nor the comprehensive inclusion of all of the important issues. Hence, there has been an effort to focus on the more fundamental issues.

Gender Role Socialization

The Gender Role Strain Paradigm suggests that, to the extent that parents, teachers, and peers subscribe to gender role stereotypes, children will be socialized accordingly. Prior to the early 1960s, traditional gender role stereotypes prevailed. Hence, children brought up in the postwar era were reared on gender tracks. In this section, we will examine some of the consequences of gender role socialization. The valuable aspects of the male role—those that deserve to be honored—have resulted from gender role socialization, but some of the problems can be traced to this source as well. These problems include: men's lesser abilities to be empathic and emotionally expressive; alexithymia; and men's greater expression of anger, rage, and violence.

To get some idea of how gender role socialization worked, think back to how it was in your own childhood. Did boys play with mechanical objects such as cars and trucks, or with very aggressive "dolls" such as military figures or superheroes, and begin to develop action-oriented attitudes, while girls played with dolls and doll houses, and started to develop nurturing attitudes? Did this gender differentiation continue throughout childhood? Were boys allowed to climb trees, roam through the woods in little packs, and come into the house covered head to toe with dirt? Were these things that girls were not usually allowed to do? On the other hand, were boys not usually asked to mind their younger siblings, nor encouraged to offer babysitting services, nor enrolled in home economics classes? Did girls visit nursing homes with their girl scout troops while boys shivered in the forests, rubbing sticks together to start a fire? These were the fairly typical experiences of childhood prior to the 1960s.

Gender-Differentiated Skills

At a more fundamental level, the current generation of adult men were trained as boys in the skills of instrumental problem solving, team work, risk-taking, maintaining calm in the face of danger, and assertiveness, those masculine skills that are still very valuable. On the other hand, boys did not learn certain psychological skills that were more the province of girls: the ability to be empathically attuned to the feelings of others, the ability to access and to become aware of their own feelings, and the ability to express their feelings.

You can see how some of this differential skill learning comes about by observing children at play (Lever, 1976; Maccoby, 1990). Young boys still typically play in groups at structured games in which skills such as learning to play by the rules, teamwork, and competition are learned whereas girls of this age may prefer to play with one other girl, their play consisting, in part, of telling each other secrets, thus fostering their learning skills of empathy, emotional self-awareness, and emotional expressivity.

This childhood training persists into adulthood. Osborne (1991), in a comprehensive review of the literature, concluded that men tend to be both less empathic and less emotionally expressive than women. The good news is that men can learn these skills as adults (Dosser, 1982; Levant & Doyle, 1983; Levant & Kopecky, 1995; Moore & Haverkamp, 1989).

Alexithymia

One of the most far-reaching consequences of male role socialization is the high incidence among men of at least a mild form of alexithymia—the inability to identify and describe one's feelings in words (Krystal, 1982; Sifneos, 1967). I would advance the hypothesis that this is a result of being socialized to be emotionally stoic. Not only were boys not encouraged to learn to identify and express their emotions, more pointedly, they were told *not* to. They might have been told that, "Big boys don't cry." In sports, they were told, "No pain, no gain." and admonished to learn to "Play with pain." These exhortations trained them to be out of touch with their feelings, particularly those feelings on the vulnerable end of the spectrum. As a result of such socialization experiences, men are often genuinely unaware of their emotions. Lacking this emotional awareness, they tend to rely on their cognition, and try to logically deduce how they should feel. They cannot do what is so automatic for most women—simply sense inward, feel the feeling, and let the verbal description come to mind.

At the Fatherhood Project, we developed a psychoeducational approach to overcoming alexithymia (Levant & Kelly, 1989). Men who are in the presence of an unrecognized emotion often experience it as a physiological sensation, which we call a "buzz," examples of which are: tightness in the throat, constriction in the chest, clenching of the gut, antsy feeling in the legs, constriction in the face, difficulty concentrating, and gritting of teeth. We found that men tend to respond to this buzz in one of four characteristic ways: (1) Distraction, which serves as a "circuit breaker," allowing men to disengage from the buzz; (2) the Rubber Band Syndrome, in which the buzz builds and builds until it erupts in an explosion of anger; (3) the Tin Man approach, which requires locking the buzz up tighter than a drum so that the man no longer feels anything; or (4) the Mixed Messenger, in which the buzz oozes out through the man's nonverbal behavior.

To help fathers in the Project overcome alexithymia, we first worked with them to develop a vocabulary for emotions, particularly the vulnerable ones, such as hurt, sadness, disappointment, rejection, abandonment, and fear, as well as the tender ones, such as warmth, affection, closeness, and appreciation. We then asked men to keep an Emotional Response Log, noting when they experienced a feeling that they could identify, or a buzz that they became aware of, and what the circumstances were that led up to that feeling or buzz. The logs were then discussed in the group, with the emphasis on learning how to apply verbal labels of feelings to emotional states. We also taught men to tune in to their feelings through watching and discussing immediate play-backs of role plays in which feelings were engendered. By pointing out the nonverbal cues and asking such questions as, "What were your feelings, Don, when you grimaced in that last segment?", the men learned how to access the ongoing flow of emotions within. The video playback was so effective at times that we came to refer to it as the "mirror to a man's soul."

Anger, Rage, and Violence

Men's lack of emotional awareness is not complete; rather, it is selective. Men are allowed to feel and become aware of emotions in the anger and rage part of the spectrum, as prescribed in the "Give 'em Hell" injunction of the male code (David & Brannon, 1976). Anger is, in fact, one of the few emotions boys are encouraged to have and, as a consequence, a lot of other feelings such as hurt, disappointment, and even fear get funneled into it. Consequently, men's anger often comes too readily.

Anger is an unruly emotion, one that too easily shades into rage and too often results in violence; men's rage and violence have ruined many families. At the Fatherhood Project, we developed techniques for anger management for men caught up in the Rubber Band Syndrome, which involve learning to identify both the vulnerable feelings that turn into anger, as well as the incipient and mild stages of anger. Being able to identify these feelings permits one to talk about them, rather than becoming "possessed" by them.

Keeping an Emotional Response Log can be particularly helpful because it provides a means by which to get a handle on the stages that lead to an eruption. Through keeping such a written record, a man might discover, for example, that his anger proceeds through four distinct stages, each with its own markers, and this information gives him a kind of early warning system. He now knows that at Stage 1 the buzz and an inability to focus signal an incipient annoyance. This means that if he takes action at this Stage, he could prevent the buzz from progressing to Stage 2, "antsyness"; Stage 3, teeth-grinding; and Stage 4, eruption.

PARENT-CHILD DYNAMICS

In this section, we will look at the psychological consequences of the separation from mother, required for the socialization of boys; we will also consider the effects of the unavailability of fathers. Here we will find need for men to undertake emotional work, work that will go much better if they have first developed the skills of empathy and emotional self-awareness described above.

Separation from Mother

The gender role socialization of boys includes the requirement that they separate from their mothers during the separation-individuation phase of early childhood in order to establish a male identity. Girls, on the other hand, can establish a female identity without this emotional rupture (Chodorow, 1978). Hence, as boys grow up, yearnings for maternal closeness and attachment, which never completely go away, bring up fears of losing their sense of separateness, and their masculine identity. Consequently, many adult men feel much safer being alone than being close to someone, a phenomenon that Pollack (1995) has termed "defensive autonomy." This may be experienced as a fear of engulfment, which often motivates the well-known clinical pattern of male distancing in marriage. On the other hand, those yearnings for maternal attachment also get expressed in marriages, in the form of husbands' (often unconscious, certainly unacknowledged) dependence on their wives.

Pollack (1995) has referred to the early separation of boys from their mothers as the "traumatic abrogation of the holding environment." This loss of the holding environment, which robs boys of the tranquility of childhood, is never acknowledged, much less mourned, leaving men vulnerable to developing what Boszormenyi-Nagy and Ulrich (1981) refer to as "destructive entitlement." Oft-criticized male selfishness may spring from these roots.

It would be interesting to see what happens to boys raised by their fathers from infancy, such as those studied by Pruett (1987). According to theory, they would not have the same need to separate from the primary caregiver in order to establish a masculine identity. What effects would this have on their abilities as adults to attach and relate intimately to women?

Father Absence, Grief, and the "Wound"

The socialization ordeal for boys also includes the requirement that they identify with their psychologically—if not physically—absent, emotionally unavailable fathers. The stress of this ordeal is further complicated by the fact that when the father is available, he is often very demanding of his son. There is such a paradox here, from the father's point of view: many men feel that their lives will not be complete unless they have a son; and then when they do have a son, they wind up being very hard on them. Part of this has to do with the father feeling that he must take an active role in enforcing his son's compliance with gender stereotypes. Developmental research has found that fathers traditionally take an influential role in enforcing sex role stereotypes with their children, whereas mothers are more gender-neutral (Lamb, Owen, & Chase-Lansdale, 1979).

The difficult father-son relationship leaves a deep impression on the man—referred to as the "wound" in the men's studies literature (Osherson, 1986)—which is manifested in myriad direct and disguised forms of desperately seeking some contact, some closeness with one's father (or his surrogate), or in being furious at him for his failures.

To illustrate, I'll describe an experience at the Fatherhood Project that would often occur during the second meeting of the group. One man would start to speak, bottom lip quivering, struggling to maintain control: "You know, the reason why I'm here. I'll tell you (pause). The reason why I am here is so that my little son Jimmy will not grow up to feel as bad about me as I feel about my own dad." This would open the flood gates, and the men would pour out their stories and their grief about their own fathers: never knowing their fathers, nor how their fathers felt as men, nor if their fathers even liked them, nor if their fathers ever really approved of them. This acutely painful feeling of father loss is very widespread and requires grief work to resolve.

CULTURAL DYNAMICS

In this section, we will consider the cultural problem of achieving manhood, and the role of shame in this process. We will also look at men's propensity for self-sacrifice, discussing the relationship between self-sacrifice and entitlement, and considering two consequences: men's dedication to work and their nonrelational attitudes toward sexuality.

Achieving Manhood

Gilmore (1990) demonstrated that in most of the cultures that he surveyed, ranging from the neolithic to the modern, masculinity is an achieved state, one that requires the passing of a series of tests. The requirements are more severe in societies where life is harsher. Women are not subjected to such tests, partly because they are under the control of men in most societies.

The tests for manhood are never finished; it is hard to find a permanent place among the community of men. A man can always slip back over the line, losing his manhood and suffering shame and disgrace by failing the next test. In fact, most men do slip over that line. The consequences of violating these sex role norms for men are quite severe (it is a fate worse than death in many societies) and usher in enormous shame. Many men harbor the feeling that they are alone in this, that they alone have egregiously violated the male code, that "all those other guys" are doing just fine, and that if anyone knew his secrets they would ostracize him completely.

Shame

This problem of never permanently attaining manhood leaves men with considerable reluctance to violate the male code lest they be disgraced and overwhelmed with feelings of shame. Krugman (1995) has noted that male culture is shame phobic—meaning that men will go to great lengths to avoid feeling ashamed. Shame thus serves as a powerful cultural mechanism for ensuring compliance with the male code, and hence a formidable obstacle to change. Therapeutic work must be informed by an awareness of the role of shame in men's lives, and take pains to avoid shaming male clients (Osherson & Krugman, 1990).

Selfless Generosity, Self-Sacrifice, and Entitlement

Gilmore found one widespread criterion for judging manhood— selfless generosity, to the point of sacrifice: "Real men are those who give more than they take; they serve others. Real men are generous, even to a fault" (1990, p. 229). Selfless generosity is clearly one of the admirable parts of the traditional male code. But male self—sacrifice is often problematic in our society. There are several facets to the problem. First, when self-sacrifice is combined with interpersonal skill-deficits and defensive autonomy, both of which make relationships difficult, workaholism may be the result. Such men often don't know what to do with themselves other than work. Second, self-sacrifice often interacts with the sense of entitlement that results from the early separation from mother, forming sacrifice-indulge cycles. These cycles can occur on a daily basis. For example, consider the man who throws himself into a fourteen-hour grueling day of work, and then comes home to make child-like demands on his family, or is abusive to them, or rewards himself with one indulgence or another. These cycles can also occur over a longer period of time, and lie at the basis of compulsive materialism, nonrelational sexuality, and chemical dependency. Self-sacrifice carried to extremes also has health consequences.

Work

As a gender, men have been "raised to work" (Pasick, 1990, p. 35). It is, for most of us, our reason for being on the planet. One of the first things that most people ask a man whom they have just met is, "What do you do?" "What is your occupation?". Men are supposed to do something, supposed to be occupied. Weiss's (1990) study is a good source of information on men who do well at work.

Now that the breadwinner ethic is passing, what do men do? What should they do? How do they define themselves? How do they measure their worth? Many men experience doubts and a terrible loss of orientation; others have attempted to renavigate the course of masculinity, by finding a balance between work and involvement with family. These are issues that deserve our attention.

Nonrelational Sexuality

Clinical experience suggests that there are fundamental differences in the way that men and women experience sexuality. Men tend to experience sexuality in a nonrelational way, that is, as unconnected lust, which is quite different from how women tend to experience it (Levant & Brooks, 1997; see also Brooks, 1995).

Lust in men stems from defensive autonomy, which makes emotional intimacy difficult, and from destructive entitlement, often amplified by self-sacrifice, in which sex and sexy women are often viewed as "rewards" for hard work. Stoltenberg (1989) argues that this sexual objectification arises from male supremacy in a patriarchal society. Unconnected lust can lead to many problems in men's lives, including sexual addiction (Carnes, 1983). Unconnected lust also contributes to men's sexual aggression against women.

No Man Is an Island

Gender role socialization leaves many men unprepared for the world of intimate relationships. Lacking ability to read his own and other people's emotions, feeling much safer being alone than being close to people, and egged on by a fear of shame, a drive to self-sacrifice, and an overriding commitment to work, many men founder on the shoals of relationship complexity. In this section, we will examine two issues: the division of family labor and the causes of marital breakdown.

Before discussing these matters, the familiar litany of criticisms of men's difficulties with intimacy must be put into perspective. They should be regarded first from the vantage point of the male role socialization process, which results in differing skill profiles for men and women, skill profiles that are to the advantage of women in relationships. Second, traditional male ways of being close, bonded, and intimate should be honored. I am referring to the feeling of "side-by-side intimacy," described by Moore (1991), that two guys might have as they spend a warm summer day leaning under the hood of a Chevy. Do they feel close? Yes. Would one of them say to the other, "You know, I really feel close to you as we work together replacing the valves on this old heap"? No way!

The Division of Household Labor

In the middle and late l960s, large-scale time budget studies indicated that husbands' participation in family work (both childcare and housework) was quite low (1.1 to 1.6 hours/day) compared to that of their wives (7.6 to 8.1 hours/day for house wives and 4.0 to 4.8 hours/day for employed wives); and that husbands tended to increase their participation only slightly (0.1 hour/day) in response to their wives' employment (Robinson, 1977; Walker & Woods, 1976). Juster and Stafford (1985) found a 20 per cent increase in the amount of time husbands put into family work over the period 1965-81. Douthitt (1989) found additional increases during the 1980s. However, the amount of time husbands spend in family work still remains only about a third of that of their wives. And, although Berardo, Shehan, and Leslie (1987) found that the type of family work that men do has shifted from yard and car work to child care and meal preparation, in the area of child care, men still tend to rely on their wives to assign tasks rather then taking responsibility for the care.

Why don't men do more? I have argued elsewhere (Levant, 1990) that one of the major reasons that men do not participate more in childcare is because of skill deficits, deficits that could be remedied through fatherhood education. But, this is clearly not the whole story. When I sit with parents who are in conflict about this issue, it is not too difficult to discern in the father the plaintiff voice of a little boy, who feels he should not have to do all this women's work, and who feels entitled to leave the truly odious jobs to his wife. Once again, we come smack up against some of the consequences of the early separation from mother, consequences which require significant emotional work.

There are compelling reasons to address the skill deficits and do the emotional work, reasons that include not only men's overloaded wives and their conflicted marriages, but also their own and their children's needs. It is of the utmost importance for men to get deeply involved in rearing their children so that their sons will not grow up with the same skill lacks and emotional problems, and their daughters can derive the benefits of parenting from their fathers. It is also important for the men themselves. I am not only referring to the obvious notion that if men do the emotional work they will function better in life, but also to Gottman's (1991) finding that husbands who do housework have better health. (See also Brooks & Gilbert, 1995.)

Causes of Marital Breakdown

We now have some pretty good longitudinal data on what causes marital breakdown. The primary factor, based on the research of Markman, Notarius, Gottman, and others, seems to be how couples handle conflict, especially hot conflict with strong negative affect.

A particularly malignant pattern, one which is more predictive of marital breakdown than measures of marital satisfaction (Markman, Duncan, Storaasli, & Howes, 1987), is one in which the wife angrily pursues the resolution of conflicts, while the husband withdraws. Floyd and Markman (1983) found that distressed wives distort their perceptions of their husbands' behaviors based on feelings of hostility, whereas husbands in distressed marriages do not attend to the negativity expressed by their wives, suggesting that they are coping by withdrawing. This pattern has been long recognized in the family therapy literature as the end stage of the distancer-pursuer cycle (Fogarty, 1979).

Recent publications make the controversial claim that this cycle may have a biological basis. Gottman and Levenson (1988) and Notarius and Johnson (1982) found that husbands experience conflict (including the anticipation of conflict) with a much higher sympathetic nervous system arousal than do wives and that husbands take much longer to return to baseline. The arousal is distinctly aversive. In situations of low conflict, husbands attempt to prevent the conflict from escalating through positive, reconciling behaviors or by being rational and logical. In situations of high conflict, husbands withdraw as a way of avoiding the arousal.

It is not yet clear what accounts for the greater physiological arousal in men. Is it the result of biological differences, or is it in some way learned? I would advance the hypothesis that men's greater arousal in conflict situations results from the skill deficits (in empathy and emotional self-awareness) and the emotional problems (defensive autonomy, unconscious dependence, destructive entitlement) discussed above that result from gender role socialization. In particular, men's relative inability to become aware of and process emotional states would make it very difficult to sort out the feelings that he was having, to say nothing of dealing with matters that may be unconscious. It is no wonder that he then becomes overwhelmed by what we have termed the physiological buzz, which may be the same phenomenon as the physiological arousal that Gottman has measured in his laboratory.[4]

Health

This section will take up the question of men's physical and mental health, and discuss the issues of men's higher mortality rates and their greater susceptibility to stress-related disorders, chemical dependency, and anti-social personality disorders.

Men die on the average seven years earlier than do women. What are the reasons for this disparity? Harrison (1978) examined the differences in life expectancy for American men and women and attempted to identify contributing biogenetic and psychosocial factors. He concluded that gender role socialization accounts for most of the variance of men's shorter life expectancies, and suggested that "the male role may be hazardous to your health" (p.65). The chief factors are men's greater susceptibility to stress-related disorders and their reluctance to seek medical attention at the early stages of a problem (Waldron & Johnson, 1976).

Recent studies indicate that both psychological distress and physical illness may be related to the quality of men's family roles. Barnett, Marshall, and Pleck (1991) found that the quality of men's marital role and of their parental role are both significant predictors of men's psychological distress. Barnett and Marshall (1991) further found that the quality of men's parental role, but not that of their marital role, was a significant predictor of men's physical health.

Men are increasingly utilizing psychotherapy to address stress-related and other emotional problems. Their increasing use of psychotherapy is certainly timely, because men are closing the gap with women on the prevalence of psychological distress. Kessler and McRae (1981) analyzed five national surveys on mental health conducted between 1957 and 1976, and found that men's rates of symptoms of psychological distress increased three times as much as women's, and that, as a result, the "gender gap" in symptoms was 38 percent smaller at the end of the two-decade period. In a later study, Kessler and McRae (1983) found a similar process occurring with regard to attempted suicides. Generalizing across a group of studies, the investigators reported that the ratio of females to males attempting suicide dropped from 2.3/1 in 1960 to 1.3/1 in 1980. It should also be noted that men continue to have substantially higher rates of completed suicides than women. Finally, a large scale NIMH study found that, although women have higher rates of affective, anxiety, and somatization disorders, men have higher rates of substance abuse and anti-social personality disorders (Landers, 1989).

Men's increased utilization of therapy presents problems, however, because psychotherapy, as traditionally employed, requires skills and behaviors that conflict with aspects of the male role. I am referring here to such male traits as difficulty in admitting the existence of a problem, difficulty in asking for help, inability to identify and express emotions, and fear of intimacy. There is, thus, a need for more gender-aware forms of therapy that take into explicit account men's sex role socialization and the problematic aspects of the definition of masculinity. There is also a need to educate men how to use psychotherapy. Literature in this area is starting to appear (Good, Gilbert, & Scher, 1990; Meth & Pasick, 1990; Pollack & Levant, 1997).

SUMMARY

In summary, the male role socialization process produces men adept at the skills of provision and protection, such as problem-solving, assertiveness, staying calm under fire, and providing for others, but lacking the abilities to know their own emotional life and to be empathic with others. In addition, men's more severe sex role socialization makes emotional intimacy threatening to them but leaves them with unmet dependency needs; it also burdens them with a sense of entitlement, a longing for their fathers, and at risk for experiencing overwhelming shame.

The reconstruction of masculinity involves several components: First, there is a need to validate the skills that men learn and the ways that men have of showing care and concern, so that men can recapture some of the lost pride of masculinity. Second, men need opportunities to learn some of the skills that women learn as girls, particularly empathy, emotional self-awareness, and emotional expressivity. Developing these skills will help balance men's emotional life, so that the outpouring of vulnerable emotions through the channel of anger is reduced. Third, aided by these new skills, men will need to do the important emotional work that will enable them to come to terms with the loss of mother, the absent father, and the fear of being shamed for not "being man enough."

One consequence of doing this work might be moderation of the mandate for self-sacrifice, which may help men put their work in a more balanced perspective. Another consequence might be reduction of sacrifice-indulge cycles, which would be of help to men caught up in the pursuit of money or objects or in the addiction to chemicals or sex. A third might be reduction of defensive autonomy and integration of dependency needs, which clears the way for the greater emotional intimacy. A fourth might be reduction of a sense of entitlement that would enable greater involvement with their children. As a result, among the possible consequences, the man might also enjoy improved health.

Thus, we come to the end of this chapter. Much has been written, yet there is much more to discuss. Fatherhood has not been addressed here in any detail; the chapter does not deal with the process and effects of divorce, including the experiences of visitation fathers or of fathers with sole- and joint-custody. Neither has it mentioned remarriage or the very difficult stepfather role. It does not speak to the corporate response to the working parent family, nor to issues of concern for gay and bisexual men. It does not comment on the dimensions of ethnicity, race, and class, for example, on the singular plight of the young urban African-American male. Finally, it has not addressed the problems of caring for aging parents or of being an older man. These are topics that merit much further exploration. My hope, however, is that I have dealt with several of the more basic issues of male psychological development and have done so in a way that is both progressive and empathic with men.

NOTES

1. See Brod (1987) for an anthology of recent work in men's studies, and Levant & Pollack (1995) for an anthology of recent work in the new psychology of men.

2. Gender role identity is not the same thing as gender identity (the knowledge that one is male or female), the latter seeming to be a fundamental requirement for personality integration and is apparently accomplished in all but the tiniest minority of cases.

3. Due to space limitations, this article will not take into account the variables of social class and ethnicity. The discussion is primarily about white middle-class men. I am aware that for many working-class and lower-class men, the traditional norms are not changing. For example, Gary Brooks has pointed out in a personal communication that, for the working class men that he sees in the Temple, Texas Veteran's Hospital, avoiding all things feminine remains a strong norm. For further discussion of these matters, see Lazur & Majors (1995).

4. The situation is even more complicated. Jacobson (1983) hypothesized that the wife demand/husband withdraw cycle is a function of power differentials within marriage, with husbands having greater power. Christensen and Heavey (1990) attempted to discern whether the demand/withdraw cycle is due to gender differences (resulting from socialization, biology, or both) or to power differences, and found that both factors play a role, with their results tending to favor the power differential hypothesis.

REFERENCES

Barnett, R. C., & Marshall, N. (1991). Men, family-role quality, job-role quality and physical health. *Health Psychology, 10*, 94-101.

Barnett, R. C., Marshall, N., & Pleck, J. (1991). Men's multiple roles and their relationship to men's psychological distress. *Journal of Marriage and the Family, 54*, 348-67.

Berardo, D. H., Shehan, L. L., & Leslie, G. R. (1987). A residue of tradition: Jobs, careers and spouse time in housework. *Journal of Marriage and the Family, 49*, 381-90.

Boszormenyi-Nagy, I., & Ulrich, D. N. (1981) Contextual family therapy. In A. S. Gurman & D. P. Kniskern (Eds.) *Handbook of family therapy.* New York: Brunner/Mazel.

Brannon, R., & Juni, S. (1984). A scale for measuring attitudes about masculinity. *Psychological Documents, 14* (1). (University Microfilms No. 2612).

Brod, H. (1987). *The making of the masculinities: The new men's studies.* Boston: Unwin Hyman.

Brooks, G. R. (1995). *The centerfold syndrome.* San Francisco: Jossey Bass.

Brooks, G. R., & Gilbert, L. A. (1995). Men in families: Old constraints, new possibilities. In R. F. Levant & W. S. Pollack (Eds.), *A new psychology of men.* New York: Basic Books.

Carnes, P. (1983). *The sexual addiction.* Minneapolis, MN: CompCare Publications.

Chodorow, N. (1978). *The reproduction of mothering: Psychoanalysis and the sociology of gender.* Berkeley, CA: University of California Press.

Christensen, A., & Heavey, C. (1990). Gender and social structure in the demand/withdraw pattern of marital conflict. *Journal of Personality and Social Psychology, 59*, 73-81.

Connell, R. W. (1991). *Men at bay: the "men's movement" and its newest bestsellers.* Cambridge: Harvard University, Department of Sociology.

David, D., & Brannon, R. (1976) (Eds.) *The forty-nine percent majority: The male sex role.* Reading, MA: Addison-Wesley.

Dinnerstein, D. (1976). *The mermaid and the minotaur: Sexual arrange-ments and human malaise.* New York: Harper and Row.

Doherty, W. J. (1991). Beyond reactivity and the deficit model of manhood: A commentary on articles by Napier, Pittman, & Gottman. *Journal of Marital and Family Therapy, 17*, 29-32.

Dosser, D. A. (1982). Male inexpressiveness: Behavioral interventions. In K. Solomon & N. B. Levy (Eds.), *Men in transition: Theory and therapy.* New York: Plenum.

Douthitt, R. A. (1989). The division of labor within homes: Have gender roles changed? *Sex Roles, 20*, 693-704.

Ehrenreich, B. (1983). *The hearts of men.* New York: Doubleday.

Eisler, R. M. (1995). The relationship between masculine gender role stress and men's health risk: The validation of a construct. In R. F. Levant & W. S. Pollack (Eds.), *A new psychology of men.* New York: Basic Books.

Floyd, F., & Markman, H. (1983). Observational biases in spouse observation: Toward a cognitive/behavioral model of marriage. *Journal of Consulting and Clinical Psychology, 51*, 450- 57.

Fogarty, T. F. (1979). The distancer and the pursuer. *The Family, 7*, 11-16.

Gilmore, D. (1990). *Manhood in the making: Cultural concepts of masculinity.* New Haven: Yale University Press.

Good, G. E., Gilbert, L. A., & Scher, M. (1990). Gender aware therapy: A synthesis of feminist therapy and knowledge about gender. *Journal of Counseling and Development, 68*, 376-80.

Goodman, E. (1991, March 14). A shining (four) star. *The Boston Globe*, p. 22.

Gottman, J. (1991). Predicting the longitudinal course of marriages. *Journal of Marital and Family Therapy, 17*, 3-7.

Gottman, J., & Levenson, R. (1988). The social psychophysiology of marriage. In P. Noller & M. A. Fitzpatrick (Eds.), *Perspectives on marital interaction* (pp. 182-200). Clevedon, UK: Multilingual Matters.

Harrison, J. (1978). Warning: The male role may be dangerous to your health. *The Journal of Social Issues, 34*, 65-86.

Jacobson, N. S. (1983). Beyond empiricism: The politics of marital therapy. *American Journal of Family Therapy, 11*, 11-24.

Juster, F. T., & Stafford, F. P. (1985) *Time, goods, and well-being.* Ann Arbor, MI: Institute for Social Research.

Kessler, R., & McRae, J. (1981). Trends in the relationship between sex and psychological distress: 1957-1976. *American Sociological Review, 46*, 443-52.

Kessler, R., & McRae, J. (1983). Trends in the relationship between sex and attempted suicide. *Journal of Health and Social Behavior, 24*, 98-110.

Kimmel, M. S. (1987). Rethinking "masculinity": New directions for research. In M. S. Kimmel (Ed.), *Changing men: New directions in research on men and masculinity.* Newbury Park, CA: Sage Publications.

Kimmel, M. S. (1991). Weekend warriors: Robert Bly's Iron John and the weekend retreat (a review essay). Unpublished manuscript, State University of New York, Stony Brook.

Krugman, S. (1995). Male development and the transformation of shame. In R. F. Levant & W. S. Pollack (Eds.), *A new psychology of men*. New York: Basic Books.

Krystal, H. (1982). Alexithymia and the effectiveness of psychoanalytic treatment. International *Journal of Psychoanalytic Psychotherapy, 9*, 353-78.

Lamb, M. E., Owen, M. J., & Chase-Lansdale, L. (1979). The father daughter relationship: Past, present, and future. In C. B. Knopp & M. Kirkpatrick (Eds.), *Becoming female*. New York: Plenum.

Landers, S. (1989, January). In U.S., mental disorders affect 15 percent of adults. *APA Monitor, 16*.

Lazur, R. F., & Majors, R. (1995). Men of color: Ethnocultural variations of male gender role strain. In R. F. Levant & W. S. Pollack (Eds.), *A new psychology of men*. New York: Basic Books.

Levant, R. F. (1990). Coping with the new father role. In D. Moore & F. Leafgren (Eds.), *Problem solving strategies and interventions for men in conflict*. Alexandria, VA: American Association for Counseling and Development.

Levant, R. F., & Brooks, G. R. (1997, Eds.). *Men and sex: New psychological perspectives*. New York: Wiley.

Levant, R. F., & Doyle, G. F. (1983). An evaluation of a parent education program for fathers of school-aged children. *Family Relations, 32*, 29-37.

Levant, R.F., Hirsch, L., Celentano, E., Cozza, T., Hill, S., MacEachern, M., Marty, N., & Schnedeker, J. (1992). The male role: An investigation of norms and stereotypes. *Journal of Mental Health Counseling, 14*, 325-77.

Levant, R. F., & Kelly, J. (1989). *Between father and child*. New York: Viking.

Levant, R. F. & Kopecky, G. (1995). *Masculinity, reconstructed*. New York: Dutton.

Levant, R. F. & Pollack, W. S. (1995, Eds.) *A new psychology of men*. New York: Basic Books.

Lever, J. (1976). Sex differences in the games children play. *Social Work, 23*, 78-87.

Maccoby, E. E. (1990). Gender and relationships: A developmental account. *American Psychologist, 45*, 513-20.

Markman, H. J., Duncan, S. W., Storaasli, R. D., & Howes, P. W. (1987). The prediction and prevention of marital distress: A longitudinal investigation. In K. Hahlweg & M. Goldstein (Eds.), *Understanding major mental disorder: The contribution of family interaction research*. New York: Family Process, Inc.

Meth, R. L., & Pasick R. S. (1990). *Men in therapy: The challenge of change*. New York: Guilford.

Moore, D. (1991). Men and emotions: Teaching men to be more emotionally expressive. In R. Levant, Chair, Men, emotions, and intimacy. Symposium conducted at Annual Meeting of the American Psychological Association, San Francisco.

Moore, D., & Haverkamp, B. E. (1989). Measured increases in male emotional expressiveness following a structured group intervention. *Journal of Counseling and Development, 67*, 513-17.

Napier, A. (1991). Heroism, men, and marriage. *Journal of Marital and Family Therapy, 17*, 9-16.

Notarius, C. I., & Johnson, J. (1982). Emotional expression in husbands and wives. *Journal of marriage and the family, 44*, 443- 89.

O'Neil, J. M., Good, G. E., & Holmes, S (1995). Fifteen years of theory and research on men's gender role conflict: New paradigms for empirical research. In

R. F. Levant & W. S. Pollack (Eds.), *A new psychology of men*. New York: Basic Books.

Osborne, R. W. (1991). Men and intimacy: An empirical review. In R. Levant, Chair, Men, emotions, and intimacy. Symposium conducted at Annual Meeting of the American Psychological Association, San Francisco.

Osherson, S. (1986). *Finding our fathers: The unfinished business of manhood*. New York: Free Press.

Osherson, S., & Krugman, S. (1990). Men, shame and psychotherapy. *Psychotherapy, 27*, 327-39.

Pasick, R. S. (1990). Raised to work. In R. L. Meth & R. S. Pasick (Eds.), *Men in therapy: The challenge of change*. New York: Guilford.

Pleck, J. H. (1981). *The myth of masculinity*. Cambridge, MA: MIT Press.

Pleck, J. H. (1995). The gender role strain paradigm: An update. In R. F. Levant & W. S. Pollack (Eds.), *A new psychology of men*. New York: Basic Books.

Pollack, W. S. (1995). No man is an island: Toward a new psychoanalytic psychology of men. In R. F. Levant & W. S. Pollack (Eds.), *A new psychology of men*. New York: Basic Books.

Pollack, W. S. & Levant, R. F. (1997, Eds.). *New psychotherapies for men*. New York: Wiley.

Pruett, K. D. (1987). *The nurturing father*. New York: Warner Books.

Robinson, J. (1977). *How Americans use time: A social-psychological analysis*. New York: Praeger.

Sifneos, P. E. (1967). Clinical observations on some patients suffering from a variety of psychosomatic diseases. *Proceedings of the Seventh European Conference on Psychosomatic Research*. Basel, Switzerland: Kargel.

Stoltenberg, J. (1989). *Refusing to be a man: Essays on sex and justice*. New York: Meridian.

Thompson, E. H., Jr., Grisanti, C., & Pleck, J. H. (1985). Attitudes toward the male role and their correlates. *Sex Roles, 13*, 483-89.

Thompson, E. H., & Pleck, J. H. (1995). Masculinity ideology: A review of research instrumentation on men and masculinities. In R. F. Levant & W. S. Pollack (Eds.), *A new psychology of men*. New York: Basic Books.

Weiss, R. S. (1990). *Staying the course: The emotional and social lives of men who do well at work*. New York: Fawcett Colombine.

Waldron, I., & Johnson, S. (1976). Why do women live longer than men? *Journal of Human Stress, 2*, 19-29.

Walker, K., & Woods, M. (1976). *Time use: A measure of household production of goods and services*. Washington, DC: American Home Economics Association.

11

Parental Development: Theory and Practice

Jack Demick

I have a seven-year-old daughter and a four-year-old son. After recently being instructed to wear a coat in below freezing temperatures, my daughter informed me that she did not have to comply with my directive because she was accountable to only two people in the world: God and Bill Clinton. During a recent dinner conversation in which my daughter was asking about foreign languages, my son's eyes piqued as he asked, "Dad, how do you say 'vagina' in Spanish?" Not usually at a loss for words, I needed several moments to regain cognitive equilibrium before attempting to respond to these novel and unexpected stimuli.

While numerous, life events have the potential to lead to higher stages of development and, specifically, to foster cognitive development, the experience of parenthood as one such life event is a relatively unequivocal example. As Berger (1994, p. 478) has noted, "From the birth of a first child, which tends to make both parents feel more 'adult'—thinking about themselves and their responsibilities differently— through the unexpected issues raised by adolescent children, parenthood is undoubtedly an impetus for cognitive growth" (Feldman, Biringen, & Nash, 1981; Flavell, 1970; Galinsky, 1981). That not only cognitive but also psychosocial development is affected by parenthood has been supported by several sources of work reported in our (Demick, Bursik, & DiBiase, 1993) recently edited volume on *Parental Development*. For example, based on Levinson's (1978) ideas concerning the periodicity or "seasons" of adult change, Palus (1993) has provided relevant findings on males' "transformative experiences of adulthood," which typically arose out of events in the realm of family/parenthood. Testing a theory of emotional development in adult life, Stevens-Long and Macdonald (1993) similarly found that adults were more likely to report the experience of empathy in response to family/parent-ing/children than to any other theme. Thus, it appears that parenthood—which occupies much, if not all, of the adult years for many—is an extremely powerful experience for the parent. Why then does the general problem area of parental development have such a short history within the fields of psychology, human development, and allied disciplines?

First, as Alpert and Richardson (1980) have described, the traditional approach of developmental psychologists to the study of parenting has, up until recently, primarily focused on the effects of parenting on the child (cf. Baumrind, 1967). However, in light of societal changes over the past ten to fifteen years, researchers have expanded the range of parental variables (e.g., maternal employment, parental choice of day care) thought to impact child functioning. With this reconceptualization has also come the revelation that these selfsame parental variables have the potential to affect not only the child, but also the parent himself or herself (cf. Barnett & Baruch, 1985).

Second, an additional body of earlier work with a heightened focus on the parent has been generated largely by sociologists, who conceptualize parenthood as: (a) a role that adults enact (Brim, 1966); and (b) occurring most always in the context of the family system (e.g., Hill & Mattessich, 1979). While these investigations have made inroads into the general problem of parental development, they remain to be complemented by conceptualization that treats the basis for continuity and change in parenthood as involving not only parental role, but also parents' transactions with all aspects of self and environment (cf. Ambert, 1992). In line with this, renewed interest in the effects of parenting on parents has been generated by the relatively recent movements of life span developmental psychology (e.g., Baltes & Schaie, 1973) and adult developmental psychology (e.g., Demick, 1994).

Third, differing conceptions of development often make it difficult to gain consensus among investigators as to the parameters of any new field of developmental inquiry, in this case, parental development. For example, Santostefano (1980) has noted that, in the general psychological and developmental literatures, development has variously been taken to refer to such phenomena as "growth, achievement of a new response, attainment of an ideal end state, change occurring over time, or any study employing children, especially if the subjects are of different ages" (p. 3).

Fourth, while our (Demick et al., 1993) recently edited volume is one of the first to contain "parental development" within its title, there have been considerably more with "parenthood" in their titles. However, these works have primarily been concerned with the processes and mechanisms underlying the experience of parenthood and parenting practices (e.g., family processes) rather than with the development of parents per se.[1]

Thus, while there has not as of yet been much research on parental development specifically, developmental psychologists have more recently become interested in related problem areas that have direct implications for the study of parental development. First, Pillemer and McCartney's (1991) volume on *Parent-Child Relations Throughout Life* has provided several chapters on, for example, the parental side of attachment, variability in the transition to parenthood, and the development of paternal maturity; however, the majority of chapters has still taken the traditional child-centered approach. Second, Cowan and Hetherington's (1991) volume on *Family Transitions* has provided information on: theoretical perspectives for understanding family transitions, examples of research programs on family transitions occurring at different periods of the life span, and statistical models for describing multi-dimensional changes in families over time. This latter work is in line with that of other investigators (e.g., Demick, 1996; Levinson, 1978; Schlossberg, 1984; Wapner, 1987; Wapner & Demick, 1991a) who have employed life transitions as a more general paradigm for the study of adult development.

How then does one attempt to provide a unified framework for the study of parental development? While Alpert and Richardson (1980) have long highlighted the need for comprehensive, empirically sound, and longitudinally based theoretical models to organize the existent potpourri of empirical findings on parenting, there still remains—with the exception of only several investigators including ourselves (cf. Belsky, 1984, who identified *personal psychological resources of parents, characteristics of child,* and *contextual sources of stress and support* as the three domains of the determinants of parenting)—a clear lack of such models. More readily available, however, are our grand theories of human functioning from which one might extrapolate implications for parental development, namely, psychodynamic,[2] behavioral,[3] and general structural-developmental[4] theories (cf. Jaffe, 1991).

PARENTS-IN-ENVIRONMENTS: HOLISTIC/SYSTEMS, DEVELOPMENTAL   APPROACH

In contrast to these theories, we (Wapner & Demick, 1990, in press a, b, c) have employed Werner's (1940/1957; Werner & Kaplan, 1963) definition of development inherent in the orthogenetic principle, namely, that the development of any given phenomenon proceeds from a dedifferentiated to a differentiated and hierarchically integrated organized state. In line with this, we have reframed the general problem of "parental development" as *developmental changes in adults' experience and action over the course of bearing and rearing children.* Such conceptualization has the potential to uncover a number of research problems heretofore unexplored (see Demick, 1993b, Demick & Wapner, 1991, and Wapner, 1993, for complete discussions).

Specifically, our approach is a direct extension and elaboration of Werner's (1940/1957) classic organismic-developmental theory, which generally emphasizes two perspectives in the analysis of human experience and action: *organismic* insofar as psychological part-processes (e.g., cognition, affect, valuation, behavior) must be considered in relation to the total context of human activity, people are directed toward ends, and they have access to alternative means to achieve these ends; and *developmental* in that it provides a systematic principle governing developmental progression (and regression) so that living systems may be compared with respect to formal, organizational characteristics. Each will be discussed in turn.

Organismic/Holistic Emphasis

We generally assume that the organism-in-environment system is the unit to be analyzed. This assumption stresses that every person is inextricably embedded in some environment. Our approach thereby adopts organismic and transactionalist perspectives (cf. Altman & Rogoff, 1987), which caution against analyzing persons and environments as separate entities; rather, such an approach treats the person's "behavings," including his most advanced "knowings," as activities not of himself alone but as processes of the full situation of organism-environment (Dewey & Bentley, 1949, p. 104).

Thus, we characteristically examine the transactions (experience and action) of person-in-environment systems. We assume that, in a holistic manner, the person's (here, the parent's) environment in such a system is comprised of mutually defining *physical* (e.g., home, work, child's school), *interpersonal* (e.g., family, coworkers, day-care provider, child's teachers/ friends/friends' parents), and *sociocultural* (e.g., household, work, school rules; community; society; sociohistorical context; cf. Sameroff, 1983) aspects. Analogously, the parent himself or herself is assumed holistically to encompass mutually defining *biological/physical* (e.g., health), *psychological/ intrapersonal* (e.g., body/self experience), and *sociocultural* (e.g., roles) aspects. These aspects of the person, in conjunction with the aspects of the environment, are assumed to constitute the parent-in-environment system.

Related to the assumption of the person-in-environment as the unit of analysis is our assumption concerning holism and levels of integration. Specifically, we assume that the person-in-environment system operates as a unified whole so that a disturbance in one part (physical, psychological, or sociocultural aspects of the person or of the environment) affects other parts and the totality. This holistic assumption holds for functioning not only among but also within levels of integration (see Wapner & Demick, 1990). For instance, on the psychological level, such part-processes as the *cognitive* aspects of experience and action (including, e.g., sensorimotor functioning, perceiving, thinking, symbolizing) as well as the *affective* (feeling) and *valuative* (prioritizing) aspects of experience and action operate contemporaneously and in an integrated manner in the normal adult.

Thus, from our elaborated perspective, a complete understanding of parents-in-environments would include consideration of a wide range of variables (listed in Table 11.1) and their interrelations. Some of the variables listed—most notably, sex differences in and contextual influences on aspects of parents' sociocultural functioning—have already received systematic attention in the literature to date. Others, however, still to be explored, have been identified through our holistic analysis. Further, those previously examined have typically been studied in isolation, rather than in relation to one another. To illustrate, we will discuss each variable in turn and conclude each section with some open empirical questions that consider some holistic relations among and within the different levels.

Table 11.1
Variables Relevant to the Study of Parents-in-Environments

Person (X Environment)	Environment (X Person)
Biological/Physical	Physical
Age	Environmental Objects (e.g.,
Sex	washing machine)*
Race*	Physical Locations*
Physical Health/Stress*	
Mode of Conception*	
Complications During Pregnancy or	
Delivery*	
Psychological/Intrapersonal	Interpersonal
Cognitive Processes	Children
Decision-making	Spouse (e.g., marital quality,
Plans and expectations*	stability)
Meaning-making*	Family of Origin
Cognitive style*	Extended Family
Affective Processes	Friends
Motivation for parenthood	Coworkers
Personality*	Day-care Provider(s)*
Mental health/stress*	Child's Teachers*
Valuative Processes	Neighbors*
General values (e.g., family vs.	General Public
career; self vs. other)*	Other Social Support Networks
Life satisfaction	
Sociocultural	Sociocultural
Socioeconomic Status (e.g., cost of	Family Developmental Tasks
children)*	Family History/Themes
Religion*	Community*
Politics*	Society (e.g., media)
Parental Role*	Legal*
Spousal Role	Educational*
Work Role	Sociohistorical Context
Gender Role	
Leisure Roles*	

*Not examined extensively in previous research

Aspects of parents: Physical/biological. Here we have included such variables as *age, sex, race, physical health/stress, mode of conception,* and *complications during pregnancy/ delivery. Age* has been relevant insofar as: there are biological considerations as to the optimal timing of pregnancy and childbearing; there may be differences in the experience of parenthood related to the parents' age (i.e., between younger vs. older parents); and there may be differences in the experience of parenthood related to whether the child is first- or latter-born (e.g., Mercer, 1986; Michaels & Goldberg, 1988).

Sex of parent has also been included as a relevant variable. Much research has demonstrated gender differences in parent-child play during both infancy (e.g., Easterbrooks & Goldberg, 1984) and the preschool years (e.g., MacDonald & Parke, 1986), with fathers' play more noisy and idiosyncratic than mothers'. Further, a growing body of literature (e.g., Belsky & Pensky, 1988) has highlighted the notions that males and females may react differentially and at different points in time to the ongoing stresses associated with first time parenthood. However, research on sex differences in later stages of parenting has been significantly less common. Analogously, one might also include *race* as a relevant variable for study here since research (e.g., Broman, 1991) has only recently begun to explore the behavior and experience of parents in other than white middle-class families.

Physical health/stress has also been included since research (e.g., Leifer, 1980) has provided evidence that pregnancy is generally perceived by expectant mothers as physically stressful. Among other things, many couples become pregnant unintentionally, husbands and wives do not always agree on the pregnancy (Cowan & Cowan, 1992), and planned children may not always arrive on schedule. Further, we have listed *mode of conception* since recent evidence (see Goldberg, 1988) documenting a rise in alternative forms of parenthood (e.g., *in vitro* fertilization, surrogate motherhood, adoption) has suggested the possibility of differential parental experience and action in such cases. Finally, we have also included *complications during pregnancy/delivery* as a moderator variable since the presence of such has been shown to impact mothers' experience of the birth process and/or baby (e.g., Leifer, 1980).

Though the majority of these studies has examined one or more of these variables in isolation, our holistic perspective leads to such questions as: What are the relationships among parents' age, sex, race, and/or general health status and their experience of the different stages of parenting? How does the relationship between parents' biological (e.g., sleep patterns, energy levels) and psychological functioning change over the course of parenthood? What impact do complications during pregnancy and/or delivery have on mothers', fathers', and children's subsequent functioning? What impact do technological advances (e.g., *in vitro* fertilization) have on mothers', fathers', and children's subsequent functioning? What are the similarities and differences among the experience and action of families generated through different modes of conception? How do all these relationships remain stable or change over the course of parenthood?

Aspects of adults: Psychological/intrapersonal. Here we include both body (e.g., feeling that one's body is inadequate) and self (e.g., self-esteem) experience. To date, the majority of literature has examined these variables in mothers (e.g., Mercer, 1986). Aspects of parents' experience treated in the literature may be divided into those examining *cognitive* (knowing), *affective* (feeling), or *valuative* (prioritizing) processes. Of these, the cognitive processes of parents have received the most attention. For example, researchers (e.g., Hoffman & Hoffman,

1973) have posited cognitive-valuative models of decision-making involved in becoming parents. Less extensive has been research on parents' expectations and plans for both their children and themselves (cf. Palkovitz & Copes, 1988) as well as on parents' life stories and processes of meaning-making (cf. Bruner, 1990; Kegan, 1982) over the never-ending course of parental development.

Affective processes as they relate to parental development have received some consideration in the literature, most notably around the transition to parenthood (cf. LeMasters, 1959, on parenthood as crisis). For example, Sirignano and Lachman (1985) have examined the effects of parents' perceptions of infant temperament on personality change pre- and post-partum; they found that new parents who perceived their infants as having an easier temperament experienced more positive change, while new parents who perceived their infants as more difficult experienced more negative change in personal control. While this study is holistic insofar as it relates cognitive and affective variables in parents, there is still the need to assess such relationships over the course of parental development. Further, studies employing parents' general personality traits as well as their mental health and stress (e.g., daily hassles and uplifts) over the course of parental development are almost nonexistent.

Research on adults' valuative processes over the course of parental development has been minimal. With the exception of work by, for example, Hoffman and Hoffman (1973) and more recently by Quirk, Sexton, Ciottone, Minami, and Wapner (1984) and Quirk and colleagues (1986), few investigators have attempted to delineate the values held by parents not only as such values enter into decisions about having children, but also as they potentially affect life satisfaction over the course of parental development.

Our approach would then suggest the following types of questions: What are some relations between prior knowledge of parenting demands and feelings about becoming and/or being a parent? What is the interplay between such variables and parental motivations for having children? What are some relations between body and self experience of mothers versus fathers across the different stages of parenting? Given our interest in individual differences (Wapner & Demick, 1991b), do field dependent and independent parents differ with respect to how they experience and act on parenting issues? What are some relations among parents' cognitive, affective, and valuative functioning over the course of parental development? What roles do planning/values play in parental development? Most generally, how do parents' specific experiences become translated into action (Demick & Wapner, 1991)?

Aspects of adults: Sociocultural. Here we have included the related variables of *parental role, spousal role, work role,* and *gender role.* As noted previously, family life cycle theorists have focused primarily on changes in parental role over the course of family development. Related to women's entry into the work force, more recent interest has revolved around the ways in which parents (primarily mothers) negotiate their parental, spousal, and work roles with the majority of studies (e.g.,

Barnett & Baruch, 1985; Verbrugge, 1983) documenting that those who combine all three roles are happier and healthier than those who do not. Further, Feldman, Biringen, and Nash (1981) have reported that adults adhere more closely to traditional gender roles when their children are young than at any other time in the life span. Still lacking, however, has been consideration of the ways in which other adult roles (e.g., in *leisure, religion, politics*) enter into the equation. We are also lacking information on the ways in which *socioeconomic status* (e.g., Streib, 1985) impacts parents' experience and action across stages of parenting.

Thus, we find the following questions among those worthy of empirical investigation: How does the adult integrate his or her various roles of parent, spouse, worker, leisurite, church member, and so forth? Are there individual differences (e.g., gender roles, socioeconomic status) in the ways in which parents negotiate these various roles? Are there similarities and/or differences in the negotiation of these roles over the course of parental development? Do gender roles change as a function of parenthood and/or do they remain stable over the course of parental development?

Aspects of environment: Physical. It may not be surprising that the physical aspect of parents' environments (*environmental objects, locations*) has received the least attention. Perhaps indirectly, studies of parenthood and employment (e.g., Brayfield, 1992) have demonstrated that, even when they work more hours outside the home, wives do significantly more housework than husbands. We (Demick & Wapner, 1988) have reported that couples practicing open adoption (some form of communication between adoptive and biological parents) may become hypervigilant to their physical surrounds (e.g., aware of possible contact). This heightened sense of vigilance toward the physical aspect of the environment was also manifest in biological parents' projective drawings prior to and following the transition to parenthood (Coltrera, 1978).

We would, thus, also be interested in the following questions: How are the ways in which parents deal with the organization of their child's physical space (e.g., bedroom) prior to and following the actual birth related to their thoughts/feelings about the transition? How do couples negotiate transactions with the physical environment (e.g., transporting of children, household chores) over the course of parental development? Do parents relate differently to the physical environment (e.g., relaxing in one's favorite chair; stopping of physical activity such as jogging; heightened appreciation of nature) at various stages of parenting? How is parents' actual location (e.g., distance between home, work, day-care) related to the functioning of all family members?

Aspects of environments: Interpersonal. Here we have included members of parents' various social support networks (e.g., *extended family, friends, coworkers, day-care provider, neighbors, teachers*), since numerous studies have shown that parenthood has the potential to affect: marital quality and/or stability particularly around the transition to parenthood (e.g., Lewis & Spanier, 1979), relationships with family of origin (e.g., Gurwitt, 1976, has speculated that the transition to parenthood may lead to a reevaluation of one's own parental relationships, particularly for men, and Troll, 1986, has referred to contemporary parents who care for their own children and their aging parents as the "sandwich generation"); and relationships with others (e.g., in our recent volume on parental development, Solomon, 1993, has identified two types of networks: one termed *affiliative*, in which mothers who associate primarily with kin maximize child behaviors oriented toward the development of sociability and compliance, and a second termed *autonomous*, in which mothers who associate with nonkin maximize child behaviors that exhibit self-reliance and social independence; within the general public, Taylor & Langer, 1977, have found an avoidance of pregnant women, particularly by men). There has been little systematic research, however, on the ways in which particular support networks (e.g., coworkers, day-care providers) aid in the development of parents at various stages of parenting.

There have been other strands of research concerning transactions with members of the interpersonal environment that may be relevant to parental development. First, parallel research on children (see Harkins, 1993, our volume) has demonstrated, from a Vygotskian (1978) perspective, that psychological processes do not develop from within but rather through the person's active relationship with the environment. Future research might consider the ways in which others structure parents' experience (e.g., child rearing advice from an older sibling or parent) leading toward development. Second, given Galinsky's (1981, p. 317) notion that caring for infants is transforming insofar as "we lose our sense of self, only to find it and have it change again and again," experimental demonstrations of self-other differentiation (e.g., see Demick & Wapner, 1980, on interpersonal distance and Porzemsky, Wapner, & Glick, 1965, on experimentally induced self-object cognitive attitudes) over the course of parental development are intriguing.

Thus, we are most interested in the following types of questions: What are the similarities and differences in the roles of maternal versus paternal grandparents? What role does the quality of one's relationship with one's day-care provider play in the psychological functioning of mothers? Of fathers? Of the marital relationship? Can coworkers function as members of social support networks? How do parents' relationships with employers impact relationships with day-care providers? Does the role of neighbors change as a function of becoming a parent? How do transactions with teachers affect parents' sense of self and other over the course of parental development? What are the nature of the relationships among the network members of mothers versus fathers? Does the general public still display an avoidance of pregnant women and/or parents with children? What are the ways in which others structure parents' experience that lead to parental development? Which experimental measures of self-other differentiation might be employed over the course of parenthood?

Aspects of environments: Sociocultural. Here we have included aspects of the sociocultural environment such as *community, society, legal, educational,* and *sociohistorical context.* For example, researchers (e.g., Leifer, 1980) have documented that prospective parents often have unrealistic expectations about parenthood, which are directly related to media portrayals. Given the recent change in demographic characteristics of families (with traditional nuclear families being replaced by other types of families including one-parent, childless, blended, adoptive, foster, and dual career families), the sociohistorical context also needs to be taken into account. Within the family itself, aspects of the sociocultural environment receiving attention have included *family developmental tasks* (e.g., Aldous, 1978) and *family history/themes* (e.g., Alpert & Richardson, 1980).

From our point of view, we would be most interested in the following types of questions: What processes underlie current societal attitudes toward various family structures? How do societal, community, and institutional beliefs about parenting and/or parental development impact parents and their children? How do these beliefs change at the various stages of parenting? Are there individual differences in the ways in which parents deal with family developmental tasks and/or family history?

Developmental Emphasis

Our view of development transcends the boundaries within which the concept of development is ordinarily applied. For most psychologists, development is limited to ontogenesis. In contrast, we assume that "Wherever there is life, there is growth and systematic orderly sequence" (Werner, 1940/ 1957, p. 125). Thus, we are concerned with both processes of formation (e.g., social network development over the course of parenthood) and of dissolution (e.g., changes in experience/action following the last child's leaving home) as parents negotiate maximally optimal relationships with their environments.

Components (person, environment), relations among components (e.g., means-ends), and part-processes (cognition, affect, valuation) of person-in-environment systems are assumed developmentally orderable in terms of the orthogenetic principle. This principle defines development with respect to the degree of organization attained by a system. The more differentiated and hierarchically integrated a system is, in terms of its parts and of its means and ends, the more highly developed it is said to be. Thus, we assume that optimal development involves a differentiated and hierarchically integrated person-in-environment system characterized by flexibility, freedom, and self-mastery (e.g., Wapner, 1987; Wapner & Demick, 1990, 1991a).

In line with these teleological notions (cf. Langer et al., 1990, who favor nonsequential models of adult development), we have described four self-world relationships ranging from a lesser to a more advanced developmental status. While these relationships have been applied to a variety of contexts (e.g., see Pacheco, Lucca, & Wapner, 1985, on application of these relationships to the acculturation of the Puerto Rican migrant to the United States), they are discussed here in the context of a problem with relevance for parental development, namely, the family systems of those practicing open versus closed adoption (communication versus no communication between biological and adoptive parents).

More specifically, adoptive families characterized by a total separation between the adopted child and his or her family of origin—as is usually the case in traditional, closed adoption—may be conceptualized as *dedifferentiated* (all family members consciously or unconsciously deny that the child has been adopted), *differentiated and isolated* (adoptive parents shelter the adoptee so that he or she will not learn about the biological parents from others and/or will not have to deal with the stigma of being adopted), or *differentiated and in conflict* (the adoptee may fantasize that the biological parents would treat him or her differently and/or may threaten to leave the adoptive family to find the "real parents" when of age). In contrast, the adoptive family, characterized by less absolute separation between the adoptee and his or her family of origin (open adoption) may be conceptualized as *differentiated and integrated* (the adoptee may be able to integrate the various aspects of his or her dual identities, possibly mitigating potential problems with identity and self-esteem. In a similar manner, the adoptive parents may be able to integrate the different aspects of the adoptee's identity so as to avoid blaming 'bad blood in the background' for any difficulties). In this way, relative to those families practicing traditional, closed adoption, those practicing open adoption may be more developmentally advanced insofar as (a) the structure of the family system may be better integrated and (b) the identities of the biological and adoptive families may be better integrated within the adoptee (Demick & Wapner, 1988).

From our point of view, developmental conceptualization of this sort might also be used to understand relations among psychological part-processes (cognition, affect, valuation, action) as well as structural relations among individuals' multiple worlds across the different stages of parenting. Such conceptualization also has potential applicability to other aspects of parenting receiving attention in the mainstream literature. For example, a developmental analysis of self-world relationships may shed light on the processes underlying attachment (cf. Bretherton, Biringen, & Ridgeway, 1991), cognitive development (cf. Vygotsky, 1978), the ecology of development (cf. Bronfenbrenner, 1979), atypical development (cf. Achenbach, 1982), parent-child relations during adolescence (cf. Steinberg, 1981), and so on.

METHODOLOGICAL   CONSIDERATIONS

Psychologists are involved in an ongoing controversy over whether the field of psychology should adhere to a "natural science" perspective (controlled experimentation and quantitative analysis, after Wundt, 1912) or a "human science" perspective (phenomenological methods and qualitative analysis, after Giorgi, 1975). While some might argue that a paradigm shift is well underway, our holistic/systems, developmental approach would advocate that both models have a place in psychological science. For us, choice of method depends in part on the level of integration to which the research question is addressed. For example, if we were concerned about describing and understanding (e.g., the sociocultural roles of parent and worker), we might opt to employ the phenomenological method. Alternatively, if we were interested in predicting (e.g., satisfaction as a parent), we might instead choose an experimental/quasi-experimental method. Within the experimental method, we would argue for the necessary complementarity of cross-sectional and longitudinal designs to understand developmental change (Wapner, 1987).

In line with our foci, we have suggested elsewhere that advances in holistic conceptualization might be obtained from the development of systematic, holistic constructs accounting for relations between and among levels of integration. With respect to the problem at hand, we would be most interested in such questions as: What are the mechanisms that underlie the ways in which phenomena at the sociocultural level (e.g., societal expectations of parents) become translated into individual functioning at the psychological level (e.g., parents' performance and self-esteem)? Conversely, how does the need for the quality of human functioning at the psychological level (e.g., the parent's energy level and/or self-concept) become actualized at the sociocultural level (e.g., through formalized parent support groups)?

Some beginning attempts to develop systematic, holistic constructs that account for the relations between/among aspects of persons and aspects of environments have been based on Wapner's (1969) earlier conceptualization of the relations among cognitive processes (sensorimotor action, perception, conception). For example, relations between cognitive operations may be *vicarious* (where use of one operation substitutes for use of another), *supportive* (where simultaneously occurring cognitive operations facilitate one another, making for greater efficiency in achievement of ends), *antagonistic* (where the operation of one function lessens the operation of another), and *correspondent* (where one level of functioning parallels another).

With respect to parents-in-environments, this conceptualization may be equally applicable. For instance, the relations between the psychological aspect of the first time mother and the interpersonal aspect of her environment *may be supportive* (e.g., the day-care provider supports the mother's decision to return to work full time when the infant is two weeks old), *antagonistic* (both the father and provider think the infant too young for full-time day-care), *substitutive/vicarious* (e.g., father and provider substitute mother's desires for their own), or *correspondent* (mother's wishes coincide with those of father and provider). Toward further illustrating some ways in which our approach frames problems on parental development, a synopsis of ongoing work in the area of parental adaptation to adoption follows.

Adaptation of Marital Couples to Open Versus Closed Adoption

Empirical research assessing the impact of open versus closed adoption on individuals' experience and adaptation has been relatively sparse. Research on traditional, closed adoption has employed either limited objective measures (e.g., quantitative questionnaire responses) or equally limited subjective measures (e.g., qualitative interview responses). This has led to perpetuation of the view that adoption is generally a monolithic event affecting all system members in precisely the same, negative ways. In contrast, it is our view—in line with our holistic emphasis—that, through the merger of both quantitative and qualitative methods, the study of individuals' overall experience pre- and post-adoption (differing with respect to whether the process is open or closed) will uncover data on the diversity of modes of experiencing and adapting to adoption. Further, studies employing families that differ with respect to the way(s) in which children have been acquired (e.g., normal biological conception and birth, complicated pregnancy and delivery, *in vitro* fertilization, surrogate motherhood, various forms of adoption) are expected to sharpen our understanding of normal processes underlying both individual and family development. We believe that both direct and indirect influences on parental development may be identified using longitudinal designs with frequent assessments. Toward identifying aspects of stability and change, we also believe that data obtained here should be compared to those obtained over the course of other person-in-environment transitions.

Armed with the hypothesis that, relative to families practicing closed adoption, those practicing open adoption would be more developmentally advanced (see previous conceptualization), we employed a variety of instruments proven fruitful in other investigations (e.g., Demick & Wapner, 1980). These instruments were chosen to sample, in a holistic manner, a range of factors indicative of developmental maturity including: general adjustment (e.g., self-esteem, life satisfaction), quality of life (e.g., perceptions of control and of stress), and potential moderator variables important in the adaptation process. Moderator variables included those relevant to the individual psychology of the parent (e.g., stress of parenting, acknowledgment of the difference between biological and adoptive parenting) and those related to the general functioning of the family as a whole (e.g., family environment variables, social interactions). An interview was also designed to assess experiential aspects of the adaptation process, which was then used to augment our understanding of the quantitative questionnaire data.

DISCUSSION OF RESULTS

In a pilot study (Demick, 1993a), both husbands and wives (15 sets under closed and 15 under open adoption; N = 60) completed the instruments within one year of adopting a healthy infant. Major analyses did not support that one form of adoption was overridingly any better or worse than the other (e.g., life satisfaction, perception of stress, and perception of control did not differ between the groups). However, the data did reveal that: (a) open adoption may help adoptive parents avoid *some* of the feelings typically associated with closed adoption (e.g., relative to those practicing closed adoption, those practicing open adoption reported less worry about attachment to their infant on Abidin's, 1983, Parenting Stress Index), and (b) there may be a selection effect for who chooses which form of adoption. On Moos and Moos', 1986, Family Environment Scale, those under open adoption reported more intellectual-cultural, and less moral-religious, emphases within the family than did those under closed adoption. These findings were corroborated by qualitative interview data.

Theoretically, although our initial findings from the early stages of the adaptation process have revealed only minor differences between the two types of adoptive families, the possibility exists that our developmental conceptualization of family processes may be more appropriate for later points in adoptive parents' development. Such a possibility is worthy of further empirical inquiry. Methodologically, the study has also suggested that future research on adaptation to adoption should routinely combine measures of individual, couple, and familial functioning. Had we limited our assessment of family functioning to only dyadic measures (i.e., parent-child or husband-wife), we would not have uncovered certain moderator variables relevant to the adaptation process. Thus, in line with our previous research (e.g., Dandonoli, Demick, & Wapner, 1990; Demick, Hoffman, & Wapner, 1985; Wapner, Demick, & Redondo, 1990), this study has reinforced the notion that a fuller picture of experience and adaptation emerges when multiple measures are employed.

Further, since our commitment to holism and to development most broadly defined is pervasive, we advocate that holistically oriented research should be conducted through reducing the number of focal families studied, rather than the number and kinds of interrelationships among aspects of family members, of the environments, and of the systems to which they belong. In addition to helping us characterize problems more in line with the complex character of everyday life, such reframing may help psychology both to see itself and to be seen by others as a unified science, that is, one concerned not only with the study of isolated aspects of human functioning, but also of problems that cut across various aspects of persons and of environments.

PRACTICAL CONSIDERATIONS

As described elsewhere (Demick, 1993b; Demick & Miller, 1993), our approach has been wedded to the notion that the distinction between basic (knowledge generating) and applied (immediate problem solving) research is an artificial one. Since theory and praxis may be seen as flip sides of the same coin, this focus has figured prominently in both Werner's original approach and in our recent elaboration (e.g., see Demick, 1993a, for discussion of the practical/legal implications of adoption research). Thus, what recommendations does such a position have for the area of parental development?

First and foremost, we would agree with previous investigators (e.g., Alpert & Richardson, 1990) that there is a distinction between the popular literature that generally focuses on the "how to" of parenting (e.g., volumes with titles such as *Preparation for Parenthood* and magazines such as *Child*, *Parent*, and *Parenting*) and attempts at intervention that are based on empirically sound research programs. For example, Azar's (1989) systematic research on cognitive errors in the thought processes of mothers who abuse their children has already been translated into specific training programs for parents. Further, although a conjoint focus on theory and practice has arguably been somewhat lacking in the field of developmental psychology, family support, education, and training programs—that teach parents well-founded psychological principles of learning, behavior modification, communication, and problem solving—are becoming increasing more available (e.g., see Gordon, 1970, and Schaefer & Millman, 1981).

For us, recommendations for the design of parent programs proceed directly from our theoretical approach and, in particular, from our holistic unit of analysis. Thus, specific recommendations would encompass all those influences on the parent-in-environment system that touch on the biological, psychological, and sociocultural levels of integration. These recommendations would include (but are by no means limited to) consideration of: the physical/ biological aspect of the parent (e.g., programs for younger versus older parents; programs for alternative forms of parenthood), the psychological/intrapersonal aspect of the parent (e.g., assessment of the interrelations among cognitive, affective, and valuative processes over the course of parental development), the sociocultural aspect of the parent (e.g., role combination/status as impacting other parts of the system), the physical aspect of the environment (e.g., negotiation of household chores/transportation of children); the interpersonal aspect of the environment (e.g., support services for children and grandparents as well as for parents), and the sociocultural aspect of the environment (e.g., neighborhood security, educational access).

Finally, toward demonstrating the conjoint focus on theory and practice within our approach, the interested reader is referred to our (Demick et al., 1993) recent volume on parental development and, in particular, to Demick (1993b). Here, attempts were made to have each contributing author delineate the practical implications of his or her empirical research for the development of parents in everyday life. Suggestions have included: identification of parental expectations in storytelling, routine moral dilemma discussion between parents and children, active reflection on family narratives and sources of social support, and educational and/or therapeutic interventions aimed at increasing parental empathy. Most interesting, however, was Miller's (1993) comparison of the behavior of mothers and strangers in an everyday life situation (i.e., an initial babysitting encounter). Although Anglo North American lore has suggested that strangers behave very differently than mothers, the strangers and mothers employed in her study, for the most part, behaved similarly except that strangers overstimulated less and consoled more. She has concluded her chapter with a provocative discussion concerning the feasibility, or lack thereof, of teaching others (particularly parents) to care for infants (cf. Spock, 1977). Such research has highlighted the need for future study on the many factors involved in the development of parents as they attempt to negotiate optimal relationships with their children in the real world.

NOTES

1. The earliest of such volumes was Anthony and Benedek's (1970) *Parenthood: Its Psychology and Psychopathology.* While a number of the psychoanalytically oriented authors contained therein examined parental functioning at various periods in the child's development (infancy through adolescence), their unit of analysis was the family system and not the developing parent per se. That is, echoing Benedek's (1959) earlier article on parenthood as a developmental phase, these authors generally characterized parenthood in terms of a set of familial processes that regularly occurs over the course of the child's development.

2. Classic Freudian (1935) theory, which has employed the developing child/adolescent with his or her sexual and aggressive impulses as the unit of analysis, has several major implications for the study of parental development. First, according to Freud, the signpost of a developmentally mature individual (i.e., one who has successfully negotiated the psychosexual stages of development) is one who "love wells and works well" (telos of development). Though Freud did not proscribe specific criteria for the fulfillment of these needs, one might speculate that the experience of parenthood serves as one means of reaching developmental maturity (cf. Erikson's, 1950, neopsychodynamic reformulation of Freud's stages to include the adult stages of intimacy versus isolation and of generativity versus stagnation, which support the Freudian notion that one expression of the ability to give of oneself to another person is through the parent-child relationship). Second, by postulating a direct relationship between childhood experience and adult psychopathology, Freud's work might also be construed as lending direction to parental behavior, particularly with respect to the need for empathic understanding of children and consideration of the role of gratification in child behavior. Further, Erikson's psychosocial reformulation has more directly implicated the role of parenting in the development of both children and parents. For children, quality of parenting (sensitivity, consistency) has been related to successful resolution of early stages; for older adults, positive evaluation of one's life has been related, at least in part, to satisfaction with the rearing of one's children.

More recent extensions of psychoanalytic notions have adopted both person- and systems-oriented approaches to parenting and/or to parental development. Examples of person-oriented approaches have included: Levinson's (1978) and Palus' (1993) notion of life crises and transformative experiences, respectively; and Miliora's (1993) application of Kohut's (1977) self psychological theory to parental development (suggesting that parents' early childhood experiences feeling understood/validated or "mirrored" at least partly determine their empathic functioning vis-à-vis their own children). Examples of systems-oriented approaches have included: Aldous' (1978) notion of family developmental tasks (i.e., familial tasks—such as the physical maintenance and socialization of family members—that meet the developing needs of both the individual and the society); and most of the contributions in the aforementioned Anthony and Benedek (1970) volume, which have conceptualized the family, at all stages of the child's development, as "a field of transactional processes . . . based on the proposition that the parents' drive motivated, emotional investment in the child brings about reciprocal intrapsychic processes in the parents, which normally account for changes in their personalities" (Benedek, 1970, p. 124).

On the most general level, psychoanalytically informed theories have addressed the roles of the child, the parent, and/or the family system in the development of parents. While these theories have made inroads into the general problem area by focusing on isolated variables important in the process, our understanding of parental development in all of its real world complexity might be augmented by complementing these theories with those that attempt more holistic and integrative formulations and analyses.

3. Behavioral theories, too, have implications for parental development. By far the most well-known, Skinner's (1953) operant conditioning and Bandura's (1977) social-cognitive variants have together highlighted for parents the roles of rewards, punishments, and modeling as important mechanisms in the socialization of children. These theories have further suggested that effective parenting requires conscious awareness of the ways in which parental behavior affects child behavior so as to avoid unintentionally reinforcing a child's negative behavior. Again, by emphasizing the environment and/or the internal representation of the environment (e.g., cognitive beliefs and expectations) as direct influences on behavior, these theories have had profound influence on practical parenting programs, but might be advanced even further through consideration of more holistic and developmental concepts that attempt to account for relations among variables.

4. Similar to psychoanalytically informed theories, both person- and systems-oriented approaches to general structural-developmental theory (cf. Kohlberg, 1969; Piaget, 1967) may help to elaborate the processes and mechanisms underlying parenting and/or parental development. Of the two approaches, systems-oriented ones have been the more common. That is, investigators (e.g., Aldous, 1978; Duvall, 1977) have applied structural-developmental principles to the family by conceptualizing stages of family life as structurally and qualitatively distinct with unique developmental issues (usually revolving around the developmental status of the child). With a specific focus on parenthood, Galinsky (1981) has identified six stages of parenting that include the stages of: *image-making* (making changes in sense of self and others while preparing for birth and parenthood), *nurturing* (changing priorities while caring for infant); *authority* (dealing with issues of power with preschooler), *interpretive* (interpreting the world for school-aged child), *interdependent* (dealing with authority and communication issues with adolescent), and *departure* (accepting one's adult child as separate).

While such theories have been important insofar as they have highlighted the transactional nature of the parent-child relationship (whereby children and parents mutually define and change one another), Alpert and Richardson (1980) have criticized such theories on the following grounds: (1) they have tended to represent general principles with little empirical support, (2) they have been more useful for descriptive rather than for explanatory purposes, (3) they have implied that development is linear rather than potentially regressive and/or spiral, and (4) they have failed to account for individual differences in family structures (i.e., presupposing an intact nuclear family rather than the diversity now found in family structure).

An example of a structural-developmental theory applied to individuals rather than to family systems has recently appeared in our (Demick et al., 1993) volume on parental development. Employing Kohlberg's (1969) theory of moral development, Lam, Powers, Noam, Hauser, and Jacobson (1993) have provided limited data that adolescents' moral development may be facilitated through interaction with two parents who themselves are at dissimilar stages of moral development. Focusing on parents, they have also posed the empirical question of whether parents (regardless of their levels of moral reasoning) might be taught (either individually or in combination) to gear moral discussions with their children toward enhancing both their own and their children's perspectives. Further, together with other articles in the volume, this work has extended the common themes that: (a) parenthood is inseparable from other areas of adult life; and (b) aspects of parenthood, like life in general, may be characterized by structural development across the life span. Again, while making inroads into the general problem area of parental development, such studies might be complemented by those that incorporate more broadly defined notions of holism, of development, of the person, and of the environment.

REFERENCES

Abidin, R. R. (1983). *Parenting stress index manual.* Charlottesville, VA: Pediatric Psychology Press.

Achenbach, T. M. (1982). *Developmental psychopathology* (2nd ed.). New York: Wiley.

Aldous, J. (1978). *Family careers: Developmental change in families.* New York: Wiley.

Alpert, J. L., & Richardson, M. S. (1980). Parenting. In L. W. Poon (Ed.), *Aging in the 1980s: Psychological issues* (pp. 441-54). Washington, DC:American Psychological Association Press.

Altman, I., & Rogoff, B. (1987). World views in psychology: Trait, interactional, organismic, and transactional perspectives. In I. Altman & D. Stokols (Eds.), *Handbook of environmental psychology* (Vol. 1, pp. 7-40). New York: Wiley.

Ambert, A. (1992). *The effect of children on parents.* Binghamton, NY: Haworth Press.

Anthony, E. J., & Benedek, T. (Eds.). (1970). *Parenthood: Its psychology and psychopathology* (pp. 275-88). Boston: Little, Brown.

Azar, S. (1989). Training parents of abused children. In C. E. Schaefer & J. M. Briesmeister (Eds.), *Handbook of parent training: Parents as co-therapists for children's behavior problems* (pp. 414-41). New York: Wiley.

Baltes, P. B., & Schaie, K. W. (Eds.). (1973). *Life-span developmental psychology: Personality and socialization.* New York: Academic Press.

Bandura, A. (1977). *Social learning theory.* Englewood Cliffs, NJ: Prentice-Hall.

Barnett, R. C., & Baruch, G. K. (1985). Women's involvement in multiple roles and psychological distress. *Journal of Personality and Social Psychology, 49,* 135-45.

Baumrind, D. (1967). Child care practices anteceding three patterns of preschool behavior. *Genetic Psychology Monographs, 75,* 43-88.

Belsky, J. (1984). The determinants of parenting: A process model. *Child Development, 55,* 83-96.

Belsky, J., & Pensky, E. (1988). Marital change across the transition to parenthood. *Marriage and Family Review, 12,* 133-56.

Benedek, T. (1959). Parenthood as a developmental phase: A contribution to the libido theory. *Journal of the American Psychoanalytic Association, 7,* 389-417.

Benedek, T. (1970). The family as a psychological field. In E. J. Anthony & T. Benedek (Eds.), *Parenthood: Its psychology and psychopathology* (pp. 109-36). Boston: Little, Brown.

Berger, K. S. (1994). *The developing person through the life span* (3rd ed.). New York: Worth.

Brayfield, A. A. (1992). Employment resources and housework in Canada. *Journal of Marriage and the Family, 54*, 19-30.

Bretherton, I., Biringen, Z., & Ridgeway, D. (1991). The parental side of attachment. In K. Pillemer & K. McCartney (Eds.), *Parent-child relations throughout life* (pp. 1-24). Hillsdale, NJ: Erlbaum.

Brim, O. G. (1966). Socialization through the life cycle. In O. G. Brim & S. Wheeler (Eds.), *Socialization after childhood: Two essays.* New York: Wiley.

Broman, C. L. (1991). Gender, work-family roles, and psychological well-being of blacks. *Journal of Marriage and the Family, 53*, 509-20.

Bronfenbrenner, U. (1979). *The ecology of human development: Experiments by nature and design.* Cambridge, MA: Harvard University Press.

Bruner, J. (1990). *Acts of meaning.* Cambridge, MA: Harvard University Press.

Coltrera, D. (1978). *Experiential aspects of the transition to parenthood.* Unpublished master's proposal, Clark University, Worcester, MA.

Cowan, C. P., & Cowan, P. A. (1992). *When partners become parents.* New York: Basic Books.

Cowan, P. A., & Hetherington, M. (Eds.). (1991). *Family transitions.* Hillsdale, NJ: Erlbaum.

Dandonoli, P., Demick, J., & Wapner, S. (1990). Physical arrangement and age as determinants of environmental representation. *Children's Environments Quarterly, 2*, 44-54.

Demick, J. (1993a). Adaptation of marital couples to open versus closed adoption: A preliminary investigation. In J. Demick, K. Bursik, & R. DiBiase (Eds.), *Parental development* (pp. 175-201). Hillsdale, NJ: Erlbaum.

Demick, J. (1993b). Parental development: Future research directions. In J. Demick, K. Bursik, & R. DiBiase (Eds.), *Parental development* (pp. 243-70). Hillsdale, NJ: Erlbaum.

Demick, J. (1994). Editor's note: The parameters of adult development. *Journal of Adult Development, 1*, 1-5.

Demick, J. (1996). Life transitions as a paradigm for the study of adult development. In M. L. Commons, J. Demick, & C. Goldberg (Eds.), *Clinical approaches to adult development* (pp. 115-44). Norwood, NJ: Ablex.

Demick, J., Bursik, K., & DiBiase, R. (Eds.). (1993). *Parental development.* Hillsdale, NJ: Erlbaum.

Demick, J., Hoffman, A., & Wapner, S. (1985). Residential context and environmental change as determinants of urban experience. *Children's Environments Quarterly, 2*, 44-54.

Demick, J., & Miller, P. M. (1993). Some open research problems on development in the workplace: Theory and methodology. In J. Demick & P. M. Miller (Eds.), *Development in the workplace* (pp. 221-40). Hillsdale, NJ: Erlbaum.

Demick, J., & Wapner, S. (1980). Effects of environmental relocation on members of a psychiatric therapeutic community. *Journal of Abnormal Psychology, 89*, 444-52.

Demick, J., & Wapner, S. (1988). Open and closed adoption: A developmental conceptualization. *Family Process, 27*, 229-49.

Demick, J., & Wapner, S. (1991). Transition to parenthood: Developmental changes in experience and action. In T. Yamamoto & S. Wapner (Eds.), *A developmental psychology of life transitions (pp. 243-65). Tokyo: Kyodo Shuppan.

Dewey, J., & Bentley, A. F. (1949). Knowing and the known. Boston, MA: Beacon.

Duvall, E. M. (1977). Marriage and family development (5th ed.). Philadelphia: Lippincott.

Easterbrooks, M. A., & Goldberg, W. A. (1984). Toddler development in the family: Impact of father involvement and parenting characteristics. Child Development, 60, 825-30.

Erikson, E. H. (1950). Childhood and society. New York: Norton.

Feldman, S. S., Biringen, Z. C., & Nash, S. C. (1981). Fluctuations of sex-related self-attributions as a function of stage of family life cycle. Developmental Psychology, 17, 24-35.

Flavell, J. H. (1970). Cognitive changes in adulthood. In L. R. Goulet & P. B. Baltes (Eds.), Life-span developmental psychology: Research and theory. New York: Academic Press.

Freud, S. (1935). A general introduction to psychoanalysis (Joan Riviare, Trans.). New York: Modern Library.

Galinsky, E. (1981). Between generations: The six stages of parenthood. New York: Berkeley.

Giorgi, A. (1975). Convergence and divergence in qualitative and quantitative methods in psychology. In A. Giorgi, W. F. Fischer, & R. von Eckartsberg (Eds.), Duquesne studies in phenomenological psychology (Vol. 2, pp. 72-79). Pittsburgh, PA: Duquesne University Press.

Goldberg, W. A. (1988). Introduction: Perspectives on the transition to parenthood. In G. Y. Michaels & W. A. Goldberg (Eds.), The transition to parenthood: Current theory and research. New York: Cambridge University Press.

Gordon, T. (1970). Parent effectiveness training. New York: Wyden.

Gurwitt, A. (1976). Aspects of prospective fatherhood: A case report. Psychoanalytic Study of the Child, 31, 237-71.

Harkins, D. A. (1993). Parental goals and styles of storytelling. In J. Demick, K. Bursik, & R. DiBiase (Eds.), Parental development (pp. 61-74). Hillsdale, NJ: Erlbaum.

Hill, R., & Mattessich, P. (1979). Family development theory and life-span development. In P. B. Baltes & O. G. Brim (Eds.), Life-span development and behavior (Vol. 2). New York: Academic Press.

Hoffman, L. W., & Hoffman, M. L. (1973). The value of children to parents. In J. T. Fawcett (Ed.), Psychological perspectives on population. New York: Basic Books.

Jaffe, M. L. (1991). Understanding parenting. Dubuque, IA: Wm. C. Brown.

Kegan, R. (1982). The evolving self: Problems and process in human development. Cambridge, MA: Harvard University Press.

Kohlberg. L. (1969). Stage and sequence: The cognitive-developmental approach to socialization. In D. A. Goslin (Ed.), Handbook of socialization theory and research (pp. 347-480). Skokie, IL: Rand McNally.

Kohut, H. (1977). The restoration of the self. New York: International Universities Press.

Lam, M. S., Powers, S. I., Noam, G. G., Hauser, S. T., & Jacobson, A. M. (1993). Parental moral stage and adolescent moral development. In J. Demick, K. Bursik, & R. DiBiase (Eds.), Parental development (pp. 75-85). Hillsdale, NJ: Erlbaum.

Langer, E., Chanowitz, B., Palmerino, M., Jacobs, S., Rhodes, M., & Thayer, P. (1990). Nonsequential development and aging. In C. N. Alexander & E. J.

Langer (Eds.), *Higher stages of human development* (pp. 114-36). New York: Oxford University Press.

Leifer, M. (1980). *Psychological effects of motherhood: A study of first pregnancy.* New York: Praeger.

LeMasters, E. E. (1959). Parenthood as crisis. *Marriage and Family Living, 19,* 352-55.

Levinson, D. J. (1978). *The seasons of a man's life.* New York: Knopf.

Lewis, R. A., & Spanier, G. B. (1979). Theorizing about the quality and stability of marriage. In W. R. Burr, R. Hill, F. I. Nye, & I. L. Reiss (Eds.), *Contemporary theories about the family* (Vol. 1). New York: Free Press.

MacDonald, K., & Parke, R. D. (1986). Parent-child physical play: The effect of sex and age of children and parents. *Sex Roles, 15,* 367-78.

Mercer, R. T. (1986). *First-time motherhood: Experiences from teens to forties.* New York: Springer-Verlag.

Michaels, G. Y., & Goldberg, W. A. (Eds.). (1988). *The transition to parenthood: Current theory and research.* New York: Cambridge University Press.

Miliora, M. (1993). Development of the capacity for empathy: A case for healthy parenting. In J. Demick, K. Bursik, & R. DiBiase (Eds.), *Parental development* (pp. 107-18). Hillsdale, NJ: Erlbaum.

Miller, P. M. (1993). Mothers' and strangers' behavior with infants. In J. Demick, K. Bursik, & R. DiBiase (Eds.), *Parental development* (pp. 159-74). Hillsdale, NJ: Erlbaum.

Moos, R. H., & Moos, B. S. (1986). *Family environment scale manual* (2nd ed.). Palo Alto, CA: Consulting Psychologists Press.

Pacheco, A. M., Lucca, N., & Wapner, S. (1985). The assessment of interpersonal relationships among Puerto Rican migrant adolescents. In R. Diaz-Guerrero (Ed.), *Cross-cultural and national studies in social psychology* (pp. 169-76). North Holland: Elsevier Science Publishers.

Palkovitz, R., & Copes, M. (1988). Changes in attitudes, beliefs and expectations associated with the transition to parenthood. *Marriage and Family Review, 12,* 183-99.

Palus, C. J. (1993). Transformative experiences of adulthood: A new look at the seasons of life. In J. Demick, K. Bursik, & R. DiBiase (Eds.), *Parental development* (pp. 39-58). Hillsdale, NJ: Erlbaum.

Piaget, J. (1967). *Six psychological studies.* New York: Random House.

Pillemer, K., & McCartney, K. (Eds.). (1991). *Parent-child relations throughout life.* Hillsdale, NJ: Erlbaum.

Porzemsky, J., Wapner, S., & Glick, J. A. (1965). Effect of experimentally induced self-object cognitive attitudes on body and object perception. *Perceptual and Motor Skills, 21,* 187-95.

Quirk, M., Sexton, M., Ciottone, R., Minami, H., & Wapner, S. (1984). Values mothers hold for handicapped and nonhandicapped preschoolers. *Merrill-Palmer Quarterly, 30,* 403-18.

Quirk, M., Ciottone, R., Minami, H., Wapner, S., Yamamoto, T., Ishii, S., Lucca-Irizarry, N., & Pacheco, A. (1986). Values mothers hold for handicapped and nonhandicapped preschool children in Japan, Puerto Rico, and the United States mainland. *International Journal of Psychology, 21,* 463-85.

Sameroff, A. J. (1983). Developmental systems: Contexts and evolution. In P. H. Mussen (Series Ed.) & W. Kessen (Vol. Ed.), *Handbook of child psychology: Vol. 1. History, theory, and methods* (pp. 237-294). New York: Wiley.

Santostefano, S. (1980). Clinical child psychology: The need for developmental principles. *New Directions for Child Development, 7,* 1-19.

Schaefer, C. E., & Millman, H. L. (1981). *How to help children with common problems.* New York: Van Nostrand Reinhold.

Schlossberg, N. (1984). *Counseling adults in transition: Linking practice with theory.* New York: Springer.

Sirignano, A. W., & Lachman, M. E. (1985). Personality change during the transition to parenthood: The role of perceived infant temperament. *Developmental Psychology, 21,* 558-67.

Skinner, B. F. (1953). *Science and human behavior.* New York: Macmillan.

Solomon, M. J. (1993). Transmission of cultural goals: Social network influences on infant socialization. In J. Demick, K. Bursik, & R. DiBiase (Eds.), *Parental development* (pp. 135-56). Hillsdale, NJ: Erlbaum.

Spock, B. M. (1977). *Baby and child care* (Rev. ed.). New York: Pocket Books.

Steinberg, L. D. (1981). Transformations in family relations at puberty. *Developmental Psychology, 17,* 833-40.

Stevens-Long, J., & Macdonald, S. (1993). Empathy, cognitive generativity, and parenting. In J. Demick, K. Bursik, & R. DiBiase (Eds.), *Parental development* (pp. 89-105). Hillsdale, NJ: Erlbaum.

Streib, G. F. (1985). Social stratification and aging. In R. H. Binstock & E. Shanas (Eds.), Handbook of aging and the social sciences (2nd ed., pp. 339-68). New York: Van Nostrand Reinhold.

Taylor, S. P., & Langer, E. J. (1977). Pregnancy: A social stigma. *Sex Roles, 3,* 27-35.

Troll, L. E. (1986). Parents and children in later life. *Generations, 10,* 23-5.

Verbrugge, L. M. (1983). Multiple roles and physical health of women and men. *Journal of Health and Social Behavior, 24,* 16-30.

Vygotsky, L. S. (1978). *Mind in society: The development of higher psychological processes.* Cambridge, MA: Harvard University Press.

Wapner, S. (1969). Organismic-developmental theory: Some applications to cognition. In J. Langer, P. H. Mussen, & M. Covington (Eds.), *Trends and issues in developmental psychology* (pp. 38-67). New York: Holt, Rinehart & Winston.

Wapner, S. (1987). A holistic, developmental, systems-oriented environmental psychology: Some beginnings. In I. Altman & D. Stokols (Eds.), *Handbook of environmental psychology* (Vol. 2, pp. 1433-65). New York: Wiley.

Wapner, S. (1993). Parental development: A holistic, developmental systems-oriented perspective. In J. Demick, K. Bursik, & R. DiBiase (Eds.), *Parental development* (pp. 3-37). Hillsdale, NJ: Erlbaum.

Wapner, S., & Demick, J. (1990). Development of experience and action: Levels of integration in human functioning. In G. Greenberg & E. Tobach (Eds.), *Theories of the evolution of knowing: The T. C. Schneirla conference series* (pp. 47-68). Hillsdale, NJ: Erlbaum.

Wapner, S., & Demick, J. (1991a). The organismic-developmental, systems approach to the study of critical person-in-environment transitions through the life span. In T. Yamamoto & S. Wapner (Eds.), *A developmental psychology of life transitions* (pp. 5-15). Tokyo: Kyodo Shuppan.

Wapner, S., & Demick, J. (Eds.). (1991b). *Field dependence-independence: Cognitive style across the life span.* Hillsdale, NJ: Erlbaum.

Wapner, S., & Demick, J. (in press-a). Developmental analysis: A holistic, developmental, systems-oriented perspective. In R. M. Lerner (Ed.), *Theoretical models of human development.* Volume 1 of the *Handbook of Child Psychology* (5th ed.), Editor-in-Chief: William Damon. New York: Wiley.

Wapner, S., & Demick, J. (in press-b). Developmental theory and clinical practice: A holistic, developmental, systems-oriented approach. In W. K.

Silverman & T. H. Ollendick (Eds.), *Developmental issues in the clinical treatment of children.* Boston: Allyn & Bacon.

Wapner, S., & Demick, J. (in press-c). Person-in-environment psychology: A holistic, developmental, systems-oriented approach. In W. B. Walsh, K. H. Craik, & R. H. Price (Eds.), *New directions in person-environment psychology* (Volume 2). Hillsdale, NJ: Erlbaum.

Wapner, S., Demick, J., & Redondo, J. P. (1990). Cherished possessions and adaptation of older people to nursing homes. *International Journal on Aging and Human Development, 31,* 299-315.

Werner, H. (1940/1957). *Comparative psychology of mental development* (Rev. ed.). New York: International Universities Press.

Werner, H., & Kaplan, B. (1963). *Symbol formation.* New York: Wiley.

Wundt, W. (1912). Principles of physiological psychology. In B. Rand (Ed.), *The classic psychologists* (pp. 685-96). New York: Houghton Mifflin.

Part III

Educating for Moral and Religious Development

12

The Conceptual and Ethical Development of Teachers

Alan J. Reiman, Norman A. Sprinthall, and Lois Thies-Sprinthall

INTRODUCTION

One of the continuing problems for teacher education and school staff development initiatives has been the absence of effective programs for improving the professional competence of such personnel. Pink (1989) has identified a litany of barriers to teacher development. Yet limited evidence suggests that attention to teachers' development has dramatic impact on teacher performance, on adoption of innovations, on student achievement, and on student promotion (Chang, 1994; Fullan & Stiegelbauer, 1991; Joyce & Showers, 1994; Stallings, 1989). Why then are effective programs not more widespread?

At least part of the difficulty has been the lack of adequate directing constructs for the process of teacher education. In fact, as late as 1986, Lanier and Little noted that teacher education programs could be characterized as representing "consistent chaos in coursework" (p. 546). They suggested that very little has changed since the seminal Conant report (1963), which documented an atheoretical, largely ad hoc approach with wide variation as the only common element. Although the most recent review by Sikula (1996) does suggest some progress in a theoretical basis for teacher education, the field is still amorphous.

In this paper, the authors describe two decades of applied research in creating educational programs within a cognitive-developmental framework applied first to adolescents and then later to adults. The effort has been epitomized by a long series of field-based studies each in turn leading to changes as we then returned for the next cycle of experimentation. It has been very much a theory to practice and practice to theory sequence.

The First Tentative Steps

As Kohlberg's work (1966) in schools and prisons (Kohlberg, Hickey, & Scharf, 1972) emerged based on the dilemma dialogue method along with a series of social role-taking studies by Mosher and Sprinthall (1970) with adolescents, an insight gradually emerged. Could one conceptualize a parallel process for teachers? Bear in mind that in the 1970s many developmental researchers were in the process of revising their schemes. Basically, the researchers all made the same fortuitous mistake of employing longitudinal samples. Cognitive-structural growth did not stop during late adolescence and Kohlberg graciously "ate crow" (Kohlberg, 1969). Piaget (1972), as well, suggested the possibility of adult cognitive growth in one of his latter works, a theme examined in detail by Arlin (1975). For some adults then, growth could continue. This raised the intervention question. If adults do not unilaterally stabilize during early adulthood, then could programs be designed to promote such growth?

Adults in this view do not necessarily face a slow slide to senility beginning sometime after adolescence. Of course, the comprehensive meta-analysis by Lee and Snarey (1988) now confirms the wisdom of the revision with their longitudinal growth pattern for both ego and moral development. They found that the process of ego and moral development continued but not at the same rate. Thus, during early adulthood, ego development was somewhat in advance of moral development, both domains were in parity in the middle phase, and moral development was in advance during later adulthood. Also, Arlin's work demonstrated the possibility of cognitive-developmental growth beyond the early Piagetian formulations. Wisdom has been conceptualized by her as a hallmark of adult development (Arlin, 1990) and is strikingly similar to Lee and Snarey's (1988) research on moral development and Erikson's (1982) theory of generativity in the later stages of adulthood. The overall result, then, has been to expand cognitive-developmental theory to comprehend adult development.

Cognitive Structural Growth for Adults: Is Higher Better?

While longitudinal research had established that stage/sequence theory could be applied to adults, a prior question arose. Does stage make a difference in the real world of adult behavior? In other words, are cognitive-developmental levels predictors, or an independent variable? Over the past twenty years there have been a series of studies and meta-analyses that validate the general question.

Miller (1981), in his review of a large number of cognitive conceptual level (Hunt's CL) and performance in teaching studies, similarly reported a consistently positive relationship. The same findings were reported by Holloway and Wampold (1986) for professional counselors. In each case the task, providing assistance to another person in a humane atmosphere where the goal is to enhance the other person's growth toward autonomy, required higher stage process by the teacher or counselor. Professional adults who process experience more complexly have a greater ability to "read and flex" with pupils, to take the emotional perspective (empathy) of others, and to think on their feet and find alternative solutions (less "functional fixedness") (O'Keefe & Johnston, 1989). Table 12.1 contains a brief summary of some of these studies as illustrative of the overall point. Jane Loevinger (1976) points out, however, that "higher is not 'happier.' "At greater levels of cognitive complexity and interpersonal maturity, an adult is more aware of the innumerable barriers to growth. Further to the point, our adult society appears at least ambivalent over promoting critical consciousness (Friere, 1981) and behavior in accord with democratic/ethical principles. Awareness of these barriers is not necessarily a path to contentment.

In general then, higher stages of cognitive development across of series of domains predict performance in complex and ill-structured tasks. Other more conventional indices such as grade point average, standardized intelligence/achievement measures, or static personality traits do not (Sprinthall & Thies-Sprinthall, 1983a).

Table 12.1
Selected Studies; the Relationships Between Developmental Stage and Behavior in Complex Situations

Group	Outcome
Accountants	Higher Stages: Greater integrity, more sensitive to client characteristics, greater competence when framing audit risk (Ponemon, 1993). Lower Stages: Interested in serving own interests, greater underreporting of financial problems (Ponemon & Gabhart, 1994)
Physicians	Higher Stages: More democratic behavior with patients (Self & Baldwin, 1994)
School Principals	Higher Stages: More democratic behavior with teachers (Silver, 1975)
School Counselors	Higher Stages: More empathetic and flexible counseling skills (Holloway & Wampold, 1986) Lower Stages: Less empathetic with handicapped pupils (Strommer, Biggs, Haase, & Purcell, 1983)
School Teachers	Higher Stages: More effective teaching strategies, more empathy, more willingness to innovate, more inter-action, broader interpretation of content knowledge (Chang, 1994; Miller, 1981) Lower Stages: More rigid in the classroom and incompetent as supervisors, less interactive with students, rigid interpretation of educational concepts (Chang, 1994; Reiman & Thies-Sprinthall, 1998; Thies-Sprinthall, 1980)
Nurses	Higher Stages: Greater willingness to accept responsibility for terminally ill patients (Eberhardy, 1982)

It should be noted that the classical view of cognitive-developmental theory as applied to adults is distinctly different from popularized views of phases of adult life by career socialization (Yarger & Mertens, 1980), or adult passages (Sheehy, 1976). Those views suggest that the process of career aging accounts for movement from phase to phase. In contrast, cognitive-developmental theory attempts to understand how individuals construct, understand, interpret, and act upon experience. Persons' meaning-making systems represent logically consistent domains of structural complexity that determine behavior. Such cognitive systems do not automatically change with age. For example, an adult who processes experience at the concrete stage on Piaget (and many still do) and at the level of social conformity on Kohlberg may go through all of the career phases and Sheehy's "passages" yet remain concrete and conformist. A cognitive-developmental stage is not a quantitative concept determined by age but rather represents a sequence of qualitatively distinct cognitive structures through which the person interprets the world. Stages are not necessarily transformed by the passage of time.

If Higher Is "Better," Can Cognitive Development Become a Dependant Variable?

With the research base clearly outlining the advantages of stage as a predictor, one turns to the intervention question. Can a cognitive developmental stage become the object of educational programs, for example, as the dependent variable? Certainly any perusal of adult base rates of development in any of the domains such as cognitive conceptual, moral reasoning stage, or ego development would hardly inspire a sense of accomplishment by the educational enterprise. For example, Hunt (1971) found university students, student teachers, and (even) graduate students functioning just below the mid-point on his scale of conceptual complexity. Kohlberg (1969) and Rest (1986) report that most adults function at the midpoint of their scales as well, somewhere between social conformity (Stage 3) and law and duty (Stage 4). Similarly, Loevinger (1976) reported that the modal stage for adults was between Stage 3 and Stage 4 on her levels of ego stage, for example, between conformity and autonomy.

Further to the point, research (Rest, 1986) has shown that standard academic instruction has marginal effect upon moral stage. The Schmidt and Davison (1983) research on reflective judgment comes to the same conclusion concerning conceptual development. The growth that does occur is modest at best. These studies and reflections led to the following observations and questions:

1. Cognitive developmental theory can be applied to adults.
2. There is a consistent predictive relationship between higher stages and performances in *complex* humane helping tasks.
3. The general stage level of pre-service, in-service professionals and adults in general is modest, about the mid-point on various indices of development.
4. Traditional or conventional education programming appears to assume rather than promote development.
5. How can we build effective developmental programs and avoid the "American Question" of hasty acceleration? Or in the John Dewey (1933) framework if we know what development is, do we know what professional education ought to be?

TOWARD A MODEL OF INTERVENTION

The original start on the intervention question was in secondary schools. The high school programs had shown that the George Herbert Mead (1934) concept of social role taking could positively affect moral and conceptual stage reasoning (Mosher & Sprinthall, 1970; Sprinthall, 1980). Basically, this was the link illuminated so innovatively by Selman (1980) with young children. Such role-taking was a bridge, a necessary condition leading to ethical growth. Lev Vygotsky (1978) explored a similar link in his brilliant microgenesis studies that led to his concept of the zone of proximal development. Moral, conceptual, and ego (self) development of adolescents was nurtured through role-taking programs in the high schools (peer and cross-age helping). In all cases, it was the helper, for example, the tutors or peer counselor who benefited from a structural growth framework. The tutees, we should quickly add, also gained from the experiences (Sprinthall & Scott, 1989).

The investigators learned from these studies that cognitive-structural growth requires at least five elements of educational programming:

1. *Role-Taking (not role playing)*. This involves selecting a helping experience in a real-world context such as mentoring, counseling, tutoring, or working in a community internship. The role-taking (action) precedes and shapes the intellectual consciousness (reflection) that grows out of it. "Time on task" need not be substantial; two or three hours per week is as potent as ten to twelve hours (Exum, 1980).
2. *Reflection*. This element requires sequenced readings, journalizing, and discussions of the role-taking experiences. Experiential learning by itself can be just as arid as listening to lectures. The research with adolescents, in fact, had shown time and again that a volunteer experience without reflection made no impact on the cognitive-developmental stage of the helper (Conrad & Hedin, 1981; Sprinthall & Scott 1989; Sprinthall, Hall, & Gerler 1992). More recently, the investigators discovered that one cannot assume a sophisticated capacity for reflection. It became obvious in both the secondary school programs and later with in-service teachers that reflection required educating. The goal, of course, was *guided reflection* rather than a stream of consciousness diary or concrete descriptions of events (Reiman, 1988, Reiman & Thies-Sprinthall, 1993).
3. *Balance*. It was important that action and reflection remain in balance or as *praxis*. Usually, this means that the helping activity is sequenced with guided reflection each week. Too great a time lag between action and reflection or the other way around appears to halt the growth process (Reiman & Parramore, 1993).
4. *Continuity*. There is an old learning truism that spaced practice is superior to massed. We found that to achieve such a complex goal as impacting the structure of the cognitions in conceptual and moral domains requires a continuous interplay of action and guided reflection. A one- or two-week workshop followed by actual helping does not shift the cognitive structure of the participants. Usually at least one semester and preferably two are required for significant structural growth to be evident (Mosher & Sullivan 1976).
5. *Support and Challenge*. In the instructional phases of the role-taking programs, the investigators essentially rediscovered Vygotsky's zone of development (1978). Piaget (1964) had documented the problems of

assimilation/accommodation and disequilibrium. Since the interventions were "requiring" the participants to engage in a more complex role with greater responsibility, we often found individuals in the middle of a "knowledge perturbation."

However, the educator cannot simply follow the "Values Clarification" format, for example, "If the experience is uncomfortable you can pass." Instead, there is a need to help the participants through the experience by a combination of support yet not eliminating the challenge. This is probably the most complex pedagogical requirement of our system, requiring assistance to be within the zone of proximal development. Vygotsky's zone or what Hunt calls the arena for a constructive mismatch does require substantial "reading and flexing" (Hunt, 1976) on the part of the instructor. Structural growth through accommodation does not come cheaply. Giving up an "old friend" of one's current preferred method of problem-solving has been greatly neglected in the developmental literature. It may be more difficult for adults than adolescents.

On an overall basis, then, the five elements are both necessary and sufficient for achieving cognitive-structural growth. When the field studies shifted from adolescents to pre-service and in-service adult teachers, however, a further refinement of the elements becomes necessary.

The First Generation

The first attempts to apply the cognitive-structural framework with in-service teachers yielded mixed results. The goal was to use the role-taking procedures to instruct teachers how to accommodate their classroom to the newly mainstreamed students (Sprinthall & Bernier, 1978; Oja & Sprinthall, 1978). Some promising trends on developmental measures and behavior were found but the data was not conclusive. Thus, the investigators hypothesized that facilitating such structural growth required a more potent format as well as a greater amount of time.

A study by Thies-Sprinthall (1980) indicated a crucial direction. She found a clear example of the negative effects of ignoring developmental stages in the process of student teaching supervision. In a version of attribute treatment interaction, she found that cooperating teachers functioning at very modest levels of development based on Rest DIT (1986) and Hunt's measure of conceptual complexity (Hunt, 1971) actually negatively and inaccurately evaluated their student teachers who functioned at higher levels on both measures. This indicated two major issues: (1) what happens when there is a negative mismatch in a learning experience such as supervision; and (2) could we make training in supervision the requisite role-taking experience to promote both conceptual and moral development? After all, it was a truism to note that curriculum materials were not teacher proof. Could we create conditions so that a similar fate would not befall a curriculum in supervision (Sprinthall & Thies-Sprinthall, 1983a, 1983b)?

The program developed and tested out by Thies-Sprinthall (1984) was the first step in that direction. She created a method of using a workshop model from Joyce and Weil (1980) in concert with our developmental conditions. Specific and focused skills of supervision and mentoring were taught to a group of experienced teachers in a sequence of rationale, modeling, peer practice, and generalization for each component. The role-taking was to become a teacher supervisor or mentor. The program was equivalent to a two-semester course to provide for continuity. In fact, one of the major goals was to help such teachers apply different models of supervision according to the developmental needs of the beginning teacher. In the Hunt sense, this meant mastering the process of systematically varying the amount of structure provided. Table 12.2 illustrates how the instructional process was varied in accord with the developmental stage of the teacher. Examples were concrete or abstract, reinforcement was immediate or spread-out, and assignments were focused or extended. These guidelines then served as the map to direct this interaction and assignments.

Table 12.2
Differentiation of Structure

Factors	High Structure	Low Structure
Concepts	Concrete	Abstract
Time Span	Short	Long
Time on Task	Multiple practice	Single practice
Advance Organizers	Multiple use of organizers	Few (if any) organizers
Complexity of Learning Tasks	Divided into small steps and recycled	Learning tasks clustered into "wholes"
Theory	Concretely matched with experiential examples	Generalized including action research
Instructor Support	Consistent and frequent	Occasional

The results demonstrated two points. It was almost impossible to provide enough structure, guided reflection, and support to help experienced teachers who initially functioned at very modest levels of development. On the other hand, for the majority of teachers, those initially at levels common to college graduates on both the Rest and the Hunt, the results were quite positive.

Second Generation: Refining Guided Reflection

It was concluded that role-taking in the form of supervision or mentoring skills was a highly appropriate means of promoting the intellectual and moral growth of in-service professionals. However, as the investigators examined the reflection component of the experience, it seemed that a rather generic method of responding each week to journals was being employed. The sentiment was that reflection was not as effective as it might be and certainly was not at the point where we could teach anyone else how to do it. Ever since John Dewey (1933), at least, educators have grappled with the problem of how to learn from experience. Certainly the current vogue in teacher education is to focus on developing reflective practitioners (Schon, 1987; Cruickshank, 1985; Zeichner & Liston, 1987). The difficulty, of course, is the sophisticated and subtle problem of how to extract complex meaning from experience. From a developmental educators' standpoint, there is the additional question of how to educate other educators in the use of guided reflection. Earlier programs had shown that conceptual, ethical, and ego complexity determines how deeply the person can perceive, analyze, and reflect. In fact, the investigators' reviews of qualitative data was a reminder of Perry's opening chapter (1970) where he describes college students at three levels of complexity with widely differing interpretations of the same questions. Quite obviously the exam question was the same but the ability to interpret the meaning was governed by the stage of the perceiver.

How to refine journal feedback became the issue or how to start where the teacher was and then to gradually mismatch. Mismatching, of course, is not as easy in practice as in theory. If we did not connect with the proximal zone in the Vygotsky sense, no growth would occur, yet such a zone varies in accord with the complexity of the teacher. It can be considered as a moving target. Thus, a flexible framework for guiding reflection was needed that itself would be differentiated.

Having been aware of the extensive work of Flanders (1970) in studying teaching, we modified that system as a basis for responding to the narrative in journals (Reiman 1988, 1997; Reiman & Thies-Sprinthall, 1993). Flanders essentially outlined seven types of instructional influence and provided an extremely large set of studies to validate teaching effectiveness as a ratio of direct versus indirect methods. If those forms worked in the classroom (Gage, 1978), could an altered version work in providing written feedback and dialogue in the journal format?

The next problem to solve was how to use the categories of response differently. For example, if the protégé has difficulty in the journal describing and discussing feelings about self and towards students, the supervisor would share his or her own feelings and even suggest some feelings that the beginner may experience. The supervisor, on the other hand, would remain less active and more indirect by accepting and perhaps clarifying the emotional themes shared when responding to more complex narratives. Each type of Flanders' influence, then, could be identified together with examples of differentiated responses according to the developmental stage of the protégé. The framework became the equivalent of an interactive lesson plan for journal entries and provides systematic guidance for the supervisor in training. The research results indicated that such a systematic reflection method for supervisors facilitates their own conceptual and moral development. First, we compared this approach to the regular method of role-taking and reflection. Both groups of teachers gained, but the systematic group demonstrated greater gains on both measures of growth (Reiman, 1988). Subsequent studies (Reiman & Thies-Sprinthall, 1993; Reiman, 1997) supported the more systematic approach to guided reflection. Table 12.3. outlines some examples of the developmental methods in journal feedback.

Thus, the current set of studies has focused on facilitating the structural growth of in-service teachers. The role-taking experience was to shift from being a teacher to becoming a supervisor of beginning teachers. All five developmental conditions were met, but the more systematic method for guided reflection yielded greater gains on the estimate of stage. Informal and qualitative information confirmed the changes. Observations of the supervisor's performance with beginning teachers further confirmed the competent behavioral interaction. These elements have been tested with in-service counselors (Peace, 1992), college tutors (Mann, 1992), pre-service teachers (Reiman & Parramore, 1993; Watson, 1995), and with beginning teachers (Watson & Reiman, 1997). In each case, the role-taking requires the learning of complex new skills, and more systematic guided reflection is included.

From these studies, the investigators have concluded that the role-taking and reflection method can be applied to adult pre-service and in-service professionals. However, such programs require a substantial commitment of time and continuity of experience along with the other developmental conditions. Probably the single most important aspect of such programs is the reflective component. It should come as no surprise to reach such a conclusion as the ability to extract meaning from experience has always been the major challenge to developmental educators throughout the ages. Oser and Schlaefli (1985), perhaps, sum it up best when they note that stage growth does "move" but very slowly. Given the complexity of such goals it could probably occur only in such a deliberative mode.

IMPLICATIONS

One major implication of this work is toward the question of theory and practice for teacher education. One of the long-standing problems in this area has been the lack of directing constructs and research for the professional education of teachers, and by implication for the education of other professional groups of action-oriented professional, for example, counselors, school psychologists, social workers, and others. There has been substantial criticism of both post-Piagetian and Kohlbergian frameworks as theoretical guides for such development. Certainly, this is to be expected, yet it is important to recall that the early and contemporary base for such claims is robust and growing. Case's (1992) cross-cultural studies clearly validate much of Piagetian stages as well as provide effective new evidence to rebut recent criticism. Similarly, the continued research summaries by Kuhmerker (1991) provide new evidence of the stage of sequence and gender free characteristics of moral stages. Also, there continue to be studies validating that "higher is better (and harder)" when the task requires empathy, perspective-taking, and a flexible choice of response in accord with the needs of the student. (Rest & Narvaez, 1994; Sprinthall, Sprinthall, & Oja, 1994; Oja & Reiman, 1997).

Table 12.3
Summary of Categories for Guiding Written Reflections

Interactions	Journal Pattern	Instructor Response
1. Accepts Feelings	1a. Teacher has difficulty discerning feelings in both self and others.	Shares own feelings.
	1b. Teacher discerns feelings in both self and students.	Accepts feelings.
2. Praises or Encourages	2a. Teacher doubts self when trying new instructional strategies.	Offers frequent encouragement.
	2b. Teacher has confidence when attempting new instructional strategies.	Offers occasional support.
3. Acknowledges and Clarifies Ideas	3a. Teacher perceives knowledge as fixed and employs a single "tried and true" model of teaching.	Relates ideas to observed events and clarifies how ideas affect students' lives.
	3b. Teacher perceives knowledge as a process of successive approximations and employs a diversity of models of teaching.	Accepts ideas and encourages examination of hidden assumptions of pedagogy.
4. Prompts Inquiry	4a. Teacher rarely reflects on the teaching/learning process.	Asks questions about observed events in teaching/learning.
	4b. Teacher consistently reflects on diverse aspects of the teaching/ learning process.	Asks questions that encourage analysis, evaluation, divergent thinking, and synthesis of theory/ practice and broader societal issues.
5. Provides Information	5a. Teacher disdains theory, prefers concrete thinking, and has difficulty recalling personal teaching events.	Offers information in smaller amounts, relates to observed practice, and reviews regularly.
	5b. Teacher employs abstract thinking, shows evidence of originality in adapting innovations to the class, and is articulate in analysis of his or her own teaching.	Relates information to relevant theory and contrasts with competing theories.
6. Gives Directions	6a. Teacher needs detailed instructions and high structure, is low on self-direction, and follows curriculum as if it were "carved in stone."	Offers detailed instructions but encourages greater self-direction.
	6b. Teacher is self-directed and enjoys low structure.	Offers few directions.

7. When Problems Exist	7a. Teacher has difficulty accepting responsibility for problems and blames students.	Accepts feelings and thoughts, uses "I" messages, and arranges a conference.
	7b. Teacher accepts responsibility for actions.	Accepts feelings and thoughts.

A second major implication is to realize that teachers in particular and education in general are focusing on increasingly more complex tasks. Most obvious is the need to broaden classrooms, to increase the accommodative capacity to respond to the legitimate educational needs of students with disabilities on one hand and the needs of an increasingly diverse student body on the other. Some seventy years of classroom interaction research simply points out the obvious. Whether we look at research reported at the turn of the century or at more recent studies (Sprinthall, Sprinthall, & Oja, 1994), the result is always the same (at least at the secondary level): we note teachers in a recitation rut, asking brief concrete questions and soliciting brief answers, a version of trivia in the classroom. These are experienced teachers. Beginning teachers have their own documented problems (Veenman, 1984) particularly in handling discipline problems, let alone in managing instruction.

Maynard Reynolds (1989) makes a clear and urgent case for teachers to improve in their competencies beyond the conventional to the state of the art. This is probably the most compelling rationale for applying cognitive-developmental approaches of teacher development. Most importantly, emerging evidence suggests that attention to teachers' development has dramatic impact on teacher performance, on adoption of innovations, on student achievement, on mentoring and supervision, and on student promotion (Chang, 1994; Fullan & Stiegelbauer, 1991; Joyce & Showers, 1994; Oja & Reiman, 1997; Stallings, 1989). Participating in school-wide innovations, mentoring programs, and diverse classrooms requires higher-order interactive humane abilities. If the teacher or counselor cannot perceive such complexity there is little hope of an effective response. Unfortunately, then the students who may require the most help receive the least, that is, the so-called "Matthew Effect" (Reynolds, 1989).

Of special note, the problems associated with adopting effective-teaching strategies have been chronicled clearly by McKibbin and Joyce (1981) and Hopkins (1990). Both studies found a clear relationship between the ability to apply innovative classroom methods and developmental stage understandings. The so-called transfer of training issue has always plagued educators, namely the inability of teachers to generalize principles beyond a single concrete example. McKibbin and Joyce (1981), in a year-long follow-up study, demonstrated that there was a linear relationship between teacher stage and effective implementation of new strategies. The lower stage teachers virtually closed their doors to innovations and they closed their minds. Developmental theory explained both outcomes. At higher stages, the teachers could "read and flex" and understand the need to change from the pupil's point of view. At lower stages, the teachers maintain the status quo and avoid the dissonance from an upsetting accommodation change. Thus, further skill training is simply a waste of time unless the focus shifts to include the cognitive-developmental structure of the participants. The failures of all those national curricular efforts (the "new" math, social studies, biology, et al.) indicate the futility of a teacher-proof curriculum that does not attend to teacher cognition.

The third implication is a realistic assessment of the scope of the teacher education problem. Diessner's (1991) review illustrates just how far we are from Arlin's (1990) goal of nurturing adult "wisdom" as a post-formal operational level. Generally, the ability (just) to identify principled reasoning remains below 50 per cent for pre-service and in-service teachers. In fact, Diessner reported that a study of educational school faculty wasn't not much higher. Certainly, it is a large step from recognizing democratic principles to acting in accord with those views. Thus, there is strong evidence that development cannot be assumed to be an outcome of existing professional education; furthermore, given the base rates, we cannot assume that we are close to achieving such growth. The down-side of Piaget's "American Question" is simply to examine the current and common developmental levels of teachers and classroom interactions. Are we really willing to accept what is as what ought to be? We have suggested elsewhere a model of developmental framework for both pre-service and in-service education (Thies-Sprinthall & Sprinthall, 1986; Reiman & Thies-Sprinthall, 1998). The basic idea would be to take advantage of the obvious role-taking opportunities in early experience, observation, pre-student teaching, and the student-teaching experience itself for beginners. Similarly, the induction phase and the continuing professional development phases for experienced teachers could be organized around the five essential elements of cognitive-developmental growth. A sequence of managed experiences could form a response to Hunt's (1976) question, is conceptual stage "malleable" (or, "modifiable", in Cronbach and Snow's phrase,1977)? Our research does establish a significant basis for just such a claim.

In sum, a helping activity such as teaching increasingly demands the ability to understand pupils and master content knowledge in at least two areas—one must know both the subject itself and the optimal pedagogy. Both are necessary, but the ability to act is also requisite. Tomorrow's classrooms will be an even greater challenge. Higher-order reflection (meta-reflection) and action by the teacher indicates a disposition to react and flex, to select an appropriate repertoire of skills and materials, to vary the instructional structure by pupil's needs, to create an empathetic yet challenging atmosphere, to adapt new strategies for new educational problems; in short, to educate in the root meaning of that word. Such effective teachers are not born, but they may be developed.

REFERENCES

Arlin, P. (1975). Cognitive development in adulthood: A fifth stage? *Developmental Psychology, 11*, 602-608.

Arlin, P. (1990). Wisdom: The art of problem finding. In R. J. Sternberg (Ed.), *Wisdom: Its Nature, origins and development* (pp. 230-243). New York: Cambridge University Press.

Case, R. (1992). *The mind's staircase.* NJ: Erlbaum.

Chang, F-Y. (1994). School teachers' moral reasoning. In J. Rest and D. Narvaez (Eds.), *Moral development in the professions: Psychology and applied ethics.* Hillsdale, NJ: Lawrence Erlbaum Associates.

Conant, J. (1963). *The education of American teachers.* New York: McGraw-Hill.

Conrad, D. & Hedin, D. (1981). Natural assessment of experiential education. *Experiential Education, 7,* 6-20.

Cronbach, L.J., & Snow, R.. (1977). *Aptitudes and instructional methods.* New York: Irvington.

Cruickshank. A. (1985). Applying research on teacher clarity. *Journal of Teacher Education, 36,* 44-48.

Dewey, J. (1933). *How we think: A restatement of the relation of reflective thinking to the educative process.* Chicago: Henry Regenery.

Diessner, R. (1991). Teacher education for democratic classrooms. Paper presented at the Association for Moral Education, Athens, GA, Nov. 1991.

Eberhardy, J. (1982). *An analysis of moral decision-making with nurses facing professional problems.* Unpublished doctoral dissertation. University of Minnesota, MN.

Erikson, E. (1982). *The life cycle completed.* New York: Norton

Exum, H.A. (1980). Ego development: Using curriculum to facilitate growth. *Character Potential, 9,* 121-28.

Flanders, N. A. (1970). *Analyzing teacher behavior.* Reading, MA: Addison-Wesley.

Friere, P. (1981). *Education for critical consciousness.* New York: Continuum.

Fullan, M., & Stiegelbauer, S. (1991). *The new meaning of educational change.* New York: Teachers College Press.

Gage, N. (1978). *The scientific basis for the art of teaching.* New York: Teachers College Press.

Holloway, E., & Wampold, B.. (1986). Relation between conceptual level and counseling related tasks. *Journal of Counseling Psychology, 33,* 310-19.

Hopkins, D. (1990). Integrating staff development and school improvement: A study of personality and school climate. In B. Joyce (Ed.), *ASCD yearbook: Changing school culture through staff development* (pp. 41-67). Alexandria, VA: Association for Supervision and Curriculum Development.

Hunt D. (1971). *Matching models in education: The coordination of teaching methods with student characteristics.* Toronto: Ontario Institute for Studies in Education.

Hunt D. (1976). Teachers' adaptation: 'Reading and flexing to students' *Journal of Teacher Education, 27,* 268-75.

Joyce, B., & Showers, B. (1994). *Student achievement through staff development.* New York: Longman.

Joyce, B., & Weil, M. (1980). *Models of teaching.* Englewood Cliffs, NJ: Prentice-Hall.

Kohlberg, L. (1966). Moral education in the school. *School Review, 74,* 1-30.

Kohlberg, L. (1969). Stage and sequence: The cognitive-developmental approach to socialization. In D. Goslin (Ed.), *Handbook of socialization theory and research* (pp. 347-480), New York: Rand McNally.

Kohlberg, L., Hickey, J., &Scharf, P. (1972). The justice structure of the prison: A theory of intervention. *Prison Journal, 51,* 3-14.

Kuhmerker, L. (1991). *The Kohlberg legacy.* Birmingham: REP.

Lanier, J., & Little, J. (1986). Research in teacher education. In M.C. Wittrock (Ed.), *Handbook of Research in Teaching* (pp. 527-69). New York: Macmillan.

Lee, L., & Snarey, J.. (1988). The relationship between ego and moral development: A theoretical review and empirical analysis. In D. Lapsley & C. Power (Eds.), *Self, ego, and identity: Integrative approaches* (pp. 151-78). New York: Springer Verlag

Loevinger, J. (1976). *Ego development.* San Francisco: Jossey-Bass.

Mann, A. (1992). *A quantitative and qualitative evaluation of a peer tutor-training course: A cognitive-developmental model.* Unpublished doctoral dissertation, NC State University, Raleigh.

McKibbin, M., & Joyce, B. (1981). Psychological states. *Theory Into Practice, 19,* 248-55.

Mead, G.H. (1934). *Mind, Self, and Society.* Chicago: University of Chicago Press.

Miller, A. (1981). Conceptual matching models and interactional research in education. *Review of Educational Research, 51,* 33-84.

Mosher, R., & Sprinthall, N.A. (1970). Psychological education in secondary schools. *American Psychologist, 25,* 911-24.

Mosher, R., & Sullivan. P. (1976). A curriculum in moral education for adolescents. *Journal of Moral Education.* 5, 159-72.

Oja, S., & Sprinthall, N.A. (1978). Psychological and moral development of teachers. In N.A. Sprinthall & R. L. Mosher (Eds.), *Value development as the aim of education* (pp. 117-34). Schenectady, NY: Character Research Press.

Oja, S., & Reiman, A. (1997). Describing and promoting supervision for teacher development across the career span. In J. Firth and E. Pajak (Eds.), *Handbook of research on school supervision.* New York: Macmillan.

O'Keefe, P., & Johnston, M. (1989). Perspective-taking and teacher effectiveness: A connecting thread through these developmental literatures. *Journal of Teacher Education,40,* 14-20.

Oser, F., & Schlaefi, A. (1985). And it does move. In M. Berkovitz & F. Oser (Eds.), *Moral education: Theory and application* (pp. 269-95). Hillsdale, NJ: Erlbaum.

Peace, S.D. (1992). *A study of school counselor instruction: A cognitive-developmental mentor/supervisor training program.* Unpublished doctoral dissertation. North Carolina State University, Raleigh, NC.

Perry, W. (1970). *Forms of intellectual and ethical developmental in the college years.* New York: Holt, Rinehart and Winston.

Piaget, J. (1964). *Judgment and reasoning in the child.* Patterson, NJ: Littlefield & Adams.

Piaget, J. (1972). Intellectual evolution from adolescence to adulthood. *Human Development, 15,* 1-12.

Pink, W. T. (1989). *Effective development for urban school improvement.* Paper presented at the annual meeting of the American Educational Research Association, San Francisco.

Ponemon, L. A. (1993). The influence of ethical reasoning on auditors' perceptions of management's competence and integrity. *Advancements in Accounting,* 1-29.

Ponemon, L. A., & Gabhart, D. L. (1994). Ethical reasoning research in the accounting and auditing professions. In J. Rest and D. Narvaez (Eds.), *Moral development in the professions: Psychology and applied ethics.* New Jersey: Lawrence Erlbaum Associates.

Reiman, A. (1988). *An intervention study of long-term mentor training: Relationships between cognitive-developmental theory and reflection.* Unpublished doctoral dissertation, North Carolina State University, Raleigh, NC.

Reiman, A. J., (1997). *Promoting reflective practice within a cognitive-structural framework: Theory, research, and practice.* Presentation at the International Council of Psychologists. Padua, Italy.

Reiman, A., & Parramore, B. (1993). Promoting pre-service teacher development through extended field experience. M. O'Hair & S. Odell (Eds.), *Diversity in teaching* (pp. 111-21). Orlando: Harcourt Brace Jovanovich.

Reiman, A., & Thies-Sprinthall, L. (1993). Promoting the development of mentor teachers: Theory and research programs using guided reflection. *Journal of Research and Development, 26*, 179-85.

Reiman, A., & Thies-Sprinthall, L. (1998). *Mentoring and supervision for teacher development.* New York: Addison-Wesley Longman.

Rest, J. (1986). *Moral development.* New York: Praeger.

Rest, J. & Narvaez, D. (Eds.) (1994). *Moral development in the professions: Psychology and applied ethics.* Hillsdale, NJ: Lawrence Erlbaum Associates.

Reynolds, M.C. (1989). *Knowledge base for the beginning teacher.* Oxford, United Kingdom: Pergamon.

Schmidt, J., & Davison, M. (1983). Helping students think. *The Personnel and Guidance Journal, 61*, 563-569.

Schon, D. (1987). *Educating the reflective practitioner.* San Francisco: Jossey Bass.

Self, D., & Baldwin, D.C. (1994). Moral reasoning in medicine. In J. Rest and D. Narvaez (Eds.), *Moral development in the professions: Psychology and applied ethics.* Hillsdale, Hillsdale, NJ: Lawrence Erlbaum Associates.

Selman, R. (1980). *The growth of interpersonal understanding.* New York: Academic Press.

Sheehy, G. (1976). *Passages: Predictable crises of adult life.* New York: Dutton.

Sikula, J. (Ed.) (1996). *Second handbook of research on teacher education.* New York: Macmillan.

Silver, P. (1975). Principals' conceptual ability in relation to situation and behavior. *Educational Administration Quarterly, 11*, 49-66.

Sprinthall, N.A. (1971). A program for psychological education: Some preliminary issues. *Journal of School Psychology, 9*, 373-82.

Sprinthall, N.A. (1980). Psychology for secondary schools: The saber toothed curriculum revisited? *American Psychologist, 35*, 336-47.

Sprinthall, N.A. , & Bernier, J. (1978). Moral and cognitive development of teachers. *New Catholic World, 221*, 179-84.

Sprinthall, N.A., Gerler, E. R., & Hall, J. (1992). Peer helping: Counselors and teachers as facilitators. *The Peer Facilitator Quarterly, 9*, 11-5.

Sprinthall, N.A., & Scott, J. (1989). Promoting psychological development, math achievement and success attribution of female students through deliberate psychological education. *Journal of Counseling Psychology, 36*, 440-46.

Sprinthall, N.A., Sprinthall, R.C., & Oja, S. N. (1994). *Educational psychology: A developmental- approach.* New York: McGraw-Hill.

Sprinthall, N.A., & Thies-Sprinthall, L. (1983a). The teacher as an adult learner: A cognitive developmental view. In G. A. Griffin (Ed.), *Staff Development, Eighty-second yearbook of the National Society for the Study of Education* (pp. 24-31). Chicago: University of Chicago Press.

Sprinthall, N.A. & Thies-Sprinthall, L.. (1983b). The need for theoretical frameworks in educating teachers: A cognitive developmental perspective. In K. Howey & W. Gardner (Eds.), *Education of Teachers: A Look Ahead* (pp. 74-97). New York: Longman.

Stallings, J. (1989). *School achievements effects and staff development: What are some critical factors?* Paper presented at the annual meeting of the American Educational Research Association.

Strommer, D., Biggs, D., Haase, R., & Purcell, M. (1983). Training counselors to work with disabled clients: Cognitive and affective components. *Counselor Education and Supervision, 23,* 132-41.

Thies-Sprinthall, L. (1980). Supervision: An educative or miseducative process? *Journal of Teacher Education, 31,* 17-30.

Thies-Sprinthall, L. (1984). Promoting the developmental growth of supervising teachers: Theory, research programs, and implications. *Journal of Teacher Education, 35,* 53-60.

Thies-Sprinthall, L. & Sprinthall, N.A. (1986). Pre-service teachers as adult learners: A new framework for teacher education. In M. Haberman & J. Backus (Eds.) *Advances in Teacher Education,* Vol. 3 (pp. 35-54). Norwood, NJ: Ablex.

Veenman, S. (1984). Perceived problems of beginning teachers. *Review of Educational Research, 54,* 143-178.

Vygotsky, L. (1978). *Mind in society.* Cambridge, MA: Harvard University Press.

Watson, B. (1995). *Early field experiences in teacher education: A developmental model.* Unpublished dissertation. North Carolina State University, Raleigh, NC.

Watson, B., & Reiman, A. (1997). *Beginning teachers developmental growth: An exploratory study.* Technical Report 97-7, North Carolina State University, Raleigh.

Yarger, S., & Mertens, S. (1980). Testing the waters of school-based teacher education. In D. C. Corrigan & K. R. Howey (Eds.) *Concepts to guide the education of experienced teachers* (pp. 139-64). Reston, VA: Council for Exceptional Children.

Zeichner, K. M., & Liston, D. (1987). Reflective teacher education and moral deliberation. *Journal of Teacher Education, 18,* 2-8.

13

Moral Development in a Postmodern World

Mark B. Tappan

In the spring of 1993, a group of white teenagers in Los Angeles, calling themselves the "Fourth Reich Skinheads," decided to start a race war by assassinating a well-known African-American. They picked as their target Reverend Cecil Murray, senior minister of the First African American Episcopal Church. The skinheads planned to shoot Reverend Murray while he was conducting a service, then throw pipebombs into the pews and spray the congregation with machine-gun fire.

An FBI sting operation thwarted the skinheads' plans, however, and three of their leaders were arrested. But, instead of prosecuting them, Assistant United States Attorney Marc Greenberg decided to try to help the skinheads develop tolerance toward their "enemies." Calling his program "Operation Grow Hair," he wanted the skinheads to meet face to face with the targets of their hatred.

Reverend Murray agreed to help, and he and other ministers from his church arranged to meet with five of the skinheads to talk openly about their thoughts and feelings. Here is an excerpt from one of those meetings[1]:

Rev. Murray: Well, you still subscribe to the basic philosophy of White power: Blacks are degenerate; separated from them, and if necessary, kill them?

Tim (skinhead): There are many Blacks who feel the same way, though, and I can—I can show you many. Walk down to Poly High School. You'll see many of them.

Rev. Murray: Are they...

Tim: Many still feel hate for me. I didn't walk around the school and say, "I'm from the Fourth Reich Skins. I'm a skinhead. White power. I don't care about you because you're black." I never said that. I would walk down the hall and people would call me "white bread" or "whitey." Just—just when I'm walking down the hall. That scared me.

Rev. Murray: We're all afraid. But out of your fear, you cannot do certain things. You cannot kill. You cannot malign. You have to keep your little prejudice within your chest. Go on and hate Black people if that's your shot, but you are not allowed to act on what you feel . . .

Turtle (skinhead): Everybody has a hate in their heart, and that's what our racism is broken down to. Everybody—if I were to ask anybody in this room if there was one thing that they hated, and everybody—you know, would have something they hate . . .

Minister: Why do you hate me just because of the color of my skin?

Tim: No, no. See, that's—that's ignorance, plain and right there.

Minister: No it's not.

Tim: I haven't showed you in any way that I dislike you, so you have no . . .

Minister: I'm talking about the skinheads . . .

Tim: Well, why don't you start judging people as individuals?

Minister: When you become part of a group, you're a part of that group and what they identify with.

Tim: We didn't just sit down one day and say, "Oh, let's call a black guy a 'coon' or a Mexican guy a 'beaner'." We didn't do that. We had all experienced some kind of prejudism [sic] towards us . . .

Rev. Murray: Mm-hmm. Mm-hmm.

Tim: So that planted hatred in our hearts, and we casted it out among other people.

I begin by describing "Operation Grow Hair," and reporting part of this conversation between the "Fourth Reich" skinheads and the ministers from the First AME Church in LA, because this effort, and these words, highlight important aspects of the contemporary world in which we live. Sadly, we do live in a world where promises of "liberty and justice for all" have not been kept; a world where racism, sexism, homophobia, and other forms of oppression are alive and well; a world "rife with contradictions and asymmetries of power and privilege" (McLaren, 1994, p. 175).

Yet, this is also a world where dialogues and discussions across differences, like those that constitute the core of "Operation Grow Hair," do take place, and do have an effect on the moral lives of both young and old alike; a world where love, courage, faith, and humility give birth to hope; a world where the only way to break the cycle of injustice and violence is to seek a kind of critical consciousness on the part of both the oppressed and their oppressors that will enable oppression to be named and thereby resisted.

Many observers have taken to calling this a "postmodern" world—to distinguish it from the "modern" world of the past 200 years or so, and to highlight the unique characteristics and qualities of contemporary life. Discussions of "postmodernism" and the "postmodern condition" have ranged widely across a variety of disciplines in recent years (including literature and literary theory, art, music, architecture, cultural studies, women's studies, legal studies, philosophy, sociology, politics, and education—see, for example, Bauman, 1992; Benhabib, 1992; Connor, 1989; Giroux, 1991; Harvey, 1989; Hassan, 1987; Jameson, 1991; Lather, 1991; Lyotard, 1984; Natoli & Hutcheon, 1993; Rosenau, 1992). Quite frankly, I am ambivalent about embracing all of the aspects of the postmodern as it has been described and debated in these and other academic and popular publications. Nevertheless, I am convinced that the contemporary world is sufficiently different from the world we knew even twenty five years ago; that it demands a rethinking and revisioning of central aspects of human life—particularly the construction and reconstruction of moral sensibility across the life-span. That is to say, I believe that the postmodern world, in spite of its problems, offers profoundly new and generative possibilities for a refocused and reinvigorated approach to moral development and education—an approach that does not simply perpetuate the status quo, but pushes, instead, toward genuine critique and authentic change.

My aim in this chapter is thus to articulate the kind of perspective on moral development to which I believe the postmodern world, at its best, gives rise. In so doing, I extend earlier efforts to sketch an explicitly "post-structural" narrative approach to moral development and moral education (Tappan & Brown, 1989; also Day & Tappan, 1996). I argue, therefore, for an approach that links postmodern insights about the discursive construction of reality (Sampson, 1993b), celebrations of difference and diversity, and critiques of the overly individualistic assumptions of the modern worldview to a dialogical conception of the moral self embedded in an inescapably relational world. Moreover, I suggest that such an approach necessarily leads to an understanding of moral community that not only answers key questions about the threat of relativism in a postmodern world, but also provides the starting point for reconceptualizing moral education as the practice of a genuinely critical and liberatory multicultural pedagogy.

THE POSTMODERN WORLD

Let me characterize, briefly, what I take to be three of the most important and salient features of the postmodern perspective.

Language, Reality, and Truth

First, postmodernism focuses particular attention on language and discourse as fundamentally constitutive of the physical and social world in which we live. On this view, words, language, and forms of discourse do not simply express or represent a predetermined or intrinsic reality, but rather give rise to that reality in the first place. As such, because language produces and reproduces its own world without reference to fixed and stable referents, our understanding of what constitutes "truth" must be radically transformed (Rosenau, 1992).

Making such claims about the discursive construction of reality entails a move from what Kenneth Gergen (1994) calls a "representationalist" view of language to a "relational" view—a move inspired, in large measure, by the work of Wittgenstein (1963): "As Wittgenstein proposed, language acquires its meaning not through a referential base but through its use in social practices. To use a word accurately is to use it within the rules of culturally specific language games, which games are embedded within broader cultural conventions or forms of life. It is not the world as it is that necessitates our callings but the relationships in which we participate" (Gergen, 1994, p. 413). Processes of social communication and social relations, in other words, which occur via words, language, and forms of discourse, are the cultural practices that constitute the "realities"—physical, psychological, and social—that we encounter in our everyday lives (Sampson, 1993b).

This postmodern focus on the ways in which language constructs both reality and truth highlights, in turn, the fundamental relationship between knowledge and power. Indeed, as Michel Foucault (1979, 1980) argues, not only are truth claims always the product of power plays, serving primarily the interests of the privileged, but language and forms of discourse, however innocuous they may seem, always link knowledge and power:

It is in discourse that power and knowledge are joined together. And for this very reason, we must conceive discourse as a series of discontinuous segments whose tactical function is neither uniform or stable. To be more precise, we must not imagine a world of discourse divided between accepted discourse and excluded discourse, or between the dominant discourse and the dominated one; but as a multiplicity of discursive elements that can come into play in various strategies. (Foucault, 1979, p. 100)

To some this postmodern inquiry into the relationship between discourse, knowledge, and power raises profound concerns about the threat of subjectivity, relativism, and nihilism. I would argue, however, following Henry Giroux (1988), that rather than raising threats to be feared, the postmodern perspective on language and discourse opens up a number of new and interesting avenues to be explored:

Perhaps the most important feature of postmodernism is its stress on the centrality of language and subjectivity as new fronts from which to rethink the issues of meaning, identity, and politics. Postmodern discourse has retheorized the nature of language as a system of signs structured in the infinite play of difference, and doing so has undermined the dominant, positivist notion of language as either a genetic code structured in permanence or simply a linguistic, transparent medium for transmitting ideas and meaning. . . . For traditionalists, the postmodern emphasis on the contingency of language represents a retreat into nihilism, but, in effect, it does just the opposite by making problematic the very nature of language, representation, and meaning. In this view, truth, science, and ethics do not cease to exist; instead, they become representations that need to be problematized rather than accepted as received canons and truths. (Giroux, 1988, pp. 20-21)

The Acknowledgment of Diversity

Let me turn, now, to a second characteristic of the postmodern world—its explicit acknowledgment of diversity, and its celebration of the reality of racial, cultural, gender, socioeconomic, and sexual differences. Perhaps the most salient feature of the contemporary world, particularly in the United States, is the dramatic increase in the range of differences that most people encounter on a daily basis. We are becoming an increasingly multi-racial, multi-ethnic, multi-cultural, multi-faith nation, with all of the attendant conflicts and tensions that accompany such a rapid increase in diversity in the midst of difficult economic circumstances.[2]

Gergen (1991) argues, moreover, that the technological advances of the past several decades have produced profound changes in the ways we experience and understand ourselves and our relationships with others: "As a result of advances in radio, telephone, transportation, television, satellite transmission, computers, and more, we are exposed to an enormous barrage of social stimulation. Small and enduring communities, with a limited cast of significant others, are being replaced by a vase an ever-expanding array of relationships" (Gergen, 1991, p. xi). Gergen uses the term "social saturation" (or the "saturated self") to capture what he takes to be this feature of the postmodern world. As a result of the process of social saturation at work in the diverse world in which we live, he argues, "emerging technologies saturate us with the voices of humankind—both harmonious and alien":

As we absorb their varied rhymes and reasons, they become part of us and we of them. Social saturation furnishes us with a multiplicity of incoherent and unrelated languages of the self. For everything we "know to be true" about ourselves, other voices within respond with doubt and derision. This fragmentation of self-conceptions corresponds to a multiplicity of incoherent and disconnected relationships, These relationships pull us in myriad directions, inviting us to play such a variety of roles that the very concept of an "authentic self" with knowable characteristics recedes from view. (Gergen, 1991, pp. 6-7)

Again, while some may be threatened by, and defend against, encounters with difference, we would argue that the explicit diversity of the postmodern world actually contains within it a myriad of possibilities for renewal and revitalization. This is primarily because the difference and diversity that have become so salient in our world offer new and powerful visions for human life: "Postmodernists are arguing for a plurality of voices and narratives, that is, for different narratives that present the unrepresentable, for stories that emerge from historically specific struggles. Similarly, postmodern discourse is attempting, with its emphasis on the specific and the normative, to situate reason and knowledge within rather than outside particular configurations of space, place, time, and power" (Giroux, 1988, p. 15).

An Explicitly Critical Perspective

These interconnected emphases on the centrality of discourse in human life, the dialectics of discourse, knowledge, and power, and the salience of difference in the contemporary world point to the third key characteristic of the postmodern—its explicitly critical perspective. In particular, postmodernism, as a form of intellectual and cultural critique, challenges the logic of foundationalism that undergirds the modern worldview, calls into question its correlative assumptions about autonomy, rationality, essentialism, and progress, and rejects its quest for a legitimate center, a solid grounding for all knowledge and value (see Bauman, 1992; Gergen, 1991; Giroux, 1991; Lyotard, 1984; Packer,

1992). As such, the postmodern perspective eschews grand narratives of progress, questions the view that universal reason is the primary foundation for human affairs, and decenters the individualistic humanist subject.

Gergen's (1991) work helps to make clear the link between the contemporary encounter with difference and the postmodern critique. If the postmodern world is marked by a plurality of diverse voices all vying for the right to name what is to be taken as reality—"to be accepted as legitimate expressions of the true and the good" (Gergen, 1991, p. 7)—both within the self and within the culture at large, then it is clear how the sense of certainty that the modern worldview offered must necessarily have vanished:

As the voices expand in power and presence, all that seems proper, right-minded, and well understood is subverted. In the postmodern world we become increasingly aware that the objects about which we speak are not so much "in the world" as they are products of perspective. Thus, processes such as emotion and reason cease to be real and significant essences of persons; rather, in the light of pluralism we perceive them to be impostors, the outcome of our ways of conceptualizing them. Under postmodern conditions, persons exist in a state of continuous construction and reconstruction; it is a world where anything goes that can be negotiated. Each reality of self gives way to reflexive questioning, irony, and ultimately the playful probing of yet another reality. (Gergen, 1991, p. 7)

Yet the postmodern critique does more than challenge the modern epistemology founded on reason and rationality. At its best, as Giroux (1991) argues, it is a profoundly moral critique that, by highlighting the role of power in the construction of knowledge, helps to make visible important ideological and structural forces, like gender, race, and class, at work in the contemporary world:

Postmodernism does more than "wage war on totality," it also calls into question the use of reason in the service of power, the role of intellectuals who speak through authority invested in a science of truth and history, and forms of leadership that demand unification and consensus within centrally administered chains of command. Postmodernism rejects a notion of reason that is disinterested, transcendent, and universal. Rather than separating reason from the terrain of history, place, and desire, postmodernism argues that reason and science can only be understood as part of a broader historical, political, and social struggle over the relationship between language and power. Within this context, the distinction between passion and reason, objectivity and interpretation no longer exist as separate entities, but represent, instead, the effects of particular discourses and forms of social power. (Giroux, 1991, p. 20)

Thus, the postmodern critique is not simply epistemological; rather, it is explicitly political and deeply normative.

This is but a cursory overview of what I take to be three of the most salient features of the postmodern world. There is more that could and should be said about the current state of affairs, but instead, I want to move ahead to consider the implications of the postmodern for the study of moral development and the practice of moral education.

MORAL DEVELOPMENT: A DIALOGICAL PERSPECTIVE[3]

In this section, I want to sketch the outlines of an explicitly dialogical perspective on the development of moral functioning across the lifespan (see Day 1991a, 1991b, 1993a, 1993b; Day & Tappan, 1996; Tappan, 1991a, 1991b, 1992, 1993). This perspective, which draws inspiration and support from the work of Mikhail Bakhtin (1981, 1986, 1990, 1993), Lev Vygotsky (1934/1986, 1978), and others (Hermans & Kempen, 1993; Holquist, 1990; Mead, 1934; Sampson, 1993a; Taylor, 1985; Volosinov, 1929/1986; Wertsch, 1989, 1991), assumes that moral functioning (like all "higher psychological functioning" [Vygotsky, 1978]) is necessarily mediated by words, language, and forms of discourse. Moreover, because such mediation occurs primarily via both private and public moral dialogue, this perspective assumes that the moral self is fundamentally dialogical in character. As such, it reflects the postmodern focus on language and discourse, and highlights the degree to which conversation and dialogue give rise to moral action. It thus differs in significant ways from the fundamentally modern cognitive-developmental paradigm that has dominated the study of moral development for the past thirty years (Kohlberg, 1981, 1984; Piaget, 1932/1965; Turiel, 1983)—a paradigm premised on representationalist assumptions about language and individualistic (monological) assumptions about the self (see Day & Tappan, 1996).[4]

Key to a dialogical perspective is Vygotsky's (1978) claim that in order to understand the psyche I must understand the "tools" that mediate and shape its functioning (see Wertsch, 1985). Language is the most important of these "psychological tools," because language, by definition, has both semiotic and communicative characteristics. Moreover, psychological tools, like language, do not simply facilitate the operation of existing mental tasks; rather the introduction of new psychological tools fundamentally transforms a given psychological function: "as soon as speech and the use of signs are incorporated into any action, the action becomes transformed and organized along entirely new lines" (Vygotsky, 1978, p. 24).

This view of the linguistic mediation of psychological functioning is essential, I would argue, to understanding the process of moral development. Moral action (acting when faced with the question "What is the 'right' or the 'moral' thing to do in this situation?") is fundamentally and irreducibly mediated action. By this I mean that for an action to be considered "moral," either by an actor or by an observer, a particular kind of meaning must be associated with that action. This obtains whether that action is as *instinctive* as rushing out into busy traffic to rescue a wayward child, or as *deliberative* as weighing the pros and cons of having an abortion. In either case, and in the myriad of others, both mundane and exemplary, that constitute the moral domain, because the designation "moral" is an *interpretation* of the action in question, generated from the shared set of understandings that constitute culture, moral action can never be unmediated. Rather, it is always accomplished with the use of "psychological tools" (most importantly, words, language, and forms of moral discourse) that enable the person to think, feel, and act in a meaningful way.

The work of Michael Oakeshott (1975) highlights this critical link between morality and language. Oakeshott argues that morality is, at its core, a "practice" or a form of "conduct" that facilitates human interaction: "The conditions which compose a moral practice are not theorems or precepts about human conduct, nor do they constitute anything so specific as a 'shared system of values'; they compose, instead, a language of colloquial intercourse" (Oakeshott,1975, p. 63). This language, claims Oakeshott, is thus fundamentally pragmatic; it is a tool used "like any other language, [as] an instrument of self-disclosure . . . by agents in diagnosing their situations and choosing their responses; and it is a language of self-enactment which permits those who can use it to understand themselves and one another" (Oakeshott,1975, p. 63):

A morality, then, is neither a system of general principles nor a code of rules, but a vernacular language. General principles and even rules may be elicited from it, but (like other languages) it is not the creation of grammarians; it is made by speakers. What has to be learned in a moral education is not a theorem such as that good conduct is acting fairly or being charitable, nor is it a rule such as "always tell the truth," but how to speak the language intelligently. (Oakeshott,1975, p. 78-79)

Moral action (or moral activity), in other words, is mediated by a vernacular moral language that shapes the ways in which persons think, feel, and act.

From a dialogical perspective, therefore, the moral self is understood not as a "prelinguistic given" that merely employs language as a tool to express internally constituted meanings, but rather as a product of language from the start—arising out of linguistic, discursive, and communicative practices (Kerby, 1991). In other words, the self's understanding of itself and its moral experience is mediated and shaped primarily through words, language, and forms of discourse, which necessarily arise out of a particular social, cultural, and historical context. The moral self is, therefore, neither "a substantial entity having onto-logical priority over praxis," nor an autonomous Cartesian agent "with epistemological priority, an originator of meaning" (Kerby, 1991, p. 4). Rather, self's morality emerges from the conflicts and struggles that obtain from her being an embodied site of contesting claims (rather than an idealized transcendental subject [see Kohlberg, 1984]). As the words, language, and forms of discourse she encounters in her own sociocultural context collide, collude, and combine, they provoke her need to establish and define a voice (or voices) of her own. Moreover, the postmodern multiplication of such discourses, and their varying claims as to how to be a person (see Gergen, 1991), both problematizes and potentially augments the process by which a person (understood as a dialogical moral self) comes to appropriate and otherwise act with reference to the voices in her world (Day & Tappan, 1996).

Two recent empirical efforts illuminate the fundamentally dialogic nature of the moral self: Day (1991a) has explored the phenomenon of the "moral audience"—the ways in which children, adolescents, and adults, in the course of telling stories about their lived moral experience, identify others (real and imagined, alive and dead) that compose an "imaginary" audience before whom they act, and by whom they are judged. And Tappan (1991a) has explored the development of moral authority, focusing on how self's representation of the words of others (in interview narratives) moves from what Bakhtin (1981) calls "externally authoritative discourse" to "internally persuasive discourse."

Ultimately, therefore, it is Bakhtin (1981) who provides the central theoretical framework for a postmodern dialogical approach to moral development. Of particular interest to Bakhtin is the process by which the words, voices, and language of others are expressed and represented by the self. This is obviously one of the primary tasks of the novelist, as he constructs and represents dialogue between different characters in the novel. It is also a crucial task for a person, as he lives and tells—as he authors—narratives of moral experience (Tappan & Brown, 1989), and thus *appropriates* the voices, words, and language of others that shape and mediate his psychological (and moral) functioning.

Bakhtin's (1981) fundamental claim is that authorship—in life and in literature—arises out of a dialogic relationship between self and other (see Day & Tappan, 1996). The "living language," he says, lies on the "borderline" of self and other, so much so that "the word in language is half someone else's" (Bakhtin, 1981, p. 293). Yet, because we are engaged in relationships with others, we must ultimately assume some responsibility and accountability for our thoughts, feelings, and actions. Thus, it is important to understand how one makes the word (language) of others one's own.

Others' words become one's own, according to Bakhtin (1981), as a result of a difficult and complicated *developmental* process. This is the process of "ideological becoming": "The ideological becoming of a human being . . . is the process of selectively assimilating the words of others" (Bakhtin, 1981, p. 341). Consequently, to understand the development of the moral self, we must understand the process by which a person appropriates others' words, language, and forms of discourse:

The importance of struggling with another's discourse, its influence in the history of an individual's coming to ideological consciousness, is enormous. One's own discourse and one's own voice, although born of another or dynamically stimulated by another, will sooner or later begin to liberate themselves from the authority of the other's discourse. This problem is made more complex by the fact that a variety of alien voices enter into the struggle for influence within an individual's consciousness (just as they struggle with one another in surrounding social reality). (Bakhtin, 1981, p. 348)[5]

The goal of development is not simply a matter, therefore, of speaking in one's own "true" or "authentic" voice. Rather, it is a matter of engaging in ongoing dialogue with the words of others, and thereby coming to a somewhat more "self persuasive," and somewhat less "authoritative," sense of self-understanding and moral responsibility (see Day & Tappan, 1994; Tappan, 1991a).

Such a dialogical perspective has profound implications for our understanding the process of moral development in a postmodern world. In particular, in its focus on language and the linguistic mediation of moral functioning/activity, it acknowledges not only that reality is discursively constructed, but also that discourse and power are fundamentally linked (see Foucault, 1980; Sampson, 1993a, 1993b). It thus offers the potential for a genuinely critical and transformative perspective on the contemporary world. And in its stress on the dialogical, and thus inescapably social, origins of moral functioning/activity, it pushes toward a distributed, collective, shared, fundamentally social view of moral development, rather than an individualistic, atomistic, isolated, fundamentally psychological view. As such, it provides a new perspective on difference, in which diversity is seen not as a problematic function of individuals, but rather as an inescapable characteristic of genuine moral communities.

In order to explore this last idea more fully, as well as to set the stage for a postmodern approach to moral education, let me turn to a brief consideration of the conception of moral community to which such a dialogical perspective on moral development necessarily gives rise.

TOWARD A CONCEPTION OF MORAL COMMUNITY

Most centrally, this perspective suggests that the communities in which moral development occurs are not composed of discrete, self-contained individuals (monads). Rather, postmodern moral communities consist of distributed, dialogical selves engaged in an ongoing process of interpretation, and committed, necessarily, to dialogue, discussion, and mutual exchange across differences: "A *community* is a group of people who are socially interdependent, who participate together in discussion and decision making, and who share certain practices that both define the community and are nurtured by it" (Bellah, Madsen, Sullivan, Swidler, & Tipton, 1985, p. 333; emphasis in original).

Unlike more traditional communities in the United States and elsewhere, however, in which similarity across a variety of intersecting dimensions (e.g., gender, race, class, culture, religious belief, sexual orientation, etc.) has been a defining feature of membership, postmodern moral communities are defined just as much by difference and diversity as they are by similarity. While there must be some "common denominator" that draws people together, that similarity is often offset, these days, by a wide range of differences across what once were understood to be common ties.

Yet, as I have indicated above, from a critical postmodern perspective, these differences within communities are not seen as threats to the integrity of those communities, but rather are celebrated as broadening and enhancing the experience of all. When members of a community share their differences openly and honestly with one another, even when those differences are threatening, everyone benefits. As Maxine Greene (1993) writes, "The community many of us hope for now is not to be identified with conformity. It is a community attentive to difference, open to the idea of plurality. Something life-affirming in diversity must be discovered and rediscovered, as what is held in common becomes always more many-faceted—open and inclusive, drawn to untapped possibility" (Greene, 1993, p. 194).

Needless to say, in order for a diverse postmodern moral community to function and sustain itself, there must be some values and assumptions that are agreed upon and shared by all the members of the community. Key to the postmodern perspective, however (as I have argued above), is the understanding that these values and assumptions are discursively constructed, and thus originate from within the community itself. Consequently, value-conflicts must be resolved through dialogue and negotiation, rather than by appeal to a priori, transcendent, universal, or ideal principles.

Postmodern moral communities thus function effectively as what Stanley Fish (1980) calls "interpretive communities." As such, they consist of persons engaged in a common effort to make meaning of (that is, to interpret) their lived [moral] experiences. But this effort is not to uncover or reveal the "true" meaning of a given event or experience. Rather, it is to jointly construct the meaning of that event or experience (or text) in a way that makes sense to the members of the community.

The assumption that meaning is made within communities, not discovered by individuals, does not, however, lead inexorably to subjectivity and solipsism, because the process of interpretation is, in the final analysis, social and conventional, not personal and idiosyncratic. Thus it is always limited by the community or institution of which the interpreter is a part: "If the self is conceived of not as an independent entity but as a social construct whose operations are delimited by the systems of intelligibility that inform it, then the meanings it confers on texts are not its own but have their source in the interpretive community (or communities) of which it is a function" (Fish, 1980, p. 335).

Consequently, a dialogical perspective on moral community resolves the problem of moral relativism that many worry is a necessary characteristic of the postmodern world. Not only does the claim that "all truths are relative" reflexively negate itself (see Lawson, 1985), but the traditional opposition between "subjective" and "objective" simply disappears within the context of an interpretive community. For, as Fish (1980) argues, when a person acts on behalf of values upon which her moral community has agreed (e.g., choosing to put an unwanted child up for adoption rather than having an abortion), she acts neither for purely objective reasons (because her values come from a particular point of view, not from access to an "objective reality"), nor for purely subjective reasons (because her values come from the practices and conventions of her community, not from her own "personal" point of view). Rather, she acts, in a sense, for both objective and subjective reasons, because her values are, indeed, a shared product of agreement among members of a community (objective), and yet the community must acknowledge that their values are not universal, but emerge from their own particular social, cultural, and historical context (subjective).[6]

This conception of moral community shares much in common with contemporary "communitarian" efforts in moral philosophy and political theory. As such, it offers both "methodological" and "normative" challenges to modern "individualistic" moral theories (Avineri & de-Shalit, 1992).[7] The methodological challenge rejects the individualistic focus on the independent, autonomous, rational agent freely choosing between different courses of action (see Rawls, 1971), in favor of a conception of dialogical, distributed selves that are thus fundamentally constituted by the relationships and communities in which they participate (see Sandel, 1982; MacIntyre, 1981; Taylor, 1985). Similarly, the normative challenge rejects the individualistic focus on autonomy and personal rights (see Nozick, 1974), in favor of a positive view of the special obligations and social responsibilities members of a community accept for one and other—obligations and responsibilities that may, in fact, impose limits on personal autonomy and individual freedom (see Miller, 1989). Communitarians argue, in short, that "it is morally good that the self be constituted by its communal ties" (Avineri & de-Shalit, 1992, p. 7).

From a dialogical/communitarian perspective, therefore, the essence of morality is *responsibility* (or "answerability" [Bakhtin, 1990]). Implicit in the idea of responsibility, argues H. R. Niebuhr (1978), "is the image of man [sic]-the-answerer, man engaged in dialogue, man acting in response to action upon him" (Niebuhr, 1978, p. 56). Responsibility thus entails responding to the needs of both others and self, within the context of a given community, and striking a *fitting* balance between them.[8] Moreover, it always involves four central elements—responsiveness, interpretation, accountability, and social solidarity: "The idea or pattern of responsibility, then, may summarily and abstractly be defined as the idea of an agent's action as response to an action upon him [sic] in accordance with his interpretation of the latter action and with his expectation of response to his response; and all of this is in a continuing community of agents" (p. Niebuhr, 1978, 65).

The moral vision to which a dialogical/communitarian perspective gives rise thus focuses on the responsibilities persons feel as members of moral communities—however those communities may be defined and/or constituted. These responsibilities, however, are not simply *chosen* or *accepted* by persons as *additions* or *afterthoughts.*   Rather, they emerge, at the start, from the fundamentally dialogic and communal character of self:

Community . . . describe[s] not just a *feeling* but a mode of self-understanding partly constitutive of the agent's identity. [Thus] to say that the members of a society are bound by a sense of community is not simply to say that a great many of them profess communitarian sentiments and pursue communitarian aims, but rather than they conceive their identity—the subject and not just the object of their feelings and aspirations—as defined to some extent by the community of which they are a part. For them, community describes not just what they have as fellow citizens but also what they are, not a relationship they choose (as in a voluntary association) but an attachment they discover, not merely an attribute but a constituent of their identity. (Sandel, 1982, p. 150)

It is, moreover, a moral vision that is at once both nonrelative and nonuniversal. It is non-relative because it emerges from social practices and shared conventions of a given community. It is nonuniversal because all communities are embedded in specific social, cultural, and historical contexts, and can not be transcended.

But what happens when the moral visions/responsibilities of different communities come into conflict? This is, perhaps, the most vexing problem of all in a postmodern world. While I cannot formulate a full answer to this question here, I would argue that once again dialogue provides the key to a solution. Certainly one community may be horrified by the deeds of another (e.g., the activities of the "Fourth Reich Skinheads"), and may even take action to stop the offending practice. But, in the postmodern world, there can be no appeal to a universal principle to justify those actions. Rather, there must be a first attempt at dialogue, discussion, and mutual exchange, so that the communities in conflict can seek a common understanding. Unilateral action is thus an option only if dialogue breaks down, and it can be justified only from within a given community. In the postmodern world, in other words, there can only be a methodological or procedural appeal to dialogue, not a normative appeal to universal principles.

CONCLUSIONS

In this chapter, I have highlighted postmodern insights about the discursive construction of reality, celebrations of difference and diversity, and critiques of the overly individualistic assumptions of the modern worldview. I have presented a dialogical conception of the moral self that reflects and incorporates these insights, and I have argued for a dialogical/communitarian vision of moral community that at once both acknowledges difference and fosters responsibility. But perhaps I have not yet fully answered the question: "What exactly does moral development in a postmodern world entail?" Let us, therefore, attempt to answer this most difficult question, before concluding with some thoughts about the approach to moral education to which I think such a conception of moral development gives rise.

The concept of "development" has traditionally been a prescriptive concept used to refer to progress toward some specified goal, endpoint, or telos that has been imbued with value (see Kaplan, 1983, 1986). In the modern worldview, which celebrated progress, development was thus assumed to entail inexorable movement up a clear hierarchy of stages or levels toward a universal goal (see, for example, Piaget, 1967; Kohlberg, 1981, 1984; Loevinger, 1976; Selman, 1980). In the postmodern world, however, development must assume a somewhat different meaning. It must retain its prescriptive connotations, but those prescriptions must be understood to apply only within specific communities, not universally. Consequently, developmental progress must be envisioned not as climbing step-by-step ever higher along a universal sequence, but rather as traversing a spiral that while it gradually increases in breadth and scope, also involves a constant revisiting of the same issues and problems (see Perry, 1970, 1981; Tappan, 1989).

I would argue, therefore, that moral development in a postmodern world, from a dialogical/communitarian perspective, entails gradual transformations in responsiveness and responsibility within a given moral community. These transformations are accomplished through the moral language learned (Oakeshott, 1975) or appropriated (Bakhtin, 1981), and thus shared by members of the community, as they engage in ongoing conversation and dialogue. Moreover, this moral language—the language of responsibility—provides both the medium for social communication and the mediational means by which moral functioning occurs.

Most importantly, however, because selves are fundamentally and inescapably dialogical, from this perspective moral development is understood less as an individual phenomenon than as a collective phenomenon. That is to say, from dialogical/communitarian perspective what develops in moral development is not so much persons as the communities to which persons belong. Of course, persons (e.g., children) must continue to provide the focus for our developmental efforts, because our attention is "recruited" (Kegan, 1982) not by groups or communities but by other human beings. But to the degree that we can move toward understanding that persons are not monological, isolated individuals, but always fundamentally dialogical, persons-in-relation (Jordan, Kaplan, Baker-Miller, Stiver, & Surrey, 1991), we will come, I would argue, to an understanding of moral development that reflects the most positive and liberating aspects of the postmodern world (see also Gergen, 1991).

This perspective clearly has profound implications for the work of moral educators in the contemporary world. In particular, I would argue that this approach, which encourages the formation of moral communities in which persons share a common moral language, while at the same time focusing on the importance of dialogue across differences, is precisely analogous to the best contemporary efforts in multicultural education, which seek to reconstruct schools as "multicultural democracies" (see Perry & Fraser, 1993; also Dickerson, 1993; Hidalgo, 1993; hooks, 1994; Mizell, Benett, Bowman, & Morin, 1993; Richards, 1993). Moreover, such an approach ultimately represents a much more powerful and productive approach to moral education than the reactionary and retrogressive "character education" approach that is so popular these days (see Bennett, 1994; Kilpatrick, 1992; Lickona, 1991). This is because instead of placing authority solely in the hands of those with power and privilege (that is, teachers), this approach envisions that students and teachers, children and parents, living together in communities, can and will jointly assume authority and responsibility for constructing and conducting the kind of critical and liberatory moral education, grounded in dialogue, that will touch people's lives and make a real difference in the postmodern world in which we all now live (see Burbules, 1993; Burbules & Rice, 1991; Freire, 1970; Noddings, 1994).

But this will not necessarily be easy; progress may be slow and victory sometimes fleeting. In the end, therefore, I return to "Operation Grow Hair." While it exemplifies the kind of effort to encourage moral development in the contemporary world for which I have argued, by promoting the difficult and often painful process of genuine dialogue across difference, it also reflects the reality that, in the last analysis, change, assisted and encouraged by the right choice of words, occurs one step at a time:

Interviewer: You chose these kids because you feared they were going to hurt other people. Do you think they will hurt other people now?

Marc Greenberg: I'm the optimist, but I don't think so.

Interviewer: Do you think these kids, in terms of their racism, have changed, genuinely changed?

Mr. Greenberg: Well, it's interesting, because [Tim] used the term 'prejudism,' which to my knowledge, isn't really a term. But if you—if you put prejudism somewhere between racism and prejudice, maybe that's where they're at.

Interviewer: You know what I saw? I saw Turtle with his head half shaved, and I thought . . ."Halfway there."

Rev. Murray: Which is better than no way there.

NOTES

Earlier versions of this essay were presented at the Annual Meeting of the American Educational Research Association, Atlanta, GA, April, 1993; the Annual Symposium of the Jean Piaget Society, Philadelphia, PA, June, 1993; and the Inquiries in Social Construction Conference, Durham, NH, June, 1993.

Thanks to Lyn Mikel Brown.

1. From "60 Minutes," CBS News, June 5, 1994.

2. These conflicts and tensions have spawned such reactionary political responses as California's Proposition 187, which denies illegal aliens access to public services.

3. In this section I draw significantly on a perspective presented first in an article coauthored with James Day (see Day & Tappan, 1996).

4. The modern vision, which privileges autonomy, rationality, essentialism, and progress, corresponds precisely to the "metaethical" and "metatheoretical" assumptions elaborated by Kohlberg (1984) in his final formulation of his theory of moral development.

5. Note the similarity here between Bakhtin's conception of the dialogic formation of ideological consciousness and Gergen's (1991) account of postmodern selves saturated with many voices—both harmonious and alien.

6. Packer (1994) argues, similarly, that "the mistake that many postmodernists make is to think that because knowledge and values can't be grounded in interpretation-free foundations they have no grounding at all. . . . Such a conclusion actually accepts the modern view of what valid knowledge and legitimate morality are, [at the same time that it] accepts the failure of the attempt to find them."

"A more coherent postmodernism," Packer suggests, is one that appreciates that the Enlightenment project looked in the wrong place for epistemological and ethical grounding—the individual subject. The place to look is the communities of practice in which individuals live, for it is these that ground our knowledge and our values. . . . Such a move leads to a recognition that there is not just one grounding but several, perhaps many. But this is not relativism, it is pluralism. And to the extent that communities share a common material circumstance (and this extent is surely growing as our world shrinks) there is a basis for communication and agreement within this plurality.

7. Such theories, of course, provide the foundation for modern approaches to moral development and moral education (e.g., Kohlberg, 1981, 1984).

8. Niebuhr (1978) contrasts responsibility to both teleology and deontology by distinguishing the good, the right, and the fitting: "teleology is concerned always with the highest good to which it subordinates the right; consistent deontology is concerned with the right, no matter what may happen to our goods; but for the ethics of responsibility the fitting action, the one that fits into a total interaction as response and as anticipation of further response, is alone conducive to the good and alone is right" (pp. 60-61).

REFERENCES

Avineri, S., & de-Shalit, A. (1992). Introduction. In S. Avineri & A. de-Shalit (Eds.), *Communitarianism and individualism* (pp. 1-11). Oxford: Oxford University Press.

Bakhtin, M. (1981). *The dialogic imagination* (M. Holquist, Ed., C. Emerson & M. Holquist, Trans.). Austin: University of Texas Press.

Bakhtin, M. (1986). *Speech genres and other late essays* (C. Emerson & M. Holquist, Eds., V. McGee, Trans.). Austin: University of Texas Press.

Bakhtin, M. (1990). *Art and answerability* (M. Holquist & V. Liapunov, Eds., V. Liapunov, Trans.). Austin: University of Texas Press.

Bakhtin, M. (1993). *Toward a philosophy of the act* (V. Liapunov, Trans.). Austin: University of Texas Press.

Bauman, Z. (1992). *Intimations of postmodernity*. London: Routledge. Bellah, R. N., Madsen, R., Sullivan, W. M., Swidler, A., & Tipton, S. M. (1985). Habits of the heart: Individualism and commitment in American life. Berkeley, CA: University of California Press.

Bellah, R. N., Madsen, R., Sullivan, W. M., Swidler, A., & Tipton, S. M. (1985). *Habits of the heart: Individualism and commitment in American life*. Berkeley, CA: University of California Press.

Benhabib, S. (1992). *Situating the self: Gender, community, and postmodernism in contemporary ethics*. New York: Routledge.

Bennett, W. (1994). *The book of virtues*. New York: Simon & Schuster.

Burbules, N. (1993). Dialogue in teaching: Theory and practice. New York: Teachers College Press.

Burbules, N. C., & Rice, S. (1991). Dialogue across differences: Continuing the conversation. *Harvard Educational Review, 61,* 393-416.

Connor, S. (1989). *Postmodernist culture: An introduction to theories of the contemporary*. Oxford: Basil Blackwell.

Day, J. (1991a). The moral audience: On the narrative mediation of moral 'judgment' and moral 'action'. In M. Tappan & M. Packer (Eds.), *Narrative and storytelling: Implications for understanding moral development* (pp. 27-42). San Francisco: Jossey-Bass.

Day, J. (1991b). Role-taking reconsidered: Narrative and cognitive-developmental interpretations of moral growth. *The Journal of Moral Education, 20,* 305-15.

Day, J. (1993a, June). Desire, risk, and the yearning for reception: Regulating vocabularies and ideology in moral and religious development. Paper presented at the Inquiries in Social Construction Conference, Durham, NH.

Day, J. (1993b). Speaking of belief: Language, performance, and narrative in the psychology of religion. *The International Journal for the Psychology of Religion, 3*, 213-29.

Day, J., & Tappan, M. (1996). The narrative approach to moral development: From the epistemic subject to dialogical selves. *Human Development, 39*, 67-82.

Dickerson, S. (1993). The blind men (women) and the elephant: The case for a comprehensive multicultural education program at the Cambridge Rindge and Latin School. In T. Perry & J. Fraser (Eds.), *Freedom's plow: Teaching in the multicultural classroom* (pp. 65-89). New York: Routledge.

Fish, S. (1980). *Is there a text in this class? The authority of interpretive communities.* Cambridge: Harvard University Press.

Foucault, M. (1979). *The history of sexuality, Vol. 1* (R. Hurley, Trans). New York: Random House.

Foucault, M. (1980). *Power/Knowledge: Selected interviews and other writings 1972-1977* (C. Gordon, Ed.). New York: Pantheon.

Freire, P. (1970). *Pedagogy of the oppressed* (M. Ramos, Trans.). New York: Continuum.

Gergen, K. (1991). *The saturated self: Dilemmas of identity in contemporary life.* New York: Basic Books.

Gergen, K. (1994). Exploring the postmodern: Perils or potentials? *American Psychologist, 49*, 412-16.

Giroux, H. (1988). Postmodernism and the discourse of educational criticism. *Journal of Education, 170*, 5-30.

Giroux, H. (1991). Modernism, postmodernism, and feminism: Rethinking the boundaries of educational discourse. In H. Giroux (Ed.), *Postmodernism, feminism, and cultural politics: Redrawing educational boundaries.* Albany: State University of New York Press.

Greene, M. (1993). The passions of pluralism: Multiculturalism and the expanding community. In T. Perry & J. Fraser (Eds.), *Freedom's plow: Teaching in the multicultural classroom* (pp. 185-96). New York: Routledge.

Harvey, D. (1989). *The condition of postmodernity.* Oxford: Basil Blackwell.

Hassan, I. (1987). *The postmodern turn: Essays in postmodern theory and culture.* Columbus, OH: The Ohio State University Press.

Hermans, H., & Kempen, H. (1993). *The dialogical self: Meaning as movement.* New York: Academic Press.

Hidalgo, N. (1993). Multicultural teacher introspection. In T. Perry & J. Fraser (Eds.), *Freedom's plow: Teaching in the multicultural classroom* (pp. 99-106). New York: Routledge.

Holquist, M. (1990). *Dialogism: Bakhtin and his world.* London: Routledge.

hooks, b. (1994). *Teaching to transgress: Education as the practice of freedom.* New York: Routledge.

Jameson, F. (1991). *Postmodernism, or, The cultural logic of late capitalism.* Durham, NC: Duke University Press.

Jordan, J., Kaplan, A., Baker-Miller, J., Stiver, I., & Surrey, J. (1991). *Women's growth in connection: Writings from the Stone Center.* New York: The Guilford Press.

Kaplan, B. (1983). A trio of trials. In R. Lerner (Ed.), *Developmental psychology: Historical and philosophical perspectives* (pp. 185-228). Hillsdale, NJ: Lawrence Erlbaum.

Kaplan, B. (1986). Value presuppositions in theories of human development. In L. Cirillo & S. Wapner (Eds.), *Value presuppositions in theories of human development* (pp. 89-103). Hillsdale, NJ: Lawrence Erlbaum.

Kegan, R. (1982). *The evolving self: Problem and process in human development*. Cambridge: Harvard University Press.

Kerby, A. (1991). *Narrative and the self*. Bloomington, IN: Indiana University Press.

Kilpatrick, W. (1992). *Why Johnny can't tell right from wrong*. New York: Simon & Schuster.

Kohlberg, L. (1981). *Essays on moral development, Volume I: The philosophy of moral development*. San Francisco: Harper & Row.

Kohlberg, L. (1984*). Essays on moral development, Volume II: The psychology of moral development*. San Francisco: Harper & Row.

Lather, P. (1991). *Getting smart: Feminist research and pedagogy with/in the postmodern*. New York: Routledge.

Lawson, H. (1985). *Reflexivity: The post-modern predicament*. La Salle, IL: Open Court.

Lickona, T. (1991). *Educating for character*. New York: Bantam Books.

Loevinger: J. (1976). *Ego development*. San Francisco: Jossey-Bass.

Lyotard, F. (1984). *The postmodern condition: A report on knowledge* (G. Bennington & B. Massumi, Trans.). Minneapolis, MN: University of Minnesota Press.

MacIntyre, A. (1981). *After virtue: A study in moral theory*. Notre Dame: University of Notre Dame Press.

McLaren, P. (1994). *Life in schools* (2nd ed.). New York: Longman.

Mead, G. H. (1934). *Mind, self, and society* (C. Morris, Ed.). Chicago: The University of Chicago Press.

Miller, D. (1989). *Market, state, and community*. Oxford: Oxford University Press.

Mizell, L., Benett, S., Bowman, B., & Morin, L. (1993). Different ways of seeing: Teaching in an anti-racist school. In T. Perry & J. Fraser (Eds.), *Freedom's plow: Teaching in the multicultural classroom* (pp. 27-46). New York: Routledge.

Natoli, J., & Hutcheon, L. (Eds.). (1993). *A postmodern reader*. Albany: State University of New York Press.

Niebuhr, H. R. (1978). *The responsible self*. New York: Harper & Row.

Noddings, N. (1994). Conversation as moral education. *Journal of Moral Education, 23*, 107-18.

Nozick, R. (1974). *Anarchy, state, and utopia*. Oxford: Oxford University Press.

Oakeshott, M. (1975). *On human conduct*. Oxford: Clarendon Press.

Packer, M. (1992). Toward a postmodern psychology of moral action and moral development. In W. Kurtines, M. Azmitia, & J. Gewirtz (Eds.), *The role of values in psychology and human development* (pp. 30-62). New York: John Wiley.

Packer, M. (1994). Postmodernism. Message sent to the electronic mail discussion, XLCHC. September 27, 1994.

Perry, T., & Fraser, J. (1993). Restructuring schools as multiracial/multicultural democracies: Toward a theoretical perspective. In T. Perry & J. Fraser (Eds.*), Freedom's plow: Teaching in the multicultural classroom* (pp. 3-24). New York: Routledge.

Perry, W. (1970). *Forms of intellectual and ethical development in the college years: A scheme*. New York: Holt, Rinehart, & Winston.

Perry, W. (1981). Cognitive and ethical growth: The making of meaning. In A. Chickering (Ed.), *The modern American college*. San Francisco: Jossey-Bass.

Piaget, J. (1965). *The moral judgment of the child*. New York: The Free Press. (Original work published 1932).

Piaget, J, (1967). *Six psychological studies*. New York: Vintage Books.

Rawls, J. (1971). *A theory of justice*. Cambridge: Harvard University Press.

Richards, J. (1993). Classroom tapestry: A practitioner's perspective on multicultural education. In T. Perry & J. Fraser (Eds.), *Freedom's plow: Teaching in the multicultural classroom* (pp. 47-63). New York: Routledge.

Rosenau, P. (1992). *Postmodernism and the social sciences: Insights, inroads, and intrusions*. Princeton: Princeton University Press.

Sampson, E. (1993a). *Celebrating the other: A dialogic account of human nature*. Boulder, CO: Westview Press.

Sampson, E. (1993b). Identity politics: Challenges to psychology's understanding. *American Psychologist, 48*, 1219-30.

Sandel, M. (1982). *Liberalism and the limits of justice*. Cambridge: Cambridge University Press.

Selman, R. (1980). *The growth of interpersonal understanding*. New York: Academic Press.

Tappan, M. (1989). Stories lived and stories told: The narrative structure of late adolescent moral development. *Human Development, 32*, 300-315.

Tappan, M. (1991a). Narrative, authorship, and the development of moral authority. In M. Tappan & M. Packer (Eds.), *Narrative approaches to moral development* (pp. 5-25). San Francisco: Jossey-Bass.

Tappan, M. (1991b). Narrative, language, and moral experience. *Journal of Moral Education, 20*, 243-56.

Tappan, M. (1992). Texts and contexts: Language, culture, and the development of moral functioning. In L. T. Winegar & J. Valsiner (Eds.), *Children's development within social contexts: Metatheoretical, theoretical, and methodological issues*. Hillsdale, NJ: Lawrence Erlbaum.

Tappan, M. (1993). Relational voices and moral development: Reflections on change. In P. Kahaney, L. Perry, & J. Janangelo (Eds.), *Theoretical and critical perspectives on teacher change* (pp. 1-14). Norwood, NJ: Ablex.

Tappan, M., & Brown, L. (1989). Stories told and lessons learned: Toward a narrative approach to moral development and moral education. *Harvard Educational Review, 59*, 182-205.

Tappan, M., & Brown, L. (in press). Envisioning a critical moral pedagogy: A postmodern perspective. *Journal of Moral Education*.

Taylor, C. (1985). *Human agency and language: Philosophical papers*, I. Cambridge: Cambridge University Press.

Turiel, E. (1983). *The development of social knowledge: Morality and convention*. Cambridge: Cambridge University Press.

Volosinov, V. (1986). *Marxism and the philosophy of language* (L. Matejka & I. Titunik, Trans.). Cambridge: Harvard University Press. (Original work published 1929).

Vygotsky, L. (1986). *Thought and language* (A. Kozulin, Eds. & Trans.). Cambridge: The MIT Press. (Original work published 1934).

Vygotsky, L. (1978). *Mind in society: The development of higher psychological processes*. (M. Cole, V. John-Steiner, S. Scribner, & E. Souberman, Eds.). Cambridge: Harvard University Press.

Wertsch, J. (1985). *Vygotsky and the social formation of mind*. Cambridge: Harvard University Press.

Wertsch, J. (1989). A sociocultural approach to mind. In W. Damon (Ed.), *Child development today and tomorrow*. San Francisco: Jossey-Bass.

Wertsch, J. (1991). *Voices of the mind: A sociocultural approach to mediated action.* Cambridge: Harvard University Press.

Wittgenstein, L. (1963). *Philosophical investigations* (G. Anscombe, Trans.). New York: Macmillan.

14

Moral and Religious Judgment Research

James M. Day and Myriam H. L. Naedts

INTRODUCTION

In recent decades, one of the more pressing questions in the psychology of human development has centered on the nature of relationships between and among various domains of development. As these individual domains have become increasingly well articulated and as measures for assessing movement within them have increased in number and sophistication, scholars and practitioners have become deeply interested in understanding how it is these discrete domains relate to one another. Some of these questions have concerned relationships between moral development and religious development, domains that have been the focus of considerable scholarly attention, public interest, and educational debate. Indeed, the questions are particularly pressing when, in the psychological domain, the development of these concepts has, at least from the time that Kohlberg began publishing work on moral philosophy, moral psychology, and moral education, been closely linked, and when, in the public domain, debate about the aims and practices of moral education is richly colored with assumptions about the intimate link of the moral and the religious.

Discussion of this matter by scholars has been accelerated by significant progress that has occurred in the rigorous investigation and assessment of the psychology of both moral and religious development. Indeed, the impact of research in moral development on work in religious development has been considerable. Advances in the empirical study of moral judgment (see Colby, Kohlberg, Candee, Gibbs, Hewer, Kaufman, Power, & Speicher-Dubin, 1987; Kohlberg, 1958, 1969, 1976, 1984; Rest, 1979, 1986) and its correlates in several behavioral domains (e.g., Gibbs, Basinger, & Fuller, 1992; Jennings, Kilkenny & Kohlberg 1983) have sparked considerable debate in theoretical and applied psychology, and have contributed mightily to the study of religious judgment and its development (Fowler 1981, 1991, 1993; Fowler, Nipkow, & Schweitzer, 1991; Kohlberg 1981; Kohlberg & Power 1981; Oser 1991; Piaget, 1976; Power & Kohlberg, 1980).

Developmental psychologists most concerned with the construction and validation of neo-Piagetian (i.e. Kohlbergian) frameworks for studying and describing religious thought have argued that moral stage advance in the hierarchy of universal socio-cognitive levels logically precedes advance in religious reasoning (Day & Naedts, in press; Fowler, 1991). On their view, moral reasoning, and the experiences required to stimulate its advance, logically precede more global transformations of the kind ascribed to religious judgment.

A central problem haunts this domain of inquiry: namely, that neither the stage formulations nor comparisons of stages outlined by religious developmentalists have been adequately validated in empirical terms (Oser & Reich, 1990). Further testing has been required in order to ascertain how stages of moral and religious judgment compare, and whether the claim of precedence attributed to moral constructs is verifiable.

The study discussed here compares levels of moral and religious judgment in a population of French-speaking Belgian adolescents and young adults. The sample consists of 194 subjects, divided almost equally by sex, and type of schooling (university-preparatory and technical high schools) (university students and students in professional training schools, and laborers, technicians, farmers, and the like) (young adults with university and other higher education and those with none), and again equally across five select ages where a significant distribution of stage assessments can reasonably be anticipated (at 12, 15, 18, 21, and 24 years). Thus, both the stage relations and the logic on which they have been proposed have been subjected to empirical investigation.

In this chapter, we dispense with overly cumbersome recitations of history and assume a working familiarity on the part of the reader with the cognitive developmental tradition, but we say something about the surrounding literature, the near history of the concepts and models that structure our research effort, and speak in detail about our methods, procedures, and findings. In sharing our work, we hope to contribute to current debates in the psychological literature concerning the utility of cognitive-developmental assumptions in the study of moral and religious development.

MORAL JUDGMENT AS A COGNITIVE-DEVELOPMENTAL CONSTRUCT

The concept of moral judgment, as we use it, makes little sense apart from the cognitive-developmental account of human development and the research and practice it has spawned. The chief proponents of this account from whom we draw, Jean Piaget (1932, 1948) and Lawrence Kohlberg (1958), carefully laid out from the beginning what they took to be the nature of moral cognition and the necessary relationships between moral judgment and moral action.

Piaget and Kohlberg, and those who advanced their work, argued that everyone is a moral philosopher. Ask a question about good and bad, what is right and wrong to do in a given situation, and people from childhood on give coherent replies. In these replies, and in more elaborate interviews about moral dilemmas—situations in which the good and the right thing to do are at issue—there is apparent in every case an underlying structure of logic which comes out no matter what the gravity of the case involved, from stopping at a red light in an empty traffic intersection to taking the life of another person where people are disputing. This logic starts off with a primitive concern with punishment and reward for what is to be done, and advances in some people over time, moving to a greater recognition of reciprocity grounded in community (what I do affects you, and you me, and the rules of my community are worth preserving because of the benefits they bring to all who abide by them). Eventually, with this principle in mind, one may come to view the world as one's community, and come to think of everyone as a neighbor, so that the rights of all individuals gain equal merit and concern for a justice that prescribes equal duties and consequences for all characterizes one's thinking. Following Piaget, Kohlberg describes this sequence of qualitative reorganizations as a development from preconventional to conventional and postconventional moral judgment. Where these movements occur they do so in sequence, and the distributions of them are roughly equal across places and cultures in which subjects have been interviewed. They are, then, held by the adherents of this position to be universal (Kohlberg, 1969, 1976, 1981; Rest, 1986).

What triggers advancement in the development of moral judgment is the respectful engagement, frustration, and linkage of one mode of thought to another, across a series of situations in which the subject takes the roles of others, and reflects on the issues involved in so doing (Jennings, Kilkenny, & Kohlberg, 1983; Selman, 1976). More specifically, five factors must be present if development is to be maximized: moral discussion, discussion in the fairness form; role-taking, group decision-making, and stage-adjacent reasoning. We cannot begin, here, to outline all of the assumptions embedded in the cognitive-developmental paradigm as it is represented in Kohlbergian work. For a further elaboration of our view, we suggest reading Day and Naedts, in press; or Day and Tappan, 1995. Readers interested in a fuller understanding of the five factors thought to be necessary to maximal moral judgment development might turn to Jennings, Kilkenny, and Kohlberg (1983).

Kohlberg also provided, as we have already suggested, a descriptive and predictive link between how people reason when confronted with a dilemma about what is good or bad, and what is right or wrong to do, and how people act. Drawing on Piaget's suppositions and the efforts by others to practice them in related fields (e.g., science education, cognitive-development, child care), and on the practical concerns of John Dewey's educational philosophy, Kohlberg asserted the value of his work for producing advances in moral life. On Kohlberg's view and those whose research claims to support it, people are less likely to yield to temptation, more likely to conform their conduct to what they say should be done, and more likely in situations of group problem-solving to be seen as morally independent, just in their appraisals of what should be done, and equitable in their fairness toward others (Day & Naedts, in press; Jennings, Kilkenny, & Kohlberg, 1983). Thus Piaget, Kohlberg, and others who forwarded their case offered a powerful architecture— one appealing to logic and to progress on account of its capacity not only to describe but also to reshape a crucial facet of being in the world.

MEASURING MORAL JUDGMENT

There exist three major instruments that have been employed in the measurement of moral judgment. The Moral Judgment Interview (MJI) involves the presentation of standard moral issues that come in the form of stock dilemmas. Subjects are asked to imagine themselves in the role of the key protagonist and to resolve the dilemma faced as the protagonist confronts the hypothetical dilemma (Colby and colleagues, 1987). The Defining Issues Test (DIT) is a computer-scoreable questionnaire that counts on the same procedure but includes a forced-choice set of responses coded according to their moral judgment level (Rest, 1979, 1986). The Sociomoral Reflection Measure (SRM) (Gibbs et al., 1992) is a questionnaire that aims to combine the advantages of the DIT with the openness of response permitted by the MJI. Like the DIT, the SRM exists in both longer and shorter versions. Subjects respond to a set of open questions in which they are invited to justify their perspective on a matter of principle in each of several domains of moral decision-making. The SRM seeks to combine ease of scoring with openness to subjects' own responses. In each of these three methods, the researcher wants to understand the prevailing stage structure present in what the subject has to say. Likewise in each of these cases, subjects' responses are coded according to the instances of deep structure that are to be found there . The MJI is a cumbersome instrument for those interested in large-scale empirical work. In the case of the DIT, the computer sorts and scores the responses selected by subjects yielding a composite score telling the researcher what percentage of the subject's selections conform to the principled, upper level of the judgment scheme. The SRM is easily distributed and collected, as in the case of the DIT, but must be scored by hand.

RELIGIOUS JUDGMENT AND DEVELOPMENT

One of the chief difficulties that besets the domain of religious development is that of how to arrive at a consensus on how to define, describe, or conceive an ideal developmental attainment. "Religious maturity" as a concept immediately introduces questions of religious context and the considerable differences that exist within and among such contexts. Indeed, some would argue that the criteria by which this maturity is defined in existing models of religious judgment development surpass what can be established in a purely psychological framework.

The two best-known figures in the field of religious development are Fritz Oser and James Fowler. James Fowler's theory of faith development and Fritz Oser's theory of the development of religious judgment can both be best understood in terms of a structuralist, cognitive-developmental perspective, and thereby assume a universally sequential and hierarchical development in which there is a series of structural transformations corresponding to an invariant series of stages. They are inspired by Jean Piaget's work and Lawrence Kohlberg's theory of moral development.

For the purposes of the research presented here, as we will explain, we chose to use Fritz Oser's work, and its elaborations with Paul Gemunder, Louis Ridez, and Helmut Reich, as the foundation for our own. Readers interested in a fuller comparison of Fowler's and Oser's theories might turn to Day and Naedts (in press), Reich (1993), and Tamminen (1994). Central to Oser's theory is the nature of the relation a human being entertains with the Ultimate, with God, and the action of the Ultimate, of God, in a human life. The relation to the Ultimate is regulated by a system of rules, by the religious consciousness of a person that is actualized by the ways, and each time the person interprets his/her life experiences, prays, studies religious texts, and takes part in religious community life (Day and Naedts, in press; Oser & Gemunder, 1988; Taminnen, 1994). Religious judgment is the way in which this relation expresses itself in verbal form.

Oser defines religious judgment as a kind of cognitive pattern of religious knowing of reality. What makes religious knowing possible is a deep "mother-structure," that is, a basic religious cognitive structure. This fundamental structure is universal and underlies whatever specific religion or even atheistic position comes into view when religious questions are discussed. Its aspects are, for example, searching for the meaning of life, hope, freedom, transcendence, eternity. Contextual factors, culture-specific and time-specific content, as well as different forms of religious socialization shape the mother-structure at least in the influence these features have on the rate of development of certain individuals, or groups of individuals in a given society (Day & Naedts, in press; Reich, 1993; Tamminen, 1994).

As Oser (1991) asserts it, and we have tried to outline it elsewhere, as religious judgment develops, it undergoes a series of qualitative transformations that reside not in the accumulation of new religious contents but in a progressively more complex and integrated cognitive pattern that is also more appropriate to resolve life situation conflicts that then result in a more mature relation to the Ultimate. This development follows a sequence of five stages. Oser's (1991) stages are described as follows :

1. *Orientation of religious heteronomy (deus ex machina).* God is understood as active, intervening unexpectedly in the world; the human being is reactive. The ultimate being is all-powerful and makes things happen.
2. *Orientation of 'do ut des' (give so that you may receive).* God is still an all powerful being, who may either punish or reward. The human being can, however, influence him by good deeds, promises, and vows.

3. *Orientation of ego autonomy and one-sided responsibility (deism).* God's influence is consciously reduced. Transcendence and immanence are separated from each other. The human being is autonomous, responsible for his or her life and the world. Religious and other authorities are often rejected.
4. *Mediated autonomy and salvation plan.* The human being has an indirect relationship with the Ultimate Being, which gives meaning and hope and the possibility of human freedom. Many various forms of religiousness emerge, all accepting a divine plan that brings things to a good end.
5. *Orientation to religious intersubjectivity and autonomy.* Universal and unconditional religiosity. Transcendence and immanence interact completely. The Ultimate Being is present in a very human commitment and in intersubjective action. Solidarity with all human beings.

Without entering into a fuller comparison of Fowler's and Oser's theories, which, as we have said, is beyond the scope of this paper and may be found elsewhere, it is useful to say that we think the concept of stage is differently conceived in each of them. We agree with Reich's (1993) observation that a well-known distinction between "soft-stage" theories and "hard-stage" ones characterizes the difference between them, and, in turn, informs our use of Oser's work. In this light, we could see Fowler's faith developmental stages are more "soft stages," while , in terms of the same criteria, Oser's stages would be considered "semi-hard" stages. The more soft the stages in a theory are, the more religious knowing and valuing is seen as an aspect of human development in general and is considered to be something requiring attention to other personality factors in order to understand it. In soft-stage theories, religion and faith come close to being synonymous with a person's worldview orientation and the way a person deals with existential issues. Such models are often more complex for the number of different operations they try to take into account. Because they try to deal with multidimensional categories and the integration of them, they may have broad applicability, but they lose in predictive precision (Reich, 1993; see also Day & Naedts, in press).

In our view (Day & Naedts, in press), any study of religious cognition first of all requires us to speak about cognition, per se, and then about how cognition especially relates to the particular domain that is religion. It is difficult, we think, given the complex nature of religious contexts, to find any developmental theory of religious cognition that attains the same degree of rigor as a "hard-stage" theory, such as Piaget's theory of cognition, does. His model describes a more content-free, invariant, clearly structural kind of universal development. The problem with religious development has to do with the way in which religious content is particular to the specific contexts in which cognition about it is to be found. We maintain, however, with Fowler and Oser, that a developmental theory of religious cognition has merit insofar as it shows how religious content in cognitive development cannot be reduced to a mere version or derivative of other (e.g. moral, ego, etc.) development.

Since the aim of our research is to compare moral and religious development, we have chosen to follow Oser's developmental paradigm rather than Fowler's for several reasons, (we originally outlined this case in Day & Naedts, in press):

First, Oser's model comes closer to meeting "hard-stage" criteria; there is a clearer relationship between structure and content in Oser's stages. Second, these clearer relationships are more suitable to the purpose of empirical testing. Third, such relationships permit us to assume a priori that we start with a more valid predictive framework for the testing of hypotheses about the likely distribution of stage scores for the subjects in a sample of the kind to which we have access in our research. This, in turn, renders religious cognition and moral cognition more comparable.

According to Oser (1991), individuals are most likely to produce religious judgments when confronted with unsettling life situations that are poignantly contingent—wherein no neat resolution is immediately apparent. This reasoning has inspired Oser and his colleagues to create a series of hypothetical dilemmas, in which a conflict occurs that puts the protagonist's relation to the Ultimate under stress. In trying to figure out a solution to the problematic situation, the subject of the study will state a religious judgment. Dilemmas have been used in the moral judgment assessment by Kohlberg and his associates, and their similar way of considering the moral and religious assessment contributes to the ready comparability of their models (Day & Naedts, in press).

To date, studies of the relationship between moral judgment and religious judgment have been problematic in three principal ways. To begin with, the numbers of subjects who have been tested has been limited (see also Reich, 1993; Tamminen 1994). This is related to a second problem, which is that the research involved has relied on the clinical method first adopted by Piaget and later extended in the work of Kohlberg, Fowler, and Oser and those whose work has followed their own. For the most part, these studies have been conducted by students trained in the assumptions belonging to the constructs that they have purported to test—thus leaving their research open to the critique that the interview methods themselves have been confounded with the findings yielded by the research; researchers trained in the notion that deep structures of moral and religious cognition exist are likely to look for them, press for them, and reduce subjects' responses to the relevant statements associated with structural criteria. Thus, one may argue that neither the numbers of subjects who have been interviewed, nor the methods that have been employed, justify the conclusion that moral and religious judgment exist in clear relationship to each other, or that one can predict the trajectory of a person's development in light of such a supposed relationship. Finally, when one considers the results that have been produced by the researchers in question, no clear relationship between moral judgment and religious judgment appears: in some cases the stage structures are equivalent in attainment in both domains; in other cases moral judgment precedes religious judgment in order of stage attainment; in yet other cases, religious judgment levels are higher than moral judgment ones. Thus, the hypothesis that moral judgment precedes religious judgment in developmental order because of the way in which religious judgment encompasses moral judgment has not been empirically verified (Day & Naedts, in press).

It thus became our task to remedy the problem of numbers, methods, and interpretation of data; a fairly monumental task at that. It fell to us to find a suitable empirical measure of moral judgment, to develop a suitable instrument for the measurement of religious judgment, to find sufficient numbers of research subjects, and to obtain enough usable data to test the hypothesis that remains in the literature that moral judgment development will be equal to or higher than that of religious judgment development in people at more than one developmental period in the life cycle.

For the measurement of moral judgment, we opted to use the Sociomoral Reflection Measure-Short Form (SRM-SF) developed by Gibbs and colleagues (1992). As described earlier, the SRM-SF combines advantages of production and response/recognition measures, covers a range of domains relevant to moral problem-solving, is robustly valid and reliable with regard to other research in the field and procedures of coding and scoring, and can be broadly distributed.

In order to have a comparable instrument for religious judgment, we created a short-form questionnaire, inspired in part by dilemmas from Oser's own work. This questionnaire is composed of seven questions that, in their content are similar to the themes we find in the Oser's dilemmas, and in their formal aspect are presented the same way as Gibbs' questions. We thus aimed to construct a questionnaire that would have construct validity in Oserian terms, and that would be satisfactory in terms of the kinds of comparisons that could be made between data yielded by subjects' responses to the SRM-SF and to our questionnaire.

Finally, we had to wrestle with the problem that not all of our subjects would define themselves as religious. We wanted to admit the possibility, asserted by Oser, Reich, and others, that religious judgments are made by all people in their efforts to resolve questions about the nature of their relationship to the meaning of life, to ultimate principles or the Ultimate being or dimension of life, while constructing questions that would pull for solutions that would be sufficiently religious to be coded as religious judgments. Therefore, the questions have to be an explicit "religious stimulus", because if they are not, then, as it is known, they fail to elicit religious answers. At the same time we had to employ religious language that is not too "confessionally" oriented—not too specifically associated with one religious set of beliefs. A common criticism of Oser's dilemmas is that they are too theologically specific to a Roman Catholic construction of the world and that they rely too much on a shared sense of the world on the part of the subject and the researcher in order to elicit meaningful responses and make reasonable coding decisions. While such a critique might seem, at first glance, to be the least obvious for researchers from a Catholic university working in largely Catholic Belgium, it certainly has seemed relevant to us as psychologists concerned to work with a large, representative sample of young people in a contemporary, multi-perspectival world.

EMPIRICAL WORK AND INITIAL RESULTS

The SMR-SF questionnaire of Gibbs and colleagues (1992) was translated into French by our research team and validated in a Belgian French-speaking population of 150 twelve-to-eighteen-year-old adolescents. Results obtained are so close to the American norms of Gibbs and his colleagues that we were able to proceed in the fullest confidence that the SRM-SF would be suitable to our research purposes. In addition, we were able to show that both highly trained coders, and students trained in a research practicum, could achieve high inter-rater reliability in coding SRM-SF protocols (e.g., inter-rater reliability between the coauthors of this paper = 0.97, between those authors and a trained research intern at UCL= 0.93, among 5 sets of students who coded questionnaires after 8 weeks of training in developmental research = 0.87, etc.). The matter of inter-rater reliability has been easier to test because of the unusually thorough coding procedures presented by Gibbs, Fuller, and Basinger (1992) in their exceptionally clear and useful book on the measurement of socio-moral reflection, and the translation of part of that manual into French (Day & Naedts, in press). On this basis, we conclude that the construct of moral judgment is well established.

Our religious judgment questionnaire was tested at three stages of its development; we used the third pre-tested version. We found that subjects during the pretests readily responded to the questions we posed. Initial reliability checks were conducted when six coders, two of whom developed the questionnaire, one of whom had participated in its pre-testing, another of whom was familiar with Oser's thought but not with our questionnaire, and two who were fully "naive" to Oser's thought and to our questionnaire, were trained in a three-session seminar on religious judgment constructs and stage descriptions, then asked to code responses to five of our questionnaires using the inductive scoring method proposed by Oser & Gemunder (1988) for scoring transcripts drawn from subjects responding to hypothetical dilemmas and associated questions constituting their Religious Judgment Interview. During these tests, reliability ranged from 98 per cent to 70 per cent. We concluded, after analyzing rates of reliability between the two most expert coders, and between those two coders and the other coders described above, that it was possible to employ Oser's inductive scoring method and to achieve reliable scoring with it.

METHODS

As we noted at the outset of this paper, we undertook to study moral judgment and religious judgment levels in a population of adolescents and young adults representing five age levels (12, 15, 18, 21, 24), equally divided between boys and girls, men and women, and evenly distributed across students in university-preparatory, and technical secondary schools, university and nonuniversity higher education, and young adults with no post-secondary education. The secondary schools, both university-preparatory and technical, span a broad range of settings from some of Belgium's most elite urban academies to regional technical schools situated in rural areas, and centrally located schools in middle-sized towns and suburbs of sprawling urban areas. Some, but not all, of the schools are Catholic schools. Some of the subjects voluntarily identified themselves (without any request on our part that they do so) as "believers," while many explicitly mentioned that they are not.

We tested three hypotheses:

1. Moral Judgment scores would be higher than or equal to Religious Judgment scores.
2. Female subjects between twelve and eighteen years of age would have higher scores than would male subjects in the same age group.
3. Students in the "college" group would have higher stage scores than would students in the "technical" group.

In all, 220 pairs of SRM-SF and RJQ's were distributed. Of those, 194 were returned with at least one completed protocol. Of those 194, 161 had a codeable SRM-SF, and 142 had both a codeable SRM-SF and a codeable RJQ.

Age Groupings

In establishing our target ages, we underestimated the impact of student failure in the Belgian school system. We discovered that the classes of "twelve"-year-olds also contained large numbers of thirteen- and fourteen-year-olds. The fifteen-year-old group also contained sixteen- and seventeen-year-olds, and so on. We did not have a sufficient number of subjects at twelve, fifteen, eighteen, twenty one, and twenty four years of age to satisfy requirements for statistical analysis, and had to create four groupings demarcated by school grade level of twelve to fourteen-year-olds (N=48), fifteen to seventeen-year-olds (N=52), eighteen to twenty-year-olds (N=37), and twenty to twenty four-year-olds (N=57). In our report, these groups are referred to as groups A, B, C, and D. Subjects are almost evenly divided by age within these groups.

Sex of Subjects

There were 123 female subjects and seventy one male subjects.

Schooling

Subjects (129) were in university-preparatory or university education or were university graduates. Of these, sixty nine were in technical school, post-secondary technical academies, or were graduates of technical schools.

We computed SYSTAT-assisted analyses of variance to study the role of the independent variables on moral judgment and religious judgment scores, and conducted correlational studies to understand the relationship of moral judgment to religious judgment scores.

RESULTS

Moral Judgment Findings

Moral judgment scores varied by age, sex, and, taken together, the variables schooling and age. Type of schooling, alone, did not account for a significant portion of the variance in moral judgment scores. Mean scores were 2.642 (combined), 2.760 (female), and 2.587 (male). Mean scores for the age groups were 2.234 (A), 2.437 (B), 2.916 (C), and 3.106 (D). Sample size was 161.

Thus, moral judgment scores increased as a function of grade level (age), female subjects had significantly higher moral judgment scores than did males except in the eighteen to twenty-year-old age group (where only a very small number of male subjects, N=6 were reported), and increases in scores, by age, were reported in both types of school groupings. Scores were higher in the university preparatory schools than in the technical schools, but not at university or post-university levels.

Religious Judgment Scores

Religious judgment scores varied by age, sex, and, taken together, school and age. Mean scores were 2.439 (combined), 2.597 (female), and 2.370 (male). Mean scores for the age groups were 1.855 (A), 2.275 (B), 2.813 (C), and 2.991 (D). Sample size was 142.

Thus, religious judgment scores increased with grade level (age grouping) in both types of school groupings, and mean female scores were higher than were mean male scores. Scores in the university-preparatory schools were higher than in the technical schools, but not at university or post-university levels.

Moral Judgment and Religious Judgment Scores

Moral judgment scores and religious judgment scores were highly correlated. Moral judgment scores were higher than were religious judgment scores, at every age level, in both male and female subjects, and in both technical and university education groups, but these differences were not statistically significant. Thus, on statistical grounds, moral judgment scores were not distinguishably of a different level than were religious judgment scores.

Mean MJ Scores: Age A=2.234; B=2.437; C=2.916; D=3.106
Mean RJ Scores: Age A=1.855; B=2.275; C=2.813; D=2.991
Scores increased most dramatically, in both moral judgment and religious judgment, between the fifteen to seventeen- and eighteen to twenty-year-old groupings.

In an effort to situate our findings vis-à-vis those of Gibbs and Oser, we compared mean moral and religious judgment scores, by age, with scores of the same-aged groups (where available) as reported by those authors.

Mean MJ scores: Age A=2.234; B=2.437; C=2.916; D=3.106

Gibbs MJ scores: Age A=2.493; B=2.962; C=3.120; E= Not Available
Mean RJ scores: Age A=1.855; B=2.275; C=2.813; D=2.991
Oser RJ scores: Age A=2.28; B=2.91; C= Not Available ; D=3.00

Mean moral judgment scores in our study were lower than those reported by Gibbs and colleagues (1992) in the twelve to fourteen- and fifteen to seventeen-year-old groups, in the former by a quarter stage, in the latter by a half stage. In the eighteen to twenty-year-old age group, our scores are lower, but not significantly so. No comparable data were available for the twenty to twenty four-year-olds we studied.

Mean religious judgment scores in our study were lower than those reported by Oser and Gemunder (1988) in the twelve to fourteen- and fifteen to seventeen-year-old groups. No comparable data were available for the eighteen to twenty-year-olds we studied. Data for the twenty one to twenty four-year-olds showed no difference between the two groups in question. The marked increase that we reported in scores from the fifteen to seventeen-year-olds to those of the eighteen to twenty-year-olds is not evidenced in either the Gibbs and colleagues' data (1992) or the Oser & Gemunder (1988) data.

In several respects, the eighteen to twenty-year-old group remains an anomaly: it is here that the technical school scores are higher than the university scores, where young men have higher scores than women do, and where there is a marked jump in mean moral judgment and religious judgment scores.

DISCUSSION

Hypothesis Testing

Readers will recall that we tested three hypotheses. First, we hypothesized that mean moral judgment scores would be higher than or equal to mean religious judgment scores. This we were able to confirm: moral judgment scores were higher at every age, in both sexes and types of schooling, than were religious judgment scores, but not so much higher as to merit the designation on statistical grounds.

Second, we hypothesized that girls' mean moral judgment scores would be higher than those of boys in the twelve to eighteen-year-old-groups. We confirmed this hypothesis. The power of this difference affected the overall statistical computation of scores across all groups enough to yield female scores higher than male scores, but a closer look indicates that female scores were higher only in the twelve to eighteen-year-old-groups.

Third, we hypothesized that students in university-preparatory schools, and at university, would have higher scores than members of their peer groups at technical schools, and that this would also be true of graduates of these different types of academic settings. This was true only of students in secondary schools. It was decidedly not the case for the eighteen to twenty-year-olds, where students in social sciences and social work studies at university scored lower than their peers in technical schools. Differences were not apparent between the graduates of university and technical schools.

Further Elaboration

We made the following further observations.

1. Coding of the religious judgment questionnaire allowed for wider variation in stage scores, per protocol, than did coding of moral judgment questionnaires. Since our inter-rater reliability was extremely good, we attribute this either to the formulation of our questions (an unlikely explanatory factor since it would not follow logically that this would elicit different structures of argumentation on the part of subjects) or to the latitude permitted by the inductive scoring method following Oser's work and employing his stage descriptions. Gibbs and his coauthors are more precise than Oser and his colleagues, despite the advances notable in the work of Kaminger & Rollet whose tentative scoring manual marks a considerable improvement over the system employed by Oser and colleagues.

2. While we were able to confirm our general hypothesis that moral judgment scores would be higher than religious judgment scores, our findings introduce an element that is not accounted for in the theoretical architecture of stage and sequence as found either in moral-developmentalists who have speculated on religious development, or in the work of religious-developmentalists. The stage and sequence hypothesis holds that moral judgment is a necessary but not sufficient condition for religious judgment at any given level, and that trans-formations in moral reasoning will provide but one component in the more embracing field of cognition represented by religious judgment. This may, of course, account in part for the effects we find. But it is interesting to note that in some cases religious judgment scores are higher than moral judgment scores, and that where religious judgment scores are lower than moral judgment scores, an interesting pattern holds in the language our subjects use to justify their responses. In short, we find that where adolescents speak of a severe, judgmental, punitive, and distant God, or a harsh, unyielding, ultimate principle or logic of organization governing the cosmos, their religious judgment scores are lower than their moral judgment scores, even on questions worded in almost the same way on the two different protocols. In contrast, subjects who speak of God as loving, tender, merciful, understanding, and approachable have religious judgment scores that are equally high, or in some cases even higher than their moral judgment scores.

Finally, we find that there are some differences that hold across all groups in the way subjects talk about moral dilemmas and religious ones. Our preliminary observation is that there are differences between males and females in ways that correspond to observations made by Day and Naedts (in press); Day, Naedts, and Saroglou (in press); Gilligan (1977, 1982); Lyons (1982, 1983, 1988); Tannen (1991); Youngman (1993) and others. We observe that females frame moral and religious dilemmas predominately in terms of relationship, while males frame them predominately in terms of principles.

We are party to the growing discussion about the nature of relationships that exist between and among different domains of psychological growth and change. In this case, we report efforts to bring empirical precision to the measurement and understanding of relationships between moral judgment and religious judgment in adolescents and young adults—subjects in which one expects to be able to find and chart significant change in moral and religious development. On the whole, we conclude that it is possible to measure religious judgment using a questionnaire instead of the clinical interviewing method developed by Oser and his colleagues at Fribourg; that moral judgment and religious judgment are highly related but that the traditional arguments for the precedence of moral judgment in the upward movement of religious judgment scores may not be verifiable; that factors having to do with God-image and relational style, corresponding in part to theological climates, the nature of religious teachings and religious institutions, and hierarchical educational and familial structures, may serve as mediating variables in understanding the relationship between moral judgment and religious judgment; that this, in turn, may augur for closer attention to variables such as world view and logical thought per se as argued by Oser and Reich; and that there may be significant sex differences in how moral and religious dilemmas are framed and resolved by subjects in our sample, which correspond to differences that have been elsewhere but likewise observed.

Educational Implications

The cognitive-developmental approach to the psychology of religious development, as we have noted, hinges on a particular set of concepts and images of the person, and strives to identify universal stage structures through which attributions about the world are constructed and transformed. As we have observed, this perspective is rooted in the work of Jean Piaget, who endeavored to elaborate, empirically, his view of the person as epistemic subject. On Piaget's view, every child is a philosopher and scientist, constantly asking hard questions about how things work, looking for answers to questions about why things work as they do, working out experimentally an ever-evolving understanding of those principles that govern the operations of the universe, ever searching for meaning and constructing pictures of the world accordingly. Piaget's claim that children pass through a universal sequence of stages in the development of reasoning, from primitive and irrational musing toward rational and scientific analysis, has had consequences throughout the world for our understanding of how children acquire knowledge, from mathematics, to literacy, to moral judgment (see also Day & Naedts, in press).

This view has also had very considerable practical consequences in a number of domains, including education, any discussion of which necessarily entails a careful and critical review of some elements essential to the cognitive-developmental paradigm itself.

Kohlberg confirmed, at least on his view and that of his adherents, Piaget's assumptions about both the nature of the stages of moral reasoning—that is, how people come to think about right and wrong, and what is good or bad to do, accordingly—and the ways in which structures of reasoning about such matters are transformed, how people move from one stage of reasoning to another. In a series of brilliant studies early in his career, Kohlberg showed that it was possible to promote development in moral reasoning in children and adults. He and his associates created programs of developmental education and rehabilitation based on their view as to how development occurs and how it can be promoted in the development of children, adolescents, and young adults. Finally, they showed how changes in reasoning can affect behavior, that development in moral reasoning inclines people to better conduct (Day & Naedts, in press; Jennings, Kilkenny, & Kohlberg, 1983).

Taking their cues from Kohlberg's success in demonstrating the efficacy of a Piagetian approach to moral reasoning and behavior, James Fowler and Fritz Oser, respectively, have tried to show empirically how religious thought develops, how structures of reasoning about God and about the meaning of life change across the human life cycle. As we have pointed out, they have tried to show that development in religious thought is related to structural transformations in other domains, including and especially the domain of moral reasoning. On their view, transformations in moral reasoning precede those in religious cognition, because religious judgments are more global in character, and more encompassing in content, including moral content. Both Fowler and Oser maintain, with Piaget and Kohlberg, that maturity in religious reasoning is characterized by commitment within relativism, clarity of purpose amidst a tolerance for ambiguity about ultimate questions, an acceptance of the historicity of particular religious practices and beliefs, a highly developed concern for others, individually and within relationships, and a simultaneous movement toward autonomy, complexity, and selfless respect and care for others (Day & Naedts, in press).

All of the Piagetian models of human development, including religious development, rely on the concept of "deep structure" and its place in human thought and behavior. On the Piagetian view, every dimension of human thought is marked by an underlying structure or logic of reasoning that most essentially characterizes the person's point of view. Across the world of persons striving to make meaning, such structures can be identified, and stratified according to age and according to specific kinds of intellectual stimulation to which those persons have, or have not been, exposed. These structures precede one another in a necessary and universal hierarchy of ever-increasing scope and adequacy. Development in human reasoning moves from pre-operational modes of thought, in which structures of cognition are subject to the immediate and the concrete, toward post-operational structures, in which people are able to think about thinking itself. In mature thought, people can abstract themselves from their immediate contexts, review their thinking objectively, and, in so doing, conform their thinking to the reality of the world as revealed by scientific investigation and analysis. People think in the ways that they do until they encounter contradictions that cannot be resolved in terms that their current structures supply, at which time they become ripe for interventions that allow their gradual appropriation and integration of more adequate ways of understanding what is going on.

These more "mature" structures are more adequate in two ways. First, they allow for greater understanding, and second, they permit more functional conduct because their comprehension is more accurate to the way the world really is. So, for example, people who reason most maturely about God and the meaning of life are closer both to the complex reality of the world's religious vitality, and are more capable of managing religious diversity in their own lives. They can accept the relativity of their own point of view, can tolerate other people as fellow meaning-makers in a world of diverse experiences, can negotiate differences more handily, and can act compassionately on account of their capacity to tolerate and enter into the different conceptions of ultimate reality, good and evil, and so forth, held by their neighbors (Day & Naedts, 1994).

As we suggested early on, in our discussion of the cognitive-developmental paradigm for understanding moral development, it behooves the educator who would learn from this model to enter into the stage-specific formulations of meaning held by his student, and invite creative re-examination of such formulations in terms of the next-highest level of formulation accessible to the student. Thus the educator must understand developmental assumptions and descriptions concerning development in order to perform his work. He must understand stage structures well enough to identify them in the thought of his students, must understand the concept of development well enough to know how to see it when it occurs and when a student is ripe for movement from one structural understanding of the world to the developmentally preferable alternative which succeeds that understanding, and the educator must have a comprehensive conception of where development is going; what the possibilities are and why certain ways of viewing the world are preferable, on developmental and behavioral grounds, than others. This, in turn, suggests that the educator in question must have some structure of support from other educators—colleagues who understand the rationale for his practice, and who can enter into practices of evaluation that are commensurate with developmental goals and possible outcomes of pedagogical engagement (Day & Naedts, in press).

The work of Caldwell & Berkowitz, Fowler, Jaspard, Kohlberg, Power, Oser, Ratliff, Reich, and others (see e.g., Ratliff, 1988) have contributed significantly to what such an education for religious development would entail. As one would expect on the grounds we have laid out here, the religious educator concerned with such questions would have to be well versed in developmental theory in order to begin her work at any given point in the life cycle, from the youngest of children in Sunday School classes to the most adept of seminarians in the most elite of training centers for clergy and theologians. An important assumption of her work would be that concepts of universal importance would be most efficaciously introduced in terms of the particulars of the student's way of understanding the world. Thus, in this picture, the compelling claims of religious engagement will make sense only in terms of the student's already existing way of thinking about religious notions. The developmental religious educator presumes that every student arrives with ideas about the Ultimate and her relationship to them, and proceeds from there. There is no "tabula rasa" to be found, no one so far from religion that she would have no idea where to begin in the process of teaching and learning (Day & Naedts, in press).

Three of the five major dynamics we cited in an earlier discussion of moral development in this article, that have been shown to promote growth of the kind envisioned by moral and religious educators in the developmental tradition are moral discussion, discussion in the fairness form, and role-taking (see Jennings, Kilkenny & Kohlberg, 1983). Essentially, these processes entail the necessity that the student have access to an ongoing forum in which moral (and for our purposes, religious) questions can be entertained; that in these discussions every participant is assured of the chance to participate actively in the resolution of dilemmas pertinent to his real-life situation; and that the various participants who are working such dilemmas through be encouraged, even required, to enter into the other participants' ways of framing the dilemmas at hand—one must step into the other person's shoes, as it were, in order to appreciate the consequences of one's own justifications for one's actions (Day & Naedts, in press).

Progress, meanwhile, would be charted accordingly; one would be able to measure the starting and ending points of students' thought in terms of stage and structure, and would modify educational media, technologies, and interpersonal interaction in terms of successes or lack of them in such measured movement from lower to higher levels of reflection on moral and religious issues. If Kohlberg's, Fowler's, and Oser's theories were to hold, it would be fundamental to any program of religious education that moral education would be part of the bargain; without encouragement of moral judgment development one could not expect religious judgment to mature—the necessary relationship in theory between moral development and religious development would have considerable consequences for religious education.

The Piagetian perspective in the domain of moral and religious development is not without its problems. Questions on whether empirical evidence bears out the claim, for example, that better moral judgment improves moral conduct, whether advances in moral judgment precede those in the domain of religious judgment, whether stages of religious judgment represent "hard" stages in the Piagetian sense of structure, sequence, and universalizability, and whether morality and religious experience are best appreciated in terms of rational judgments or broader notions of cognition, continue to be the source of research and debate (see, e.g., Blasi, 1980; Day, 1993; Day & Naedts, in press; Power, 1988).

In addition, there is some empirical evidence that the stage descriptions and directions of the Piagetian model, and the instruments used to measure development within it, fail to account for the richness and diversity of moral and religious experience, and discriminate against those whose voices do articulate autonomy as the endpoint and criterion measure of development. Carol Gilligan's (see, e.g., Gilligan 1982; Gilligan, Ward, & Taylor, 1988; Brown & Gilligan,1991) research on the moral experience of women defines a critical moment in this area of research. Her work shows how, when given the chance, women's strategies for making and articulating moral decisions, and for conceiving of self and relationship, defy the categories devised by Piaget, assumed by Kohlberg, Fowler, and Oser, and, more generally, embedded in psychological conceptions of women's development. On our view, Gilligan's methods for attending to lived moral experience in the lives of her interviewees have consequences far beyond the ones originally envisioned in her work, and we think it can be demonstrated that serious attention to Gilligan's critiques of standing developmental frameworks of stage and structure will require work toward a different conception of relationships among language, action, and mind.

Appropriating the work of Mikhail Bakhtin (1981, 1986), Jerome Bruner (1986, 1990), Kenneth Gergen and Mary Gergen (1986), Theodore Sarbin (1990), Lev Vygotsky (1978), James Wertsch (1989, 1991), and others, we have tried, in concert with Mark Tappan, to show that moral and religious speech, on which developmental and other kinds of interviews and psychotherapy are based, are as much performative as they are informative, that they are irreducibly conversational, that they are defined as much, or more, by their narrative form as they are by logical deep structure, and that they require a different way of thinking about moral and religious development (Day, 1991a, 1991b, 1991c, 1993, 1994a, 1994b; Day and Tappan, 1995, 1996; Tappan 1989, 1990, 1991a, 1991b, 1992; Tappan & Brown, 1989). We have called this different approach to moral and religious development a narrative approach. Interested readers might turn to Day and Naedts (in press) or to Brown, Tappan, Gilligan, Miller, and Argyris (1989) for a more detailed exploration of this point of view. While it does not fall within the scope of this chapter to outline this approach in fine detail, perhaps a few broad constructs to it, and their consequences for education and psycho-therapy, are worth mentioning.

People Talk in Story Form

People may be able, when pressed, to do rational-scientific talk, but even then, they incorporate such talk into the broader framework of plot, character, and the larger vocabulary of life as theatre that they know. People are incapable of living without stories. When their life stories break down, so do they. Religious education, in part, is a process by which a coherent narrative framework for understanding the meaning of life and the roles and actions required of its participants is transmitted and remade. Psychotherapy is, for the client, the effort to make, or remake, a story worthy of their lives, and faith, as Fowler, has noted it, is, in part, the effort to constantly negotiate the dramas of the self in terms of the master narrative of religion. Whether, in our time, such master narratives can compel loyalty or provide frameworks for integrity of personal lives is open to question. Perhaps a large part of our problem in contemporary culture is that we are continually exposed to "too many" narrative propositions as to what life and we, ourselves, ought to be about. Perhaps all talk of master stories or narratives is by definition hopelessly nostalgic. Perhaps the task of therapy is to help us find ways to live the different selves we are, according to the different stories we have to, or want to, live. Perhaps the task of religious education will be, in the end, to free us for ways in which we must live in multiple frames of reference simultaneously; a process in which the notion of ultimate values and continual change might be reconciled more adequately than they have been until now.

Talk Is Action, And As Such, Is Inherently Performative

Talk is not a mediator between a realm of thought outside of action, and something that "really" is action. Talk is done to accomplish something. As such, we can only say that it achieves something or not, that codes of talk are associated with certain kinds of conduct. We cannot say that talk tells us something about the essence or mind of another, except as that mind itself is conceived as patterns of talk. We talk according to what we imagine will be the story that can be told about us later, we talk ourselves into being using stories as our guides. Our talk tells about the context in which codes of speech have utility or lack it, but not about us, if by "us" we mean some beings apart from what we say.

The Purpose of Talk Is Relationship

We talk in order to accomplish social ends and to shape relationships. We talk in order to establish, maintain, and reconcile place in relation to other talkers, in relation to other human beings. Apart from talk we have no selves, apart from talk we know no selves, apart from talk we die, are left, have no way to make a place or to survive in the world. We learn, thus, that talk, that our signs, that the fine tuning of these, is what will keep us alive and connected to other people, and that some ways of being are more desirable than other ones (some keep us related, some make more likely our abandonment). We talk the way we do to keep contact or keep distant, depending on our needs for both.

When We Talk About Mind, We Talk About Behavior

There is no mind we can see, no set of essences or functions, that we have access to apart from talk. We think in terms of talk, and when we learn to talk, we speak in terms of voices that we know, have heard, and have practiced watching the consequences of. Our minds are the conversations we hear and have in private and that we sometimes make accessible to others through the signs and voices we have; thus the border of self and mind is not a wall between essences, not the shell of body inhabited, as it were, by ghosts inside of our machines. Our borders are borders of access, recognition, and intelligibility. Without such acts of recognition, we will have no conversation of which to be a part, and that will be our death, our end. Religious conversations are not so much about "ultimate things" as they are about the conditions of ultimate being. They claim that certain kinds of talk make the conversation and the self of which it is a part go on indefinitely, and they show how to remain a part of that, how to tailor that to an experience of utter recognition, reception, and continuity. There's a place for you beyond the changes you will certainly face on life's way; here's a code you can speak to keep going;

here's the language you need to know in order to be known and cared for, forever; there is a talk you can learn that is the talk of the world, that finds its echo there, which is spoken back to in recognizable form, in words meant just for you, this conversation is bliss like the bliss of your best correspondence, speaking it will free you from division, you will talk and be heard unto eternity. Religious talk is what makes the transitions possible, makes the picture appear whole, gives the talking self the illusion of indestructibility, of continuity, of eternal merit and recognition. Take performative speech away and religion is nothing. All the religious "things" in your mind have voices attached to them, all the "ideas" you have are constructions of speech, all the signs that make sense in your faith are a function of the relationships they make possible. Thus, for the therapist, the question is not what do you believe, but for whom are you talking about belief in the way you do. We are always talking to, talk is always talking to, talk is social, talk is live, talk is going somewhere, now.

CLOSING REMARKS

In keeping with the narrative turn we have taken, we would be so bold as to say that what develops in human growth and change is the way we talk, the kinds of conversations we can have, whether our talk places us or disinherits us from the larger conversations of which we want and need to be part, the kinds of stories we can construct, whether or not we can tell acceptable stories about ourselves, and whose voice counts among the many we hear as our minds. The child is "small" in developmental terms, not because her mind is far from reality, not because she doesn't know things; not because of what she can't do, but because, as talkers par excellence, we see her as being outside the bounds of our conversations. We have talked ourselves into a world of definitions that she doesn't yet know how to enunciate, and we take it as our task to show her how to use her talk to do things, how to talk herself into acceptability, how to use words to forge her way. We want her to speak in and perfect the language we know, because we can't know her, or she us, apart from it. We want her to hear our voice in her mind, and she does. But she is exposed along the way to multiple voices and stories and ways and what we expect her to do in the time of post-modernity is quite paradoxical. We expect her to have an "open" mind, that is, a mind in which she recognizes that there are many ways of talking. At the same time, we expect her to speak as though she is, herself, the author of her mind. She is supposed to persuade others that she is the origin of the self she is among them. To do this, we talk her into talking the language of autonomy, and control, of independence, and most of all, choice. She is supposed to be capable of choosing, which means she has to convincingly talk the language of choice. Meanwhile, the system of talk is starting to break down. She suffers because she is written on by a thousand codes of choosing, among which she is supposed to choose, which means there is supposed to be a self who could choose, which, perhaps, she recognizes, she is not. She is all her strategies of justification of the choices she could make, none of which add up to a real self of the kind she has heard she is supposed to be. There is no self where she looks for one, there is no master narrative to which to resort in the time of her confusion. She is more stories than her body can hold, she is an entangled web in a cacophony of voices, she is the embodied site where discourses contest, she is looking for a resting place and at the same time for that relationship where she can talk herself into a coherent state of being, where the tales she can tell about herself have some semblance of mutual justification, where the jumbled selves of her time can be surpassed by a set of terms that will last.

Thus the lack of a religious alternative as master play or narrative for self-recomposition as a self in need of reconciliation in the relational cacophony of multiple voice, pitted against the false code of autonomy and choice, is itself central as a religious problem to the educational and therapeutic conundrums of our day. How to transmit certainty in a world that is sure to confuse it, how to speak of ultimate things in a world in which the transience of our conceptions is so much at issue, how to speak of what abides when change so clearly governs what it means for us to live—these are some of the very problems our research subjects insist on our recognizing. That we can confirm certain hypotheses within a cognitive-developmental framework does not render either the paradigm or initial conclusions based upon it sufficient.

In this chapter, we have tried to show how a compelling, canonical paradigm in the psychology of moral and religious development makes possible and necessary empirical work for the testing of claims about relationships between moral and religious reasoning. We have suggested that the outcomes of such research, on terms specific to the cognitive-developmental paradigm, have consequences for our thinking about constructs such as religious judgment, and for practical pursuits such as moral and religious education. We have also suggested that some of the questions posed by the problems inherent to the cognitive-developmental paradigm and our research from which it springss require a rethinking of how it is that people think, speak, and act.

We conclude by reaffirming our interest in moral and religious development, acknowledging our debt to the cognitive-developmental tradition in which we have been nurtured, and suggesting that our students and research subjects continue to confound, meaningfully, the prospects afforded by the structuralist canon.

ACKNOWLEDGMENTS

We gratefully acknowledge the support of Professors Christiane Vandenplas-Holper and Jean-Marie Jaspard, for the time, resources, and liberty necessary to the work we have outlined here. Were it not for the funding obtained from the National Science Foundation of Belgium and the Funds for Scientific Development of our University and of the French-Speaking Community of Belgium, this work would not have been possible. Professors John Gibbs of The Ohio State University and Helmut Reich of the Universität Fribourg have been exceptionally generous in sharing ideas, materials, and appraisals of our work in the fields of the psychology of moral and religious development. We owe them both a considerable debt.

REFERENCES

Bakhtin, M. (1981). *The dialogic imagination.* (M. Holquist, Ed., C. Emerson, & M. Holquist, Trans.) Austin, TX: University of Texas Press.

Bakhtin, M. (1986). *Speech genres and other late essays.* (C. Emerson & M. Holquist, Eds., V. McGee, Trans.) Austin TX: University of Texas Press.

Blasi, A. (1980). Bridging moral cognition and moral action: A critical review of the literature. *Psychological Bulletin.* 1-45.

Brown, L., & Gilligan, C. (1991). Listening for voice in narratives of relationship. In M. Tappan & M. Packer (Eds.), *Narrative and storytelling: Implications for understanding moral development. New Directions for Child Development, No. 54,.* pp. 27-42.

Brown, L., Tappan, M., Gilligan, C., Miller, B., & Argyris, D.(1989). Reading for self and moral voice: A method for interpreting narratives of real-life moral conflict and choice. In M. Packer & R. Addison (Eds.), *Entering the circle: Hermeneutic investigation in psychology.* Albany, NY: State University of New York Press.

Bruner, J. (1986). *Actual minds, possible worlds.* Cambridge, MA: Harvard University Press.

Bruner, J. (1990). *Acts of meaning.* Cambridge, MA: Harvard University Press.

Caldwell, J., & Berkowitz, A. (1987). The development of religious and moral thinking in a religious education program. German trans. in *Unterrichts-wissenschaft, 15,* pp 157-76.

Colby,A., Kohlberg, L., Candee, D., Gibbs, J. C., Hewer, A., Kaufman, K., Power, C., & Speicher-Dubin, B. (1987). *The measurement of moral judgment.* New York: Cambridge University Press.

Day, J. (1991a). The moral audience: On the narrative mediation of moral judgment' and moral 'action.' In Mark Tappan & Martin Packer (Eds.), *Narrative and storytelling: Implications for understanding moral development* (New directions for child development, No. 54, pp. 27-42). San Francisco: Jossey-Bass.

Day, J. (1991b). Narrative, psychology, and moral education. *American Psychologist, 46,* 167-8.

Day, J. (1991c). Role-taking revisited: Narrative and cognitive-developmental interpretations of moral growth. *The Journal of Moral Education, 20,* 305-15.

Day, J. (1993). Speaking of belief: Language, performance, and narrative in the psychology of religion. *The International Journal for the Psychology of Religion, 4 ,* No.3.

Day, J. (1994a). Narratives of "belief and unbelief" in young adult accounts of religious experience and moral development. In Dirk Hutsebaut & Josef Corveleyn (Eds.), *Advances in the psychology of religion: Psychological studies of belief and unbelief.* Amsterdam: Rodopi.

Day, J. (1994b). Obligation and motivation: Obstacles and resources for counselor well-being and effectiveness. *Journal of Counseling and Development, 73,* 108-11.

Day, J. (in press, a). Knowing the good and doing it: Moral judgment and action in young adult narratives of moral choice. In Detlef Garz, Fritz Oser, & Wolfgang Althof (Eds.), *Der kontext der moralisches urteilen-moralisches handeln.* Frankfurt, Germany: Suhrkamp.

Day, J. (in press, b). Exemplary sierrans: Stories of the moral. In Ralph Mosher, Davic Connor, James Day, Kathy Kaliel, Marc Porter, & John Whiteley. *Character in young adulthood.* San Francisco: Jossey Bass.

Day, J., & Naedts, M. (1994). *Questionnaire sur la reflexion religieuse.* Universite Catholique de Louvain: Louvain-la-Neuve, Belgique.

Day, J., & Naedts, M. (in press, a.). Moral development and religious development: Theoretical, empirical, and practical considerations. In W. van Haaften (Ed.), *Advances in the study of moral development and education: Philosophical and psychological approaches.*

Day, J., & Naedts, M. (in press, b). A reader's guide for interpreting texts of religious experience: A hermeneutical approach. In J. Belzen (Ed.), *Hermeneutical approaches to the psychology of religion.* Amsterdam: Rodopi.

Day, J., Naedts, M., & Saroglou (in press). Reading interview texts for gender, self, and religious voice. *The International Journal for the Psychology of Religion.*

Day, J. & Tappan, M. (1995). Identity, voice, and the psycho/dialogical. *American Psychologist, 50,* 47-48.

Day, J. & Tappan, M. (1996). The narrative approach to moral development: From epistemic subject to dialogical selves. *Human Development, 39,* 67-82.

Fowler, J. (1981). *Stages of faith: The psychology of human development and the quest for meaning.* San Francisco: Harper & Row.

Fowler, J. (1991). Stages in faith consciousness. In F. Oser & W. Scarlett (Eds.), *Religious development in childhood and adolescence. New Directions for Child Development,* No. 52.

Fowler, J. (1993) Response to H. Reich: Overview or apologetic? *The International Journal for the Psychology of Religion, 3 ,* 173-79.

Fowler, J., Nipkow, K., & Schweitzer, F. (Eds.) (1991). *Stages of faith and religious development. Implications for church, education, and society.* New York: Crossroads.

Gergen, K., & Gergen, M. (1986). Narrative form and the construction of psychological science. In T. Sarbin (Ed.), *Narrative psychology: The storied structure of human conduct.* New York: Praeger, 1986.

Gibbs, J. C., Basinger, K. S., & Fuller, D. (1992). *Moral maturity: Measuring the development of sociomoral reflection.* Hillsdale, NJ: Erlbaum.

Gilligan, C. (1977). In a different voice: Women's conceptions of self and morality. *Harvard Educational Review, 47,* 481-517.

Gilligan, C. (1982). *In a different voice: Psychological theory and women's development.* Cambridge, MA: Harvard University Press.

Gilligan, C., Ward, J., & Taylor, J. (Eds.) (1988). *Mapping the moral domain: A contribution of women's thinking to psychological theory and education.* Cambridge, MA: Harvard University Press.

Jennings, R., Kilkenny, R., & Kohlberg, L. (1983). Moral development theory for youthful and adult offenders. In W. Laufer & J. Day (Eds.), *Personality theory, moral development, and criminal behavior.* Lexington, MA: DC Heath-Lexington Books.

Kohlberg, L. (1958). *The development of modes of moral thinking and choice in the years 10 to 16.* Unpublished doctoral dissertation, University of Chicago, Chicago, IL.

Kohlberg, L. (1969). Stage and sequence: The cognitive-developmental approach to socialization. In D. A. Goslin (Ed.), *Handbook of socialization theory and research* (pp. 346-480). Chicago, IL: Rand McNally.

Kohlberg, L. (1976). Moral stages and moralization: The cognitive-developmental approach. In Likona, T. (Ed.), *Moral development and behavior. Theory, research and social issues* (31-53). New York: Holt, Rinehart & Winston.

Kohlberg, L. (1981). *The philosophy of moral development.* San Francisco: Harper & Row.

Kohlberg, L. (1984). The meaning and measurement of moral judgment. In L. Kohlberg (Ed.), *Essays on moral development: Vol. II. The psychology of moral development.* San Francisco, CA: Harper & Row.

Kohlberg, L., & Power, C. (1981). Moral development, religious thinking, and the question of a 7th stage. In L. Kohlberg (Ed.), *The philosophy of moral development.* San Francisco: Harper & Row.

Lyons, N. P. (1982). *The manual for analyzing responses to the question: How would you describe yourself to yourself?* Unpublished manuscript, Harvard Graduate School of Education.

Lyons, N. (1983). Two perspectives: On self, relationships, and morality. *Harvard Educational Review, 53,* 125-45.

Lyons, N. P. (1988). Two perspectives: On self, relationships, and morality. In Gilligan, C., Ward, J. & Taylor, J. (Eds.), *Mapping the moral domain.* Cambridge, MA. Harvard University Press.

Naedts, M. (1994). Gender, identity, and religion in readings of selected interview texts. Unpublished paper.

Oser, F. (1988). Genese und Logik der Entwicklung des religiosen Bewuessteins: Eine Entgegnung auf Kritiken. In K. Nipkow, F. Schweitzer, & J. Fowler (Eds.), *Glaubensentwicklung und Erziehung.* Guttersloch, Deutschland: Gerd Mohn.

Oser, F. (1991). The development of religious judgment. In F. Oser & W. Scarlett (Eds.), *Religious development in childhood and adolescence. New Directions for Child Development,* No. 52.

Oser, F., & Gemunder, P. (Eds.) (1988). *Der Mensch: Stufen seiner religiosen Entwicklung: Ein Struckturgenetischer Ansatz.* Gutersloch, Deutschland: Gerd Mohn.

Oser, F., & Reich, H. (1990). Moral judgment, religious judgment, world view, and logical thought: A review of their relationship; Part One. *British Journal of Religious Education, Vol. 12,* 94-101.

Piaget, J. (1932). *The moral judgment of the child.* New York: Harcourt.

Piaget, J. (1948). *The moral judgment of the child.* Glencoe, NY: Free Press.

Piaget, J. (1976). *The child and reality.* New York: Penguin.

Power, C. (1988). Development of faith and of religious judgment: Hard or soft stages? In J. Fowler, K. Nipkow & F. Schweitzer (Eds.), *Stages of faith and religious development: An intercontinental debate.* New York: Crossroads.

Power, C., & Kohlberg, L. (1980). Religion, morality, and ego development. In Brusselmans, C. & O'Donahue, J. (Eds.) *Toward moral and religious maturity,* (pp. 343-73). Morristown, NJ. Silver Burdett.

Ratliff, D. (1988). *Handbook of preschool and religious education.* Birmingham, AL: Religious Education Press.

Reich, H. (1993). Cognitive-developmental approaches to religiousness: which version for which purpose? *The International Journal for the Psychology of Religion, 3,* 145-71.

Rest, J. (1979). *Development in judging moral issues.* Minneapolis, MN: University of Minnesota Press.

Rest, J. (1986). *Moral development: Advances in research and theory.* New York: Praeger.

Sarbin, T. (1990). The narrative quality of action. *Theoretical and Philosophical Psychology, 10,* 49-65.

Selman, R. L. (1976). Social-cognitive understanding: A guide to educational and clinical practice. In T. Lickona (Ed.), *Moral development and behavior:*

Theory, research, and social issues (299-316). New York: Holt, Rinehart, & Winston.

Tamminen, K. (1994). Comparing Oser's and Fowler's developmental stages. *Journal of Empirical Theology, 7.*

Tannen, D. (1991). *You just don't understand: Women and men in conversation.* London: Virago.

Tappan, M. (1989). Stories lived and stories told: The narrative structure of late adolescent moral development. *Human Development, 32,* 300-15.

Tappan, M. (1990). Hermeneutics and moral development: Interpreting narrative representations of moral experience. *Developmental Review, 10,* 239-65.

Tappan, M. (1991a). Narrative, authorship, and the development of moral authority. In M. Tappan & M. Packer (Eds.), *Narrative and storytelling: Implications for understanding moral development* (New directions for child development, No. 54). San Francisco: Jossey-Bass.

Tappan, M. (1991b). Narrative, language, and moral experience. *Journal of Moral Education, 20,* 243-56.

Tappan, M. (1992). Texts and contexts: Language, culture, and the development of moral functioning. In Lucien Winegar & Jaan Valsiner (Eds.), *Children's development within social contexts: Metatheoretical, theoretical, and methodological issues.* Hillsdale, NJ: Lawrence Erlbaum.

Tappan, M., & Brown, L. (1989). Stories told and lessons learned: Toward a narrative approach to moral development and moral education. *Harvard Educational Review, 59,* 182-205.

Vygotsky, L. (1978). *Mind in society: The development of higher psychological processes* Cambrige, MA: Harvard University Press.

Wertsch, J. (1989). A sociocultural approach to mind. In W. Damon (Ed.), *Child development today and tomorrow.* San Francisco: Jossey-Bass.

Wertsch, J. (1991). *Voices of the mind: A sociocultural approach to mediated action.* Cambridge, MA: Harvard University Press.

Youngman, D. J. (1993). *Autre temps, autre morés? Life-span restrospectives on moral presence in the relational self: A contextual interpretation.* Vol. 1 & 2. Unpublished doctoral dissertation, Boston University.

Suggestions for Further Reading

Alexander, C., & Langer, E. (Eds.) (1986). *Beyond Formal Operations: Alternative Endpoints to Human Development.* New York: Oxford University Press.

Archambault, R. (1964). *John Dewey on education.* Chicago: University of Chicago Press.

Baltes, P. B. (1987). Theoretical Propositions of Lifespan Developmental Psychology: On the Dynamics Between Growth and Decline. *Developmental Psychology, 23,* 611-626.

Baltes, P.B., & Brim, O.G. Jr. (Eds.) (1984). *Life-Span Development and Behavior.* Vol. 6. New York: Academic Press.

Basseches, M. (1984). *Dialectical thinking and adult development.* Norwood, NJ: Ablex Publishing.

Birren, J. E., & Schaie, K. W. (Eds.) (1977). *Handbook of the psychology of aging.* New York: Van Nostrand Reinhold.

Bornstein, M. H. & Lamb, M. E. (1988). *Developmental psychology: An advanced textbook.* 2nd Edition. Hillsdale, NJ: Lawrence Erlbaum Associates, Publishers.

Bowlby, J. (1980). *Attachment and loss: Volume 3, Loss, sadness, and depression.* New York: Basic Books.

Bronfenbrenner, U. (1979). *The ecology of human development.* Cambridge, MA: Harvard University Press.

Buhler, C. (1935). The curve of life as studied in biographies. *Journal of Applied Psychology, 19,* 405-09.

Commons, M. L., Richards, F. A., & Armon, C. (Eds.) (1984). *Beyond Formal Operations: Late Adolescent and Adult Cognitive Development.* New York: Praeger.

Datan, N., Greene, A. L., & Reese, H. W. (Eds.). (1986). *Life-span developmental psychology: Intergenerational relations.* Hillsdale, NJ: Lawrence Erlbaum Associates.

Erikson, E. H. (1959). *Identity and the life-cycle: Selected papers by Erik H. Erikson.* New York: International Universities Press.

Erikson, E. H. (1997). *The life cycle completed.* Extended version. New York: W. W. Norton & Company.

Friedan, B. (1993). *The fountain of age.* New York, NY: Simon and Schuster.

Freud, S. (1961). *Civilization and its discontent.* New York: W. W. Norton & Company.

Goulet, L. R., & Baltes, P. B. (Eds.). (1970). *Life-span developmental psychology: Research and theory.* New York: Academic Press.

Jordan, J. V., Kaplan, A. G., Miller, J. B., Stiver, I. P., & Surrey, J. L. (1991). *Women's growth in connection.* New York, NY: The Guilford Press.

Kegan, R. (1994). *In over our heads: The mental demands of modern life.* Cambridge, MA: Harvard University Press.

Kurtines, W. M., & Gewirtz, J. L. (Eds.) (1984). *Morality, moral behavior, and moral development.* New York: John Wiley and Sons.

Lerner, R. M. (1986). *Concepts and theories of human development.* New York: Random House.

Lerner, R. M. (1996). Relative plasticity, integration, temporality, and diversity in human development: A developmental contextual perspective about theory, process, and method. *Developmental Psychology, 32.,* 781-786.

Loevinger, J. (1976). *Ego Development.* San Francisco: Jossey-Bass.

Miller, J. B. (1976). *Toward a new psychology of women.* Boston, MA: Beacon Press.

Neugarten, B. L. (1964). *Personality in middle and late life.* New York: Atherton Press.

Neugarten, B. L. (Ed.) (1968). *Middle age and aging: A reader in social psychology.* Chicago: University of Chicago Press.

Neugarten, B. L. (Ed.) (1968). Toward a psychology of the life cycle. In B. L. Neugarten (Ed.), *Middle age and aging: A reader in social psychology.* Chicago: University of Chicago Press.

Packer, M. J., & Addison, R. B. (Eds.) (1989). *Entering the circle.* Albany, NY: State University of New York Press.

Parke, R. D., Ornstein, P. A., Rieser, J. J., Zahn-Waxler, C. (Eds.) (1994). *A century of developmental psychology.* Washington, DC: American Psychological Association.

Piaget, J., & Inhelder, B. (1969). *Psychology of the child.* New York: Basic Books.

Pressey, S. L., & Kuhlen, R. G. (1939, 1957). *Psychological development through the life-span.* New York: Harper & Row.

Reese, H. W., & Franzen, M. D. (1997). *Biological and neuropsychological mechanisms: Life-span developmental psychology.* Mahwah, NJ: Lawrence Erlbaum Associates, Publishers.

Rest, J. R. (1984). The major components of morality. In W. Kurtines & J. Gewirtz (Eds.), *Morality, moral behavior and moral development.* New York: John Wiley.

Riegel, K. F. (1975). Toward a dialectical theory of development. *Human Development, 18,* 50-64.

Rosnow, R. L., & Georgoudi, M. (Eds.) (1986). *Contextualism and understandings in behavioral science.* New York: Praeger.

Sinnott, J. (1996). The developmental approach: Postformal thought as adaptive intelligence. In F. Blanchard-Fields & T. M. Hess (Eds.), *Perspectives on cognitive change in adulthood and aging* (pp. 358-86). New York: McGraw-Hill.

Tennant, M., & Pogson, P. (1995). *Learning and change in the adult years.* San Francisco, CA: Jossey-Bass Publishers.

Vaillant, G. E. (1978). *Mind in society: The development of higher psychological processes.* Cambridge, MA: Harvard University Press.

Vygotsky, L. (1962). *Thought and language.* Cambridge, MA: MIT Press.

Vygotsky, L. (1978). *Mind in society: The development of higher psychological processes.* Cambridge, MA: Harvard University Press.

Index

About the Contributors

LYN MIKEL BROWN is Associate Professor and Cochair of the Education and Human Development Program at Colby College, Waterville, Maine. She received her Ed.D. from Harvard University's Graduate School of Education and is a founding member of the Harvard Project on Women's Psychology and Girls' Development. Her book with Carol Gilligan, *Meeting at the Crossroads: Women's Psychology and Girls' Development,* was a 1992 New York Times Notable Book of the Year. She has written numerous articles on girls' and women's psychological development, girls' education, and feminist research methods, and is a 1994-95 recipient of a National Academy of Education Spencer Foundation Fellowship. Her new book, *The Politics of Girls' Anger: Class Accents and White Femininities*, was published in 1998.

MARIANNA LAWRENCE CAYTEN received her doctorate with highest honors from the University of Pennsylvania, where she received the Alice Paul Award for "outstanding contributions to the quality of university and community life. " She has taught at the University of Pennsylvania and has been Adjunct Assistant Professor at Fordham University. She was also Acting Director and Psychotherapist at the Counseling and Personal Development Service at Pace University. At Barnard College, she was an Associate at the Center for Research on Women and was a post-doctoral fellow and Psychologist in the Mental Health Service. She presently has a practice as a licensed psychologist, with offices in New York City and Westchester County. She is currently leading a group for women who have been battered and a support group for those who have had cancer. Her continuing research is on the empowerment of African-American professional women.

JEANNE S. CHALL is Professor Emerita at the Harvard University Graduate School of Education. Formerly the director of the graduate programs in reading and the Harvard Reading Laboratory, she has written widely, including *Learning to Read: The Great Debate, Stages of Reading Development, The Dale-Chall Readability Formula, The Reading Crisis: Why Poor Children Fall Behind,* and *Creating Successful Readers.* She is a member of the National Academy of Education and past president of the Reading Hall of Fame.

JAMES M. DAY is Professor of Human Development and the Psychology of Religion at the Universite Catholique de Louvain, Belgium. He holds degrees from Oberlin College, Harvard University, and the University of Pennsylvania, and has been a visiting scholar at Cambridge, Columbia, Union Theological Seminary (New York), and Princeton. In addition to his research interests in the relationship between moral development and religious development, Professor Day conducts research on discourse processes related to moral and religious decision-making, and how contextual variables such as gender, religious affiliation, ethnicity, social class, and family history figure in languages of moral and religious experience. Professor Day is a member of the editorial boards of *The Journal of Moral Education, Pedagogia et Vita, The Journal of Adult Development, Pedagogies,* and the *Religion and Culture* book series published by Kok Verlag. He also serves as a reviewer for a number of other scholarly journals, including *L'Annee Psychologique, Behavioral Processes, The Journal for the Scientific Study of Religion,* and *The International Journal for the Psychology of Religion.* He has recently been the Annual Lecturer in Education and the Christian Faith at St. Andrew's College of the University of Glasgow (Scotland), the annual guest lecturer in the Post-Graduate Training Program in Psychotherapy at the University of Cambridge (England), and the annual invited lecturer in Counseling Psychology, in the Master Psychotherapist series at Rollins College, Florida.

JACK DEMICK received his Ph.D. from Clark University and is currently a full professor in, and the chair of, the Department of Psychology at Suffolk University in Boston. Prior to Suffolk, he held teaching appointments at Clark University and Harvard University. His research interests include both cognitive development (e.g., cognitive style, environmental cognition) and social development (e.g., adaptation to adoption) across the life span. He is also the editor of the *Journal of Adult Development.*

HENRY DUPONT has served both as Professor of Psychology at the University of Wisconsin, Eau Claire and as Chair of the Department of Special Education at the University of Hawaii. Among his publications is the book *Emotional Development: Theory and Applications, a Neo-Piagetian Perspective,* which was published in 1994. He is presently semi-retired but provides psychological services from his private practice in Blairsville, Georgia.

CAROLE E. GREENES is Associate Dean for Research, Development, and Advanced Academic Programs, and Professor of Mathematics Education at Boston University's School of Education. She is senior author of *Exploring Your World*, a K-8 mathematics textbook program; *TOPS*, a problem-solving program for students in pre-kindergarten through grade 12; *MEGA Projects*, interdisciplinary investigations for students in grades 1-8; *Mathletics, Gold Medal Problems*, for middle and high school students; the *Spotlight Series* for college students; and *ATTACK* and *Prime Times*, two mathematics programs for students with learning difficulties. She is a member of the Mathematics Equity 2000 Committee and the Ad Hoc Committee for Curriculum for the College Board, the management team for the Boston University/Chelsea Public Schools Partnership, and advisory boards of several funded projects. Dr. Greenes is currently working on interactive CD-ROM mathematics-science explorations for middle and high school students, and software for assessing student understanding of graphs, proportionality and motion. She has taught at the elementary, secondary, and college levels.

PETER HABERL is completing his doctoral degree in the Department of Developmental Studies and Counseling at Boston University's School of Education. Like his mentor, Professor Zaichkowsky, Peter has taught at Boston University and works as a sport psychology consultant with collegiate, Olympic, and professional athletes. His research interests, as a former professional athlete himself, are in team building and the psychology of optimal experience.

ROSELMINA INDRISANO is a Professor of Education and Chairman of the Department of Developmental Studies and Counseling at Boston University, School of Education. She is a member of the management team for the Boston University/Chelsea Public Schools Partnership. Professor Indrisano is a recipient of Boston University's Metcalf Award for Excellence in Teaching and was the 1996 Boston University Scholar/ Teacher of the Year. She is Past President of the International Reading Association and the Reading Hall of Fame. Dr. Indrisano is a Fellow of the National Conference on Research in English.

RONALD F. LEVANT earned his doctorate in Clinical Psychology and Public Practice from Harvard in 1973 and has served on the faculties of Boston, Rutgers, and Harvard Universities. He is currently Dean, Center for Psychological Studies, Nova Southeastern University. Dr. Levant has authored, coauthored, edited, or coedited over 130 publications, including eleven books and sixty five refereed journal articles and book chapters in family and gender psychology. His publications include *Between Father and Child* (coauthored with John Kelly), *Masculinity,*

Reconstructed (coauthored with Gini Kopecky), *A New Psychology of Men*, (coedited with William Pollack), and *Men and Sex: New Psychological Perspectives* (coedited with Gary Brooks). In addition, he has served as guest editor for special issues of *The Counseling Psychologist, Psychotherapy*, and *The Journal of African American Men*. He serves on the editorial boards of seven journals and as Editor of the *Journal of Family Psychology*. Dr. Levant was the 1984 recipient of the Jack Krasner Memorial Award from Division 29 of American Psychological Association (APA), the 1994 winner of the Heiser APA Presidential Award for Advocacy, the 1995 recipient of the Ezra Saul Psychological Service Award from the Massachusetts Psychological Association, the 1996 recipient of the Distinguished Service Award from Division 51 of APA, and the 1997 recipient of the Family Psychologist of the Year Award from Division 43 of APA. He is a Fellow of the APA, a Diplomat of the American Board of Professional Psychology, and a Distinguished Practitioner of the National Academies of Practice. Dr. Levant has also served as President of the Massachusetts Psychological Association, President of APA Division 43 (Family Psychology), cofounder and the first President of APA Division 51 (the Society for the Psychological Study of Men and Masculinity), Chair of the APA Committee for the Advancement of Professional Practice, member of the APA Council of Representatives, and is presently a Member-At-Large of the APA Board of Directors. He has just been elected to a three-year term as Recording Secretary of the APA.

RALPH MOSHER was Professor Emeritus in the Department of Developmental Studies, Boston University, having begun his teaching career as an Assistant Professor in the Department of Counseling and Curriculum Development at Harvard. His many professional interests over the years have included teacher development; supervision of beginning and advanced teachers and helping professionals; curriculum development—particularly to promote socio-moral and civic development in adolescents; and reform of school governance, policy-making, and justice structures to enhance the adolescent's understanding of democracy. He was the editor of *Adolescents' Development and Education* (1979) and *Moral Education* (1980) and coauthor of *Democracy with Children* (1981), *Preparing for Citizenship* (1994), *Moral Action in Young Adulthood* (1998), and other books and articles.

MYRIAM H. L. NAEDTS is a clinical psychologist affiliated with The Center for Neuropsychiatry and Psychotherapy, Brussels, Belgium. Before assuming her post there, she was Clinical Research Psychologist at the Cliniques St. Luc of the Faculte de Medecine of the University Catholique de Louvain. From 1993 to 1995, she was Research Fellow in the Human Development Laboratory and Center for the Psychology of Religion at Louvain. Her published work includes a number of coauthored articles in *The Journal of Education* and *The International*

Journal for the Psychology of Religion as well as chapters in two forthcoming books.

GIL G. NOAM, Ed.D., DIPL. PSYCH. is Associate Professor of Psychiatry/ Psychology and Education, Harvard University and Director of the Laboratory of Developmental Psychology and Developmental Psychopathology, McLean Hospital. He is Director of the Harvard RALLY Program (Responsive Advocacy for Life and Learning in Youth). This is a model program that identifies at-risk children and prevents school failure and delinquent behavior through a comprehensive, school-based, community-resource program of fostering psychological resilience. He received his Clinical Psychology degrees at Freie University in Berlin, and Fribourg University in Switzerland, and his developmental training at Harvard University. His research interests are in the development of adolescents and the evolution of psychological strengths and resilience throughout the life span.

MICHAEL J. PARSONS, Ph.D. is a Professor in the Department of Art Education at The Ohio State University. He is the author of *How We Understand Art: A Cognitive-Developmental Account of Aesthetic Experience* (1987) and coauthor with H. G. Blocker of *Aesthetics and Education* (1993).

ALAN J. REIMAN is Assistant Professor in the Department of Curriculum and Instruction at North Carolina State University. From 1988 to 1996, he served as a clinical assistant professor, and worked closely with the Model Clinical Teaching Program and Mentor Network—a consortium of school systems interested in innovative approaches to teacher education, mentoring, and ongoing teacher professional development. Dr. Reiman has studied teacher development, mentoring, and guided reflections from multiple perspectives. In 1997, he was invited to coordinate the Clinical Teaching Network, a consortium of twelve North Carolina universities creating innovations in clinical developmental teacher education.

DAWN E. SCHRADER is an Associate Professor in the Department of Education at Cornell University in Ithaca, New York. She is Past President of the Association for Moral Education (AME) and was the dissertation award recipient from the AME in 1989.

BETSY SPEICHER received her Ed.D. in Human Development at Harvard University, where she studied under Lawrence Kohlberg. Dr. Speicher was a Research Associate and Research Scholar at the Henry A. Murray Research Center at Radcliffe College. She served as Assistant Professor in the School Psychology Program, Department of Psychology, University of Rhode Island and in Boston University's Department of Developmental Studies and Counseling before returning to the private practice of psychotherapy. She is now also a licensed psychologist for the public schools in Lexington, Massachusetts. Her publications include: *Measurements of moral judgement, Vol. 2* (1987); Adolescent moral judgement and perceptions of family interaction, *Journal of Family Psychology, 6,* 128-38 (1992); and Family patterns of moral judgement during adolescence and early adulthood, *Developmental Psychology, 30,* 624-32.

NORMAN A. SPRINTHALL, Professor Emeritus at North Carolina State University, received his Ed.D. from Harvard University in 1963. His early research focused on the MAT program at Harvard with a colleague team of Mosher, Purpel, Weller, and others. These investigations examined teacher and counselor flexibility as predictors of performance. Gradually, as a result of collaborations with Larry Kohlberg and Bill Perry, the framework shifted more toward cognitive-developmental stage theory as a framework for intervention strategies for both adults and pupils. In the 1970s, he moved to Minnesota and teamed with his wife, Lois Thies, in teacher supervision. More recently, they worked at North Carolina State University as they continued to build theory, research, and practice for teaching, counseling, and supervision. He has coauthored *Educational Psychology: A Developmental Approach,* 6th edition, and *Adolescent Psychology: A Developmental View,* 3rd edition.

MARK B. TAPPAN is Associate Professor and Cochair of the Education and Human Development Program at Colby College in Waterville, Maine. He received his doctorate in Human Development from Harvard University in 1987 and has taught at the University of Massachusetts, Boston, Trinity College, Clark University, and the Harvard Graduate School of Education. He is the coeditor (with Martin Packer) of *Narrative and Storytelling: Implications for Understanding Moral Development* (1991), and the author of *Ethically speaking: Discourse, Dialogue, and Moral Development* (soon to be published). He has also published numerous articles and book chapters in the areas of moral development, moral education, interpretive methodology, gender differences, and adult development.

LOIS THIES-SPRINTHALL, Associate Professor Emerita at North Carolina State University, began her career in education in the elementary classrooms of Iowa and Illinois in the 1950s and 1960s. It was her graduate work at Minnesota and at Northern Colorado, however, that created an interest in teacher education as innovative practice. She managed Project Sixty at Minnesota with a cadre of young assistant professors, including Ken Howey, David Peason, and Roger Johnson. This was followed by appointments to S. Cloud State and more recently to North Carolina State University. Her work has continued to focus on supervision for student teachers and mentoring for beginning teachers. In 1987, the collaborative teacher education program she directed won the AACTE award for innovative practice in school-university collaboration. She has published numerous articles and book chapters detailing her applied research and is a coauthor with Alan Reiman of the book *Mentoring and Supervision for Teacher Education* (1998).

DEBORAH J. YOUNGMAN is an Assistant Professor in the Department of Developmental Studies and Counseling in the School of Education, Boston University, where she also serves as the Clinical Coordinator for the graduate program in Counseling. She supervises clinical interns working with infants, children, adolescents, and adults in both conventional and alternative educational settings. A primary interest in life span moral development has led to research on moral presence in later life, interactive psychiatric illness and substance abuse in adolescence, and educational and vocational development in persons who are homeless and mentally ill. Over the past five years, she has also directed the study of applied ethics at the Sackler Graduate School at Tufts University. Her current research focuses on challenges to moral life in the emerging democracies of Eastern Europe.

LEONARD ZAICHKOWSKY is Professor of Education at Boston University. His research interests are in the psychology of development, learning, and performance. He is currently president of the Association for the Advancement of Applied Sport Psychology.